Streams of Renewal

Streams of Renewal

Revised Edition

Peter Hocken

paternoster

First Edition published 1986 in the UK by Paternoster Press
Revised Edition 1997

03 02 01 00 99 98 97   7 6 5 4 3 2 1

Paternoster Press is an imprint of Paternoster Publishing,
P.O. Box 300, Carlisle, Cumbria CA3 0QS UK

British Library Cataloguing in Publication Data

A catalogue record for this book is available from the British Library.

ISBN 0-85364-805-0

This book is printed using Suffolk Book paper which is 100% acid free.

Typeset by WestKey Ltd., Falmouth, Cornwall
Printed in Great Britain by Clays Ltd., St. Ives plc

Contents

Introduction

There is no shortage of literature on the Charismatic movement, and Britain is no exception to this general observation. However, this abundance of literature characterizes the more developed phases of the movement in the late 1960s and the 1970s, and one tends to be unaware of the relative scarcity of information publicly available on its beginnings. The pursuit of this research into the origins and first years of the Charismatic movement in Britain has uncovered much little-known material, and illustrates that the roots of the new movement lie further back than had been previously assumed.

The cut-off date for this study at the end of 1965 was chosen for a number of converging reasons. By that date, the main outlines of the new movement are clear, and all the major instruments used by the Holy Spirit are manifest. After this date the sources are more numerous and better-known.

A major place is deliberately given to the witnesses of early participants in this movement of the Spirit. This reflects firstly my concern to discover what happened. When people were baptized in the Spirit, what actually took place? What changes resulted from this experience? I have assumed that details in direct testimonies to events are in general reliable, especially in those which were given within a year or two of the events. Such eye-witness details need to be distinguished from interpretations subsequently placed upon them, which are more likely to be influenced by received patterns of exegesis and theology. Such received patterns may also influence the terminology in which the basic experiences are described, and so the descriptions of spiritual experience couched in non-technical terms have stronger authority as evidence.

On the basis of what happened, the basic questions concerning the meaning and significance of the events are then asked. This second level of investigation, on the basis of the collected data, is the particular thrust of the conclusion.

Secondly, the inclusion of witnesses suggests the desirability of a wider use of narrative in presenting this history. In recent years, scholars have become increasingly aware of the irreplaceable role of narrative in conveying the sense of events. Narrative does not merely convey the flavour of what was happening (though that is itself valuable), but it alone can do justice to all the dimensions of the experience. Narrative respects the individuality of each participant's history, and this is why it is possible to make general judgments on what was common to all or many, without stereotyping their experience.

The period examined in this study divides readily into four parts:

1. Pioneer figures who were not committed to renewal of the historic churches but who were clearly not simply Pentecostals
2. Initial spread to the historic churches
3. The coming together of hitherto independent streams and
4. The continuing contribution of independent sources.

In order to provide some analysis of the emerging patterns, the first three sections all follow a common pattern; Chapters 7, 16 and 20 each bring together and compare the data cited in each chapter within the preceding section. This makes it possible to limit the conclusion (Chapters 23 and 24) to substantive issues concerning the meaning and significance of the Charismatic movement as a whole. Chapter 25 then compares the origins in Britain with the origins of the same movement in North America.

Two explanatory points should be made about the terminology used in this study. First, the adjective 'Pentecostal' has been used with a capital when reference is being made either to anything associated with the Pentecostal movement from its origins early in this century or to what later characterizes the Pentecostal Churches, and those accepting the doctrines and practices of those denominations. The adjective 'pentecostal' without a capital refers to those blessings and characteristics that in the period covered by this study are common to both the Pentecostals and the Charismatics.

Secondly, the terms 'Pentecostal movement' and 'Pentecostalism', though often used synonymously, have slightly different senses in this work. By 'Pentecostalism' is indicated that complex of doctrines, practices and convictions shared de facto within the various Pentecostal churches and which reflects a more advanced stage of institutionalization than the phrase 'Pentecostal movement', which is used of those periods and places where the movement-character of the Holy Spirit's work among Pentecostal Christians is more evident. 'Pentecostal movement' would then represent something more flexible and less fixed than 'Pentecostalism'.

Finally, I want to express my gratitude to all those who have contributed in any way to this study. My first thanks therefore are to Almighty God, Father, Son and Holy Spirit, without whose loving provision nothing would exist, let alone the church or any movement of the Holy Spirit, and without whose grace and light no real understanding of his works is possible. I am particularly indebted to Professor Walter J. Hollenweger of the University of Birmingham, under whose guidance this dissertation was begun and has been completed, for all his kind assistance and steady encouragement. I am also most grateful to all the people I interviewed and with whom I corresponded. They generously provided information and/or written source material not readily available. In this respect, I wish particularly to thank Cecil Cousen, Michael Harper, Benedict Heron, David Lillie, Philip Smith, Richard Trout, and Basil Varnam of the Assemblies of God office in Nottingham. I wish to thank Fr. James Connelly, CSC for access to the archives of the Congregation of the Holy Cross, South Bend, Indiana, to which I owe the information not generally available concerning Van Nuys. My thanks are also due to Charles Clarke and Bill Grant, who both died in the summer of 1984.

I am particularly grateful to the brothers and sisters of the community to which I belong, Mother of God in the Washington, D.C. metropolitan area. Without their support, practical help and encouragement, the completion of this study would not have been possible. I thank Dr. John Dillon and Judith Tydings for their comments and suggestions throughout the work, Angela Burrin for her patience and hours of typing and Sr. Georgina Foyster for her meticulous proof-reading of the typescript. I pray that this study may contribute to a fuller knowledge of the love and mercy of Almighty God.

Abbreviations

Organizations and Corporate Bodies

AoG	Assemblies of God
ALC	American Lutheran Church
APFR	Anglican Prayer Fellowship for Revival
BPF	British Pentecostal Fellowship
BRF	Baptist Revival Fellowship
BTS	Blessed Trinity Society
CFO	Camps Farthest Out
CIM	China Inland Mission
CMS	Church Missionary Society
EPCRA	European Pentecostal-Charismatic Research Association
FIEC	Fellowship of Independent Evangelical Churches
FGBMFI	Full Gospel Business Men's Fellowship International
IVF	Inter-Varsity Fellowship
IVP	Inter-Varsity Press
LHM	London Healing Mission
MRF	Methodist Revival Fellowship
OM	Operation Mobilization
OSL	The Order of St. Luke
PWC	Pentecostal World Conference
SPF	Students' Pentecostal Fellowship
WCC	World Council of Churches
WEC	World Evangelization Crusade

Periodicals

A	America (New York, weekly)
APFRQB Quarterly	Anglican Prayer Fellowship for Revival Bulletin (London, mostly quarterly)

AVFA	Voice of Faith (Bradford, quarterly)
AVWA	Voice in the Wilderness (Granada Hills, California, quarterly or bi-monthly)
BT	Baptist Times (London, weekly)
BW	British Weekly (Edinburgh, weekly)
C	The Churchman (London, quarterly)
CEN	Church of England Newspaper (London, weekly)
CH	The Christian (London, weekly)
CL	Christian Life (Wheaton. Illinois, monthly)
CPL	Clark Prayer Letter (Worthing, quarterly)
CR	Crusade (London, monthly)
CT	Church Times (London, weekly)
CTO	Christianity Today (Washington, D.C., fortnightly)
D	Dunamis (Thelwall, Cheshire, then Bradford, quarterly)
DdPN	David du Plessis Newsletter (Oakland, California, four to six times a year)
E	Eternity (Philadelphia, monthly)
EC	English Churchman (London, weekly)
EDHN	Evangelical Divine Healing Newsletter (Braughing, Herts, approx. quarterly)
EE	Elim Evangel (London, weekly)
ET	The Expository Times (Edinburgh, monthly)
F	Fulness (Canterbury, then Cobham, irregular)
G	Greetings (Worthing, twice yearly)
GR	Grassroots (Post Green, Dorset, bi-monthly)
IAN	Intercessors for America Newsletter (Elyria, Ohio, monthly)
LC	The Living Church (Milwaukee, Wisconsin, weekly)
LF	The Life of Faith (London, weekly).
LHML	London Healing Mission Letter (London, three times a year)
LW	Life and Work (Edinburgh, monthly)
M	The Ministry (London, quarterly)
MHN	Michael Harper's Newsletter (London, every one or two months)
MR	The Methodist Recorder (London, weekly)
NRT	Nouvelle Revue Theologique (Louvain, monthly)
OiC	One in Christ (London, quarterly)
P	Pentecost (London, quarterly)
PE	The Pentecostal (Dublin, only four issues published)

PN	Pneuma (Oklahoma City, then Pasadena, California, twice yearly)
Q	The Quest (Halesowen, then Ely, quarterly)
RG	Ripened Grain (Hadleigh, Suffolk. then St. Austell, approx. quarterly)
RHE	Revue d'Histoire Ecclesiastique
RN	Renewal (London, bi-monthly; later Crowborough, monthly)
RPFN	Revival Prayer Fellowship News Sheet (London, bi-monthly)
RS	Restoration (Bradford, bi-monthly)
RT	Redemption Tidings (London, then Nottingham, weekly)
RV	Revival (London, monthly from second issue)
SR	Sound of Revival (MRF, quarterly)
T	Trinity (Van Nuys, California, initially quarterly)
TR	Theological Renewal (London, then Nottingham, three times a year)
TT	The Torch (Cowes, Isle of Wight, quarterly)
V	Victory (Houston, Texas. irregular)
W	The Witness (Glasgow, monthly)

Other

CCD	Crockford's Clerical Directory
EDH	Evangelical Divine Healing
QF	Questionnaire Findings on the Mamhead Park Conference S.P.R.
USA	United States of America

Report on Stoke Poges Prayer Conference 1964
Belstone Report on a Conference held at Belstone, Sept. 1961
Exmouth
Report on a Conference held at Exmouth, May 1958 Mamhead
Report on a Conference held at Mamhead, Sept. 1962

Preface

The Spirit's Call to Repentance

The Pentecostal Movement is now 80 years old. The Charismatic Movement in Britain is 30 years old. It is now time to take stock. Two centres for such research have been emerging, the one at the Catholic University of Louvain in Belgium, the other at the University of Birmingham.

In spite of the international significance of the British Pentecostal and Charismatic pioneers, very little research has been done on these two movements so far. Not that there is a lack of literature on the subject. But most of it does not belong to the genre of research.[1]

Dr. Peter Hocken fills an important gap with the present volume. His research shows that the Charismatic Movement in Britain was not imported from the United States, although it was highlighted and publicized by the media once the American Charismatic Movement hit the headlines.

In his painstaking and patient uncovering of the early history of the Charismatic Movement, Peter Hocken shows its simultaneous beginnings in different places in Britain and the subsequent attempts at discovering each other. The early cohesion of the movement was not of the nature of an organization but rather of the nature of an emerging network of friends. The importance of this oral spirituality escaped the attention of the mainline church headquarters just as it was overlooked by the secular and religious press. The reason for this is that it was and still is a grass-roots movement. Therefore Peter Hocken could not rely entirely on written material. He had to visit and speak to the early pioneers. He thus was able to write a piece of British church history 'from the underside', an emerging ecumenical grass-roots spirituality.[2]

In contrast to most writers on the baptism of the Spirit, Hocken

sees in this crisis experience a cognitive element. The fact that
people from evangelical to catholic backgrounds, from conservative
to liberal theological persuasion, have undergone an experience
which is considered identical, asks for a new look at our received
theologies.

This was certainly the case for the ecumenical pentecostal pioneer
David du Plessis. He correctly stated that Pentecostals are not simply
to be understood as the left wing of Protestantism. There are too
many Catholic elements in their history and spirituality. Therefore
it is foolish – in the opinion of du Plessis – to exclude either the World
Council of Churches or Rome from the sphere of the Spirit's visitation.[3]

It is, however, true that neither Pentecostals nor mainline
churches are equipped to deal with the theological queries which
arise from such an observation. Peter Hocken writes:

> While there was a genuine communion in the Spirit between the Spirit-bap-
> tized, there was not a common understanding of the movement and of its
> purpose in God's sight. The possibility of a common understanding was
> dependent on the participants being willing to allow their received theolo-
> gies, especially their ecclesiologies, to be challenged and expanded in com-
> mon fidelity to the grace of baptism in the Spirit and in parallel fidelity to the
> work of God at the heart of each tradition.[4]

This hermeneutical approach can be defended as Roman Catholic.
But in the context in which Peter Hocken presents his findings this
hermeneutics can also be called pentecostal, protestant or Anglican.
In fact it reveals a critical edge in relation to any ecclesiology,
including the Roman Catholic.

Thus Peter Hocken sees the uniqueness of the Charismatic Movement in the fact that for the first time since the Reformation, an
ecumenical grass-roots movement emerged which crossed the frontiers between evangelicals and catholics. This indeed is of high
significance both for historical and theological research. The basis of
this ecumenical approach is the fact that Christians discover a common experience, which is at the heart of their spirituality – and this
in spite of their differing theologies and interpretations of this experience.

Having failed to throw it out of their churches altogether, no
doubt denominational theologians are busy on all sides proving that
the baptism in the Spirit can be 'contained' within the traditions of
their denominations.[5] And it is right that they try to do so, because

it is always easier to accept something new by showing that it is in fact not that new.

But if this work is of the Spirit, as its adherents believe, then the discovery that the Spirit might teach us new hermeneutical possibilities for the new crisis of our day, comes as no surprise to Christians. In other words the baptism of the Spirit introduces a critical and cognitive element into the evangelical and liberal camp. Evangelicals discover that it is possible to be a committed and spirit-filled believer without accepting evangelical theological propositions. Critical liberals discover that the oral evangelical tradition is a vehicle of communication which can carry important ecumenical and social insights in a milieu which the liberals can never reach.[6] Catholics discover that there might be a possibility to be a fully-fledged 'catholic' without accepting the jurisdiction of Rome. Protestants discover that Roman Catholic priests take Scripture and in fact the Reformation tradition just as seriously as they do.

Because theology has not only to do with the critical interpretation of Scripture and tradition but also with the critical interpretation of Scripture's and tradition's reception by men and women in the churches, Peter Hocken's dissertation is not only a welcome historical study but it is also a call to rethink our received theological positions.

WALTER J. HOLLENWEGER

One

A Startling Prophecy

In 1906 the Pentecostal movement caught fire and became more than a local revival in the American Midwest. In a ramshackle two-storey wooden building in the industrial section of Los Angeles, California, in turn Methodist chapel, livery stable and tenement house – the saving, healing and reconciling power of the Spirit of God was experienced with a force that recalled the events described in Acts 2. Under the leadership of a black pastor, William J. Seymour, an astonishing mixture of people of many races and ethnic backgrounds testified to a new revelation of the glory of Jesus Christ, and to the power of God manifested in spiritual gifts of tongues, healings and prophecies.[1] The message 'Pentecost has come' went out from Azusa Street to thousands of Christians whose hopes and expectations had been raised by the news of the Welsh Revival of 1904–05. Visitors flocked to Azusa Street from distant parts, and in turn carried 'the message of Pentecost' to their own churches.

Moreover, a remarkable number of people went forth from Azusa Street as missionaries to distant lands, firmly convinced the message must be proclaimed to all peoples before the expected return of the Lord. This primary impetus from Azusa Street was supported by the results of Charles Parham's autumn mission in Zion City, Illinois, in the same year.[2]

By the year 1936, the Pentecostal movement was a full generation old. The enthusiastic, spontaneous movement of 1906 had become a cluster of new Pentecostal denominations, regarded with suspicion and disdain by the older churches, which had almost universally refused to countenance, within their ranks, speaking in tongues and the other spiritual gifts associated with this Pentecostal outpouring. Spurned and despised, the Pentecostals had in turn denounced the older churches as barren and rejected by the Lord. A new generation of Pentecostal believers was growing up, who had never known the trans-confessional phase of the movement before the hard lines were drawn and the new Pentecostal denominations emerged.[3]

One of this new generation was the young general secretary of the leading Pentecostal denomination in South Africa, the Apostolic Faith Mission, David John du Plessis.[4] At the beginning of 1936, he was a month short of his thirty-first birthday. By his own admission, du Plessis was a sectarian Pentecostal, seeking only to draw people out of the 'false Churches' into the Full Gospel truth of Pentecostalism. As a young man, he had been puzzled and saddened by all the competing and hostile denominations he saw, and he recalls having prayed 'Lord, help me to change this.' But in all other respects, du Plessis' mind was as closed as other Pentecostals to the possibility of the Holy Spirit working in power beyond and outside the Pentecostal assemblies.

One morning in January of that year du Plessis was in his office early, opening the day's post. Suddenly the door burst open and in marched Smith Wigglesworth. Wigglesworth, the Pentecostal evangelist from Bradford, Yorkshire,[5] gave no greeting, but commanded du Plessis: 'Come out here.' Du Plessis had hardly rounded his desk, when Wigglesworth placed hands on his shoulders, pushed him against the wall and began to speak. Du Plessis knew instantly it was a prophecy.

> There is a revival coming that at present the world knows nothing about. It will come through the churches. It will come in a fresh way. When you see what God does in this revival you will then have to admit that all that you have seen previously is a mere nothing in comparison with what is to come. It will eclipse anything that has been known in history. Empty churches, empty cathedrals, will be packed again with worshippers. Buildings will not be able to accommodate the multitudes. Then you will see fields of people worshipping and praising together. The Lord intends to use you in this revival. For you have been in Jerusalem long enough. The Lord will send you to the uttermost parts of the earth. If you are faithful and humble, the Lord will use you and if you remain faithful and humble, you will see the greatest events in Church history.[6]

A full twenty-five years elapsed before du Plessis publicly shared this message.[7] By that time its fulfilment was under way and du Plessis' new ecumenical vocation had begun some nine or ten years earlier.[8] Over the intervening years, he had only confided in a few people, with whom he sensed an affinity of spirit. These included his wife Anna, his younger brother, Justus, Dr. Charles S. Price of Pasadena, California,[9] Kenneth Ware[10] and the British Pentecostal leader, Donald Gee. Du Plessis had been responsible for inviting Gee to speak in South Africa, where he had then acted as Gee's interpreter into Afrikaans. It was at this time that a spiritual bond was first formed between these two men, almost a generation apart. It was Gee who had recommended Wigglesworth to du Plessis as another Pentecostal speaker worth inviting to South Africa. So it was not perhaps surprising that du Plessis shared this news with Gee when they next met in Memphis, Tennessee, in 1937.[11]

Du Plessis did discuss the prophecy when he met Wigglesworth again in England after World War II. He told du Plessis:

> I feel the time is very near. I am not going to live much longer. I have asked the Lord if I could have a part in this or help you and the Lord said, 'No, you will not be alive when this begins.' After I pass on, then I believe the Lord will speak to you.[12]   note 12 says different from place in 1946

Wigglesworth died on 12 March 1947 at the age of eighty-seven. The following year, du Plessis was involved in a serious accident at a railroad crossing in West Virginia. In the following months of extended medical care and convalescence, he prayed for understanding about the Wigglesworth prophecy, 'an event so powerful at its birth and yet beginning to dim ever so slightly because of time and distance.'[13] While at prayer du Plessis heard the word, 'The time for the fulfilment of the prophecy Smith Wigglesworth gave you has arrived. It is time to begin. I want you to go to the leaders of the churches.'[14] There followed a dialogue in prayer in which du Plessis argued with the Lord that the mainline churches were dead, that their leaders were enemies; and how could he love people whose doctrines and practices he could not countenance? Du Plessis tells us the answer the Lord gave him:

> I never gave you authority to justify anybody. I only gave you authority to forgive. And if you forgive, you will love them. And if you love, you will want to forgive. Now you can choose.[15]

Du Plessis chose to love and to forgive. His life-story shows how this process began with the Protestants and later, to his complete surprise, extended to the Catholics. His ecumenical vocation, prophesied by Wigglesworth, had begun.

THE SIGNIFICANCE OF WIGGLESWORTH'S PROPHECY

The reason that this account of the origins of the Charismatic movement in Great Britain begins with Wigglesworth's prophecy to David du Plessis is because that event suggests a possible framework within which to interpret the movement not only in Britain but throughout the world.

Firstly, the Wigglesworth prophecy places any discussion of the Charismatic movement into an international context. What is described in the pages that follow is only one small national segment of a much larger international reality.[16] Some of the leaders mentioned in the British history had extensive influence in other countries,[17] and some Christians from abroad, most notably David du Plessis, played a significant role in Britain.[18]

Secondly, the prophecy points to a basic identity and continuity between the Pentecostal movement and the future Charismatic movement. This is implicit in the prophecy being given by a Pentecostal to a Pentecostal. It is explicit in different phrases in the various versions available.[19]

Thirdly, the prophecy implies that the denominationalization of the Pentecostal movement represented a narrowing of the divine purpose and a subsequent loss in its dynamic movement character. By contrast, the new Charismatic developments will manifest an element of reversal of this narrowing trend.

Finally, the prophecy indicates that the future Charismatic movement will touch all the traditional churches. This fact will illustrate its unparalleled ecumenical significance.

It will be helpful to bear these four points in mind, as the story of the origins of the Charismatic movement in Britain unfolds.

Two

Expelled by the Pentecostals

Smith Wigglesworth had pioneered the Pentecostal work in Bradford at a mission in Bowland Street until he became a full-time itinerant preacher around the end of the First World War. A number of the Bowland Street believers then joined the Apostolic Church, a recently-formed Pentecostal denomination just beginning its work in Bradford – a city which soon became one of the new church's main centres. Among these Christians were the Cousens, whose son Cecil was to play a significant role in the origins of the Charismatic movement in Britain.[1]

Cecil Cousen, born in 1913, had been baptized in the Spirit at the age of ten at a tarrying meeting, and he retained many memories of the power and vitality in the first generation of the Apostolic Church. 'I was brought up in that almost semi-revival state where the movings of the Holy Spirit were real, were miraculous and were almost normal with us.' Exceptionally for a Pentecostal, Cousen was sent to university, obtaining a lacrosse blue as well as an MA degree at Cambridge. From 1934 until 1948, he worked in the textile business founded by his father, as well as being very active in pastoral ministry in West Yorkshire. Though a successful businessman, he always sensed that one day he would become a full-time worker for the Apostolic Church.

In 1948, the family business was sold and Cousen offered to serve as Apostolic pastor in Hamilton, Ontario, for a year. This offer was approved, though the term was fixed at two years through a prophecy given in the council meeting.[2] Cousen ministered in Hamilton from 1949 to 1951.

During his stay in Canada, Cousen came into contact with the Latter Rain movement, which was being experienced in various locations in North America as a return to primitive Pentecostal power.[3] He was initially touched by a sermon of Dr. Thomas Wyatt of Portland, Oregon, at Hornell in New York State. The Latter Rain movement was characterized by the restoration of the ministries of apostles and prophets, by an emphasis on deliverance, by the laying-on of hands for baptism in the Spirit[4] and specific spiritual gifts, by the occurrence of extraordinary signs and wonders and by an opposition to human organization. For Cousen, the immediate impression was 'This is like what it used to be.'

Cousen was soon led to put some of his renewed convictions into practice. In his own words:

> I was new and at the bottom of the hierarchy. Hierarchy was very important. The Lord had shown me this. He had woken me up in the middle of the night, which was quite unusual for me and revealed this to me: in scripture and in experience – you should lay hands on for the baptism. . . . The Holy Spirit said, 'Tomorrow morning [which was the big day, the national holiday], you are going to speak and you have got to preach this and then put it into practice.' Well nobody had even heard of it before in our circles. I said, 'That is impossible, Lord. I can't preach, it's the big day, all the big guns will be preaching.' 'Well leave that with me.' So off I went to sleep.

The next day, about forty minutes before the big dinner, to everyone's astonishment and without any prior warning the president said, 'Now, we are going to ask Cecil to preach.' Cousen preached on laying-on hands for baptism in the Spirit and invited those wishing to receive to come forward. He asked his fellow-pastors to join him in the imposition of hands. They said, 'You preached it, you go down.' So Cousen went down, and all twelve seekers received the baptism.

Thus began an energetic ministry seeking to open up the Apostolic Church to recovery of Holy Spirit life and power. In Canada, it met with considerable success. On his return to England in February 1951 it also found a welcome among many of the ordinary church members among the Apostolics, thirsting for the old-time vitality they sensed they had lost.[5]

At the next Council meeting of the Apostolics in Britain in May 1951, there was a form of stalemate between those favouring the Latter Rain movement and the leaders of the Executive. In a surprising decision following a prophecy, Cousen and a close friend Philip Rhodes were freed to work together wherever they chose and to report back to the Executive. This permission had no precedent and was not allowed for in the Constitution of the Apostolics. It allowed Cousen and Rhodes to have further success in their preaching of revival with pentecostal fire.

However, those on the Executive who were opposed to the Latter Rain development secured a worldwide Council for the Apostolic Church in 1953. The president ruled that each person present at the Council should reaffirm his allegiance to the Constitution of the church. While having no problem with the tenets of the denomination, Cousen now saw its Constitution as a millstone round its neck, largely responsible for the throttling of its spiritual life and vigour. Together with James McKeown, a missionary to the Gold Coast (later Ghana), Cousen refused on the grounds of conscience to make the reaffirmation. Both were required to hand in their ordination certificates, and all Apostolic platforms were henceforth closed to them. Philip Rhodes, who – certain that Cousen would be expelled – had not attended the Council, had already pledged his loyalty to his friend come what may.

Cousen and Rhodes had no immediate plans to form any independent congregation. The next Sunday they arranged to worship at Rhodes' house with their families. Some thirty people turned up in the morning, and fifty to sixty at night. Soon a deputation of these ex-Apostolics came and said: 'We are not going back. They have rejected this move of God. We want to go on with you. You had better get a place and look after us.' They soon obtained a building in the centre of Bradford. Such was the beginning of the Dean House Christian Fellowship.

While the Apostolic leadership was denouncing Cousen, he was also receiving countless letters of interest and sympathy. This led to his issuing a newsletter reporting on his work.[6] After a few years, the need for such clarification disappeared, and Cousen replaced it with a new magazine, *A Voice of Faith*,[7] intended primarily as a vehicle for teaching. An early issue includes a sermon to the Christian Fellowship at Dean House by Philip Rhodes, defending their existence; it was based on Ezra 5:9: 'Who commanded you to build this house?'[8] A prefatory note by Cousen remarks:

> It will be sufficient for the reader to know that God visited us personally with Deliverance and Restoration. Thereupon we began immediately, in faith, to rebuild our spiritual temple. Unfortunately, however, such a ministry was unacceptable in certain quarters and so Christian Fellowship came into being as an independent local assem-

bly and a centre somewhat similar to the pattern of Antioch in the book of Acts. Already many have joined us locally and many others have visited us from the British Isles and other countries – all for one reason, they long for a new move[9]

The title of the magazine deliberately reflected Cousen's emphasis in the 1950s. A prophecy over Cousen in Toronto in 1950 had declared he would be a man of faith,[10] and it was the faith of Dr. Wyatt that made such an impression on Cousen. The first issue of *A Voice of Faith* declared:

> In particular, this ministry is specifically dedicated to create faith in the Name of Jesus Christ of Nazareth (the Son of God) for spiritual, emotional and physical healing.[11]

Evidently some readers sensed that this work could be in danger of focusing excessively on one truth, for the editorial comments in the next issue reassure such critics:

> The emphasis of AVF is on no particular truth in the ordinary sense of that word. True, we seek to create faith, especially for 'healing', but we immediately enlarge that word to cover body, soul, and spirit so that it covers the full range of God's purposes with man in Christ Jesus. But the real emphasis God has put into our zeal is not so much on 'healing' as on 'faith'. It is a voice of FAITH.[12]

Cousen saw his new life in terms similar to Luther's discovery of justification by faith. The discovery of faith replaces the effort to earn salvation and prove oneself before God. 'It takes away all the years of striving and the groaning that we should be good enough. Oh, my friends,' he told those present at the 1958 Exmouth Conference, 'for twenty-five years I've moved in circles where men and women with all the deep sincerity of their heart have been groaning and praying and agonizing that they may be good enough, that they may attain to some stature, some level of righteousness, for God to use them.'[13]

Cousen and Dean House refused to describe themselves as Pentecostal. AVF described the work as 'undenominational in spirit.'[14] Indeed in these early years, there was much more mention of faith than of the Holy Spirit and hardly any mention of baptism in the Holy Spirit. This may have represented a desire to appeal to a wider evangelical audience, but more evidently it reflected a conviction that doctrinal and dogmatic rigidity had been the ruin of the Pentecostal movement.[15] The pentecostal baptism was a victim of this process.[16] It is clear however that Cousen still believed in the baptism of the Holy Spirit, and that the spiritual gifts of 1 Corinthians 12:8–10 were in operation at Dean House. As he began to exercise a wider teaching ministry, he regularly preached and ministered the baptism in the Spirit,[17] though this does not become explicit in AVF until 1961.

This marked change was the result of a growing awareness that other Christian circles were becoming open to the pentecostal life. This awareness was particularly a result of the Evangelical Divine Healing Convention at High Leigh in September 1960, when several people were baptized in the Holy Spirit,[18] and of the first news of the pentecostal outpouring among the Episcopalians in the USA.[19]

The January 1961 issue of AVF begins: 'It had to come! Sooner or later it was inevitable. I refer to an AVF issue with an emphasis on the Holy Ghost.'[20] In fact, every issue of AVF from that point is a Holy Ghost issue. It now becomes the first magazine in Britain with a charismatic message, that is to say, a teaching of the baptism in the Spirit and the spiritual gifts expecting and receiving acceptance beyond the framework of Pentecostal-type churches.[21] AVF eventually achieved a circulation of 11,000.[22]

It will be clear from this description that Cousen did not bring the full 'Latter Rain' message back to England. He never attempted for instance to build Dean House on a basis of apostles and prophets. Rather, the Latter Rain movement was the occasion for Cousen recovering a measure of pentecostal fire and vitality, in which the central concept was faith. The one practice he did bring from Latter Rain was that of the laying-on of hands for ministering the baptism in the Spirit.

A near neighbour of Cousen in Bradford was Pastor G. W. North, later to be a prominent figure in one of the strands of the House Church movement.[23] It was during Walter North's period as pastor of the Calvary Holiness Church in Bradford (1952–65) that he began to attract attention as a preacher and teacher of baptism in the Spirit.[24] Cousen and North had quite regular fellowship during these years, and Cousen published some teaching articles by North in AVF.[25]

While Cousen's reaction to the rigidity of the Apostolics led him (at least for a time) to deprecate all forms of Christian organization, a parallel reaction led him away from Apostolic exclusiveness to much wider Christian fellowship. He became a regular participant in the Ministers' Fraternal in Bradford, and was invited to speak there about baptism in the Spirit and about healing. Cousen's ministry in the early years of Dean House was largely limited to ex-Apostolics, but through AVF his teaching gifts became more widely known. His contribution to the emerging Charismatic movement grew with his participation in conferences organized by other groups, whose rise and development will be described in succeeding chapters.

Three

Developments in Devon

Another circle of Christians combining pentecostal experience with a refusal to be categorized in Pentecostal terms already existed in Devon before the formation of Dean House in Bradford. In this circle the leader was David G. Lillie.[1]

Lillie was born in 1913 to a devout family belonging to the main group of Plymouth Brethren, known as the Open Brethren. At the age of nineteen, he moved from his native Sussex to London to work in a bank. The following year an open-air speaker at Tower Hill gave him some booklets, one of which asserted that all the gifts given by the Lord to his church were still available to his people today. Lillie realized that this was not what the Brethren had taught him to believe, but sensed it might well be true.

In 1934 he was moved by his bank to Exeter, where he joined the local Brethren assembly. In a Brethren Bible class he met a man who behaved in un-Brethren-like ways, wearing plus-fours and punctuating the teachings and prayers with 'Hallelujah' and 'Praise the Lord'. Lillie came to know this man, Ren Jackman by name, and discovered he was a Pentecostal, who received the baptism in the Spirit through the ministry of the famous Pentecostal revivalist, George Jeffreys. Jackman had joined the local assembly of Jeffreys' Church, the Elim Foursquare Gospel Alliance, though he later resigned, objecting to its centralized church government.[2]

Lillie and Jackman had many lively discussions, though Lillie was not ready to accept Jackman's argument that he needed a further experience of the Holy Spirit. Gradually, however, he came to sense that his resistance stemmed from a troubled conscience. He came to acknowledge the authenticity of the spiritual gifts that he had not yet experienced.

In the late 1930s Lillie met the Pentecostal missionary, Willie Burton,[3] who came to Exeter to minister among Jackman's circle.

Lillie tried without success to persuade the Brethren leaders to meet Burton. Instead this led to Lillie's suspension from all active ministry in the Brethren assembly.[4] As a result he moved four miles outside Exeter to Topsham, where he lodged with a family who had entered into 'the blessing of the Holy Spirit' and who were part of a small Christian fellowship led by Jackman. By this time Lillie was definitely seeking the inner experience which Jackman preached. It was during a small prayer meeting early in 1941 that he received this fullness. His recollection for the present author provides a classical description of what Pentecostals call the baptism in the Holy Spirit, even though Lillie himself called it an 'infilling':[5]

In the course of this time I became aware suddenly of a physical phenomenon which was new to me. Actually I felt a sort of pins and needles in my toes and feet. I never had this before and it gradually moved up my body and as I was actually, I believe, praying at the time, praising the Lord audibly, possibly along with several others. I can't remember just what was going on, suddenly my lips were taken over by a power that was not of me and I found myself speaking in an entirely new language. And it was a language, it wasn't mumbo-jumbo. It was a clearly enunciated language of tremendous clarity and phrasing. I say I found myself doing this, but that is only the subjective aspect of my thinking . . . the more important and objective aspect of what was going on at that moment was that the heavens opened and I became conscious of the presence of God in a way that I had never ever known before. And so I was filled with the Spirit of God and along with that infilling there was given to me the facility to express to my Lord the worship that was welling up in my heart.

Jackman and Lillie worked closely together in the small fellowship at Topsham, until 1949 when Lillie moved to Countess Wear, closer to Exeter. Here, arising out of a Sunday School which Lillie pioneered on a large housing estate, a new group slowly emerged under his leadership, yet still in close association with the original group at Topsham. At Countess Wear, Lillie was able to give himself more freely to the realization of his vision of the church according to the New Testament. Whereas Jackman was in many ways an independent Pentecostal,[6] Lillie brought to his pentecostal experience a distinctive emphasis on the restoration of the church. A major influence here was G. H. Lang, a Brethren writer and teacher, of an independent cast of mind, whom Lillie first discovered when Willie

Burton lent Jackman a book of Lang's on the local church. As Lillie
narrates:

> He (Lang) became a kind of spiritual father to me although he wasn't
> at all favourably disposed to the modern Pentecostal movement.
> Although he accepted doctrinally the teaching that the ministry and
> gifts of the Holy Spirit are for today, he wasn't prepared to admit or
> recognize that this was working out practically in Pentecostal circles.[7]

Helped by Lang in his reading and interpretation of the New
Testament, Lillie saw the outpouring of the Holy Spirit and the
recovery of spiritual gifts as given for the restoration of the New
Testament church.[8] In practice, he firmly believed that such a view
was incompatible with accepting the concept of denominations,
though he refused to identify with Jackman's anti-denominationalism.

As a result, the Countess Wear fellowship represented something
other than an independent Pentecostal assembly. It was a fusion of
the distinctively pentecostal (a filling with the Spirit distinct from
conversion and the recovery of spiritual gifts) with elements coming
from another tradition, namely the Brethren understanding of the
Church and the priesthood of all believers. The Countess Wear
group has then some claim to be a forerunner of the Charismatic
movement in its combination of pentecostal and traditional elements. What this fusion represents will be discussed further when
the Devon Conferences of later years are examined.

David Lillie also knew another former Plymouth Brother from the
West Country who had been baptized in the Spirit at the end of the
1940s. This was Sidney Purse of South Chard, Somerset, who formed
a house church in his home following his departure from the Brethren.[9] Although Lillie and Purse always remained on friendly terms,
their assemblies developed on different lines.[10]

A significant event in the development of Lillie's ministry was his
meeting with Arthur Wallis in 1952.[11] Wallis, ten years younger than
Lillie, had also been brought up among the Brethren, although his
father subsequently left, put off by their apparent narrowness. He
had also been much influenced by G. H. Lang, though he was more
influenced by Lang's emphasis on holiness and discipleship than by
his teaching on the church.[12] When he first met Lillie, Wallis still
moved a good deal in Brethren circles, and Lillie recalls that he bore
'the unmistakeable Brethren stamp'. But the Brethren understanding

of the church in the New Testament meant little to him. He was much
more interested in revival along Keswick lines, as his father had been
before him. In March 1951, Wallis had an experience of being filled
with the Holy Spirit, with an awareness of new power and freedom
in his life and ministry, though without speaking in tongues. He had
then visited the Outer Hebrides to see the effects of the Lewis revival,
and in 1956 had published a book on revival, *In the Day of Thy Power*,
which became one of the best-selling of his books.

Lillie and Wallis soon found they had much in common, sharing
a firm belief in the importance of biblical foundations and a vision
and burden for revival. However, there were also differences in
emphasis, and in May 1953, they held 'A Bible Study Conference on
the Holy Spirit' at Lillie's home in Countess Wear mainly to clarify
the differences between their positions.[13] Although Lillie's testimony
concerning spiritual gifts, especially tongues, did not initially make
much impact on Wallis, his vision – not just for the awakening of
individual Christians, but for the renewal of the church as an expression of the body of Christ – began to grip him.[14] Although Wallis
came to see the genuineness of the spiritual gifts, it was not until 1962
that he personally entered into their exercise.[15]

Through the agency of Edgar Parkyns,[16] a former member of the
Apostolic Church living in Exeter, Lillie and Wallis were introduced
to Cecil Cousen, probably early in 1954. He was immediately invited
to a day conference in the Lillies' house, that was held in July 1954.
These day conferences at Countess Wear had been by invitation only,
but by 1955 Lillie and Wallis opened them up to any interested
believers. These Saturday Conventions, aimed at spreading their
convictions about the renewal of the church in the power of the
Spirit, were initially somewhat irregular, but in the late 1950s they
were held about four times a year, with Cecil Cousen generally the
main speaker. These local Devon conventions proved to be a preparation for the larger leaders' conferences they began in 1958.

Lillie and Wallis, on the one hand, and Cousen, on the other hand,
complemented each other. Having been brought up in the most
church-oriented of the British Pentecostal denominations – the Apostolic Church – Cousen had some sympathy with the corporate
renewal sought by Lillie and Wallis. However, Cousen's contribution to the conferences sponsored by Lillie and Wallis was in the area
of ministry in the Spirit. Cousen immediately struck them as having
wisdom, vitality and maturity in an area where they were both

relatively inexperienced.[17] Lillie and Wallis, without being mere theoreticians, were always more interested than Cousen in theological issues, especially in ferreting out a deeper understanding of the church from the Scriptures.

In the summer of 1957, Lillie shared with Wallis the idea of gathering men from all over the country who shared this concern for a renewed expression of the church.[18] Their convening letter emphasized the serious spiritual plight of the nation:

> Almighty God has ceased to be a reality in the minds of the mass of His human creatures, and in this land alone a generation is arising which has so little grasp of the significance of any moral standards that one wonders how the present social order can survive apart from a spiritual revival.[19]

Almost all the leaders they approached welcomed the idea of such a conference, and in May 1958 approximately twenty-five people came together in Exmouth 'to wait on God and to exchange ideas'[20] on the topic 'The Church of Jesus Christ: Its Purity, Pattern and Programme in the Context of To-day'.[21] The three main speakers spoke on their distinctive emphasis: Cousen on the Power, Lillie on the Pattern of the Church and Wallis on the Purity.

The platform for the Exmouth Conference was not Pentecostal or charismatic, though the convening letter hinted at new moves of the Holy Spirit:

> There is a growing conviction that God will yet grant, in response to believing prayer, another gracious visitation of the Holy Spirit in reviving grace. Many are being stirred to pray to this end, and a spirit of expectancy, born surely of the Spirit of God, is in many hearts. It is also our conviction that God is now raising up men, taught of the Spirit according to the Word, who will thus be prepared for the unfamiliar conditions and perils attendant upon a time of revival.[22]

This gathering did have some influence in spreading the pentecostal-charismatic fire.[23] Two future leaders present at this meeting were Graham Perrins[24] and Roger Forster.[25] Two factors contributed particularly to this influence.

First, Cecil Cousen's address on 'The Power of the Church'[26] directly raised the issues of baptism in the Holy Spirit and spiritual gifts. Cousen began from the concept of 'a new line of manhood' revealed in Jesus Christ. To be in Christ is to have this new line of

manhood, to be able to do through faith and the Spirit what Jesus
did through the Spirit. 'If our faith can only rise to this reality, then
it is merely a matter of asking, and we are baptized in the Holy
Ghost.'[27] Cousen went on to speak of this baptism as an event distinct
from and usually subsequent to conversion:

> . . . the body is a means of expression of the personality which is
> within, and at the Baptism of the Holy Ghost the Spirit of God comes
> within and takes possession of the body. God thinks tremendously of
> the body, and it is the last and the hardest thing for us to yield to Him.
> It is far easier to yield the rest of our personality than our body. 'I
> beseech you . . . yield your bodies a living sacrifice'. God is wanting
> hands, and feet, and lips, that are indwelt by the power of the Holy
> Ghost, so that supernatural things may be done all the way along the
> line. Our members functioning under divine control – supernaturally,
> through not necessarily spectacularly: the touch of God upon every-
> thing.[28]

Cousen then concluded, 'When the Holy Spirit Himself comes,
He brings with Him the gifts of the Holy Spirit.'[29] While there was
no public ministry 'to receive the baptism' at Exmouth or subsequent conferences, there was some private ministry, in particular
by Cousen.

Secondly, Lillie was led to a public exercise of the gift of tongues
during this Conference. His own description conveys some of the
atmosphere of the meeting:

> We had already decided, Arthur (Wallis) and I, beforehand that there
> was to be no display of spiritual gifts that would be likely to embarrass
> any of those who came, because at this point they were just people
> that were seemingly reasonably open in their minds but certainly not
> Pentecostal in their experience or as far as we know in some cases in
> their convictions. Extraordinarily enough though in the midst of one
> of our sessions during a time of prayer the Holy Spirit came upon the
> meeting in a most compelling way and I found myself absolutely
> obliged to exercise my gift of tongues which was totally out of
> character for me, but I did it . . . the extraordinary thing is that I knew
> exactly what I was doing. I knew exactly the kind of reaction one
> might expect from some of those men, but I had no fear, and felt that
> I was in the will of God in using the gift in that way.

In fact, only one participant reacted visibly against this 'pentecostal element'. This element was to increase somewhat and to

feature in public discussion at a second conference organized by Lillie and Wallis in 1961.

The second conference was also held in Devon at Belstone near Okehampton, and was devoted to the theme 'The Divine Purpose in the Institution of the Church'.[30] Forty people attended Belstone, with a slight increase in those with a pentecostal or charismatic interest.[31] Among these were Pastor Rae Shaw of the Good Shepherd Mission, Bethnal Green in London's East End[32] and two close friends, Ben Allen and W. B. Grant, who will feature later in this history.

The combination of restoration (of the New Testament church) and pentecostal elements is indicated in the introduction to the Conference report:

> It was our conviction that such a church must arise in this end time, endued with power from on high, equipped with the manifold gifts of the Spirit, and with a much fuller understanding of her proper function and purpose in the divine plan.[33]

This report has more explicit references to the Pentecostal movement. In his address on 'The Divine Idea of the Local Church', Wallis spoke of the two movements particularly flowing into these conferences:

> The two church movements that one might expect to offer most may provide the two greatest dangers to such New Testament churches arising in this end time. I refer to the peril of 'Brethrenism' and that of 'Pentecostalism', with emphasis in both cases on the 'ism'. I say this without wishing to minimize the revelation that God has given through those two movements.[34]

This quotation indicates salient elements in the understanding of the two conveners of the Devon Conferences. Firstly, they were influenced significantly by both the Brethren and by the Pentecostals, or (as they would emphasize) by what the Lord has given to his people through these two movements. Wallis located the particular gift of Brethrenism in 'church order'[35] and that of Pentecostalism in 'the baptism in the Holy Spirit and . . . the supernatural gifts of the Spirit'.[36] Secondly, they believed that God was now leading believers into something greater than either of these forebears. Not all participants in these Devon Conferences were as open to both influences as were the organizers of the programme.[37] Allen and Grant were among those present who were being touched by the pentecostal current but hardly at all by the Brethren ecclesiology. As at Exmouth, Cousen gave a teaching, ending with the practical necessity of receiving the baptism in the Spirit[38] and was active in private ministry to 'receive the baptism'.[39]

By the time of the Belstone conference, participants were aware of the neo-pentecostal movement among Episcopalians in the USA.[40] The interest aroused led to the 1962 conference held at Mamhead Park, near Exeter, being devoted to the theme 'The Present Ministry of the Holy Spirit'.[41] It attracted a record attendance of seventy. It was at Mamhead Park that Wallis first met the young Welshman, Bryn Jones, later to be his close colleague in the Harvestime group of assemblies (or house churches).[42]

At Mamhead Park, the distinctive issues raised by the new pentecostal developments were directly addressed. Cecil Cousen devoted his entire address entitled 'The Holy Spirit and the Personal Need of the Believer'[43] to the baptism in the Holy Spirit. He covered three aspects:

1. What is the scriptural ground for an expectation of a personal filling with the Holy Spirit?
2. What is the nature of this experience, and how may we know that we have received it?
3. What are the prerequisites of such a filling?[44]

Lillie introduced a Bible study on 1 Corinthians 14, and thus directly confronted the question of tongues.[45] He posed the challenge, which he then answered in the affirmative:

> 'Is this gift of tongues divine; has it been divinely bestowed upon the church?' We have only to face up to that simple question and most of our problems dissolve. If this gift is from God, then it is holy; it is sacred; it ought to be desired and coveted; and we as believers and members of local fellowships ought to be concerned to see it operating in the churches for the glory of Christ.[46]

In a shorter contribution under the heading of 'News and Views', Ben Allen spoke of 'The Gift of the Spirit in His Two Phases.'[47] Allen here quotes from the Speaker's Commentary on John 20:22, to the effect that the relation of the paschal to the pentecostal gift is that of quickening to endowing. 'The one answers to the power of the resurrection, and the other to the power of the ascension. The one to victory and the other to sovereignty.'[48] Allen adds a comment that implicitly endorses the Pentecostal movement:

> Surely we have here the Scriptural solution to the problem of misunderstanding between the Pentecostal Movement and the Holiness Movements and others.[49]

The three conferences convened by Lillie and Wallis show a slow but steady increase in the pentecostal or charismatic element in both teaching and practice. The findings of a questionnaire given to participants at Mamhead Park show a high level of appreciation, though a few participants were unhappy with the pentecostal features.[50] However, the very fact that noisy praise seemed to be a bigger problem for a minority than the manifestation of spiritual gifts indicates the considerable evolution of the conferences from Exmouth to Mamhead Park. Lillie and Wallis in their comments conclude regarding the three conferences:

> In the main those attending have shared with us the conviction that; 1) There is a baptism of power (whether individual or corporate) available to the believer, which the early church knew, but to which most Christians today are strangers. 2) There are supernatural spiritual gifts which the early Christians enjoyed and exercised . . . and which are still given in response to earnest prayer and living faith. 3) There is a need for a wholehearted and full-blooded return to the principles of N.T. church life and witness, if the blessing of the Spirit in revival is to be made permanently effective, and the fruits conserved and developed. In short, we need REVIVAL AND REFORMATION.[51]

The first two of these convictions were to be shared with other participants in the emerging Charismatic movement. The third, in which the Brethren influence is paramount, was to become a ground for dispute and a point of separation within the movement in later years.

By the time the conveners' comments on Mamhead Park were written, Wallis had himself received the gift of tongues. Cousen had previously told Wallis, 'Arthur, when you are baptized in the Spirit, you will not only speak in tongues but you will prophesy.' And so it was.[52] Wallis did not publicize this event immediately as he knew it would lead to many doors being closed to him, especially among the Brethren.[53]

After Mamhead Park, there was only one more Lillie-Wallis conference, and that was some two and a half years later and not in Devon.[54] One reason for the series winding down was the sense that smaller and more localized conferences were needed after Mamhead Park.[55]

The Devon Conferences held by Lillie and Wallis have a particular significance in the history of the Charismatic movement in Britain. Not only were they conferences by invitation only and largely attended by people who were leaders with influence over others, but they are well documented and explain much about subsequent developments and tensions within the movement.

Four

Healing First

While participants in the Charismatic movement of the 1970s and early 1980s in Britain would be likely to know the names of Cecil Cousen and Arthur Wallis, though possibly not that of David Lillie, it is virtually certain that they would not know that of David Rushworth Smith. Some would have known of David Smith, but that would have been David Smith first of Gillingham and later of York.[1]

In 1952 David R. Smith was a student at the Methodist Cliff College in Derbyshire, when he had an unsought and dramatic introduction to the ministry of healing. Smith recalls this event:

> One of the students came to my room and said to me, very simply, 'The Lord Jesus has told me that if I come to you and you pray for me I shall be healed.' Now he had got a very serious disease and in fact he really should not have been at college any longer. He should have gone home . . . They were being very patient with this illness. I said, 'Well, it's funny the Lord Jesus hasn't told me that.' And he said, 'But I insist. This is absolutely true. If you pray for me, I shall be healed.' So I said, 'All right, then, let us pray.' So I did pray for him, and instantly and immediately he was healed.[2]

Smith subsequently discussed this episode and its implications with his tutor, who advised him not to get too involved with healing.[3] Another student who had heard of the healing told Smith about a conference held in London in the late 19th century by a body calling itself 'the Evangelical Divine Healing Fellowship'.[4] Smith discovered that the EDHF was still in existence, at least nominally, and he became a member.

Smith immediately began to read and to collect books on the subject of healing. He also made contact with a number of American evangelists with a healing ministry, including A. A. Allen and T. L. Osborn. He received their magazines, and exchanged letters with them. Growing acquaintance with their Pentecostal teaching led Smith into a process of re-evaluation of his understanding. This was further complicated by his decision in 1953 to leave the Methodist Church, disturbed by the anti-supernatural views of Donald Soper, the well-known London preacher. Smith now moved to Suffolk, where he pastored a Congregational chapel near Hadleigh.[5]

From the time of his conversion in 1947, Smith had believed that the gifts of the Spirit did not cease with the apostles. Now with the experience of healing as a present-day reality, he urged an openness to the full range of God's gifts. In consequence other spiritual gifts besides healing were soon in evidence. Now Smith and his wife found themselves 'in the middle of what may be honestly called a genuine evangelical religious awakening in Suffolk'.[6] Into the midst of this excitement came a WEC missionary to preach about the religious awakening in the Congo. He was surprised to find the same phenomena in East Anglia. Smith describes his reaction:

> He was surprised and excited by this discovery. He wanted to know what we called this 'movement', and was told that it had no name, and that nobody had thought of giving it one. He pressed us to call it something . . . Our reply may now seem to have been unwise, but it was made sincerely: 'In some ways, this is a new form of pentecostalism, but it might better be described as a dynamic evangelicalism'.[7]

It was at this time in the mid-1950s that Smith came to play a definite supportive role in the life of a young Christian, Donald Double, later to become one of the most influential of the independent Pentecostal evangelists.[8] Double had been converted in October 1954 during a campaign in Hadleigh, Suffolk, led by Peter Scothern, an independent Pentecostal evangelist, invited there by Smith.[9] About 1955, Smith moved to Ipswich, where he began a house church in his home. Here, following a further campaign by Scothern, Double began to attend house meetings and was in fact prepared by Smith to be prayed over for 'the fullness of the Spirit.'[10] Double's actual baptism in the Spirit was however on the occasion of a Scothern crusade in Ipswich.[11]

Besides Scothern, Smith was also in at least occasional contact with other evangelists of Pentecostal convictions. One was Vic Ramsey, at that time with the Assemblies of God,[12] and another was Henri Staples, a Christian businessman from Newark, Nottinghamshire who ran what he called 'Glory Meetings'.[13]

Smith does not fit into any clear category – a position he was careful to maintain as the emerging neo-pentecostal or charismatic movement began to take shape. He refused to be called a Pentecostal, regarding a second baptism after conversion as unscriptural, although in the 1950s he clearly taught a post-conversion experience of being filled with the Spirit.[14] After a period of admiring the Pentecostal healers, Smith decisively rejected their 'Prosperity Gospel' and the view that God wills to heal all sickness. In 1955, he turned down an invitation to be T. L. Osborn's European representative.[15]

Beginning with the years in Ipswich, Smith and his wife Doreen became prolific writers of booklets and leaflets on Christian topics. These they published themselves, many in a series entitled 'Some Light'.[16]

As Smith became active in the ministry of divine healing, he was able to reactivate the EDHF, of which he became the secretary. This became a larger part of his ministry from 1959, the year in which Smith knew he must get back inside a major denomination, lest he be guilty of schism. 'It came to me as a revelation from God . . . I had this terrible conviction that I was guilty of schism.' Smith tried without success to join the Baptists, and finding the Congregationalists were the only people who would have him, he became the minister of the Congregational Church at Braughing, near Ware in Hertfordshire.[17]

In July 1959, Smith attended the Fourth International Conference on Divine Healing in Glasgow, where he felt ill at ease with the non-evangelical elements in this conference. It was there that Smith first met David du Plessis, driving him around to various meetings, and they put each other on their mailing lists.

Smith saw a need for a preaching of the evangelical message with the power of the Spirit manifested in healing and the other gifts. Moving nearer to London provided him with greater opportunities for a wider ministry, and in September 1960 he convened at High Leigh the first Evangelical Divine Healing Convention. Among the speakers at High Leigh were Cecil Cousen, of whom Smith heard through AVF, and Ben Allen, a near-neighbour in Hertfordshire to whom Smith was introduced by Bill Grant.[18]

The convention programme as well as Smith's welcoming address[19] show that his own focus was particularly on healing. This does not mean that Smith ignored the rest of the gospel in the promotion of healing. His published works clearly indicate otherwise.[20] However, healing has been a constant special interest for Smith, and it is evident that he saw the significance of High Leigh 1960 in terms of healing, not in terms of a neo-pentecostal or charismatic movement.

Nonetheless the Evangelical Divine Healing Conventions, beginning with High Leigh, did make a contribution to Charismatic beginnings in Britain. Once again, Cousen preached directly at High Leigh about baptism in the Holy Spirit.[21] During the convention, Cousen and Smith laid hands on Ben Allen, Bill Grant and Eric Houfe[22] for the pentecostal blessing, though none of them evidently received on that occasion. Others did, however,[23] and it is clear that there was a public charismatic character to much of this convention.

Soon after High Leigh, Smith began to issue an EDH bulletin[24] and the first issue announced the second convention to be held at Herne Bay, Kent in May 1962. Cousen and Allen were again among the speakers,[25] who also included another minister later active in the Charismatic movement, Stephen Wyatt of Bournemouth.[26] Again it had an evident charismatic dimension, later recalled by Bill Grant:

> I have been to a number of Healing Conventions run by different bodies, but the two conventions arranged by the independent evangelicals were far and away the most outstanding, both as regards depth and soundness of teaching and unity of those present . . . The Holy Spirit was present in power at the second convention last year. At one of the early meetings three girls (women rather) – all Anglicans, one from All Souls, another from Hay-on-Wye and the third from Yorkshire – sitting together all cried out and afterwards declared they had been filled with the Holy Spirit. That something terrific had happened there is no doubt whatsoever. Two days later at one of the morning lectures Cecil Cousens [sic] digressed from his theme and started talking about the lordship of Christ. Soon most of those present were broken before the Lord. A man from All Souls sitting next to me was in tears, so was I, and a Vicar from Somerset had his head between his knees sobbing his heart out. God was striving in many hearts. Then a Pentecostal given to starting choruses, chose to start one: and everything went flat. Blessed as choruses can be, they do not always help.[27]

Thus, at the time when the Charismatic movement was just coming into public awareness, David R. Smith was seen by many as one of the leading promoters of the new move, even though he himself was not thinking in those terms.

Five

Two Friends from South Africa

In 1955 two men who were close friends, and who had both been touched by the power of God in South Africa, moved with their families to Britain in response to a definite sense of God's call. Both were to play a role in the subsequent history of the Charismatic movement.

Campbell McAlpine, unlike his friend Denis Clark, was not a native of South Africa.[1] As his name indicates his roots lay in Scotland, where he was born in 1918. Though his father had been an evangelist and he was brought up among the Brethren, he subsequently fell away and had no active Christian faith during his six years in the army during World War II. Within a year of demobilisation, Campbell was persuaded to attend a mission in Troon, his home town, by a famous Scottish evangelical preacher. He recalls:

> From the minute the minister began to speak, I disliked him, and resented him. But, in spite of that, the Holy Spirit convicted me of sin, and later that night I wept my way to Jesus.[2]

That same year (1946), the newly-converted Campbell McAlpine went to South Africa to take up a responsible post in the John Laing Engineering firm, and quickly became involved in the local Brethren assembly. There he learnt the importance of commitment to a local church and gaining experience in evangelism. It was during these years that he first met and then became a close friend of Denis Clark.

Denis G. Clark was born in Johannesburg on 29 April 1920.[3] As a young man of sixteen he was converted under the ministry of Dr. J. Edwin Orr. Following this experience, he belonged to a Baptist Church for a number of years. Eventually however he left the Baptists for the Brethren, persuaded that the latter's practice and teaching were more scriptural. From 1938 Clark became active in *Youth for Christ*, while training to be an accountant. In 1952 he resigned his responsibilities as a business executive, becoming in 1953 the full-time director of *Youth for Christ* in South Africa. All through this period Clark retained his close links with the Brethren. Meanwhile McAlpine was still in business, though giving much of his free time to Christian service.

In the South African summer of 1953–54, Clark was with his wife Beth on holiday in the Karoo, a semi-desert area in South Africa. Beth Clark recalled in an interview:

> It was there as we were really seeking the Lord and asking the Lord to show us things in our lives which were not pleasing to him, that we were preparing ourselves for the baptism of the Spirit. Having been brought up in the Brethren, this subject was taboo, and therefore we were not taught, and yet Denis knew that there was something more. There was a man in the Brethren, whom God used mightily, and whose power was resting upon him. Denis went to him to enquire, but he couldn't put a name to it. He just had said God had blessed him in this particular way, and Denis wanted what his friend had, he wanted the power of God in his life. Just through reading through the Scriptures, and meditating and studying, he knew there was a further experience after the new birth. So therefore while we were in the Karoo together, we asked the Lord to fill us with his Holy Spirit.

There was no immediate manifestation of spiritual gifts, but after returning from holiday, Clark sensed that the Lord was calling on him to pray for the sick. Beth Clark describes her husband's struggle:

> Working in Brethren circles, he knew if he did that [pray for the sick], that would be the end of his ministry in the Brethren. He tried to hedge it and dodge it, but God's word was so explicit on this particular evening where he was having a campaign in a Baptist Church in Germiston in the Transvaal, that he just said to the Lord, 'All right, Lord, if you ruin my ministry, that's up to you.'

At the service that night, Clark invited any sick people present to come forward for ministry. Three did so, one being a woman dying of cancer.[4] She was healed, and Clark took this as the Lord's confirmation of this ministry. Brethren circles were now closed to him, as he had feared. From this time, people came to Clark in increasing numbers to be prayed with for the baptism in the Spirit.

Some received the manifestation of tongues, even though the Clarks did not yet have this gift.

McAlpine soon followed Clark into his experience of a greater fullness of the Spirit. He was baptized in the Spirit on 11 November 1954. In his printed testimony, McAlpine recalls:

> Two Scriptures were specially impressed upon me: 'And Jesus being full of the Holy Ghost, was led by the Spirit into the wilderness' (Luke 4:1); and 'He that saith he abideth in Him ought himself also to walk even as He walked' (1 John 2:6). Linking these together I saw that I needed to be filled with the Holy Spirit, and that this was my right. But I had been warned against such things. Yet the longing remained. Had He not promised to fill the thirsty soul?
>
> One morning at business I became ill, and returned home and went to bed. I was soon prompted to get up and pray. God showed me how impossible it was to be filled with the Spirit while my heart was so full of rubbish and sin. I saw the need for specific confession instead of my former vague half-confession: 'Lord, if I have sinned against you, I claim the blood to cleanse me.' I cried now: 'Search me, O God, and know my heart.'
>
> How wonderful to know His cleansing and forgiveness as one by one those sins were uncovered, confessed and forsaken! I now pleaded with the Lord to fill me with His Spirit. Words are inadequate to describe what followed: the love of God filled me, and flowed through and over me like a mighty wave. Suddenly the Lord had become real; I loved Him with all my heart with a love that He had given me. Kneeling at His feet I praised and worshipped Him.
>
> I knew little then about speaking with tongues, beyond hearing it was something to be avoided. Later I was led to study the Word on this subject. The same night as I was lying in bed praising and thanking the Lord, I found myself praising Him in a new language. It seemed 'natural' as the indwelling Holy Spirit took my lips and the words flowed forth in praise of the Lord.[5]

McAlpine now had a deep desire to spend his life in the Lord's service, so he asked what the Lord wanted to do with his life. His answer came from Jeremiah 1: 'Do not say, 'I am a youth,' for you shall go to all to whom I send you, and whatever I command you, you shall speak.' He decided to spend a weekend in prayer to seek the Lord's will as to where he was sent, and Clark asked if he could come. During the weekend the two men heard the words from Ruth: 'Arise, let us go back to our own people, and to the land of our nativity.' McAlpine knew he had to return to Britain.

The following year, the McAlpines and the Clarks moved to Britain in obedience to the leading they experienced, and both families settled in Worthing on the Sussex coast. Initially, they threw themselves into service in the Billy Graham Crusade. Clark naturally linked himself with *Youth for Christ* in Europe, being initially invited to speak in Copenhagen, Denmark, as a last-minute substitute for an American speaker. This soon led to his becoming European Director, a post he held for the next five years. McAlpine and Clark worked closely together until June 1959, when the McAlpines left for New Zealand where Campbell had some close relatives.[6] Campbell McAlpine had first met Arthur Wallis around 1957–58, and Arthur introduced Campbell in turn to David Lillie and Cecil Cousen, thus opening up wider fellowship with other Christians baptized in the Spirit.

In the meantime the Clarks 'still . . . sensed an inward restriction'[7] from which they sought release. Because some close friends had received the full pentecostal blessing at the Good Shepherd mission in Bethnal Green, the Clarks went there in the spring of 1960 to receive ministry. The pastor Rae Shaw[8] and an associate Fred Smith[9] told Clark he needed the gift of tongues.[10] Clark describes what happened:

> My wife and I were in London, and some brethren to whom we disclosed our need, laid hands upon us both, and prayed. Immediately my wife began to speak with a new tongue, as an accompaniment of a wonderful inward release. Clinging desperately to the Lord, at last He began to fill this poor vessel with such power I thought I should succumb. It was however four days before I experienced the full release in my inner being as my tongue was loosened to praise the Lord.
>
> My wife and I testify that this precious experience of the Holy Spirit has revolutionised every part of our lives both in the home and in the ministry. We stand by the imperative of Acts 1:8.[11]

This was the year in which Clark resigned as European Director of *Youth for Christ* and launched out into a full-time evangelistic and teaching ministry.

Clark's role in helping others to be baptized in the Spirit now increased significantly. Stanley Jebb, a close associate of Clark's in the 1970s, first met Clark and was introduced 'to a charismatic experience in 1960 in connection with the World Youth for Christ Congress in Bristol, which was followed by a mission in which Denis preached with tremendous power'.[12]

By this time, Clark was producing an occasional newsletter for his friends and supporters under the title of *Greetings*.[13] The newsletter shows the basic evangelistic thrust of Clark's ministry at this time. In 1961 he visited Scandinavia three times, holding campaigns in Denmark and Sweden.[14] Clark was now openly preaching the need for baptism in the Spirit:

> 'Preach that Christ saves, and the people believe and get saved: preach that He heals, and they believe for healing: preach that He delivers, and devils depart' . . . we quote Dr. Graham. 'We need to learn once again what it means to be Baptized with the Holy Spirit.'[15]

It was in July 1961 that one of the more extraordinary outbreaks of spiritual power occurred in connection with Clark's ministry during a crusade in Matlock, Derbyshire. A local Pentecostal pastor whose assembly co-operated in this crusade provides the fullest account of what happened:

> A young man of the local Brethren assembly, impressed by the earnestness of young Pentecostal believers in the town, went home to pray and read the Scriptures by his bedside, when suddenly he was baptized in the Spirit, praising the Lord in other tongues. The hunger of God grew, and one night in an after meeting about sixty people gathered in the Brethren Church to wait on the Lord. There were Methodists, Wesleyan Reform, Congregationalists, Salvationists, Pentecostals and Brethren, and numbers received the Baptism of the Spirit including an elder of the Brethren Assembly. It was after midnight when this meeting ended long after last buses ceased to run – but time didn't matter, the blessing of the Lord mattered more.[16]

Clark's influence on the origins of the Charismatic movement is hard to evaluate. First, he never adopted a predominantly Pentecostal or charismatic platform, but taught the distinctively charismatic convictions as part of a basic Christian evangelism. Secondly, he was always on the move, and it is difficult to determine what later charismatic currents in a place might have been influenced by an earlier Clark visit. However, some witnesses and correspondence of the early 1960s indicate that Clark was often instrumental in opening believers to a new dimension of life in the Spirit.[17] To one or two places, notably Farnborough[18] and Hermon Baptist Church in Glasgow, he paid several visits. The two factors that make evaluation difficult may themselves have contributed to Clark having a wide influence. His 'non-charismatic' platform made him acceptable in many places closed to men like Scothern, Double and Ramsey, and his travels brought him into contact with many people.

McAlpine and Clark first came to know Cousen, Lillie and Wallis around 1957–58. Neither was present at any of the Devon conferences, hosted by Lillie and Wallis, although McAlpine was certainly invited to those at Belstone and Mamhead Park. Clark and Wallis shared a strong concern for revival in the nation, which was to lead to close association in the years after those covered in this study.[19] Clark also exercised a significant influence through Prayer and Bible Weeks, of which the first was held in his home in Worthing at the New Year in 1964.[20]

In the long run however McAlpine had a greater influence on the Charismatic movement in Britain than Clark. While both developed widely-appreciated teaching ministries, only McAlpine became closely associated with the Fountain Trust in the years from 1964, almost immediately after his return from New Zealand.[21] This contrast did not represent any division or indeed lessening of collaboration between the two men. Rather it was an amicable recognition of some differences in their specific spheres of ministry.

Six

From Local Preaching to a National Ministry

In the history of the Charismatic movement in Britain, Edgar Trout of Plymouth deserves particular mention.[1] Several people involved in the mid-1960s regard Trout as the key figure of that period. His story is different in many respects from those of the leading figures mentioned in previous chapters. Prior to 1964, a relatively late date in this story, he had little or no interaction with other leaders in the emerging movement, even his fellow Devonians, Lillie and Wallis.[2] The glowing tributes at his death in 1968 point to the sheer impact of Trout's contribution in the last four years of his life.[3]

Edgar Trout's life was interspersed with major trials and with dramatic evidence of divine activity. His earliest years from his birth in 1912[4] were marked by bronchial weakness, which made survival seem unlikely, and which then retarded his formal education. Trout's parents were devout Methodists. At the age of eleven, he was taken by his father to hear the famous evangelist Gipsy Smith, who made a deep impression on young Edgar. That night he resolved that Jesus should be the Lord of his life. The following year, he received the first intimation of future calling in what he later described as a vision. His son reports:

> But whatever the form of this revelation, its content remained immovable in his memory: at an appointed time in his life, God would call him into full-time service for himself; and by the end of his life, he would see miracles performed by the power of God, as in the days of Christ's earthly ministry – including the direct healing of the sick.[5]

Trout left school two months before his fifteenth birthday. A few years later, when others urged him to become a Methodist lay preacher, he had to overcome feelings of inferiority because of his educational limitations. This call he accepted, becoming fully accredited as a lay preacher in March 1935. The lay preachers' test was the only public examination Trout ever passed. Trout ministered in Plymouth and in neighbouring Cornish circuits for over twenty-five years. His son notes that from the beginning, Edgar Trout's preaching had three characteristics that remained throughout his life: an abundant use of illustration, an appeal for a wholehearted Christianity and an element of direct challenge to the hearer.[6] After working in his teens as an apprentice to a firm of wholesale ironmongers and builders' merchants, at the age of twenty Trout went into partnership with his father in a small knitwear business in Plymouth.

For the next twenty years until the mid-1950s, Trout combined his Christian commitment with forms of public service. From 1935, his involvement with Toc-H, a Christian organization for public and social service, extended his Christian contacts beyond Methodist circles; and this was where he first came to know and respect some Anglican believers.[7] During the war, when he was exempted from military service, first by reason of reserved occupation and later on medical grounds, Trout gave political expression to his Christian idealism. He joined the Common Wealth party, and fought the 1945 Election as Common Wealth candidate for the Drake division of Plymouth, losing his deposit in the process. Later he won local success at the polls, becoming a Labour Councillor in the City of Plymouth in 1953.

Thrown back on his faith by a severe business crisis in 1954, Trout experienced a breaking of his self-will and his dependence on his self-energy. It was however another two years before there was a dramatic change in his life. In April 1956, Trout was driving his family to Penzance when his car was hit by another vehicle that was out of control. He alone was seriously hurt.

Three weeks later Trout was lying flat on his back, almost totally paralysed from the neck down and in considerable pain, awaiting return to hospital, when he received an unlikely visitor, the anglo-catholic vicar of the local parish of Eggbuckland.[8] While shopping in the town, the vicar sensed that God was telling him to go and visit Mr. Trout immediately. He challenged Trout directly: 'Do you believe God can heal today, as in New Testament days?'[9] Trout told him about two previous healings in his life,[10] but saw his present state as more extreme, not one of sickness but of broken bones, indeed of a fracture of the first lumbar vertebra. Challenged that he was limiting the power of God, Trout expressed his willingness if healed to serve God with all his energy and strength.

The vicar prayed for Edgar Trout's healing, and then left. Trout suddenly realized that all the pain had gone. After a 'pins and needles' sensation had gone right down his body, he found he had suddenly sat up. After sitting, he stood; after standing, he walked. He then astonished his wife by carrying his tea tray downstairs to the kitchen. Within ten days, Trout was preaching and within another week he was back at the wheel of his car.

Partly as a result of this remarkable healing (he was then a public figure as a city councillor), Trout was invited to lead a fortnight's mission that autumn in the small Bath Street mission hall, belonging to the non-denominational Plymouth City Mission. Apprehensive, because this represented a drastic change from the respectable city suburbs to the heart of Plymouth's 'red-light' district, Trout knew that he must accept, in fidelity to the promise made before his healing.

Before the mission began, he received an anonymous phone call. His son tells the story:

'I hear you've got a mission coming off in October', said the gruff old voice on the other end.

'Yes, that's right', said Edgar coolly. 'But who are you?'

'This town's been packed full of missions ever since the war', the voice pursued, unperturbed. 'It's packed full of Christians, too. But nothing ever happens. When are you going to get the outsider in?'

'That's what we're wanting to do', countered Edgar, trying hard to keep his temper, 'but how do you suggest we do it?'

'Oh, I'll tell you how you can do it, all right. But it all depends on your carrying it out . . . Have your normal evangelistic rally by all means, and have it full of church-types as usual – it might even do 'em good. But then at 10.30, when the pubs are turning out and there are plenty of people on the streets, send a bunch of Christians out with invitations to come in and have a cup of tea and a bun free. That'll shock them. Speak to them for a couple of minutes, perhaps, but then just hand the meeting to the floor. Open yourself up to be asked any question at all on the Christian Faith. And if you can't answer, then you're not as good as the Communist – he at least knows what he believes and why. If you promise to do this, I'll send you twenty pounds to pay for the tea and buns.'[11]

Trout knew this was a confirmation of some previous pointers, so he did precisely what the caller said. His trust and dependence on God's power and wisdom were soon put to the test as the dingy hall was filled by a crowd of inebriated sailors out for some fun. Trout's faith was more than equal to the challenge. To the first question 'Why does Jesus want me for a sunbeam?', asked to a tittering accompaniment, Trout gave an inspired response: 'My friend, if you hadn't been to Sunday School in the first place, you wouldn't have known that he wants you.' The burly questioner was reduced to a stunned silence and then to uncontrollable sobbing.[12] The success of the mission, during which a number of people were converted, led to Trout holding regular weekly services at Bath Street.[13] One of the converts from these days, Harry Greenwood, then in the Navy, was to have a significant ministry within the charismatic movement in Britain.

It was in dealing with disturbances at the Bath Street mission hall that Trout came face to face with the power of Jesus Christ in deliverance and exorcism. Although Trout's evangelism would have no doubt rejoiced the heart of John Wesley in its reaching out beyond the normal ranks of churchgoers, it was not well received by all his fellow Methodists.[14] He was forced to choose between Bath Street and running the Bible class in his own church, an ultimatum which led to his resignation from the latter.

Trout's explicit introduction to the pentecostal dimension of Christian life was just as remarkable as some of the earlier incidents already narrated. One evening at Bath Street early in 1958 a woman handed him a grubby piece of paper on which was written the message, 'Come to this address next Thursday evening, Mr. Trout, and you'll get a blessing from the Lord.'[15] Dismissing the lady in his mind as a 'poor old soul', he carried on with his business. Later that evening however he was convicted in conscience about his treatment of the woman. He felt God telling him:

> 'Tonight you treated one of My children as if she did not count, as if she did not exist. Who are you to judge, just because she appeared to you a bit eccentric? I sent her. She was My messenger to you'.[16]

Again Trout obeyed the unknown messenger. He went to the hall, even though in the meantime he had discovered that it was the meeting-place of a rowdy Pentecostal group known as the 'Gloryland' Assembly.[17] His first impressions confirmed his worst fears of unbridled emotionalism, exhibitionism and superficiality. He was astonished to see in the congregation several of 'his' converts from Bath Street, as well as others touched by his Sunday preaching in

Methodist chapels. It was only when a small, elderly lady began singing in a strange language that Trout sensed a reverence and something of God's peace. When the pastor issued an altar call, Trout felt no inclination to respond. But he was astonished to see his staid Anglican companion leave his seat. With somewhat mixed feelings he followed suit. When the pastor came to pray for Trout, the extraordinary happened.

> For in the next instant he was suddenly overwhelmed, and well nigh knocked off his knees, by an almost unbearable consciousness of the presence of God. It was as if he had been transported, in the twinkling of an eye, to the purest realms of everlasting light, and was kneeling right before the very Throne of the Father. All he could do was weakly bow his head in awe and worship, as light and love broke over him. At first he was too choked to speak. What he was experiencing, within himself and without, was too deep and holy, too immeasurably vast, too intensely real, for shallow, shadowy words to express . . . Then all at once his whole being let out its love and adoration in an ecstatic gush of sound. They were words indeed that were pouring from him, but words in a language he had never before heard and could not for the life of him understand. He only knew that his spirit was communing with God in a way more direct, more fundamental, more basic to his innermost nature, than he had ever thought possible.[18]

Trout was baptized in the Spirit, without having previously considered the question of baptism in the Spirit or having encountered the phenomenon of tongues. He soon spoke of this experience of God to his colleagues at Bath Street but had a mixed response. The refusal of some to welcome Trout's experience meant that he could not express anything explicitly pentecostal or charismatic at the mission. As a result, Trout began a prayer fellowship in his home in 1959. This gradually grew in size while his attachment to Bath Street diminished. The gatherings in Trout's home initially consisted of an open meeting on a Friday night, with some singing and a message, followed about ten p.m. by a prayer meeting with those members of the Bath Street team who had welcomed the new pentecostal dimension. It was particularly at this late-night meeting that the spiritual gifts were exercised. One close associate of Trout's from the inception of the prayer fellowship was John Hutchison of Paignton.[19] Hutchison, then a member of the Brethren, was baptized in the Spirit in the summer of 1957,[20] following an intensive prayer of seeking the Holy Spirit. He soon

made contact with Trout, and became a trusted friend and counsel-
lor. Another Devon colleague in Trout's developing ministry was
Rex Pointz-Roberts, whose farm at Avonwick was also used for
prayer meetings.

The first instance of a healing through Trout's ministry came in
Bristol in early 1960, when he prayed very reluctantly over a woman
with spinal trouble. Also in 1960, he finally resigned his business
position, and came out in full-time ministry.

It was in April 1960, in Holy Week, that Trout had an experience
which shaped his ministry for the remaining eight years of his life.
For a second time he had a vision of a lighthouse sending its beams
of light out from Plymouth over a darkened land. And then he heard
words, which he recognized as the Lord's, telling him, 'Build thou
My underground army, and lay the sticks for revival.'[21] Around this
time, evidently linked to this vision, Trout knew he had to resign
from the Bath Street mission. He subsequently described the inner
struggles he experienced over this decision, in a way that reveals
much about the spiritual purification he went through:

> When, after five years in that Mission, God told me to resign because
> He had other work for me to do, I did not have the courage. I enjoyed
> the work at the Mission . . . and Christians, you can be worshipping
> the work that you are doing and not the Lord; you can be worshipping
> your church organisation instead of the Lord; and preachers, you can
> worship your preaching, and not the Lord! For twelve months I
> resisted God's command, and then suddenly, I lost my voice. For
> weeks I could not speak. Even in that time of rebellion I would go in
> faith to take certain meetings, and the Lord gave me back my voice
> just to preach, and as soon as I had finished it would go again. It took
> me six weeks to learn the lesson. Eventually, I asked the Lord what
> was wrong, and in a very clear way He told me that I had been
> disobedient. I had been told to leave the Mission and I had not done
> so. Then the Lord showed me the reasons why I had not obeyed:- 1.
> If you leave, you think people will criticize you. It is what God says
> that matters. 2. You are afraid that the Mission will shut if you come
> out . . . If it has only been kept alive by you, it is just as well that it
> does shut down! 3. You are trusting in past reputation; you have been
> on radio and TV and are well-known at the Mission. If you leave, you
> will not be known, and you are afraid to trust Me for the unknown.
> 4. I told you to preach Sanctification and Holiness and you have not
> done so because it is not popular.[22]

So at the end of 1961, Edgar Trout gave up his association with the Bath Street mission, and in January 1962 officially established the All for Christ Fellowship, based on his home. The All for Christ Fellowship was interdenominational, and its development led to a lessening of Trout's ties to local Methodism. Trout's preaching engagements on Methodist circuits in East Cornwall were taken over by the Fellowship. Although this continued through 1962 and into 1963, there were increasing complaints about the raw young preachers sent out from the Fellowship. Trout defended his young-sters, and one local Methodist superintendent felt obliged to ask him to withdraw the Fellowship from this ministry.[23] As a result, the All for Christ Fellowship became more of a house church, even though not given this designation. Sunday services were now held, and some members lived for a while in the Trout household.

In September 1962, Trout organized a small residential conference in Paignton at Torbay Court Hotel, which by this time was managed by John Hutchison as a Christian enterprise.[24] From 1964, Trout held Torbay conferences each autumn, and the members attending stead-ily increased. These conferences then gave him further contacts beyond the South-West of England and were an opening to a wider ministry throughout the country. Another contact of Trout's which developed from attendance at Torbay Conferences was that with G. W. North of Bradford.

As Trout's faith deepened, and he became more experienced in the use of the spiritual gifts, he became known for many remarkable instances of prophetic words and of spiritual discernment. A num-ber of people have borne testimony to these gifts.[25] He became known as the person to consult in matters of occult bondage. How-ever, Trout was under no illusion about the dangers of dabbling in deliverance, and he emphasized the need for holiness in each Chris-tian life. As he said at a later conference:

> Without holiness, power is dangerous. There is too much evidence of
> people taking the gifts of the Spirit and playing with them as though
> they were toys.[26]

Following the word he received in Holy Week 1960, Trout's last years were marked by a growing burden for revival in Britain. Besides the need for repentance from obvious sin preached by virtually all revival-conscious preachers, Trout called on the 'good Christians' to repent if revival was to come and God's voice be heard: 'Christians, we need a Christian repentance in our churches today. Repentance for not listening to God's Voice as we ought, for not reading his Word, for not spending as much time as we ought with God.'[27] It was through his concern for revival that Trout came into touch with Bill Grant,[28] another contact that opened the door to audiences beyond the West Country.

Seven

A Pattern Emerging

All the developments in Britain described thus far indicate an experience of God in pentecostal blessing and spiritual gifts outside the Pentecostal churches well before the end of the 1950s.[1] None of the main figures involved thought of themselves as Pentecostals and none would have identified wholly with the declarations of faith of the main Pentecostal churches. These two factors differentiate these men from others who were in effect independent Pentecostals; that is, from those men, mostly travelling evangelists, who were de facto not part of any Pentecostal denomination, but who thought of themselves as Pentecostal and/or identified themselves with the doctrine of one or more of the Pentecostal churches.[2]

What was it that made these men – Cousen, Lillie, Wallis, David R. Smith, Clark, McAlpine, Trout – different? They clearly differentiated themselves from the classical or denominational Pentecostals. Cousen and Smith were quite adamant in refusing the Pentecostal classification though for quite different reasons. Cousen, having been expelled from his Pentecostal denomination for his protest against its formalization, had no problems with basic pentecostal convictions. Rather, he saw the Pentecostals as having lost their earlier fire and thus becoming less authentically Pentecostal. Smith, on the other hand, while enjoying the distinctive pentecostal blessing and the exercise of the spiritual gifts, objected to the distinctive Pentecostal doctrines.

Lillie and Wallis, and to a lesser extent Clark and McAlpine, refused absorption into Pentecostalism on different grounds. While accepting the necessity of the pentecostal blessing and endowment, they believed that this needed complementing by other input from the Holy Spirit. Lillie and Wallis saw the Lord restoring his people through both the positive elements in the Brethren movement of the nineteenth century and the Pentecostal movement of the twentieth.[3]

All the ex-Brethren, but particularly perhaps Wallis and Clark, saw the urgent need for a nation-wide revival in the original sense of a sovereign outpouring of God's grace transforming the face of whole communities and touching the life of the nation.[4] In this, they saw the pentecostal contribution as a divine provision of necessary tools, but not as the revival itself.

Trout did not see himself as a Pentecostal, partly because of his strong Methodist background, partly because he had little contact with Pentecostals in the years immediately after his baptism in the Spirit. He too shared the conviction that the Spirit-baptism of individuals was but a preparation for a real revival.

There was another significant way in which these men consciously differed from the Pentecostals. They did not suffer from the limited horizons that almost inevitably mark groups of believers isolated from the mainstream of national and ecclesiastical life and consequently dismissed as insignificant or marginal. Such minority groups easily expect rejection, and as a result they cease to anticipate having any major influence on society. The pioneer figures in this section all manifested a confidence that this new surge of the Holy Spirit would not only touch multitudes (Pentecostals characteristically 'think big' numerically) but would also penetrate new milieux and would open a new phase in Christian impact on society. They tended to have access to people and circles not ordinarily open to anything seen as sectarian. For example, Cousen's *A Voice of Faith* by 1960 was reaching quite a range of evangelicals not particularly sympathetic to Pentecostal claims, and this readership was not lost when Cousen introduced a new Holy Spirit emphasis in 1961. Clark as European director of *Youth for Christ* had access to circles closed to the Pentecostals, and Trout was another example of a man whose thinking was not restricted by sectarian-type limitations.[5]

However, despite the reluctance or refusal of these men to be called Pentecostals, there was a considerable Pentecostal influence in most of their personal stories. Cousen had been brought up and formed as an Apostolic. Lillie was influenced by Jackman and Burton, and Trout was baptized in the Spirit at the Gloryland Assembly. Smith had contact with Pentecostal healing evangelists. Clark received tongues at Bethnal Green, an independent Assembly influenced by Pentecostals. None of these men denied the importance of God's outpourings among the Pentecostals, though some, especially

Cousen, were concerned about Pentecostal decline from former glory.

Here there is an initial link with the prophecy of Smith Wigglesworth. For just as that prophecy implied a restoration of God's original purpose in the Pentecostal movement, so in an unformulated manner did the basic sense of these men that this new move was Pentecostal (the blessing was that received by the Pentecostals), but not 'Pentecostalist', that is to say, it went beyond the contemporary vision of the Pentecostal churches.

However, while the pioneer figures of Section I were clearly not Pentecostals, neither were any of them committed to relating their pentecostal experience to the life of an historic denomination. Cousen and the four ex-Brethren were independents, initially by force of necessity and then by their own choice. Lillie and Wallis retained grave doubts about the ability of the old wineskins of the historic churches to receive and retain the new wine of the Holy Spirit. Moreover, they held a view of the New Testament church that excluded denominational renewal.[6] Their independence was thus more doctrinally-based than that of Cousen, Clark and McAlpine.

David R. Smith was outside the main-line traditions until convicted about his independence towards the end of the 1950s. However, of all those studied in these chapters, Smith was the one least inclined to see the pentecostal blessing as constitutive of a new movement. Hence his joining the Congregational Church did not really represent any attempt to relate the distinctively pentecostal with the distinctively Congregational.

Of those studied to date, Edgar Trout was the one with the deepest roots in a main-line tradition, that of the Methodists. However, his charismatic ministry led to looser connections with local Methodism, and his generally pragmatic bent did not favour the kind of historical interest that had to undergird any serious attempt to relate to distinct Christian traditions.[7]

Even at this time however it was clear that not every aspect of these emerging streams was traceable to Pentecostal influence. Smith's first experience of divine healing, as well as Trout's own healing in 1956, point to an element of divine sovereign intervention. The concern of men like Wallis, Clark and Trout for revival reflects other currents of spiritual life that will be examined in more detail in later chapters.[8]

Are the developments described in chapters 2 to 6 really the beginnings of the Charismatic movement in Britain, or are they more accurately seen as preparatory elements, better termed 'pre-Charismatic'? If the Charismatic movement is to be strictly defined in terms of the occurrence of distinctively pentecostal blessing and endowments (baptism in the Holy Spirit and the nine spiritual gifts) within the historic churches, then the developments so far described are at best only 'pre-Charismatic'. None of the streams mentioned represent a real acceptance of pentecostal experience within a mainline church.

However, there are grounds already evident for questioning the adequacy of this definition of the Charismatic movement. The factors which differentiate the men here studied from those described as independent Pentecostals point to the fact that something genuinely new is happening, that is not simply a continuation of Pentecostalism. In particular, the vision of Lillie and Wallis represents a fusion of traditions, linking the Brethren vision of the true non-hierarchical church of the New Testament with the pentecostal endowments of baptism in the Holy Spirit and the spiritual gifts. Although the Brethren had in fact rejected and expelled all those acknowledging any pentecostal experience, the Lillie-Wallis thrust was just as much a concern to relate the power of God in the pentecostal experience to a received tradition, albeit a confessedly iconoclastic tradition as far as the main-line denominations were concerned. In this combination, the Lillie-Wallis stream represented a facet later characteristic of the charismatic renewal.

Although these considerations point to the developments described in Section I being seen as part of the Charismatic movement rather than being merely preparatory, it is somewhat premature to speak of a Charismatic movement in Britain in the 1950s. While the elements that would later be recognized as distinctive of this movement are here present on a small scale, there were lacking the social links and recognition between the various streams that would constitute a new movement in the sociological sense. Prior to 1960, there was not much awareness of streams beyond one's own. The closest links before 1960 were between Cousen and the Devonians, Lillie and Wallis, who also were just beginning to get acquainted with Clark and McAlpine. Cousen was the man who first began to develop wider contacts and who first saw signs of something distinctively new happening in the country. This was partly because he was editor of *A Voice of Faith*, which elicited letters from those having a similar experience.

From 1960 however there are signs of a growing awareness of streams beyond one's own. Partly, this was due to the further factors to be examined in Section II, but in this broadening of contacts, Cecil Cousen played a greater part than the other figures so far mentioned. In September 1960, he taught at David R. Smith's EDH Convention at High Leigh, and this undoubtedly contributed to a growing sense of something new being in gestation. Thus Smith writes in his EDH Newsletter, quoted by Cousen:

> There is no doubt about it at all; there is a stirring in the church. Whether you belong to this denomination or that one matters little – the move is on throughout the whole Body.[9]

The accounts given in Chapters 2 to 6 tend to end around 1962–63, when it was becoming clearer that a new Charismatic movement of the Spirit was under way, touching the historic churches of Great Britain. In God's providence, the men so far mentioned were by that time in a particularly advantageous position to exercise a significant influence within the emerging movement. For they had some years of experience in pentecostal blessing, without being suspected of trying to lure other Christians out into Pentecostal assemblies. The way in which these men contributed to this work of the Spirit will become apparent as the story further unfolds.

Eight

The Pentecostal Pioneers

Before recording how the pentecostal blessing came to penetrate the historic church traditions in Britain, it is appropriate to return for a moment to David du Plessis and how the Holy Spirit prepared the Pentecostal world for 'Pentecost outside Pentecost'.[1] We shall find that the Pentecostals were aware of this new surge beyond their boundaries before there was any real knowledge among Anglicans and Free Church people of such a development. This Pentecostal awareness was almost entirely the work of two men, David du Plessis and Donald Gee.[2]

By 1950, David du Plessis was already a well-known figure among Pentecostal Christians. After twenty years of service as General Secretary of the Apostolic Faith Mission in South Africa, and playing a prominent part in the first Pentecostal World Conference in Zurich in 1947, he was named secretary with the responsibility of organizing the second world conference in Paris in 1949.[3]

In 1951 du Plessis heard an inner summons to visit the offices of the World Council of Churches in New York. His immediate reaction shows how little his mind was then prepared for a pentecostal move of the Spirit within the mainline churches.

> Lord, I have preached so much against them. What do I say to them now? They will not listen to me. Their churches have put our people out of their fellowship. That is why we have now a separate Pentecostal Movement. The churches were not willing to listen to the testimony of those who speak with tongues.[4]

This response demonstrates the standard Pentecostal attitude towards the historic churches, prior to the outbreak of the Charismatic movement. Du Plessis' many testimonies regularly bear witness to how his own attitudes were changed. The transformation came about as he obeyed the inner directives, and found an unexpected interest and welcome among the churchmen he visited.

Du Plessis' first ecumenical encounters in New York took place in January 1952, and quickly led to a meeting with Dr John A. Mackay, the president of Princeton Theological Seminary. In Mackay, du Plessis met that rarity among church leaders, a man who had already been impressed by and who deeply respected the Pentecostal movement.[5] The friendship between du Plessis and Mackay was to be the main point of entry for du Plessis into the world of the historic churches and the ecumenical movement in the 1950s. This entry was slow and gradual, though highly significant, in the years between 1951 and 1958.[6]

In these years, the Pentecostal who was most supportive of du Plessis' pioneering ministry was Donald Gee. By this time, Gee was ideally placed to exercise a strong influence on his fellow Pentecostals. Uniquely among Pentecostals, Gee combined status and position in official church bodies, an internationally-recognized teaching ministry and a knowledge of Pentecostal history not restricted to his own country. He held key positions in the Assemblies of God in Great Britain and Ireland,[7] he had been one of the leaders responsible for the convening of the Pentecostal World Conferences,[8] and he was editor of the only international Pentecostal magazine, *Pentecost*.[9] In the midst of a movement renowned for dramatic preaching rather than sober, reflective teaching, Gee had established an unrivalled reputation as a Pentecostal teacher.[10] His teaching had included material on the history of the Pentecostal movement, which led to the production of the history now known as *Wind and Flame*.[11]

The same qualities which contributed to Gee's reputation among his fellow Pentecostals made him reflect frequently on the history and significance of the Pentecostal movement. The main locus for these reflections was the editorial page in *Pentecost*. More than any other Pentecostal leader, then or since, Gee pondered, with some concern, about the denominationalization of the movement.

Gee saw the Pentecostal movement in basically evangelical terms as a *revival*. An early editorial in *Pentecost* expressed concern that Pentecostals were too 'movement-conscious'. Gee concluded:

> Before we became so Movement-conscious we thought more often of the Pentecostal Revival as a means of grace to quicken whomsoever the Lord our God should call. Denominational loyalties were a secondary consideration. Let them remain such. The vital necessity of the

Movement is that it shall continue and grow as a Revival. Nothing less deserves to be called 'Pentecostal'.[12]

Gee was well aware that the Pentecostal movement preceded the Pentecostal denominations. This awareness made it easier to conceive the possibility of the pentecostal blessing occurring and remaining within other churches. This conclusion was explicitly drawn by Gee as early as 1953 in an editorial in which he wrote concerning a preacher who had 'gone back to the churches' after receiving a personal pentecostal experience:

> Let us beware of making it our supreme aim to drag people into our own denomination. If they can maintain unsullied and intact their Pentecostal witness where they are, then let them do it. Our experience causes us to expect that they will have difficulty. Our hope is that such difficulty will grow less as truth wins its certain victories. Our prayer will henceforth be that the floodtide of Pentecostal grace and power that should follow speaking with tongues may be manifested in any and all of the churches. For Pentecost is more than a denomination; it is a REVIVAL.[13]

Whereas Pentecostals ordinarily regarded it as axiomatic that mainline churches would expel any who spoke in tongues, Gee was less dogmatic and said truthfully that 'our experience' suggested such people would have 'difficulty' within their churches.

In a 1954 editorial supporting Billy Graham's London campaign, Gee made explicit reference to pentecostal blessings crossing Pentecostal frontiers: 'We are wholeheartedly in the fight for a conception of the Pentecostal Movement as a REVIVAL rather than just another denomination. For that reason we specially welcome news of Pentecostal outpourings of the Holy Spirit outside the generally recognised "Movement".'[14]

It does not seem that this is a reference to anything in Britain. One instance in Gee's mind was immediately cited, namely a WEC mission station in Central Africa.[15] But it is also likely that he was getting news from his friend du Plessis, with whom he was in regular correspondence.

In his final editorial of the 1950s Gee looked ahead to the 1960s with genuine foresight, sensing that the new decade would see the Holy Spirit poured out beyond the Pentecostal churches. He observed that in the process of rejection by the historic churches and denominationalization among the Pentecostals, 'very soon the vision of a gracious revival to refresh the whole Church faded'. Accordingly Gee repeats, 'The idea that we have to 'come out from among them' and come 'into Pentecost' as we say, is largely a hang-up from an era passing away.' That this is not mere conjecture is apparent from a later remark: 'Best of all is the news that leaders in these other circles of Christian work and witness are receiving a personal Pentecost and even speaking in tongues.'[16]

It would not seem that at this time Gee had heard of any of the developments described in Section I of this study. His editorials generally give some indication of news that he had received.[17] It is possible that he had picked up echoes of events in Holland.[18] It is more likely however that du Plessis had conveyed this sense of a growing movement when he visited Britain for the Fourth International Conference on Divine Healing at Glasgow in September 1959.[19] This was du Plessis' first appearance as Pentecostal advocate to other Christians in Britain. A few months later he passed through London and addressed a meeting of Pentecostal ministers.[20]

A more significant visit by du Plessis took place in the summer of 1960. He began his European tour at the end of June with two packed days, during which he met the Executive Council of the Elim Churches and heard Fred Smith's account of the Holy Spirit touching members of the historic churches in Britain.[21] The most important meeting was however at the end of the tour, in early August, when he and Gee attended as observers the meeting of the Faith and Order Commission of the WCC at St. Andrews in Scotland.[22] It was at St. Andrews that du Plessis first met several British church leaders, including Archbishop Michael Ramsey.[23] It was also, significantly, his first meeting with a prominent Roman Catholic, a contact that was to open the door for du Plessis to be invited to the Second Vatican Council as an observer.[24]

By the time of his visit to St. Andrews, du Plessis had heard of the pentecostal developments among Episcopalians in California, which became public in the spring and summer of 1960.[25] This was reflected in du Plessis' address at the Faith and Order Conference.[26] He recognized the distinctive character of the new phase: 'I am privileged to share in two Pentecostal revivals: one still outside the World Council of Churches and the other more recent one, inside the historic churches within the Ecumenical Movement.'[27]

In a subsequent discussion during the St. Andrews Conference, du Plessis spoke of the importance of witnessing by believing

Christians. In his contribution, he showed an awareness of the danger of the Pentecostals losing one of their most precious assets.

> It seems we in the Pentecostal Movement are seeking to develop a stronger ministry and the Churches are seeking to get back to a more effective witnessing of the laity. We had that . . . that is why the Movement has swept the world in less than half a century! Brethren . . . In the name of Christ, I plead, let us not lose the best we ever had . . . the witness of all members who are filled with the Spirit . . . or have we now only tongues and have we lost the power?[28]

As subsequent developments occurred, Gee and du Plessis were in close touch. *Pentecost* regularly published du Plessis' latest news of Charismatic growth.[29] While du Plessis was actively promoting this new work outside the Pentecostal ranks, Gee was defending him and striving to open Pentecostal minds and hearts to this unexpected blessing.

Perusal of the main Pentecostal journals in Britain makes it clear how attuned the Pentecostal public was being made to these new charismatic outbreaks. News items concerning pentecostal outbreaks in other British churches began in 1960.[30]

Thus, almost entirely through the vision and the efforts of du Plessis and Gee, the Pentecostals were alert to these developments beyond their churches well before any such awareness arose among other Christians. Few other Christians knew of these occurrences, and those who did saw them at that stage as merely disconnected instances of glossolalia and other phenomena. Gee and du Plessis, however, saw in them a connection and a unity reflecting the one work of the same Spirit. This does not mean that other Pentecostals were as open as du Plessis and Gee in their expectations. Many Pentecostals expected the tongues-speakers in the older churches to be expelled, or at best saw Pentecostal approval as a short-term tactic that would eventually swell their own ranks.

Donald Gee's developing thought presents in a more ordered and rational manner the same ideas that were expressed in the prophecy of Smith Wigglesworth to David du Plessis. Gee too had a clear sense of the original Pentecostal movement having lost something through the process of denominationalization. He saw that God's reviving purpose concerned 'the whole Church'.[31]

The truly extraordinary range of Gee's sympathies has recently become more manifest through the making public of Gee's friendship and correspondence with a Roman Catholic priest, Dom Benedict Heron,[32] at that time resident in Belgium. Gee and Heron were introduced to each other by John Lawrence at an ecumenical meeting in Chelsea in January 1960. A few days later Heron went to visit Gee at Kenley Bible College, and realized after some minutes that Gee had assumed he was an Anglican. The discovery of Heron's Catholic allegiance did not deter Gee from getting to know his new acquaintance further. From January 1960 until Gee's death in 1966, Gee and Heron were in sporadic contact, either by correspondence[33] or by Heron's calling at Kenley on his visits to England. In June 1960, Gee wrote to Heron saying: 'I am more convinced than ever of the essential unity of those truly in Christ Jesus, even when members of communities as utterly diverse as Roman Catholic and Pentecostal. This is really an amazing thing and perhaps more of a miracle than the things we mutually call miracles.'[34] Although the spread of pentecostal blessing to the Catholic Church occurred after Gee's death, the sentiments expressed in his letters to Heron show clearly that he would have rejoiced in this news.[35]

Du Plessis' distinction at St. Andrews between the old and the new Pentecostal revivals was based on those outside the ecumenical movement and those within. At first sight this may seem somewhat clumsy, and be attributable to looseness of language in spontaneous utterance. However, it may have been rather more prescient. Du Plessis had been moving in ecumenical circles for several years. By 1960 he evidently sensed the significance of the ecumenical movement in the reconciliation of those for whom their traditions were important. While du Plessis himself had never been a particular admirer of tradition for its own sake, he did grasp the difference between on the one hand receiving the pentecostal blessing into an existing tradition while retaining that loyalty, and on the other hand receiving this new power in a free-floating situation which imposed no obligations towards the past or towards fellow church members. In this we find a contrast which will continue as the story unfolds in the 1960s. But du Plessis was clear that both were 'Pentecostal revivals'. The two were aspects or phases of one work of God. This conviction was shared by Donald Gee, who saw this as a marvellous opportunity that must not be lost.

> The 'old' and the 'new' within the one heaven-sent revival must now watch against threatening temptations . . . It will be a thousand pities if a division occurs between the two streams of the one Revival.[36]

Nine

'Brother Bill'

Of the streams flowing into the Charismatic movement in Britain that have not yet been mentioned, that involving the Rev William Wood and the London Healing Mission certainly goes back as far as any. This stream does not belong to Section I of this study, primarily because Wood only became an active promoter of the movement in the early 1960s. Unlike the men studied in Section I, Wood was firmly rooted within a historic Christian tradition – that of the Church of England. While he only became a voice for the new work of the Spirit in the 1960s, Wood's earlier interests, thinking and contacts all point to the gestation of the Charismatic movement in the 1950s.

William Wood was born in Australia in 1903.[1] As a young man he shepherded sheep for five years and became a believing Christian only at the age of twenty-five.[2] He then entered a seminary and in 1932 was ordained priest in the Anglican Church of Australia, being of high church and sacramental convictions. In 1937, he came to Britain 'to learn more of Jesus and His healing ministry'.[3] In 1949, Wood was appointed warden of the newly established London Healing Mission to carry on the work of Fr John Maillard.[4] The LHM was one of two healing agencies among Anglicans[5] that traced its lineage back to the pioneering healing ministry of the lay preacher James Moore Hickson.[6] The LHM developed the catholic and sacramental line through Maillard and the Prayer Healing Fellowship, while the Divine Healing Mission of Rev. George Bennett continued the more Protestant and evangelical emphasis.[7]

Brother Bill, as Wood came to be known, became aware of the phenomenon of glossolalia soon after his arrival at LHM. An early visitor was an American evangelist Harvey McAlister, who had been baptized in the Spirit.[8] At the first LHM Conference (called a 'Healing Advance') one of the speakers was an Anglican layman from Canada with a healing ministry, Albert Cliffe.[9] Cliffe had received the gift of

tongues, although he never mentioned this in public. Possibly stimulated by this awareness, Wood began to look increasingly beyond
the healing of the individual to the healing of the church. An editorial
in the LHM Newsletter in 1954 spoke in pentecostal terms of the Holy
Spirit's stirring:

> Do you realize what is happening, for the initiative is with God? . . .
> Can you read the signs of the times? The Blessed Trinity is meeting
> the human need in the 20th century. He is stirring His Spirit in the
> Church. The Ecumenical Movement of the last 50 years is pricking our
> conscience over the sin of our 'unhappy divisions' in the Body of
> Christ. The Church is being healed, and we are all realising something
> of what God is doing. . . . Hungering and thirsting after righteousness,
> it is knowing Pentecost in the Twentieth Century. The small clouds
> on the horizon showed in Wesley's and Keble's days. In 1906–07 in
> the Parish Church of All Saints, Sunderland, in Los Angeles, India and
> Chile, the fire of the Holy Spirit manifested. In 1908, the prophet,
> James Moore Hickson, was listened to by the Anglican Bishops at the
> Lambeth Conference.[10]

Several points from this unusual Anglican-Pentecostal lineage
deserve comment. First, Wood was conscious of the Holy Spirit
stirring among God's people in a particular way in the twentieth
century. Secondly, this move is related both to the event of Pentecost and to the Pentecostal outpouring of the first decade of this
century.[11] Very few other Anglicans of the 1950s knew anything
about the ministry of Alexander Boddy at All Saints, Sunderland
from 1907 and his role in the origins of British Pentecostalism.[12]
Thirdly, Wood independently echoes du Plessis in correlating the
ecumenical and the Pentecostal movements. He returned to this
topic in the following issue of LHML:

> This experience is Pentecostal. It was not until after Pentecost that the
> first disciples entered into the Resurrection Life of their Saviour.
> Throughout the ages Saints have achieved this experience of holiness
> and power. What is happening today is that the multitude are becom-
> ing saints. What was recognized as the fulfilling of the Prophecy of
> Joel in New Testament times, is being abundantly manifested in this
> Twentieth Century.[13]

What was causing Wood to write with such enthusiasm, when
he did not yet lay claim to any experience of Spirit-baptism? It
seems that around this time Wood read Stanley Frodsham's life of

Smith Wigglesworth,[14] in which he learned of Alexander Boddy[15] and was introduced to the more dramatic world of pentecostal healing.[16]

Another sign of Wood's being impressed by what he was learning about Pentecostals was his invitation to Donald Gee to speak at the second International Conference on Divine Healing held at High Leigh in the summer of 1955.[17] In 1956, Wood visited the USA, attending the first OSL Conference in Philadelphia.[18] Here he met Agnes Sanford, an Episcopalian pioneer in the divine healing ministry, who told him privately about baptism in the Spirit and the gift of tongues.[19] On a return visit in 1958, Wood was prayed over among a group of twenty-five people in a hotel bedroom during the annual OSL Conference, and though he did not then receive tongues, he received some form of inner healing, which gave him a new lease of life and energy.[20]

At least as early as 1958, isolated instances of glossolalia were reported from the LHM circles of intercessors. Wood's positive attitude to the Pentecostal movement and his American experience enabled him to respond to this news without any anxiety. By this time, he also knew of tongues-speaking among healing ministers on the Continent.[21]

In July 1959, Wood met David du Plessis for the first time at the Fourth International Conference on Divine Healing in Glasgow.

> When I met David du Plessis at the Glasgow International Conference I knew at once that he was born again of the Spirit. Like knows like. The Spirit cried Abba.[22] Du Plessis showed his characteristic gift for remaining in touch with his new friends. The following year he sent Wood a copy of his leaflet *God has no Grandsons*, which Wood then sent to all subscribers to the LHM Newsletter as his 'personal Christmas present'. He tells them that they can read 'what has been happening in 1959 and 1960 in 'Pentecost outside Pentecost' if you ask him for this letter from the address printed at the back of the leaflet'.[23] This was almost certainly the first time any member of a mainline church in Britain recognized in print and publicized the existence of a pentecostal movement outside the Pentecostal churches.

A significant result of Wood's contact with du Plessis was the latter's coming to speak at the LHM Healing Advance at High Leigh in Herts in June 1961. As was not unusual with du Plessis in these earlier days, he was not advertised in advance as a speaker, and his coming was a last-minute achievement by Wood.[24] Du

Plessis' talk at High Leigh was much more of a personal witness to his ecumenical vocation than his previous talks. Although it was not mentioned in the printed account of this talk,[25] du Plessis recalls that it was at High Leigh in June 1961 that he first made public the Wigglesworth prophecy.[26] Du Plessis again made a big impression. Wood reported 'This first day of witness opened the Advance to the power and peace of Our Lord's presence as never before. In the prayer group work and in private seekings, several were baptized in the Holy Spirit. All previous Healing Advances had only prepared for this year's experience.'[27]

The next letters from LHM do not convey a sense of the momentum generated at High Leigh, though reports of du Plessis' activities receive regular mention.[28] Wood travelled to the Philippines in 1962, returning via the USA. On this journey he visited van Nuys in the Los Angeles area, and met Jean Stone and others associated with the charismatic outbreak among the Episcopalians.[29] Wood heard there of *Trinity* magazine, edited by Stone, and he advertised it in the LHM Newsletter the following year.[30] This role of publicizing charismatic events and publications by the LHM was of significance in 1963 and 1964 until the setting up of the Fountain Trust rendered these services unnecessary.

In October 1963, du Plessis was in London[31] and met with 'Brother Bill'. He wrote in his newsletter: 'Here I learned that I had many more friends among Anglican ministers than I was aware of till now. Eight of them have already received the Baptism.'[32] Wood's open support for this movement of the Spirit became even more evident from 1963, from which time the LHM Newsletter carried regular items relating to people being baptized in the Spirit, to the gift of tongues, to David du Plessis and to other Pentecostal-charismatic topics.

During the 1950s Wood had become chaplain to the OSL[33] in England and OSL concerns feature frequently in the LHM Letter.[34] In the early 1960s, the practice and more especially the promotion of glossolalia became a controversial issue within OSL in the USA, as the newly-emerging Pentecostal movement within the historic churches became a matter of public knowledge. At the annual OSL conferences in Philadelphia, there was increasing debate behind the scenes on tongues-speaking, and the matter came to a head in 1963 with a ruling that glossolalia be excluded from all OSL activities.[35] Wood obeyed this directive as far as OSL meetings in England were concerned, but he felt he would be stifling the Holy Spirit if he outlawed glossolalia under the auspices of the LHM. The American leaders of OSL disapproved of Wood's stance, and after some other disagreements[36] Wood was eventually required to sever his connection with OSL.[37]

Wood was also closely associated with the British work of Camps Farthest Out, another movement of American origin,[38] whose activities in Britain were also regularly advertised in the LHM Letter. In the USA, particularly from the mid-1950s, CFO meetings were a frequent occasion for private ministry for baptism in the Spirit, sometimes by the invited speakers.[39] There is no evidence suggesting that CFO exercised a significant influence on the origins of the Charismatic movement in Britain, but the question of glossolalia evidently arose within CFO by 1963 when their National Advisory Council Ring felt obliged to adopt a policy on this matter.[40] One early English participant in the Charismatic movement, Howard Cole, then vicar of St. James the Less, Bethnal Green, first learned of the spiritual gifts through a friend made at CFO.[41]

Wood's Christianity was more firmly catholic and sacramental than that of any of the other charismatic pioneers examined to date in this study. The LHM Constitution stipulated that 'the methods and means of healing shall be sacramental including corporate prayer, intercession, the laying-on-of-hands with prayer, Holy Anointing, Absolution, Holy Communion, according to the needs and dispositions of the sick and suffering.'[42] Wood's lending the support of the LHM to the Charismatic movement – a policy which continued with his successor[43] – represented the first instance in Britain since Alexander Boddy of Christians combining pentecostal and sacramental convictions. Another Anglican priest of similar churchmanship associated with LHM to come into the baptism in the Spirit was Roy Parsons, vicar of St. Martin's, Ludgate Hill.[44]

Wood also provides the first British example of a Christian being led into the pentecostal or charismatic dimension after many years of experience in the ministry of healing.[45] His pattern is somewhat different from that of David R. Smith.[46] Whereas Smith's first experience of healing had a strongly charismatic character and he very soon experienced other spiritual gifts, and subsequently focused on the ministry of healing, Wood had specialized in the area of healing virtually since his ordination in the 1930s.

Although Wood never became a prominent figure in the emerging Charismatic movement, he played a significant role in its origins.

His new-found charismatic commitment was not to the liking of all LHM supporters, but he did not adjust his convictions according to the pressures of the moment; this is evidenced by the various quotations and references in this chapter. The LHM Letters provide evidence of supporters questioning the constant mention of Pentecostal-Charismatic items in LHM literature.[47] Wood answered the critics and doubters by emphasizing the essential link between healing and the Holy Spirit. 'The Holy Spirit is our protection from all the counterfeit forms of healing. The promised power from on high to enable the disciples to preach the gospel and heal the sick is the Holy Spirit.[48] In 1965, having remarked that 'without collusion' all the speakers at the LHM Healing Advance that year were 'in the fellowship of the Holy Spirit',[49] Wood concludes: 'Personally, I can no longer minister to the sick in the name of Jesus Christ and withhold my witness to Jesus as the Lamb of God and the Baptizer in the Holy Spirit.'[50]

Ten

Other Pentecostal Influences

In addition to the prophetic pioneering work of du Plessis and Gee, there were some lower-level Pentecostal influences on the origins of the Charismatic movement in Britain. This chapter examines three such strands, all of which are traceable back into the 1950s.

THE ST. BRIDE'S PRAYER MEETING

Around 1957 or 1958[1] a group of Pentecostal businessmen in London began to hold a lunch-hour prayer meeting each Thursday at St. Bride's Institute off Fleet Street.[2] This meeting arose from discussions in an inter-Pentecostal fellowship on the need to reach out to lost souls. The impetus to start a prayer meeting came from a pastor who remarked, 'Isn't it about time we listened to God and stopped telling Him what to do?'[3] The result was a largely silent prayer meeting, at least in the early days, involving men with an evangelistic zeal. 'They were deeply concerned about the impotence of the churches and the godlessness and lawlessness of the nation, and they too were praying for Revival.'[4] Among the first participants were Reg Down, who combined a London business with the Assemblies of God pastorate in Purley, Surrey,[5] and Frank Birkenshaw, then of the Elim Church in Clapham.[6] Though beginning with only half a dozen participants, the meeting rapidly grew to some seventy people and had to be moved to a larger room. As it grew, it attracted many who were not Pentecostals, including Rae Shaw and Fred Smith of the Good Shepherd Mission in Bethnal Green,[7] Andrew Milliken, a Congregationalist businessman,[8] and H. J. (Jim) Rattenbury who at that time belonged to Westminster Chapel, pastored by Dr. Martyn Lloyd-Jones. Grant recalled that 'the majority of those attending had Anglican, Baptist,

Methodist, Brethren, FIEC or some other non-Pentecostal background or church membership.'[9]

Although these early meetings were not obviously pentecostal,
having no corporate praise and no public testimonies to baptism in
the Spirit, the Pentecostals made an impact on the other Christians
present. Often a sense of awe at the greatness of God dominated the
prayer. As the meeting grew, it took on a more pentecostal character.

> The meeting grew in numbers, and the gifts of the Spirit were in
> operation from time to time. Sometimes a prophecy or the interpreta-
> tion of a tongue appeared to have, and afterwards proved to have, a
> personal application. There were truly wonderful answers to prayer
> and numerous testimonies to healing.[10]

In January 1960 Grant himself received a healing when he was
about to enter hospital for a double hernia operation. He was
prayed over by Rattenbury at the St. Bride's meeting; by the time
the hospital sent for him, the problem had disappeared.

Grant's own involvement led to the Thursday meeting at St.
Bride's Institute becoming more widely known, because he had a
wide range of evangelical contacts and acquaintances through his
association with the Nights of Prayer for Worldwide Revival.[11] These
meetings made more of a contribution to the beginnings of the
Charismatic movement in Britain than most other Pentecostal initiatives. Being a lunch-hour meeting, it did not pull participants away
from their churches. Moreover, the Pentecostals largely saw its aim
as sending people back to their churches with a revitalized faith and
the power of 'the baptism'.

One particular instance, which has been documented, of people
at St. Bride's being prayed over for the baptism in the Spirit, was the
visit of David du Plessis on 27 March 1962. Du Plessis did not arrive
at the expected time, and during the wait Grant told those present
of the news he had just received of the movement of the Holy Spirit
in Prince Rupert in British Columbia. When du Plessis arrived, he
spoke about the events at Prince Rupert, though he did not know of
Grant's earlier sharing. One result of du Plessis' delayed arrival was
that an Anglican priest working for the Leprosy Mission, F. Roy
Jeremiah, was able to hear the whole talk. Jeremiah has described his
experience on that occasion in a small book, *Divine Healing: the Way
of It*. During du Plessis' address on baptism in the Spirit, Jeremiah

was 'in terrible turmoil'[12]. He knew he must ask to be prayed over, but he experienced great difficulty in so doing.

> Then came a clear, strong whisper deep in my ear, and at once I knew it was different from the others; it was the voice I had heard in my morning quiet time. I've often wondered just why it said what it did. 'If you don't get up now, this will be your last chance in this life!'[13]

Jeremiah eventually made his request, and he was prayed over for 'the baptism' by du Plessis and Vic Ramsey,[14] together with two others who came forward, Bill Grant and a South African nurse.[15] Jeremiah and the nurse quickly received. Afterwards two separate people, unknown to each other, Anne White[16] and Vic Ramsey, both told Jeremiah he would have the gift of healing.[17] After two years in South Africa,[18] Jeremiah became an assistant to Bill Wood at the LHM in 1965[19] and his successor as Resident Chaplain in January 1968.[20]

By the autumn of 1963, the success of the St. Bride's lunch-hour meeting and the growing number of people coming to seek God in pentecostal fullness led the organizers to see the need for some scriptural teaching on the subject. Some after-work meetings were organized, also at St. Bride's, and were much more crowded than anticipated. Cecil Cousen was the speaker at the first of these teaching meetings in November 1963.[21]

RICHARD BOLT AND THE STUDENTS' PENTECOSTAL FELLOWSHIP

A more Pentecostal outreach in the early days of the Charismatic movement in Britain that occasioned some controversy was the ministry of Richard Bolt and the work of the Students' Pentecostal Fellowship.

In 1957, Richard Bolt was an Anglican theological student of evangelical convictions from the parish of All Souls, Langham Place, in London's West End. He was halfway through a degree course at Durham University after two Years at Oak Hill Theological College.[22] He was also prayer secretary of the Durham Christian Union,[23] apparently successful in ministry to young people – and yet he knew that something was missing in his spiritual life.

One day in my College room, I dared to admit this to the Lord, and cried to Him for help. Soon after, a spirit of prayer came upon me with groanings that could not be uttered. I believe the groanings were the Spirit's intercession for this my unconscious need. I could not ask for the Gift of the Holy Ghost, because I did not know of it; the Spirit was 'helping mine infirmity' (Rom. 8:26).[24]

This was in November 1957. Only three days later, Bolt recalls, he set out through the streets of Durham to find the meeting place of the Open Brethren. The hall that he thought was Brethren belonged to the Assemblies of God, about which Bolt knew nothing. Bolt's description highlights the stark contrast between the stately majesty of the established Church of England and the backstreet world of the Pentecostals, all the more marked in an historic cathedral city:

The Assembly Hall was a small and out-of-the-way place, almost rickety compared with the huge Cathedral, with its extravagant towers and pinnacles, on view from the Assembly doorway. Only a few were there, but the praises, prayers, singing, ministry and fellowship were impregnated with a lively glory, indicative of a spiritual reality beyond anything I had met before in the finest of the church buildings and Christian groups where I had been.[25]

Asked by the pastor[26] after the meeting whether he had received the Holy Ghost since he believed, Bolt as a good evangelical replied 'Yes'. The pastor then explained to him the baptism in the Holy Spirit and the sign of tongues. Bolt asked the pastor to pray with him, which the latter took as a request for 'the baptism'. His account of what followed echoes many Pentecostal testimonies:

He began to pray, and I began to drink. Suddenly, as I drank so I was made to drink. [?]THE HOLY GHOST, the breath of life, came sweeping over me; through my nostrils into my body, with a sound of a rushing mighty wind. A tingling fire began to burn through my limbs and fingers; prelude to an unspeakable joy welling up from within. The presence of the Lord . . . Jesus, so real . . . living water to a parched, thirsty soul . . . an actual glorious fragrance almost unbearable! As I yielded in faith, beginning to speak and expecting the Holy Ghost to give the words, so I found myself making simple unintelligible utterances, only a few, over and over again it seemed – in an unknown tongue. Simple, but definite and exquisitely satisfying I swayed as I walked to the back of the hall wonderfully drunk with the New Wine of the Holy Ghost. I noticed that each part of the experience dovetailed with the description in Acts.[27]

Bolt carried his new pentecostal exuberance with him as he went to Clifton Theological College in Bristol to complete his preparation for ordination. During this time he valued the chances he had to worship with Pentecostals. In the first half of 1959, two other students at Clifton received the pentecostal baptism through Bolt's ministry. These happenings, particularly Bolt's influence on other students within the College, provoked controversy which led to his being asked to leave.[28] A letter from the College Principal, headed 'To Whom It May Concern' stated that 'his [Bolt's] view of the Holy Spirit conflicted with the doctrine of the Holy and Undivided Trinity',[29] an accusation that seems to lack foundation.

When Bolt was turned out of Clifton, he was unwelcome at home; his father had strongly disapproved of his Christian commitment. He was immediately befriended and given a second home by an accountant, David Foot,[30] who also left the Church of England to join the Pentecostals.

On his departure from Clifton, Bolt went immediately to the Assemblies of God Conference, where he gave his testimony,[31] which evoked a high level of interest and even excitement. The concern to help him in a difficult time of transition led to the offer of the temporary pastorship of an Assemblies of God Church in Colchester. Right from the start Bolt's major interest was ministry to college students, and an early report states that 'in addition to his work as pastor . . . and evangelist, he has, in between conducting campaigns, etc., constantly visited the universities and colleges.'[32] He was enabled to continue at Colchester, where his stay became more than temporary, because there was a woman in the congregation who was able to pastor the congregation in Bolt's absence.[33]

Richard Bolt immediately used his evangelical connections to witness to the baptism in the Spirit. Just as quickly there was evangelical opposition to his ministry. In early 1960, Bolt ministered at a Crusaders House Party, and the Crusaders Union was expressing disapproval of his ministry.[34] He served as padre each summer from the early 1960s at an evangelical school camp for the schools of Croydon, whose director wrote of Bolt that 'The Lord is pleased to use him mightily in our midst.'[35] Several tapes of Bolt's teaching were circulated by the Evangelical Tape Fellowship.

Bolt's concern for the universities (a field in which the Pentecostals had not previously shown much interest) encouraged others particularly in Dublin and Wigan who had been praying for a fellowship to be established for Pentecostal students.[36] As a result, the Students' Pentecostal Fellowship came into being in 1961.[37]

From its inception the SPF saw the movement of the Spirit within the historic churches as a God-given opportunity to make the full blessings of Pentecost more widely known. The aims of SPF were initially defined as:

> Firstly, to link together for Pentecostal fellowship, ministry, etc., students who are baptized in the Holy Spirit, including those from or within the historic churches. In addition to the College weekday meetings, members of the Fellowship are linked to the local Pentecostal Assemblies or Churches.
>
> Secondly, the SPF is a corporate witness to the Full Gospel in the Universities, and aims to bring other students into the Pentecostal experience.[38]

The mention of 'those from or within the historic churches' together with the statement that 'members . . . are linked to the local Pentecostal Assemblies or Churches' suggests a certain ambiguity in the SPF's response to the new situation. This ambiguity reflected some tensions within SPF, particularly between older Pentecostal church leaders, the younger leaders who had first been student participants, and someone like Richard Bolt, with a greater theological sophistication. The expectation of the majority was that those joining the Fellowship would end up by joining Pentecostal churches.

Oxford and Cambridge were particularly favoured spheres for SPF expansion, the former having one of the most forceful groups from the SPF's inception.[39] The strategy of the SPF was to work through the Christian Union, with which Bolt was familiar from his Durham days and in which other SPF leaders had been active.[40] Bolt was made the travelling secretary of SPF, and in 1962 he relinquished his pastorate to do this work full-time.[41]

Bolt's evangelistic work in SPF was especially focused on particular universities and colleges. Outside the home counties, he gave particular attention to Newcastle in the north-east, and to Matlock in Derbyshire, where his success at the Teachers' Training College led the Principal eventually to ban any further visits from Bolt.

A leaflet put out by the SPF after this date[42] to describe its aims and activities gave added space to the outpouring of the Spirit in the historic churches.

> During the last few years God has especially been pouring out His Spirit in the Universities and Colleges of our land.
>
> Many students have received the Baptism in the Holy Spirit with the speaking in other tongues (Acts 2, 10, 19, etc.), and Spiritual Gifts (1 Corinthians 12–14, etc.).
>
> Those who have received these blessings have mostly remained in fellowship with the Christian student bodies to which they already belonged. As no other collegiate Christian organisation provided opportunity for the spiritual study and use of Spiritual Gifts, however, it became necessary to form the Students' Pentecostal Fellowship . . .
>
> The SPF is interdenominational, its members being drawn from all sections of the Christian church. The programme of the Fellowship is in no way intended to interfere with the activities of the local church, which, of course, members are encouraged to attend.

While SPF statements sought not to antagonize those 'who have mostly remained' in their existing fellowships, SPF activities undoubtedly contained some elements of 'Come-Outism'. Bolt was not the only SPF leader to have experienced rejection at the hands of non-receptive evangelicals. This background explains why the editorial in the first issue of an SPF magazine[43] blamed general Christian ignorance of the Pentecostal movement on 'the majority of evangelical leaders' who 'have persistently opposed and rejected the revival since it began in the early years of this century'.[44] The editorial continues:

> It is apparent that so far the cost of admitting that this revival is of God has proved to be too great for these leaders . . . The evangelical compromise with the nominal church in its desire to make the Gospel respectable evidences an attitude which is utterly opposed to seeking an outpouring of the Holy Spirit whose ways are never modified to make them acceptable to the darkened reasonings of fallen man.[45]

Not surprisingly, SPF was not seen as an ideal ally by those committed to the renewal of their historic denominations in the power of the Spirit. Bolt's other main sphere of Pentecostal evangelism, among his Anglican contacts, became an area of contention and controversy. Bolt's home had been within the parish of All

Souls, Langham Place, where his father. though not an evangelical believer, was the medical practitioner for the clergy. Richard had been one of the numerous ordinands coming forward from this centre of Anglican evangelicalism. In 1960, he had prayed over one of the All Souls' curates, who was seriously ill.[46]

So it was natural that one Anglican group with whom he would share his experience of God and of the Spirit's power would be the young people of All Souls. Bolt's contacts there evidently continued over the succeeding years; several young people from All Souls, who had been baptized in the Spirit through Bolt's influence, later left the Church of England and joined the Central London Full Gospel Church formed by Bolt in April 1964.[47] This assembly, which met in the board-room of David Foot's office under the leadership of Bolt, Stuart Stranack (also active in SPF) and Foot, was formed following the success of Bolt's campaigns at Orange Street Congregational Church in December 1963 and March 1964.[48] One of those baptized in the Spirit during the March campaign was Dr. Muriel Adams, a Harley Street specialist and a former missionary to Egypt. Dr. Adams, who had long associations with the Open Brethren but had for some years belonged to the independent Honor Oak Fellowship in South-East London, had been running a Bible study in her home near Baker Street, and she brought a number of other women from this group into Bolt's Central London Church.[49]

Another Anglican centre influenced by Bolt was the parish of St. Paul, Beckenham, in the Kent suburbs of the London metropolitan area. The vicar, George Forester, had been led, through his experiences with a parish group concerned with healing, to see the lack of power in the modern Church.[50] By June 1963, Forester was convinced there was a baptism in the Spirit distinct from and subsequent to conversion and regeneration, and he determined to go anywhere to seek this baptism.

Forester visited an Apostolic church and went to a London crusade held by the American evangelist Morris Cerullo.[51] On the last night (27 July) when several from Beckenham attended, one of the Sunday School teachers was baptized in the Spirit and spoke in tongues.[52] Two weeks later on 12 August, Forester's wife, Daphne, received when she was prayed over by some Pentecostal friends.[53] Others received over the following weeks,[54] and Forester himself received through the ministry of Bolt in the second week of Septem-

ber.[55] Asked what impact the baptism in the Spirit had upon his life,
Forester replied:

> For me personally it's made the Lord Jesus very much more real
> although we certainly knew him before. We feel that we know the
> third person of the Trinity as a person in His own right. We are far
> more conscious of sin . . .[56]

By mid-autumn, fifteen members of the parish had been baptized in the Spirit and spoken in tongues,[57] some of these through
Bolt's ministry.[58] Events at Beckenham soon attracted attention and
became a cause of some controversy. Forester's promotion of baptism in the Spirit was more public and overt than in Burslem and
Gillingham.[59] The wider publicity was partly the work of another
Pentecostal, Selwyn Hughes,[60] who also saw in this new move of
the Spirit an opportunity for wider Pentecostal evangelism. In
January 1963, Hughes had begun a magazine *Revival*,[61] and its
November issue published an interview with Forester.[62] This article
was picked up by the *Church of England Newspaper*, which immediately printed an item ' "Baptism of the Holy Spirit" ' at Beckenham.'[63] This short report on what it called 'this 'glossolalia'
movement' triggered off a correspondence which lasted for several
weeks.[64]

Beckenham continued to be a source of controversy, for in March
1964 Michael Harper felt it necessary to enclose with his Newsletter
a report by George Forester entitled 'Baptism in the Holy Spirit at
Beckenham'.[65] Harper noted: 'False rumours have been circulating
which have not been God glorifying. Here is the truth.'[66]

Forester's report had a more Pentecostal tone in some respects
than other Anglican witnesses and suggests he was more influenced
by Bolt than by other Anglican friends. For example, he speaks of
tongues as 'the initial evidence' and distinguishes, as many Pentecostals but few charismatics do, between the initial manifestation at
baptism in the Spirit and the gift of tongues available for use on
subsequent occasions.[67] The complaint against Beckenham was particularly that the movement was divisive. Forester defended himself
by acknowledging: 'The Baptism in the Spirit is proving to be a
divisive experience in the twentieth century church which is living
in experience on the right side of Easter, but on the wrong side of
Pentecost.'[68] After noting that the Reformation, Wesley, Keswick and
the Ruanda Revival were also divisive, Forester concluded:

Yes, it is divisive, but that does not mean it is wrong. Division is sometimes caused by the 'have nots' far more than by the 'haves' and that has certainly been the case at Beckenham. Nevertheless, if this experience brings division, it also brings a unity amongst Christians who share in it which is sounding the death knell of denominationalism.[69]

Towards the end of 1964, Forester resigned his living, though still intending to remain in Anglican orders.[70] While believing that 'the gifts and the outpouring of the Spirit were compatible with Anglican formularies',[71] Forester felt unable in conscience to continue the practice of infant baptism. He admitted that others at Beckenham had been troubled over the same question and had sought adult baptism elsewhere in Baptist and Pentecostal churches.[72]

There is no doubt that many committed Anglicans, who had been baptized in the Spirit, saw what happened at Beckenham as a serious setback, capable of ruining the reputation of the nascent movement in the eyes of other Anglicans. Bolt was seen as one of those responsible for this outcome. However, when any assessment is made, it must also be borne in mind that Bolt was probably responsible for more people receiving the baptism in the Spirit than any other person with access to Anglican circles at this time. Not all of those to whom Bolt ministered left their churches of origin, one notable example being Gordon Strachan, a minister of the Church of Scotland, whose story is more appropriately included in the chapter on Scottish origins.[73]

As the Charismatic movement became more visible and produced its own leadership, Bolt and the SPF exercised less influence outside strictly Pentecostal circles. Their influence on its origins belongs to the period up to mid-1964, especially from late 1962.

ST. JOHN'S BURSLEM

The third instance of clear Pentecostal influence on the origins of the Charismatic movement in Britain stretching back into the 1950s comes from the Potteries. In this instance, Pentecostal influence led to charismatic convictions being held and taught within an Anglican parish.

In June 1959, a young man in the Potteries still at grammar school, Ron Bailey, was baptized in the Spirit, receiving the gift of tongues.

Eight months earlier, Ron had been converted to faith in Jesus Christ through seeing the Billy Graham film *Souls in Conflict* in his parish, St. John's, Burslem. At school, one of his closest friends belonged to a Pentecostal Church, and Ron knew his Pentecostal friend had something he still lacked.[74] Now he himself wanted this gift, and summoned the courage to speak to his rector, Philip Smith, half-expecting severe disapproval. Instead, Smith encouraged Ron to seek this blessing, but advised him not to visit the Pentecostal church for the purpose. As a result, Ron was prayed over and received the baptism in the Spirit on the playing field of his school.[75]

From this point, Ron Bailey was a pentecostal activist among the youth at St. John's, impressing the rector with his zeal. At Bailey's instigation, a successful open-air campaign was held in Burslem in the summer of 1961, by which time other young people in the parish were being touched by Bailey's zeal. Over the following year, the pentecostal nucleus at Burslem grew in unexpected ways. A young lady in the parish, Margaret Wilson, a student at Matlock Teachers' Training College, was baptized in the Spirit through the ministry of Richard Bolt during a campaign at the Matlock Assembly of God in the first half of 1962. By the summer of 1962, four young people in Burslem, all under twenty-one, had received the baptism in the Spirit, and were meeting together to pray for the rest of the parish.[76] A young man in the army, Barry Sillitoe, while on a posting in British Honduras (later Belize) met up with two Pentecostal missionaries. He wrote to tell Smith that he had been told about the baptism in the Spirit and that he was most impressed.[77] Then in September 1962, the organist of St. John's, David Garner, announced to Smith that he had been baptized in the Holy Ghost.[78]

While all this had been happening in his parish, Philip Smith's heart was divided. He could see the real faith and joy of the young people baptized in the Spirit, and he did not want to quench their enthusiasm. However, his evangelical orthodoxy and his Anglican sense of decorum made him dubious about extending a full welcome to the Holy Spirit in this pentecostal form. Having had his interest aroused, Smith particularly noticed newspaper items about the outpouring of the Spirit of Pentecost in other places, and he began to keep a file of cuttings on this topic.

The event that finally broke Philip Smith's resistance to the pentecostal blessing was the publication of Philip Hughes' editorial in *The Churchman* for September 1962.[79] That such a respectable and learned evangelical spokesman as Hughes should be impressed by what he saw among the Episcopalians in California was sufficient to dispel Smith's evangelical qualms about the movement.[80] He and his wife, Norah, were prayed over by Ron Bailey and Margaret Wilson, by now Bailey's fiancée, on 28 September, 1962, and received the baptism of the Holy Spirit.[81] A few months later Norah Smith wrote:

> There was the initial evidence of 'tongues' and, for my husband particularly, tremendous joy. The power of the Holy Spirit was there, concern for souls, and new liberty in witnessing. The keynote was PRAISE. Praising heart and praising lips.[82]

Smith's pentecostal blessing soon became known, particularly through the enthusiastic witnessing of the charismatic nucleus in his parish.[83] Corporal Sillitoe spread the word at meetings he attended in the south of England, and it was through Sillitoe's visiting Gillingham in January 1963 that Michael Harper heard the news from Burslem.[84] The word spread that the rector of Burslem was a pentecostal Spirit-filled Anglican, and he began to receive enquiries from interested seekers. One such was Amos Edwards, then a neighbouring Methodist minister in Stoke-on-Trent. Edwards describes his baptism in the Spirit after two hours of prayer in the Burslem Rectory with Philip and Norah Smith:

> Still we waited and prayed until about 2.0 p.m. [sic]. Then somehow I remembered a word of Maquire [sic] . . .[85] that the Holy Spirit speaking through a tongue did not use the mind, i.e. the person did not think out the words or ideas but the heart praised and spoke as it were apart from the mind. This was how it happened to me. I began to speak in another tongue. What it was I do not know – but somehow it was expressing all the things I felt deep down within.
>
> Sometimes it was just groaning out a longing, sighing out release, pouring out words of deep thankfulness, and bringing within a deep love. There were words of gratitude to God for his servants; there were longings for God's love. There was no vision, no image of Jesus, just a tongue that kept speaking and speaking quietly at first, then louder and more confidently . . . and I was loathe to cease. After this experience I sat down and my friends praised God and embraced me, and the tears of joy and relief came flowing forth as I realised the great thing that God had done, the gift He had given.[86]

Another clergyman who came to Burslem seeking ministry for 'the baptism' was the Rev. John Bradberry, then vicar of St. Mark's,

Siddal, Halifax. He and his wife received on 4 November, 1963.[87]
Also a recipient through Smith's ministry (around 1965) was Bob
Dunnett, later associated with the Birmingham Bible Institute.

Another place touched by a spark from Burslem was Emsworth
in Hampshire. While attending a managerial course in the Potteries,
Trevor Longman, a young Baptist from Emsworth, came into contact
with St. John's through one of their Youth Rallies organized by the
Baileys. His interest was aroused and before long he was baptized
in the Spirit following the laying-on of hands.[88] Longman witnessed
to his experience at Emsworth Baptist Church, where four young
members soon received:

> You will rejoice to hear that one little spark of Revival Fire has fallen
> on our Emsworth Baptist Church, and touched four of our group of
> young people, of whom there are some twenty or more, I think, in the
> Church. Only four, so far are affected. The change in the lives of three
> of those four is remarkable. They have spoken in tongues! We have
> had them to our home to question them, and to make sure that this is
> no 'strange fire', and we are convinced that this is of God . . . We are
> keeping quiet about it at present, lest opposition should be aroused.

A letter sent from Emsworth to the Ingrams, who produced the
newsletter for the Nights of Prayer for World-Wide Revival, reported:

> It started with one young fellow who is away working at or near
> Stoke-on-Trent, who comes home on weekend leave occasionally. He
> has planned to come home again on the weekend May 10–12, and
> bringing another with him who has also received the fullness of the
> Holy Spirit.[89]

This pattern of spontaneous expansion was happening to vary-
ing degrees wherever Christians in the historic churches were
being baptized in the Spirit. It is more easily traced in the case of
Burslem, primarily due to Smith's extended correspondence and
his careful preservation of the data.

Philip Smith himself exercised a certain caution as to how he
presented his pentecostal baptism. He made no attempt to introduce
any pentecostal elements into the church services, the exercise of
charismata and free praise being reserved for prayer meetings in the
Rectory and other homes.[90] Smith combined a willingness to give his
testimony whenever he was asked[91] with a desire to avoid media

attention. Thus his basic testimony printed first in the Assemblies of God weekly *Redemption Tidings* was published anonymously under the title 'A New Work of the Holy Spirit in a Church of England Parish' by 'The Rector.'[92] This was soon reprinted in several other journals.[93] The article created widespread interest, being the first account in the British church press of the pentecostal movement re-entering the Church of England.[94]

Not only were the charismatic beginnings at Burslem brought about under the influence of Pentecostals, but Philip Smith himself was happy to acknowledge this influence. He became a close friend of Leslie Knowles, the pastor of Ball Green Assembly of God, where Ron Bailey had been touched, and he also spoke on a number of Pentecostal platforms.[95]

Eleven

Revival-Minded Anglicans and Langham Place

One particularly significant preparation for the Charismatic movement was the formation and growth of various fellowships to pray
for revival. The first revival prayer fellowship within which Baptism
in the Spirit was seen as a possible answer to this prayer was the
organization known as Nights of Prayer for Worldwide Revival.[1] It
was also the only interdenominational group among the various
revival fellowships in Britain.

The servant of God behind NPWR was a retired missionary,
George Skinner Ingram.[2] After many years of service in India with
the CMS during which he was awarded the MBE for his work among
the 'untouchables', George and his wife, May, returned to England
in 1952. He was already over seventy years of age, but one of the
most important of his initiatives still lay before him.

Within a week of their return to England, the Ingrams were asked
to join the prayer committee for the Billy Graham crusade due to be
held at Harringay in London in 1954. One of the centres for the
pre-Harringay prayer was St. Paul's, Portman Square, where Prebendary Colin Kerr was vicar. There resulted a close liaison between
Kerr and the Ingrams, which was to last beyond the Graham Crusade. Nights of prayer were held, as many people could not manage
ordinary working hours. When the Harringay Crusade was over,
Billy Graham went on to crusades in other places and countries
which were just as much in need of prayer and revival. So further
nights of prayer were arranged for Graham's campaigns in Glasgow
in 1955 and in India and the Far East in 1956. It was George Ingram
who then suggested that the nights of prayer become monthly
occurrences, and be simply for worldwide revival.[3]

Ingram had long possessed a burden for revival, and this concern had been at the centre of his intercessory prayer for many

years. It was recognition of his passion for revival that led to the invitation to join the pre-Harringay prayer committee. Ingram knew the desperate need of the world for revival. He knew that it is a sovereign act of God, who pours out his Spirit to bring the nations and peoples to repentance and new life in Jesus. Crusades, like those of Billy Graham, were not themselves revival, and at best could prepare the ground by multiplying the number crying out to God for his mercy. 'You have to organise a mission; you have to work it up, but you have to pray a revival down from heaven. Evangelism could well be a preparation.'[4] With these convictions, it was entirely consistent that Ingram should see the pre-Harringay gatherings as an opportunity to launch an ongoing crusade of prayer for worldwide revival.

The first night of prayer under the name of Nights of Prayer for Worldwide Revival was held in May 1957, and it was the start of regular meetings on the night of the first Friday of each month from ten o'clock at night until six in the morning. Soon a substantial correspondence was flowing in from all parts of the world telling the Ingrams of the evident fruit of this prayer. As a result May Ingram began to produce a news-sheet with extracts from these letters. This sheet began with a print of 150 copies, but had reached almost 6,000 by the time of George Ingram's death in 1969.[5] It was its rapid expansion that drew others into this work, especially Bill Grant and Ben Allen.

W. B. Grant though qualified as an engineer was managing director of a Christian publishing firm in the city and was in his mid-fifties at the beginnings of NPWR. Grant was a convinced evangelical within the Church of England, and had held strong British Israelite views[6] 'for most of his life. During World War II, he had been editor of the British Israelite journal *The National Message*.[7] With time, Grant's concern for revival grew, and his British Israelite views became less central. Eventually, his widened involvement in NPWR and his subsequent charismatic experience led him to abandon the British Israelite theory.

Ben Allen was a few years younger than Grant, and had shared his British Israelite convictions. Allen had an interest in healing, which dated back to 1952 when a dying girl of seventeen, whom he knew, had been healed. This interest may also have been stimulated by his own ill-health, about which he was very reticent and which led to his early death in the summer of 1964.

It was Allen who discovered May Ingram addressing hundreds of envelopes by hand, and arranged for the mailing list for the NPWR news sheet to be put on to an addressograph system. Soon arrangements were made for the Ingrams to receive more help. In 1959 Allen began to assist in promotion for NPWR and Grant, who had some experience in journalism, assisted in administration and in preparation of the news-sheet, a task he was to continue after the Ingrams' deaths.

For these revival-conscious evangelicals, 1959 was a special year. Their expectations were roused by this centenary of the 1859 revival in Wales, in Scotland and Northern Ireland. They also knew that the 1859 revivals in Ireland and Scotland had been sparked off by news of the 1858 revival in the USA, which had spread from a small mid-day prayer meeting of businessmen in New York.[8] As 1959 approached, so the prayer at the NPWR intensified for a gracious outpouring of God's Holy Spirit on a similar scale in 1959. Throughout 1959, one of Britain's most renowned Protestant preachers, Dr. Martyn Lloyd-Jones of Westminster Chapel, spoke every Sunday on the 1859 Revival and the nature of revival.[9]

In the light of the 1857 precedent in New York, it was perhaps not surprising that the leaders of NPWR should begin lunch-hour prayer meetings for city workers. Two venues were chosen, one in Westminster and the other at St. Bride's Institute off Fleet Street. The Tuesday St. Bride's meeting, with which Grant was closely associated, began in late 1958.[10] It was there that Grant had his first close knowledge of Pentecostal Christians, through hearing of and then attending the Thursday prayer meeting in the same room, which has already been mentioned.[11]

Also encountering pentecostal phenomena for the first time at St. Bride's Institute with Grant was a close friend of his and Ben Allen's, Eric Houfe. Houfe, an architect with a leading London firm and a resident of Ampthill, Bedfordshire, had, like Allen, been interested in healing for many years. Grant and Houfe soon shared with Allen their excitement about the occurrence of pentecostal gifts today. Allen was already convinced from his Bible study that there were no scriptural grounds for restricting to the apostolic age any blessings described in the New Testament.

There then began for these three friends, all lay Anglicans, a period of persistent seeking for the pentecostal fullness in their lives. All three were prayed over by two Pentecostals for baptism in the

Spirit on 16 June 1960, but only Houfe experienced an anointing of the Holy Spirit which later he recognized as his baptism in the Holy Spirit.[12] They were prayed over again by David R. Smith and Cecil Cousen at the EDH Convention at High Leigh in September 1960, but without any tangible results. On 10 August 1961, Ben Allen was praying in a Hertfordshire field in a strong wind in which he sensed the voice of God saying, 'Go where the wind blows.' The next day, Eric Houfe phoned Ben Allen concerned about the next step in their quest, and Ben answered, 'Go where the wind blows.' On that same day, 11 August 1961, Allen and Houfe, together with Bill Grant, visited Peniel Chapel in Kensington and the following day went to the Elim Church in Clapham. A pentecostal interest had been strongly aroused.

Meanwhile, in 1959, Ingram sensed that a revival prayer fellowship ought to be formed among Anglicans, specifically to pray for revival in the Church of England. This was not seen as an alternative to praying for worldwide revival, and the APFR formed at the end of 1959 existed alongside of and as a smaller body than the NPWR.

The setting up of APFR established closer links between Grant and the leading Anglican evangelical parish of All Souls, Langham Place, where the occasional meetings of the fellowship took place.[13] This was the parish from which Richard Bolt had come and where some of the young people were coming under his influence.[14] The Ingrams were already parishioners, and Grant, though living in Hammersmith, now became a regular worshipper at All Souls. In January 1960, a quarterly bulletin appeared for the APFR with Grant as editor.[15] The second issue has an article by Grant on the 1859 revival entitled 'The Second Evangelical Awakening in Britain'.[16]

The Ingrams, Grant and Houfe (the last-named had his office near Langham Place) had all begun to pray for the clergy at All Souls to receive the full blessing of the Spirit. George Ingram understood by the baptism of the Spirit an experience of entire sanctification, such as he had received while an undergraduate at Cambridge many years before.[17] Grant and Houfe now understood this in more pentecostal terms.

Among the several clergy at All Souls, they singled out Michael Harper for particular prayer. Harper, at that time around thirty years of age and recently arrived at his second curacy since ordination, was particularly opposed to the ministry of divine healing. Houfe made this discovery on his first meeting with Harper on 19 May 1960 when, at St. Peter's, Vere Street, a daughter church of All Souls, Harper introduced two lunch-hour talks by Houfe which touched on healing.[18] Harper responded by preaching against divine healing in a series of sermons at All Souls shortly afterwards.[19] George Ingram made no secret of his prayer for Harper, who recalls that familiar elderly voice on the phone pleading 'Brother – please don't travel second class to heaven, will you?'[20]

In 1961, the NPWR prayer meeting at St. Bride's Institute was amalgamated with the Thursday meeting started by the Pentecostal businessmen. When David du Plessis came to speak at this meeting in March 1962, Grant was one of the three people prayed over for 'the baptism'.[21]

> I did not speak in a new tongue: but I was filled with love and joy and peace, so much so that I was hardly aware of the journey home by Underground. Following this experience, new avenues of service opened up for me.[22]

Although Houfe and Grant knew that their contacts with Pentecostals had led to many blessings, they also sensed something was lacking until they received the gift of tongues. Houfe has written of this period (1960–62):

> I had been seeking the blessing with my friends for at least two years. Our concern for divine healing had driven us to a re-examination of Pentecostal power. We studied the Word, read books and began to associate with Pentecostals and others who had received the blessing with the manifestation of tongues.[23]

Houfe was to receive the gift of tongues earlier than Grant, Allen apparently not at all. Houfe's reception was a sequel to the du Plessis visit to the City. Du Plessis had recalled a story of a preoccupied businessman seeking the baptism in the Spirit, but too tense to receive. Du Plessis advised him to ask the Lord to baptize him in his bath, when he would be at his most relaxed.[24] Houfe was to remember this incident, and himself received the gift of tongues in his bath on 27 August 1962, after excitedly reading the latest issue of *Trinity* magazine from America on the train home. He recalls 'Although I could not speak a word of English, I nevertheless was giving praise to Jesus with my conscious mind.'[25] It was another year before Grant eventually prayed in tongues.

In late August 1963 I was walking on a heather-covered common in Hampshire on a beautiful afternoon. I could not help lifting up my voice to praise God for the wonders of His creation. The desire came strongly upon me that my praise should be in the Spirit, and I raised my voice and uttered a cry, not a word I understood, and other words followed. It was all over quite quickly and I returned to London relaxed and happy. But soon Satan was raising his accusing finger and saying: 'You did that yourself. It was not of the Spirit.' However, over the weekend, through both the written and spoken word, Luke 11:11 was given me on three occasions, and Satan's artifice was defeated. Some days later while praying during my morning quiet time, with no thought of the recent happening in mind, I found myself speaking in a new tongue with great fluency. I did not, of course, understand what I was saying, but my heart was just overflowing with love and praise for the Lord Jesus.[26]

In the meantime, the prayers for Michael Harper were being answered. Harper's first breakthrough came during a weekend conference on Ephesians at a conference centre at Farnham, Surrey in September 1962.[27] Harper describes how he experienced the revelation of God in his mind over that weekend:

Then I went to the Conference. To my utter amazement I began to experience what St. Paul had prayed so many years before. I was "filled with all the fullness of God" and had to ask God to stop giving me more – I could not take it. For a fortnight I found it impossible to sleep, so filled was I at one moment with "joy unspeakable and full of glory", and then deep conviction of sin as the Holy Spirit revealed areas of my life and ministry which had not been under His sovereign control, and then wonderfully fresh revelations of truth in His Word. I experienced as I had never before the love of God literally poured into my heart, so that I loved people I have previously only just tolerated. I found liberty and power in my ministry which I had never thought possible. The Bible came alive to me, and for several months it was the only book I wanted to read. Prayer was a new experience of intimate communion with my Master and the element of worship, which had been almost totally absent before, became an important part of my devotional life.[28]

When Harper described his experience at a church meeting at All Souls, another curate there recognized that the same had happened to him two years earlier.[29] Immediately Harper's praying friends realized that something was different. Someone reported Houfe's baptism in the Spirit to Harper and his wife, Jeanne, who by then had had a similar experience. The Harpers invited Houfe to their flat, and listened to his witness.[30] This was the first time they had heard of tongues as a contemporary gift. Before leaving, Houfe handed the Harpers a copy of *Trinity* magazine.[31] Until now they had not known of the existence of a pentecostal movement among Episcopalians in the USA. Although Harper had not yet received the gift of tongues, he recognized the similarities between his recent experience and those of the tongues-speakers he met and read about.

As these events occurred to Houfe, Grant, the Harpers and others, George Ingram and his wife rejoiced to see their prayers answered. Harper tells of his visit to tell Ingram of his recent blessing:

> That was the first of many tea-time meetings, as we shared together the news that was coming in from all around the world of revival breaking out, sometimes in the most unlikely places. In spite of increasing frailty, George never stopped praying for revival, and he lived to see the first stages of it in his own country.[32]

This extract shows the importance of the NPWR connection with All Souls, Langham Place, for the initial understanding of the new movement among 'pentecostal evangelicals' in London and the Home Counties. The influence of George Ingram and NPWR ensured that the first experiences of pentecostal blessing in their midst were interpreted in terms of the first showers of revival. This was a different context from the other 'neo-pentecostals' studied in previous chapters. The prior instances were either from Pentecostal influences, in which case the normal understanding was of reception of 'Pentecost' continuing the pattern of the Pentecostal movement,[33] or they were scattered sovereign interventions of God's grace, without any immediate awareness of wider occurrence.[34] The only leader to date who had a strong concern about revival prior to his baptism in the Spirit was Arthur Wallis.[35]

Because George Ingram reported all such blessings in the NPWR bulletin, and he received revival news from all continents, the people in his circle quickly developed a sense of a new work of God spreading throughout the world.[36] This vision tallied well with, though it was not identical to, that being spread by David du Plessis. Whereas du Plessis began from baptism in the Spirit as a basic datum of Scripture and of the Pentecostal movement, the NPWR and Langham Place group touched by the Spirit of

Pentecost began from revival, and saw baptism in the Spirit as the new factor in realized revival.

Michael Harper however did not immediately speak of baptism in the Spirit. Following his Farnham experience, he preached frequently on the power of the Holy Spirit. For the next six months, the experience he commends is that of being 'filled with the Spirit'. This can be seen from his writings between autumn 1962 and summer 1963.[37]

Harper soon wrote to inform Dr. Martyn Lloyd-Jones of his recent experience of the Spirit. Lloyd-Jones' response was to desire a meeting without delay,[38] and on April 9, 1963, he met with Harper, John Collins of Gillingham and David Watson of Cambridge.[39] This was the beginning of fairly regular – about twice-yearly – meetings between Harper and the man known to many as 'the doctor'. One result of this first meeting was that Lloyd-Jones sent Harper a list of ministers to invite to the talk by Rev Frank Maguire from the USA at the beginning of May.[40]

Because of the prominent place of All Souls in the world of Anglican evangelicalism, news of events there spread with particular rapidity. Further, it was a training ground for able young evangelical clergy; and so the staff at Langham Place tended to have a network of close associates, who had moved on elsewhere after their period of apprenticeship as assistants at All Souls. One such alumnus was John Collins, the rector of St. Mark's, Gillingham. Harper's visit to Gillingham in January 1963 played a part in the beginnings of what became a centre for evangelical charismatic life within the Church of England.

After hearing from Corporal Sillitoe of Philip Smith and the developments in Burslem, there began a fairly regular correspondence between the Harpers and the Smiths. This correspondence is a valuable source of information on Harper's developing understanding of this move of the Spirit. By the early summer of 1963, Harper is beginning to use the terminology of 'baptism in the Spirit'.[41] He thinks in Spirit-movement terms, seeing these as 'early days'.[42] He has heard of the origins of the Pentecostal movement in Britain at Sunderland, and sees the new outpouring in continuity with that Pentecostal beginning.[43] Harper affirms 'I am convinced that this blessing is for all denominations.'[44]

The Harpers and the Smiths finally met on 4 August, 1963, in Cambridge, during the latter's holidays.[45] Although Harper attributes the release of his own gift of tongues to the help of the American Lutheran Larry Christenson, who was in London three weeks later,[46] it is clear from his correspondence that the beginnings of this gift came when they had hands laid on them by the Smiths in Cambridge.[47]

Another of the curates at Langham Place, Martin Peppiatt, was to be baptized in the Spirit on the occasion of Christenson's visit, when he was prayed over by an American Pentecostal.[48] Hopes were high among the newly-blessed at Langham Place that John Stott, the rector, a weighty voice in evangelical circles within the Church of England, would follow suit. Stott came to hear some visiting speakers witness to their pentecostal experience,[49] but these hopes were finally disappointed at the Islington evangelical clergy conference early in 1964.[50] Before a record attendance attracted by the topic of the Holy Spirit and by news of this new movement, Stott repudiated the concept of a post-conversion Spirit-baptism.[51]

The fact that these developments occurred at All Souls, Langham Place, immediately made the incipient movement in Britain less of a fringe phenomenon. Not only was this occurring within the Church of England, but it was happening in evangelical high places, with close connections to the national establishment. Oxbridge men who had served at Langham Place were Anglican to their bones. Not only did the events of 1962–63 at Langham Place provide a focal point for the movement, but they ensured that it was firmly within the national church.

Twelve

A Wesleyan Contribution

In all the streams flowing into the Charismatic movement, that we have so far discussed, nobody had been led into baptism in the Spirit by way of a deeper grasp of his own church tradition. Charles J. Clarke, the father-figure among Methodist charismatics in Britain, provides the first example of such a pattern.[1] Whereas many first received the baptism in the Spirit, and only subsequently sought to relate this experience to their own tradition of theology and spirituality, Clarke's pentecostal pilgrimage was spread over many years of rediscovering the heart of Methodism as Holy Spirit revival, and reached its climax in his baptism in the Spirit.

A native of Essex, Clarke had witnessed in his teens a remarkable revival in his home village of Great Wakering[2] This memory accompanied him as a young Methodist minister when he went to the world of the industrial north in 1936. He was in Bradford for several years, pastoring a former Wesleyan Methodist Church from 1936–40, and a former Primitive Methodist Church, the Bradford Central Hall, from 1940–43[3] It was during his years in Bradford that he received a visit from a man who had belonged to Samuel Chadwick's church in Leeds. So began Clarke's fascination with the life and teaching of one of the greatest Wesleyans of the previous generation.[4]

Chadwick had worked in a Lancashire cotton mill from the age of eight, and had remarkable results in bold evangelism before entering theological college at the age of twenty-one. The power of the Spirit of Pentecost was made manifest to him from those years, particularly in the revelation to Chadwick that the key to revival in any place was the conversion of its most notorious sinner, a principle of which he then demonstrated the truth.[5] As his ministry developed, Chadwick preached more and more on the transforming power of the Holy Spirit. Significant in the light of the later development of the Charismatic movement was Chadwick's regular intercession for the spiritual renewal of the Roman Catholic Church.[6]

A collection of Chadwick's sermons, originally published as a series of articles in the Cliff College magazine *Joyful News*, eventually appeared in book form as *The Way to Pentecost* in the year of Chadwick's death. In *The Way to Pentecost*, Chadwick taught a post-conversion experience of entry into the fullness of the Holy Spirit, and he describes this experience as 'Pentecost'[7] and as 'the Baptism of the Holy Spirit'.[8] In his teaching, Chadwick was fully in the line of the Holiness movement with its emphasis on a second experience of the Spirit for entire sanctification.'[9] However, there was more in Chadwick than many Holiness teachers that prepared the way for a Pentecostal pattern of experience. First, he spoke of the spiritual gifts of 1 Corinthians 12:8–10 as still available and operative.[10] This included the gift of tongues[11] about which Chadwick wrote with remarkable accuracy, when one considers that apparently he never received the gift himself.[12] Secondly, there was in Chadwick and his preaching a strong concern for the power of the Spirit to be manifest in evangelistic ministry. It was not then surprising that some later Methodists should be led into charismatic experience through the influence and teaching of Samuel Chadwick.[13]

Clarke read *The Way to Pentecost* six times before he left Bradford, and was deeply impressed by what Chadwick had written about a baptism of the Holy Spirit for holiness and power. From that time forward, Clarke taught on the Holy Spirit wherever he went, and formed small groups that prayed for the baptism of the Holy Spirit. In doing so, he knew that this concern with Holy Spirit revival in evangelism and sanctification was the heart of the Methodist movement from its origins.

No doubt aided by Chadwick, Clarke was open to contact with Pentecostal Christians. It was while he was at Bradford Central Hall that he first met Cecil Cousen, and invited Cousen and his singing group of Apostolics to come to Central Hall. From Bradford, Clarke went to Endike Hall in Hull,[14] where his 'Quest' for the fullness of the Spirit led to further contact with Pentecostals.

> We went to Hull after this to a flourishing work at Endike Hall. Here I pursued the quest with great determination. An interesting contact was David Ruddock who had been a Pentecostal Pastor and described to me the experience of the baptism of the Holy Spirit as enjoyed by

the Pentecostals. This was most intriguing but also puzzling. Here I met and talked to two Pentecostal leaders, Donald Gee and George Jeffreys, and I read through the history of the Pentecostal Movement by Donald Gee.[15]

Clarke was introduced by Ruddock to a local Assemblies of God pastor, who prayed with him without success to receive 'the Baptism'. Though not looking in a specifically Pentecostal direction in the years that followed,[16] Clarke nonetheless pursued his 'Quest'. His burden for revival increased, and he became known among Methodists as a speaker and writer on this topic.[17] 'For many years' Clarke stated, 'I have brooded over the contradiction between the promise of power our Lord made to His Church and the appalling powerlessness of modern Christians in a world which is sliding down into atomic doom.'[18] Clarke's concern for revival meant that his 'Quest' was not an isolated spiritual search but was experienced as part of a longing for God to manifest himself to his people.

For a number of years, Clarke preferred the term 'Resurgence'[19] to that of Revival, in the belief that the latter designation had become debased by its application, especially in the USA to organized crusades – even to a series of regular evening services. Something of the flavour of Clarke's convictions can be sensed from the following passage, evidently protesting against a loss in the original meaning of revival:

> Let it be quite clear, however, what we mean by this term [Christian Resurgence]. We do not mean that some popular Vicar has persuaded more people to attend his church by some ingenious device; or that a big bazaar has raised a deal of money. We do not mean even that the church attendance has increased; or that enthusiastic Christians have done some good social work and earned the applause of the world. We do not mean either that all the evangelicals have united in organizing a very efficient and highly publicized crusade. We mean that the original power of Christianity has been rediscovered by humble, broken Christians who have waited upon God in passionate pleading importunate prayer. We mean that God the Holy Spirit is manifesting his supernatural Presence once more and is working through a prayerful, anointed Church which has become once more a Body of Christ, vibrant with His own divine power to bless and heal and save the people.[20]

How did Clarke's continued reading of Chadwick[21] and his developing interest in revival lead him to the pentecostal experience of baptism in the Spirit manifested in the sign of tongues? It would seem that the death of his first wife, Helen, in May 1959 spurred him to a renewed search for the fullness of the Holy Spirit. In September 1961, Clarke was moved from the Isle of Wight to Halesowen, just outside Birmingham.

> Then I came to Halesowen and determined to use my loneliness to renew my Quest. Alone in my bereft Manse I sought afresh with great tenacity.[22]

Clarke already belonged to the Methodist Revival Fellowship[23] before moving to Halesowen. As Clarke renewed his 'Quest' in his new church, he became more actively involved in MRF, and was a major influence in the Birmingham branch.

One immediate result of Clarke's new spiritual thrust was the launching of a quarterly mimeographed magazine, appropriately named *The Quest*, of which the first issue appeared in October 1961.[24] Unlike his previous magazine, *The Torch*, which was simply a local church publication[25] *The Quest*, from the start had a wider public in mind. Clarke was already aware that his message had emphases that were not so fully expressed in the MRF and its publication, *Sound of Revival*.[26] The difference lay in the stronger awareness of the full power of the Holy Spirit so central to Chadwick's teaching.

In *The Quest* Clarke continued his practice of publishing his personal notes under the heading 'Dominie's Diary'. In an entry for November 1961, Clarke refers to a message of David du Plessis[27] that 'the leaders of the ecumenical movement are receiving the Pentecostal blessing'[28] He goes on to say:

> I have just had a telephone call from Pat Nixon to tell me of blessing that is coming to the MRF. group in Birmingham. It is a Pentecostal blessing and the Pentecostal gifts are given.[29]

Those so blessed in Birmingham were young people[30] and they then asked Clarke to teach them about the spiritual gifts. The result was the formation of the 'Halesowen Resurgence Group' which met each Saturday evening. Clarke recalls:

> I soon had a praying group again, made up mostly of young people who came from different parts of Birmingham. We met on Saturday nights and prayed for three or four hours. Often wonderful blessing descended upon us and sometimes the Lord stretched out His hand to heal.[31]

When this group began, Clarke did not know of the pentecostal blessing being received in other parts of the world. This exciting knowledge, so rejoicing the heart of this man praying fervently for worldwide revival, came from Bill Grant, with whom Clarke had made contact because of their common concern and prayer for revival. Clarke visited London on 7 September 1962 for the monthly NPWR,[32] and renewed contact with Bill Grant, whom he had first met at a MRF Conference at Swanwick. The following month, a Birmingham group of NPWR, with Clarke as one of the organizers, held its first vigil.[33] Grant gave Clarke a supply of what would later be called charismatic literature, amongst which was *Trinity* magazine from the USA.[34] Not surprisingly, Clarke comments: 'News of the Pentecostal Revival amongst the Anglo-Catholics of America has deeply stirred me.[35] As I read of their joy and power in the Holy Ghost I knew that this was "it".'[36] It was however still a few months before Clarke himself received the baptism in the Spirit. But at the end of January 1963, Clarke tasted the longed-for fullness, and he was able to tell the readers of *The Quest*: 'Now – the big blessing I have read about in the Bible and in Christian History and Biography is Mine!'[37]

Clarke does not describe his Spirit-baptism primarily in terms of power, but as a new level of knowledge of God and his love:

> Imperceptibly, the BIG blessing has been growing up inside me. I feel it mostly in the morning quiet time. It wells up within me as a warm, indescribable joy. It seems so natural, yet I know it is Supernatural. There is no reason for it, except Romans 8:16. I have done nothing to deserve it. It is pure, unmerited grace. Its essence is the sense of being beloved. It is the 'caress of God' spoken of by Brother Lawrence:
>
> > Oh, this full and perfect peace,
> > Oh, this transport all divine
> > In a love which cannot cease
> > I am His and He is mine.
>
> Sometimes I cannot keep this glory in. It seems to force itself out in clapping hands and dancing feet – sometimes in heavenly language as praise flows out in a torrent of joy.[38]

From this point, *The Quest* becomes an unofficial journal for the incipient Charismatic movement among British Methodists.[39] Within days of Clarke's baptism in the Spirit, the Halesowen Resurgence Group met elsewhere: at Edgbaston, where two people, one a student for the Methodist ministry, told how they and others had recently been filled with the Spirit at a Youth for Christ weekend in Derbyshire, with some speaking in tongues.[40] Others were prayed with for the blessing, and a seventy-three-year-old lady was healed of deafness when Clarke laid hands on her.[41]

Two weeks later, Clarke was at a regional MRF Conference in Birmingham, dominated by news of this pentecostal blessing.[42] In May Clarke spoke at a MRF Conference in Cornwall, where he met Cecil Cousen, whom he had not seen since his Bradford days.[43] This contact led to Cousen's reprinting part of Clarke's witness in AVF.[44] In November, Clarke was one of the principal speakers at the annual Conference of the MRF at Swanwick. Here he spoke on the Holy Spirit as the agent of revival, but felt a need to present his convictions in a non-provocative manner.

The Chairman of the MRF was the Hon. Roland Lamb, from Callington, Cornwall, one of the local superintendents in whose district Edgar Trout's youthful assistants had been preaching. In his annual report, Lamb explicitly addressed the question of 'Charismatic Gifts'[45] and showed how the realm of the miraculous was less foreign to many Methodists than to most other Protestants. Lamb argued for one of two possibilities, both accepting the legitimacy of spiritual gifts in principle.[46] Lamb urged the need for discernment, and appealed to members of MRF to keep in touch with him on this topic. It is clear that the charismatic issue was prominent throughout this Conference. Reports in *The Quest* indicate that several people were then baptized in the Spirit.[47]

The MRF continued to be a forum where Methodists were faced with the challenge of the new movement, though not without some raising of hackles. The annual conference the following year had two charismatics out of three speakers, David Pawson from Gold Hill, Chalfont St Peter[48] and John Collins from Gillingham.[49] The next following Chairman of MRF also addressed the topic of the charismatic movement[50] and *The Sound of Revival* published a few articles by charismatics.[51]

Some branches of MRF were more open to the charismata than others, and the Birmingham branch perhaps most of all. Though initially influenced by Clarke, the Birmingham MRF continued with a charismatic emphasis after Clarke's departure from Halesowen[52] as the Secretary was Pat Baker, one of the original group of young people who had contacted Clarke in 1961.[53] Until 1965, Amos Edwards was also Secretary for the West Midlands Region, of which Birmingham district was a part.

Not long before moving to Ely in September 1964, Charles Clarke re-married, his second wife being Mary Collins[54] who had been baptized in the Spirit the previous year.[55] For a number of years, Clarke was the principal spokesman for the Charismatic movement among Methodists, a role to which he was able to give more time following his retirement in 1967, when the Clarkes returned to C.J.'s native village near Southend.

Clarke certainly did not seek to promote his own name and ministry. Twice he ceased his own publication to merge his charismatic contribution within the pages of new magazines, first with *Renewal*[56] and later with *Dunamis*.[57] Clarke's most important contribution may however have been his love for the great figures in Christian history. He knew how many saintly Christians of the past had been able to do great things for God within their own traditions.[58] Interestingly, his knowledge extended to some Roman Catholics such as Teresa of Avila, the Curé d'Ars, and Brother Lawrence.[59] Clarke's knowledge of Chadwick's influence within Methodism was probably a formative influence in this respect.

As a result, Clarke was able to counsel Methodist charismatics to remain within their church, if at all possible, without implying any dilution of their ideals.[60] His knowledge of Christian history, particularly the history of the Holy Spirit's workings, gave him perspective, without diminishing his conviction that the new movement was a distinctive work of the Spirit without obvious parallel.

Thirteen

North of the Border

As in other places, so also in Scotland, there were individuals baptized in the Spirit and remaining in their churches before any public outbreaks became news. One such instance was that of Gordon Ross, the organist of a Church of Scotland church in Aberdeen. Ross was baptized in the Spirit in the mid-1950s through the ministry of an Apostolic Church pastor, but himself always remained Presbyterian.[1]

Another development was the small group that met in the early 1960s at the home of Dr. Jack Kelly in Glasgow. Kelly, a relative of Campbell McAlpine,[2] was a consultant heart physician at Paisley Infirmary[3] and a member of Hermon Baptist Church.[4] Brought into this work of the Spirit through the ministry of Denis Clark, Kelly led meetings in his Glasgow home throughout the early and mid-1960s. The meetings were held outside the time of normal church services, so as not to cause division.[5]

The strand in Scottish charismatic origins which led to the movement's public emergence can be traced to the arrival at New College, Edinburgh in the autumn of 1961 of Bill McLean from New Zealand. McLean's wife had been healed, his own faith had been enkindled and his call to the Presbyterian ministry aroused through contact with Pentecostal Assemblies in New Zealand. In Edinburgh, McLean shared his story with a fellow student, C. Gordon Strachan, who had been convinced of the reality of the miraculous in the Scriptures some three years before, and who also had been finding the theological college atmosphere spiritually stifling. McLean and Strachan gathered a few friends together and met weekly in the McLeans' home throughout the winter of 1961–62.[6] Strachan reports:

> Being students we were very theological. We had to be when amongst most of our friends and professors, this new doctrine of Pentecost and the Holy Spirit was nonsense. Half our meetings were spent in prayer and praise – 'Let the fire fall', but little happened.[7]

Strachan soon wrote to tell his friend, Brian Casebow, minister in Motherwell,[8] about this new group studying the Holy Spirit. For some months Casebow had felt increasingly discouraged over the ineffectiveness of his ministry, but Strachan's letter pointed him to the Holy Spirit as the answer to his failure. In February 1962, Strachan visited Casebow, who now heard for the first time about the Holy Spirit coming upon believers and their speaking with tongues as in the Acts of the Apostles.[9] The Edinburgh group had heard of the pentecostal blessing among mainline Protestants in America, and so now did Casebow, who began to pray that he might receive the baptism in the Spirit. During the next months, Casebow's faith was built up, as he read *Trinity* magazine and the stories of various healing of ministries.

On the evening of Sunday May 27, Casebow was reading an article in *Trinity* magazine, when he fell to his knees.

> Suddenly I was on my knees and speaking a language which sounded remarkably like Russian – speaking it with emotion and power.[10]

That week Casebow was in Edinburgh, attending the General Assembly of the Church of Scotland.[11] Casebow told Strachan of his experience, but he was unsure whether it was authentic, as he had never heard anyone else speaking in tongues.[12] McLean and Strachan both thought at that time that authentic tongues couldn't be doubted.[13] Casebow doubted for a full week.

> Then I prayed in tongues again and this time received such a strong personal conviction of seeing the cross itself that I had no more doubts. This was food! The Holy Spirit does not detract from Jesus. It is in fact the Spirit of Jesus leading us into a truer worship of Himself.[14]

Later that week Strachan went on holiday to London and made a point of speaking to Donald Gee, who reassured him 'Don't worry, you'll receive all right.' Gee told Strachan of the ministry of Richard Bolt, who was then conducting a crusade in the Derbyshire village of Eastwood.[15] Strachan's desire for the baptism in the Spirit was such that he travelled to Derbyshire, making it for the last night of the crusade.

> On the last night of the mission I heard them testify to healings, savings and also receivings. After the meeting we went upstairs, and following excellent instruction we were all baptized in the Holy Spirit. I have never heard such a noise coming from a church meeting. On

the way home to Edinburgh on the night train I watched myself in the carriage mirror speaking in tongues.[16]

Soon, there were small prayer meetings at both Motherwell and Edinburgh. Motherwell was to become the better known, when the Scottish Daily Express in 1963 published an item on 'The man who "speaks in tongues" '.[17] The Glasgow Sunday Mail also reported on Motherwell under the heading 'Strange new sect in Scottish kirk' making the memorable comment that they practised 'a form of worship bordering on the supernatural'.[18]

About this time, the editor of the *Scottish Baptist*, who was also from Motherwell, asked a neighbouring Baptist minister, Douglas McBain,[19] to visit and evaluate Casebow's prayer meeting. McBain was not in the least attracted to the idea. Most Church of Scotland parishes were deserts of non-evangelical theological aridity to an evangelical Baptist like McBain.

McBain found the Motherwell prayer-meeting a disturbing experience. In some ways he was impressed. He could not deny the signs of spiritual life that he saw. Yet he felt ill at ease when they prayed over a twelve-year-old paralysed deaf mute, who they said would be healed. McBain was sure the boy would not be cured and he was right. It was then that something happened within him. He recalls:

> I was just at this point of self-congratulation when God really con-
> victed me . . . He said, 'All right, you are the man who knows your
> Bible. This fellow doesn't —he's a liberal. What would you have done
> if the parents of that boy brought him to you rather than to him?'

When McBain got home, he told his wife that it was possible God was doing something at that prayer meeting, but that he wasn't going to have anything more to do with it. But that same night, he said he would pray about it, and, when praying, he found that unknown words and phrases were coming into his mind, and crying out for utterance. He tried in vain to get this out of his mind. Eventually McBain offered it up to God, and had an immediate sense of release and of the coming of the Spirit. 'I felt as though Jesus was right there in the room beside me, and was just doing business with me.'[20]

With both Casebow and McBain in the Motherwell area, it became for a while the centre for charismatic promotion in Scotland. Visitors from the USA would include Motherwell on their itineraries. One was Jean Stone, the editor of *Trinity* during whose visit some forty to fifty people were baptized in the Spirit.[21]

As in England and America, there were Christians in Scotland rediscovering the ministry of healing. Foremost among these was the Rev. J. Cameron Peddie, a minister of the Church of Scotland.[22] Peddie had come to believe that 'a baptism of the Holy Spirit' was needed if men are to receive and transmit the healing grace of God.[23] He was instrumental in the starting of a weekly meeting of ministers interested in divine healing, the so-called 'Glasgow Group of Ministers'.[24] Another milieu in Scotland with an increasing interest in healing was the Iona Community.

One young minister of the Church of Scotland, Keith Edwards, was possibly the only person who was both a member of the Iona Community and involved in the Glasgow Group of Ministers. Around 1963–64, Edwards, then minister of Laurieston in Renwick,[25] saw that there was a logical link between healing, which he accepted, and the other gifts of the Spirit mentioned in 1 Corinthians 12:8–10, which he had much more difficulty in accepting. He was helped in this by being sent an evangelical monthly from the USA called *Christian Life*, which featured regular articles on the new movement of the Holy Spirit with the restoration of the charismata.[26] Soon after this, he made contact with Casebow and Strachan. A prayer group for healing in his parish began to manifest other gifts, and some members were baptized in the Spirit. Within a year, Edwards himself had received the baptism in the Spirit, and in the summer of 1965, was the first minister in the Charismatic movement encountered by Rev. Thomas A. Smail, later one of the best-known Scottish figures within the renewal movement.

Another Scottish Presbyterian baptized in the Spirit by 1965 was John B. Burnet, the recently-ordained minister of Burra Isle in the Shetlands.[27] One evening when praying, Burnett found himself praying effortlessly in an unknown tongue in a spirit of praise. Burnett wrote of his experience:

> When praying in the Spirit in an unknown tongue, the words flow effortlessly, filling the prayer with the sound of praise, raising one into an intimate communion with God. The phrase 'in Christ' becomes a reality as one is caught up with Him. He gives such a love for Jesus Christ as never before experienced. There is joy in believing. The word of God becomes a living word. The desire for holiness becomes overpowering.[28]

Elspeth Shaw, the wife of a future minister of the Church of Scotland, provides an example of someone baptized in the Spirit without any evident human agency and without knowing at the time anything about baptism in the Spirit. She received this blessing in 1964 when taking her confirmation vows, and for some years used to sing in tongues when doing the 'hoovering' so that no one else would hear.

The Charismatic movement in Scotland was slower to develop than in England. This probably reflects the cautious conservatism of the Kirk, as well as some suspicion of an impulse originating in America or at least south of the border. Moreover, the first protagonists of the new movement in Scotland, Casebow, Strachan and McBain, were all young ministers, only ordained a few years and unlikely to carry much weight within the country. So by the end of 1965, there was only a tiny handful of people in the historic churches in Scotland who had been baptized in the Spirit, a much lower percentage than in England. The main development of the movement in Scotland was to occur after the period examined in this study.

Fourteen

St. Mark's, Gillingham

Philip Smith of Burslem was the first Anglican priest in Britain since the days of Alexander Boddy to hold what would later be called charismatic prayer meetings in his parish. St. Mark's, Gillingham, was the first Anglican parish to be corporately influenced by this move of the Spirit and the first parish to which sympathetic enquirers were directed to see this renewal in action.[1]

Behind the beginnings of the Charismatic renewal in St. Mark's lay some years of soul-searching on the part of its clergy. St. Mark's, Gillingham, is an evangelical parish in a dockyard area, to which John Collins came as vicar in 1957, after spending the first six years of his ministry at All Souls, Langham Place. Also in 1957 there arrived a new curate, David MacInnes, who was to be joined in 1959 by a second curate, David Watson.

Between 1959 and 1961, when MacInnes left for a curacy in London,[2] close relationships developed among the three clergy at St. Mark's.[3] They shared their trials and disappointments, and rejoiced together in their spiritual blessings and discoveries. Collins was aware of the inconsistencies in his life, and began to spend some days at a house in the country seeking God's face. He was increasingly struck by the gap between what he read of great Christians in the past, and what he experienced and saw around him. He reasoned that either the people in the past knew things that he did not or they were exaggerating.

Not long before MacInnes left, Watson came to a new awareness of the meaning and importance of Paul's teaching in Romans 6 about being dead to sin and alive to Christ. This gave a new power to his preaching, which the others then lacked.[4] While Collins was still seeking the answer to his dilemma, he was taken aback by a remark that it was ridiculous how some people pray for the healing of a patient with cancer, when they don't have faith to believe that God can cure a common cold. At that very time, Collins had a severe cold, and he was praying for someone with cancer. That evening he anointed himself with oil and the fellowing morning the cold was gone.

Watson moved to Cambridge in 1962,[5] but his Romans 6 discovery had kindled some response in Collins, who preached a series of sermons on that chapter. Some who heard Collins at the time knew that something was happening to him, but recognized – from the way that inspiring sermons were ending without real application – that this work was unfinished.

From his contacts with All Souls, Langham Place, Collins knew George Ingram and the Nights of Prayer for Worldwide Revival. In his own mind the search for what the saints of old had known was inseparable from thirst for revival. The idea for a Night of Prayer in Gillingham however came from Arthur Harris, a businessman in the town. Collins was finally persuaded to support this idea, but he thought it should be for the whole town, not just for St. Mark's. A preliminary meeting of ministers and helpers was arranged for Saturday 26 January 1963 with Ben Allen as visiting speaker. Allen fell ill and had to cancel, so Collins called Michael Harper, who was at a conference at Herne Bay a few miles to the east. Harper agreed to stand in for Allen, but severe winter conditions delayed his arrival. While the group waited, Collins invited any people present with experience of spiritual blessing to share their testimony. It was then that Corporal Barry Sillitoe stood and told the gathering of the events at St. John's, Burslem and how he personally had been baptized in the Spirit and had spoken in tongues. Collins was reminded of the possibility of pentecostal-type revival, of which he had read the previous autumn in Philip Hughes' editorial in *The Churchman*.

The vigil had been arranged for the following Friday night, February 1. At five o'clock that evening it began to snow, and by ten o'clock, when the Night of Prayer was to start, the snow was deep. About thirty of the most committed people from the Medway valley came, one only being another clergyman, a pastor of the Nazarene Church. The night was divided up into periods, and at 2 a.m. Collins gave a short talk on Luke 11:9–13, which ends with the words 'If you, then, bad as you are, know how to give your children what is good for them, how much more will the heavenly Father give the Holy Spirit to those who ask him.' At about twenty past two, all present were caught up in a sense of the glory of God, and were filled with a joy that led people, unacquainted with such behaviour in church, to skip and leap about in their rejoicing.[6]

Over the next few days, several conversions and healings took place.[7] One couple from St. Mark's, present at the Night of Prayer, were David and Jean Smith. Jean experienced a filling of the Spirit, and began to praise God in her own words. A few nights later, she woke in the middle of the night with a desire to praise God and suddenly found herself praying in tongues. Her husband David after a spell of recurring bad memories from World War II was prayed over by Jean and a friend in the parish, John Freeth. He recalls the occasion:

> As the three of us were sitting there praying, we had a time of deep prayer together and the Spirit of God came mightily upon me, and welled up within me . . . There was a bright shining light which just filled the whole room, and filled my whole being.

A few evenings later, when praying together, David received an interpretation of Jean's utterance in tongues. Then David had a picture of a small match and a big hand, bearing the message:

> You are the match. I am the hand. I want to use you to light little fires throughout the whole land. Wherever I send you, start a small fire.

A small prayer group with exercise of the spiritual gifts was now held at the Smiths' home on a Monday evening, while a 'non-pentecostal' parish prayer meeting was held on Tuesdays. As the Monday group grew, it was transferred to the vicarage which could accommodate more people. For a time, the Monday meeting was changed to become an optional extension of the parish meeting. It was known that the second hour was 'pentecostal' and people were free to stay or leave after the opening hour.

St. Mark's had a vigorous youth work, and John Collins had pioneered there a hostel where young men could test a call to ministry in the church. One young man, Mike Evans, who had gone from this hostel to work in France for Operation Mobilization,[8] was baptized in the Spirit on the Continent before February 1963, and witnessed to this on a return visit. John Freeth was another baptized in the Spirit who went on from the hostel to train for full-time ministry.

After February 1963, word spread quickly in evangelical circles about the 'goings-on' in Gillingham. Though Collins himself was careful to avoid media publicity as far as possible,[9] he did witness to the parish experience in speaking engagements, which included the Christian Union at Cambridge and at Oxford.[10]

Developments at Gillingham in the spring and summer of 1963 were evidently somewhat slow. Sillitoe reported a dry spell there,[11] and a correspondent of Philip Smith's wrote of a student from Ridgelands Bible College[12] at Bexley, Helen Guttery, who was in touch with Gillingham.

> Helen is going to see John Collins next week-end 27–29th September about the Baptism. Apparently she has gained the impression that he and his group there have received a mighty annointing [*sic*] from the Lord but have not spoken in tongues. They realise their lack of real lasting power and want Helen, Sylvia and Evelyn, (another student at Ridgelands) to talk and pray with them.[13]

At that time, September 1963, neither John Collins nor his wife Diana had received tongues. Diana Collins had not long to wait, as she received after David du Plessis' visit to the Londoner Hotel the following month. The February 1964 NPWR at St. Mark's, the first anniversary of these vigils, was also a memorable occasion. The Harpers reported to the Smiths of Burslem:

> They had a great time at Gillingham night of prayer last Friday. Thomas Collett White the Curate entered in – praising the Lord in tongues. At 4 a.m. they had holy mirth in the Spirit.[14]

A significant step forward occurred during a youth club house party run by the Harpers and the Smiths at Lindfield in the summer of 1964.[15] The young people of the parish were generally resistant to the new pentecostal life through the influence of other evangelicals and despite the youth club being under the leadership of David Smith. After several days of intense struggle and resistance, a break-through occurred and the week ended with almost all the fifty young people present being baptized in the Spirit.[16] Early the following year, these young people made a strong impression on Tom Walker, then a travelling secretary with the IVF and later to become a recognized leader in the Charismatic movement.[17] Following his weekend in Gillingham, his objections to tongues severely dented by the witness of the youth of St. Mark's, Walker himself received the baptism in the Spirit, while driving to Brighton. He later testified that:

. . . there and then there was an overwhelming, flooding, filling, wholly absorbing, penetrating experience of joy and praise. Words were inadequate to express a proper response of gratitude to God; and I found myself praying and praising in tongues, shouting aloud in the car and almost leaping in the driving seat with worship and gladness.[18]

The outreach from St. Mark's, Gillingham was intensified by the close connections with the former curates, David MacInnes and David Watson, as well as by David Smith leaving his carpenter's job to become a full-time evangelist.

Both MacInnes and Watson had begun their search at Gillingham with John and Diana Collins with whom they continued to be in close touch. A decisive moment for MacInnes came during a lengthy time of prayer that quite unknown to him was the same evening as the first NPWR at St. Mark's. He was made aware how up to that point in his ministry he had been as much concerned with the impression he was making as with the proclamation of the gospel. Through some hours of prayer, MacInnes was led to a deeper surrender of his ambitions and to an inner peace. At du Plessis' talk in October 1963, he was faced with the question of tongues, but it was only the following year that MacInnes received tongues after his fiancée, another student at Ridgelands Bible College, had received immediately on first hearing about this gift.

Watson had received at Cambridge a few months before MacInnes, shortly after he had been visited by Ben Allen and Eric Houfe, who witnessed to the baptism in the Spirit.[19] David Watson's adjustment to his new experience had its difficult side. He was soon instrumental in bringing students into blessing, informing Collins that several in Tyndale had received 'the fullness of the Spirit'. Watson was well aware of the potentially explosive reaction to the new movement in the university and college setting, particularly concerning speaking in tongues, so he decided to keep quiet about his experience of this gift. This did not prevent him being barred from Tyndale, because the authorities there had heard that he used tongues in his private devotions.[20] Saunders and Sansom remark that 'in Cambridge they made great issue out of tongues, perhaps particularly because they were an assault on the use of the mind, to which many intellectuals took very grave exception.'[21] There was strong opposition within the InterVarsity Fellowship,[22] and Watson also suffered from rebuffs or coolness from old evangelical friends.

Another element in David Watson's inner wrestling with the charismatic experience was his unhappiness with the terminology of baptism in the Spirit and any doctrine of a second blessing. He agreed with John Stott's criticism of Pentecostal teaching about 'the baptism', which made his difficulties with other evangelicals in Cambridge all the more ironic. He chose instead the language of 'filling' and 'fulness'. He had a strong dislike of controversy, and desired only that Christians open up to the full life of the Holy Spirit, bringing alive the love of God in the believer and the power of God in ministry, including the spiritual gifts, on whose availability he insisted.

The events at Langham Place and Gillingham with their connections meant that by the end of 1964 there was a solid, if not numerically large, group of evangelical Anglicans, baptized in the Spirit and consciously part of a new movement of a pentecostal type within the historic churches. Because Watson and MacInnes became well-known leaders in the Charismatic movement – Watson internationally – the role of John Collins, who is less widely-known, could easily be overlooked. Those who know Collins well hold him in great respect. He sees the new understanding of Romans 6 that came with his baptism in the Spirit as a grace of God that prevented him subsequently from separating the power of the Holy Spirit from the centrality of the cross.

St. Mark's, Gillingham came to be regarded by many Anglican charismatics as a model for the integration of the charismatic and the (evangelical) Anglican, in contrast to the experience at St. Paul's, Beckenham, where the vicar, George Forester, was seen as more overtly Pentecostal, resigning his living towards the end of 1964.[23] However, this judgment seems to have been made after Forester's departure rather than during 1963 and 1964, when this work of the Spirit was developing in both places.

Fifteen

Other Developments in the South of England

Another Anglican parish in the South of England where people began to receive the baptism in the Spirit in 1963 was in Farnborough, Hants. The first impulse came through a full-time parish worker at St. Peter's, Miss Ellita Howell Williams. Although the churchmanship of the parish was liberal-broad, Miss Williams was herself an evangelical, and indeed not a confirmed Anglican. She moved to Farnborough in September 1962 following six years' service in a parish in Worthing. In March 1962, Miss Williams had been convicted of her need for the Holy Spirit after becoming aware of the Spirit's transforming power in the lives of Christians from various churches in Worthing. During her final six months there, she became a close friend of Denis and Beth Clark, and received blessing through their ministry.[1]

Miss Williams arrived in Farnborough still seeking the manifestation of the Spirit and soon found a couple equally thirsty. A parish prayer meeting was begun in October and soon Miss Williams invited Denis Clark to speak one Sunday. Despite Miss Williams' apprehensions, this turned out to be 'a glorious day and the small beginnings of future outpouring'.[2] One of those unexpectedly appearing on this Sunday was Corporal Barry Sillitoe. It was Sillitoe's first meeting with Michael Harper on 26 January[3] that led Harper to write to the rector of Farnborough, Canon Ben Hutchinson, proposing a meeting which took place during the Church Assembly in mid-February.[4]

Clark returned for a day in June, to which about thirty people came, twenty-one from Farnborough. Clark told Harper about this day:

> They were not ready to receive the baptism, and therefore we sowed much and deeply, for a future day, as we have no interest in producing

false fire. Some of the letters we have had back from those present seem to indicate that God has set something in motion in several hearts.[5]

That Clark's judgment was correct is indicated by the fact that several members of the Farnborough Congregation were baptized in the Spirit by the time of his next visit for a weekend in the latter half of September.[6] By this time too, some of the Brethren had received 'the baptism' and been duly expelled, and the group at the parish church had made contact with the Elim Church in Aldershot. The pastor there, Joseph Smith, was introduced to Canon Hutchinson, who was at that time becoming increasingly sympathetic to the charismatic message without having received the baptism in the Spirit.[7]

From this point, the initiative in the Farnborough group seems to have passed to Bob and Norah Love, who were among the first to receive 'the baptism'. While on a trip to Birmingham to hear the American healing evangelist, T. L. Osborn, Bob Love met Harry Greenwood, by now based in Looe, Cornwall.[8] Greenwood visited Farnborough during that autumn, considerably increasing the level of excitement over what was going on.[9]

Clark returned to Farnborough twice in the summer of 1964[10] and reported that 'about seventy-five have now been baptised with the Spirit in this congregation'[11] The parish was also included in David du Plessis' itinerary in May 1964, when he preached in the church on Pentecost Sunday.[12]

During 1964 the Loves felt themselves constrained in conscience to be baptized in water, and on September 16, they were baptized in Frensham pond by Don Double.[13] Canon Hutchinson had been notified of the Loves' intention and apparently had not sought to dissuade them. However, another baptismal immersion in November caused some friction, and the Loves were asked by Hutchinson that none of their house group should teach any further in the youth work at the parish church.[14] This was the beginning of the Loves' withdrawal from the Church of England, and in 1965 Bob Love moved to Exeter where he became the leader of a house fellowship.[15] Several others from the Farnborough beginnings joined the local Baptist Church after the arrival of Michael Pusey as minister.[16]

One place to be ignited by a spark from Farnborough was Ridgelands Bible College, an Anglican foundation at Bexley in the

Kentish suburbs of the London metropolitan area. To Ridgelands in 1962 came a new principal, Mrs. Molly MacKenzie, who had been for many years a missionary in Ethiopia. Mrs. MacKenzie, brought up in a family opposed to all forms of Christianity, had had a conversion experience in Kenya in 1931, which she has long regarded as her baptism in the Spirit. She recalls having first spoken in tongues on that occasion. But she never really understood that experience until she was on furlough in 1947, and stayed with some Pentecostals in Bournemouth. At that time she began again to pray in tongues. By the time she was appointed to Ridgelands, she was attending the NPWR meetings and was hearing from Bill Grant and others how the pentecostal blessing was being received by many in the historic churches.[17]

Mrs. MacKenzie had taken over at Ridgelands in 1961 with only twelve students after a period of decline in the old age of her predecessor. While she herself urged the girls to go on with the Lord and discover more of the Holy Spirit, the number of students enrolled steadily increased, reaching forty-eight by 1965.

While some students from Ridgelands were baptized in the Spirit during their summer holiday in 1963[18] and a few others during the following year,[19] the biggest impact on the College came when six girls went to lead a Sunday school teachers' weekend at Farnborough Parish Church run by Ellita Howell Williams in the summer term of 1964.[20] Ridgelands was in fact the College where Miss Williams had her first experience of the Spirit back in 1952. All six girls returned from this week-end baptized in the Spirit and came back 'completely alive'.[21]

Mrs. MacKenzie sought both to encourage these girls in their new spiritual growth and to discourage them from speaking openly to other girls of their experience, unless they were asked first. The Council administering Ridgelands College was not very sympathetic to these developments in the student body, being somewhat disturbed by the news from nearby Beckenham. Nonetheless, Mrs. MacKenzie invited Michael Harper to conduct a 'quiet day' at Ridgelands, which he did on 14 January 1965.[22] Within a year of the Farnborough visit, over 90 per cent of the students at Ridgelands had received the baptism in the Spirit. Difficulties with the Council of trustees increased, and Mrs. MacKenzie was asked to leave, which she did in 1966.

Not far from Ridgelands, similar stirrings were occurring at Liskeard Lodge, the men's training college of the CMS in Chislehurst. To Liskeard Lodge in January 1964 came a couple recently baptized in the Spirit, Martin and Cynthia Peppiatt.[23] Peppiatt had been a fellow curate at All Souls, Langham Place with Michael Harper; now he and his wife were offering themselves for missionary service in Kenya. Within a month George and May Ingram came to visit. Ingram was praying for 'a revolutionizing work of the Spirit in the college'.[24] Within some weeks another couple destined for Kenya, Tom and Mary Fisher, received the baptism in the Spirit and were then instrumental in bringing other residents into the same blessing.[25] Thus by mid-1964, there were other centres of charismatic ferment to the South-East of London in addition to Beckenham and Gillingham.[26]

As the accounts of Ridgelands and Liskeard Lodge have shown, evangelical Anglican centres tended to experience charismatic stirrings around the period 1963–64. Another place, and one that exerted a considerable spiritual influence in Anglican circles mostly though not exclusively evangelical, was Lee Abbey in North Devon. Two people in particular were responsible for the initial interest of members of the Lee Abbey Community in the work of the Holy Spirit in the Charismatic movement: Deaconess Kristeen Macnair, a resident chaplain, and Leslie Sutton, one of the founders of Lee Abbey[27] who by the early 1960s was living in retirement at Dawlish, the other side of the moors on Devon's south coast just south of Exeter.

Sutton, a former WEC missionary forced to return to Britain by ill-health, had long been convinced of God's power to work miracles and transform lives. When he heard through *Trinity* magazine of the pentecostal blessing among Episcopalians in North America, Sutton saw this as part of the fulfilment of his prayers for Holy Spirit revival.[28] When in 1963 he heard of Michael Harper's experience, Sutton began a correspondence and tells Harper:

> The immediate fellowship and desire that springs up between those who are eager to know God's fulness of the Spirit is proof that this is of Him.[29]

Sutton's deep convictions are clear in these letters. He tells Harper:

> The outpouring of the Spirit is the only answer to the present increasing apostacy [sic] – but it may be healthy in the reaction against the stuffy lifeless religion which goes for Christianity.[30]

Sutton was soon in regular touch both with Beckenham and Farnborough,[31] as well as having regular fellowship with Rex Pointz-
Roberts, a Devon farmer and associate of Edgar Trout.[32] Although
spending two months at Lee Abbey in the summer of 1963, Sutton
was not apparently aware of the interest of Kristeen Macnair, one of
the Abbey's chaplains. Macnair was a former missionary in China
with the China Inland Mission,[33] and while there 'had some experience of this aspect of the Spirit's Work'[34] and in 1963 had re-read
Lesslie Newbigin's *The Household of God*, which speaks of the three
major Christian streams – all of which need each other – as the
Catholic, the Protestant and the Pentecostal.[35]

During 1964, this work of the Spirit was more evident at Lee
Abbey. Macnair reports on Whit Sunday:

> Things have been happening down here and we had a very significant
> visit from Edgar Trout the week before last in connection with a very
> difficult case of demon possession.[36]

Agnes Sanford spoke at two Clergy Recesses at Lee Abbey in the
early summer.[37] By the autumn, the Warden in his annual report to
the Abbey Council reported that more than a dozen numbers of the
Community were now praying in tongues.[38]

It was during a Lee Abbey Families Houseparty in the summer of
1964 that John Perry, an Anglican priest from St. Andrew's, Chorleywood in Hertfordshire, had an experience of the Holy Spirit in
repentance and reconciliation.[39] Perry had attended du Plessis' talk
at the Londoner Hotel the previous October, to which he had mixed
reactions. He had agreed with John Stott's theological objections to
a post-conversion baptism in the Spirit at the January Islington
Conference, but now at Lee Abbey his pursuit of the fullness of the
Spirit was rekindled. That autumn he ran a series of Bible studies in
his parish on the person and work of the Holy Spirit and invited
Michael Harper to speak to this group.

Harper came to Chorleywood at fortnightly intervals at the end
of 1964[40] and on his final visit[41] Perry said his reservations about the
fullness of the Holy Spirit had been removed and Harper should feel
free to speak his full mind.[42] Harper later recalled:

> So my prepared talk went by the board, and instead I told them about
> the blessing of Pentecost, and how they could be filled with the Holy
> Spirit. There was a memorable hush and stillness over the entire
> meeting. No one moved a muscle. You could feel the hunger that was

arising. I was just itching to lay my hands on them! But I felt the very
definite restraint of the Spirit.

We had a time of silent prayer afterwards, which was broken by
the vicar, who began slowly and deliberately to confess his own need
and faults. One by one people expressed their needs, and what they
wanted. And that was that. I told them afterwards that the Lord had
stopped me praying for them, and that He had a programme worked
out. They were not to worry, but in His time they would all receive
what they were seeking.

And they did. The vicar was the first; that very night he was filled
with the Spirit; and then one by one the people who had attended the
meetings.[43]

These beginnings at Chorleywood were marked by an absence
of divisiveness, most of the leaders in the various parish activities
being among those baptized in the Spirit. The impact of the Spirit
was further deepened and extended by visits from Edgar Trout[44]
and by the coming of Nicky Cruz[45] at the end of 1965.

Another area in the South of England where people were being
baptized in the Spirit in 1963 was South Bedfordshire, where word
was being spread by Eric Houfe, whose home was at Ampthill. One
of the first Anglican priests in this area to receive the baptism in the
Spirit was John Gravelle, then rector of Toddington.[46] Soon to follow
was the Anglo-Catholic rural dean of Woburn Sands, Michael
Meakin. In the autumn of 1962, Meakin had 'a rather shattering
realisation' that he had no gospel to give others, but on 2 September
1963, he heard a tape by Dennis Bennett and told his wife 'This is
it!'[47] Houfe and Gravelle spoke at Woburn Sands on 17 November
1963 to 'quite a sizeable group', which included Meakin's brother
Rex Meakin, rector of Emmanuel Church at Loughborough, Leicestershire.[48] Michael Meakin received the baptism in the Spirit before
Rex, who spoke in a tongue following the visit of Jean Stone to
Woburn Sands in April 1964.[49] Other clergy in Bedfordshire who
were baptized in the Spirit in 1963–64 were Bob Dunstone, a former
missionary to Trinidad[50] and Leonard Moore, vicar of All Saints,
Bedford.[51]

Another Anglo-Catholic priest to receive the baptism in the Spirit
by the summer of 1964 was John Gunstone of the diocese of
Chelmsford. the priest in charge of St. Augustine's, Rush Green,
Romford. Gunstone was a close friend of Reg East, the vicar of East
and West Mersea on the coast, who was a more 'middle-of-the-road'

Anglican. Sometime in 1963 the Easts first heard of this move of the Spirit through Leslie Sutton and soon after received a copy of *Trinity* magazine. After several months' searching, and growing contact with local Pentecostals, East received the baptism in the Spirit when he was prayed over by a young Pentecostal minister. He describes what happened on that day (25 April 1964):

> I breathed in the Holy Spirit as he and a friend laid hands on me, so I felt the power filling me, till I thought I would burst. I kept moving myself up and down and then it burst out through my lips. The sound was extraordinary!!! I went on and on simply yelling. Then gradually I began to control it and the tongue came in natural voice.[52]

Gunstone, as a close friend, was impressed by what he saw happening to the Easts (Lucia East had received a few days after her husband), and soon he asked East to lay hands upon him to be baptized in the Spirit. About a week after this ministry, Gunstone received an overwhelming sense of the presence of God and began to pray in tongues.[53] Gunstone was later to become the most articulate spokesman for the Charismatic movement in the more catholic wing of the Church of England.[54]

Sixteen

Out into the Churches

Section II chronicles a second stage in the emergence of the Charismatic movement in Great Britain, with the appearance of pentecostal patterns of blessing within the historic churches. The men studied in Section I, e.g. Cousen, Lillie, Wallis, Clark, McAlpine,[1] were generally characterized by a combination of receiving the baptism in the Spirit, not seeing themselves as Pentecostals and yet not having a committed relationship to any of the historic church traditions. Most of the people, whose stories are recounted in Section II – Wood, Parsons, P. L. C. Smith, Grant, Houfe, Harper, Clarke, Collins, MacInnes, Watson, McBain, Casebow, Strachan, MacKenzie, Macnair, Perry, the Meakin brothers, East and Gunstone – differ from those in the first list in that from the start they were convinced that God was calling them to live out their new life in the Spirit within their own churches.[2]

Whereas the narratives in Section I all clearly begin in the 1950s and the influence of those there described is felt by 1960, the accounts in Section II mostly belong to 1962 and 1963, or at least begin by the end of 1963. In several cases, however, the explicit search for a greater fullness in Christian life goes back at least to the late 1950s (Wood, Grant, Houfe, Allen, Clarke, Collins). None of these entered into the exercise of spiritual gifts before 1962. Nonetheless a number of people, not in leadership positions but members of mainline denominations, evidently did receive the baptism in the Spirit with the sign of tongues before 1962, for example at the EDH Convention in 1960, at the LHM Healing Advance in 1961, among the first young people at Burslem and at the St. Bride's Institute prayer meeting. Even if the Charismatic movement is defined in terms of pentecostal patterns of blessing within the historic churches (a position that has already been questioned[3]), the beginnings in Britain clearly ante-date 1962.

Of the events recorded in Section II, a significant percentage occurred between August 1962 and February 1963 (the baptisms in the Spirit of Houfe, P. L. C. Smith, and Clarke; Harper's Farnham experience; the Night of Prayer at Gillingham; and the beginnings at Farnborough). There is an evident connection between some of these events and the publication in September 1962 of an editorial about the pentecostal movement among American Episcopalians in the evangelical Anglican quarterly *The Churchman*.[4]

It is also clear from the data in Section II that the greatest impact of the nascent movement at this stage was upon the world of the Anglican evangelicals. With the possible exception of the Open Brethren, the Anglican evangelicals represented the only segment of English Christianity that by late 1963 was conscious of facing a new development in its midst. By early 1964, the charismatic question had surfaced in all the major publications produced or favoured by Anglican evangelicals, most obviously in the *Church of England Newspaper*,[5] but also in the *Life of Faith*, the weekly of the Keswick movement,[6] the *English Churchman*[7] and the monthly *Crusade*.[8] Moreover, there is evidence of the charismatic issue arising in evangelical student bodies such as the Inter-Varsity Fellowship of Christian Unions,[9] as well as in such evangelical institutions as Oak Hill Theological College,[10] Ridgelands Bible College, and the CMS house at Liskeard Lodge. Mention has already been made of the question being debated at Lee Abbey.

The difference in the movement's impact between evangelical Anglicans and those of a 'higher' churchmanship at this time can be seen from the contrasting accounts of the January 1964 Islington Clerical Conference in the two major Anglican weeklies. The evangelical *Church of England Newspaper* gave extensive coverage to this evangelical gathering, reporting on the front page both John Stott's opening address under the heading ' "Baptism of the Spirit" should unite, not divide' and the Presidential address of Rev. R. Peter Johnston, presenting as his major point Anglican relations with the Free Churches and the Church of South India.[11] The *Church Times*, representing a higher churchmanship, did not mention Stott's address, but made a major item of Johnston's remarks on the Vesture of Ministers Measure shortly to be debated in the Church Assembly.[12]

However, despite the predominance of Anglican evangelicals in the early days of the nascent Charismatic movement in Britain, there were already sufficient signs that the movement as a whole could not be seen as essentially an evangelical phenomenon. By the middle of 1964, there is a recognizable cluster of priests baptized in the Spirit from the more catholic and sacramental wing of the Church of England (Wood, Parsons, Meakin, Gunstone). Moreover, the publicity about the movement in the USA stressed that the Episcopalians involved mostly came from a High Church background.

As with the pioneers mentioned in Section I, the influence of Pentecostals on those covered in Section II was considerable. Their influence was major in the case of those associated with the St. Bride's prayer meeting in London (Rattenbury, Grant, Shaw, Milliken), as well as on Jeremiah, P. L. C. Smith, Houfe and MacKenzie. It is also significant in the stories of Wood, C. J. Clarke, the Loves of Farnborough, Peppiatt, Strachan and East. It appears to be minor in the cases of MacInnes, Watson, the Meakins and Casebow and non-existent in the initial experience of Harper, Collins and David Smith. The surprise is the relatively restricted influence on these people of the pioneers mentioned in Section I. While several of these men make an important teaching contribution in 1964 and 1965, they play very little part in the story of the origins among those committed to the historic churches. Indeed, the only one to feature prominently in any of the stories in Section II is Denis Clark with the beginnings at Farnborough. One explanation for this lack of influence is that both McAlpine and Wallis were absent in New Zealand for extended periods during the years covered in Section II. Another factor is that these men for the most part were more noted as teachers than as evangelists, and they only came into their own as the newly-established charismatic groups began to look for teaching.

The years covered in Section II are evidently the period during which the Charismatic movement in Britain emerged from being a random range of unco-ordinated blessings, mostly unknown to other recipients, to being consciously a single new movement of the Spirit. The factors promoting the conscious unity of the movement will be examined in Section III. The evidence, however, already indicates that the new development of people outside the Pentecostal churches receiving the baptism in the Spirit was being seen as a distinct movement and not just as the further expansion of the Pentecostal movement. This movement-aspect was particularly communicated by those producing regular journals or bulletins, such as Wood, Grant and Clarke.

By the end of 1963, however, the emerging movement was somewhat unevenly spread across Great Britain. The area of least penetration appears to have been the North-East and the North-West of England,[13] together with Wales.[14] The North of England was less affected even than Scotland. There was a smattering of charismatic revival in the Midlands (Charles Clarke, A. Edwards, P. L. C. Smith) and by 1964 in Loughborough and in Yorkshire (C. Cousen, G. W. North, J. Bradberry). In relation to general population distribution, there was a remarkably strong incidence in the South-West (Lillie, Wallis, Trout, Pointz-Roberts, Hutchison, Sutton, Macnair).[15] The strong showing in London and the Home Counties is perhaps less remarkable, granted the higher density of population and the greater facility of communications and travel in the area close to the Capital, that attracted more visits of speakers from other lands. It no doubt also reflected the more middle-class character of the Charismatic movement compared to the Pentecostals.

Seventeen

News from North America

Already one can sense from some of the accounts recorded, a growing awareness that the blessings being received were not scattered graces without any essential interconnection. Rather they formed part of one overall movement of God the Holy Spirit. This consciousness grew as 'non-Pentecostals' receiving the baptism in the Spirit came to know each other, and as news arrived of similar blessings being received in other parts of the world.

The first news from abroad indicating that something dramatically new was occurring concerned American Episcopalians being baptized in the Spirit and speaking in tongues. Although numbers of people including ministers in the mainline Protestant churches of the USA had been receiving the pentecostal baptism for some years before 1960, it was in that year that the news made the headlines, following Dennis Bennett's public profession of his receiving 'the fullness of the Spirit' and his subsequent resignation from his parish in Van Nuys, California.[1]

THE US NEWS REACHES BRITAIN

Knowledge of the events at Van Nuys must first have reached Britain through the reports in *Newsweek* and *Time*.[2] But there is no evidence that these items had any influence on the beginnings in Britain. However, in 1961 the American developments received mention in the British church press, on three occasions in the *Church of England Newspaper*.

In April 1961 an article was published entitled 'Glossolalia – a phenomenon rather unusual in contemporary Anglicanism' by the Ven. J. Ralph Deppen, Archdeacon of Chicago.[3] Deppen had been the chairman of the special commission appointed by the Bishop of

Chicago to report on glossolalia, which was seen as the most prob-
lematic aspect of the first pentecostal outbreak among Episcopalians
at Wheaton, Illinois.[4] His article simply records the work and findings of the commission, with the bishop's endorsement, and does
not refer at all to the outbreak at Van Nuys.[5] However, it was
noteworthy enough to attract editorial attention; the same issue
included an editorial comment entitled 'Sound of "tongues" '.[6]
Though faithfully evangelical in stressing conformity to the word of
God, the editorial was characteristically Anglican in urging an openness to this phenomenon.[7] Despite Deppen's article, later British
accounts show no awareness of Wheaton as a precursor of Van Nuys.
However, it was noticed by David Lillie, who mentioned it at the
Belstone Conference in September 1961.[8] It was also read with interest by Bill Grant and Philip Smith.[9]

The second and third articles in CEN both had the same heading,
'Tongues and Healing'; one was by an unnamed 'US correspondent'
on 4 August[10] and the other was by Dennis Bennett on 8 September.[11]
Unlike Deppen's, the article by Bennett has a definite witness element. Even so it does not seem to have made much impact, for it isn't
mentioned in personal testimonies in the same way as the visits of
du Plessis or the early issues of *Trinity*. One further article on the
topic appeared in CEN in 1962.[12]

THE ARRIVAL OF TRINITY MAGAZINE

While the news that American mainline Protestants were being
baptized in the Spirit undoubtedly fostered a sense of a new movement of God's Spirit touching people in many diverse places, this
consciousness owed more to the magazine *Trinity* published by the
pentecostal Episcopalians than to the occasional column in CEN.[13]
The first issue of *Trinity*, dated Trinitytide 1961, was published in the
autumn of 1961.[14] Copies reached England through David du Plessis
who gave Bill Grant a copy at the Fleet Street prayer meeting in
March 1962. Grant then wrote off to California for more copies, and
was surprised to receive fifty in return. He gave several to George
Ingram as well as single copies to John Stott, Eric Houfe and Charles
Clarke among others.[15] Jean Stone, the editor, then asked Grant if he
would act as the British agent and distributor for *Trinity*, but Grant
declined.

It was from *Trinity* that Clarke first heard of the pentecostal outpouring among Episcopalians in California, which he then reported in *The Quest*.[16] He sent Jean Stone a copy and suggested *Trinity* obtain a British agent.[17] She then proposed Clarke, who agreed and served as British agent from the summer of 1963 until *Trinity*'s demise in 1966.[18]

Trinity raised consciousness of the existence of a new move of the Holy Spirit across the churches because it was specifically founded to publicize and promote this work of the Spirit within the historic churches. Thus it had an immediate appeal to many committed churchmen. Several prominent figures in the movement in Britain recognized its role in their lives. Eric Houfe and Brian Casebow were baptized in the Spirit after reading *Trinity*, while Michael Harper first read details of Dennis Bennett's experience from the same source[19].

The Christmastide 1962 issue was the first to include an item from Britain with Casebow's witness.[20] It was over a year before further British news appeared with Philip Smith's witness[21] and reprints of two articles of Harper in the Septuagesimna 1964 issue.[22] From this point, articles from British authors appear in almost every remaining issue.[23]

The extent of *Trinity*'s influence in Britain was however limited by its price. At 10s. 6d. a copy, it was much more expensive than any comparable Christian magazine in the country. At its peak, the British circulation was approximately.[24]

THE CHURCHMAN EDITORIAL

Probably the biggest factor in the publicizing of this neo-pentecostal movement in Britain at this time was the editorial, which Philip Hughes, a prominent evangelical scholar, wrote for *The Churchman* of September 1962.[25] Hughes had been in the USA earlier that year and had received an invitation from Jean Stone to visit California and see what was happening. He was impressed by the prayer meetings he attended and by the people he met.

> The serene joy, love and devotion which marked these gatherings made a profound impression on me. They adore their Lord and Saviour; they feed eagerly upon his Word; they seek in the power of the Holy Spirit to be his witnesses daily in all their living, and they testify to the most remarkable answers to their prayers in the lives of

others, in bodily healing and spiritual blessing. Dare we deny that this is a movement of God's Sovereign Spirit?[26]

The Churchman editorial was written on Hughes' return to England. He wrote of his visit in the third person:

> What he witnessed points only in one direction, namely, that the Breath of the Living God is stirring among the dry bones of the major, respectable, old-established denominations, and particularly with the Episcopalian Church.[27]

Hughes as a sympathetic observer had less difficulty than some participants in recognizing the new developments as a distinct movement. 'It is a movement, moreover, within the heart of the Church, not away from the Church.'[28] Because he was known as an evangelical scholar, not given to mindless enthusiasm, Hughes' highly positive evaluation made a definite impression. Grant, who had been shown a copy by John Stott, immediately saw its potential to win over evangelicals to the new movement. Grant obtained Hughes' permission to reprint and Ingram's agreement to send a copy to the two thousand recipients of the NPWR News Sheet and the smaller number of members of APFR. The demand for the reprint was so great that thirty-nine thousand copies were printed.[29] Denis Clark and Bill Wood were among those who sent a copy of the Hughes leaflet to all on their mailing lists.[30]

Besides the much wider circulation of this leaflet than that of *Trinity*, the reprinted editorial had the added advantage of the American events not just being described but also endorsed by a British scholar. This combination did much to overcome the deep-rooted British suspicion of imported American religion. As a result, the 'neo-pentecostal' movement was placed firmly before many British Protestants, especially Anglican evangelicals as a serious issue. One consequence was the record attendance at the Islington Clerical Conference, an annual gathering of Anglican evangelical clergy, in January 1964, when the topic was the Holy Spirit.[31] John Stott's eagerly-awaited talk on 'The Individual Christian and the Fullness of the Holy Spirit'[32] was a severe disappointment to Harper, Grant and their friends. Stott rejected on exegetical grounds any concept of a distinctive 'second blessing', and the idea that Christians today should seek the spiritual gifts. Stott's negative stance towards the new movement ended the period of relative evangelical openness that had begun with Hughes' editorial. For several years after this, evangelical parishes identifying with the new move of the Spirit, such as St. Mark's, Gillingham, were suspect in the eyes of most fellow-evangelicals within the Church of England.

For a period after the publication of his editorial, Hughes was invited on various occasions to speak about his experiences in the USA. It was at one such talk at Michael Harper's flat in January 1963 that Harper first met David Lillie.[33]

A VOICE IN THE WILDERNESS

David Lillie was largely responsible for making known in Britain another American publication publicizing this new charismatic move of the Holy Spirit.[34] This was *A Voice in the Wilderness*, a bi-monthly – later a quarterly – that had begun publication early in 1960. While most of the articles in AVW were teaching articles, there were occasional items with news concerning the charismatic revival.[35] It combined a commitment to corporate church restoration with a conviction that the Pentecostal revival of the first decade of this century was a vital grace of God that had largely been lost in the subsequent development of Pentecostalism.[36]

FIRST AMERICAN VISITORS

In retrospect, it is surprising that no American participants in the new movement visited Britain and spoke on its beginnings before the summer of 1963. One reason may be that they did not know whom to contact in Britain. The first visitor to witness to events in the USA was in fact on holiday – on his way to visit his parents in Northern Ireland. This was Frank Maguire, the rector of the Episcopal Church of the Holy Spirit, Monterey Park, California. It was in Maguire's parish that the charismatic beginnings among Episcopalians in California took place, and it was there that Dennis Bennett was baptized in the Spirit.[37]

Maguire flew to London in May 1963 en route to Ireland. Michael Harper heard from John Stott that he was coming; Stott already knew Maguire from previous visits to All Souls. Harper arranged a meeting and sent out some invitations privately. Maguire spoke to an audience of about fifty, which included two famous and contending evangelicals, John Stott and Dr. Martyn Lloyd-Jones.[38] Maguire also spoke at the Church Army Training College,[39] at a small meeting in the Oxfordshire village of Cogges, near Witney[40] and at Warley Woods Methodist Church in Smethwick.[41]

Although Maguire never achieved the celebrity of some later American visitors, he undoubtedly exercised some influence on Michael Harper. Harper acknowledges his indebtedness to Maguire, who was the first person to help him understand baptism in the Spirit in the context of full initiation instead of the normal Pentecostal view of two crisis-experiences. Maguire also warned Harper not to welcome uncritically every travelling American charismatic. 'Be very careful of these people that come through. Some of them are good and some of them are not so good. I'll help you and tell you who is coming.'[42]

The first visitor Maguire commended was Larry Christenson of the American Lutheran Church and pastor of Trinity Lutheran in San Pedro, California.[43] Christenson was taking part in the Lutheran World Federation Conference in Helsinki in August 1963, and Harper arranged for Christenson and his wife to pass through London on their return journey. Christenson spoke twice on 26 August, in the afternoon to a gathering of clergy and in the evening to a meeting to which laity were also invited.[44]

While Maguire evidently recounted the origins among the Episcopalians,[45] Christenson, at least in his address to clergy, spoke more of the significance of this move of the Spirit for the churches at this point in history.[46] Christenson spoke very much in terms of a movement within the historic churches, seeing God choosing to begin in the most unlikely place, among the highly respectable Episcopalians. He spoke of the Holy Spirit calling Christians to repentance, both for their personal sin and for the sins of the whole church. Here we find a note, missing among the Pentecostals, and accompanying a firm church commitment, namely a sense of responsibility for the weak sickly state of the churches. Christenson described this as a new discovery, that he like Daniel should kneel before God and repent for the rebellion of the people, including himself.

It was during this visit that Christenson gave advice that helped Harper with speaking in tongues. A few months later Harper arranged for Christenson's articles on tongues already published in the USA to be printed as a pamphlet in Britain.[47] Christenson was responsible for recommending David du Plessis to Harper.[48] It is a measure of Harper's newness to the movement at this time that he needed such a recommendation.

Agnes Sanford was another American who visited Britain in the summer of 1963.[49] Mrs. Sanford spoke at St. John's, Bromley in Kent and at St. Mary Magdalene's, Reigate in Surrey.[50] Mrs. Sanford's visits to Britain[51] almost certainly contributed to the spread of the Charismatic movement,[52] though as in America she only spoke in private of baptism in the Spirit and the spiritual gifts.[53]

Maguire and Christenson in particular communicated to their hearers a sense of a definite move of God's Spirit on Christians within the historic churches and of their own commitment and loyalty to their own traditions. This was wholly in line with du Plessis' message that God was pouring out his Spirit on all flesh, including the historic churches. They presented a vision of old churches renewed in the Holy Spirit more clearly than anyone in the movement in Britain had done up to this time.

Eighteen

Michael Harper and the Fountain Trust

Not only did the visits of Maguire and Christenson in 1963 spread the sense of a new and recognizable movement of the Holy Spirit within the historic churches but they contributed to the emergence of Michael Harper as a spokesman for the movement in Britain. This in turn helped to make the rise of the movement more visible, and awareness of its existence more widespread.

The process of sending out invitations for these meetings helped Harper to find out who were the people, especially the clergy, already baptized in the Spirit or showing signs of real interest in this work of the Spirit. Being at All Souls, Langham Place, he was at a focal point in the Anglican evangelical world and ideally placed to hear of evangelicals sympathetic to this pentecostal wave. Moreover, Harper was in regular touch with Bill Grant, who had wide links among evangelicals of all types concerned about 'Pentecost'. Immediately after the Maguire visit in May 1963, Harper told Philip Smith that 'a small group of clergy interested in or having experienced the baptism is arising in the South'.[1] To follow up on the Christenson gathering, he organized a meeting in September of 'those who are in 100% agreement and sympathy – for mutual encouragement, prayer and waiting on the Lord.'[2]

Immediately after the Christenson visit, no doubt encouraged by his new freedom with the gift of tongues, Harper spent a few days in the country reading and writing. 'I have written two articles – one on "prophecy" and another on "the new revival". I am thinking of offering the latter to the CEN.'[3] The CEN article, which appeared in two parts,[4] came out first and was a reflection on Lesslie Newbigin's prophetic analysis in The Household Of God (1952) in the light of the first stirrings of the movement in Britain. Newbigin had argued that besides the Catholic and Protestant streams in Christianity, there is a third, the Pentecostal, all three being in need of each other.[5] Harper wrote particularly of Anglo-Catholics rediscovering the living word of God and evangelicals coming to a dynamic conception of the body of Christ. The two CEN articles brought Harper quite a batch of correspondence and did much to increase the range of his contacts. The other article on Prophecy became Harper's first pamphlet, *Prophecy -A Gift for the Body of Christ*, published in May 1964.

In October 1963, Harper hosted a talk by David du Plessis at the Londoner Hotel.[6] Afterwards several people were prayed over for the baptism in the Spirit at the Harpers' flat.[7] As a result of Harper's meeting with du Plessis, he was asked to arrange du Plessis' itinerary for a longer stay in Britain the following summer.[8]

At the beginning of 1964, Harper began to send out a regular newsletter to all interested parties. These letters advertised tours of visiting speakers, new publications and tapes, and gave news of Harper's own activities, as well as explaining his own convictions concerning this move of the Spirit. The first letter identified three urgent concerns of Harper: (1) Christian initiation as including baptism in the Spirit; (2) The church as the body of Christ; and (3) Gifts for the church. He concluded: 'This is to pinpoint three desperate deficiencies in modern Christianity. There are probably many others. (1) is the key to (2) and (3).'[9] The newsletter also advertised some events sponsored by leaders from other streams flowing into this movement.[10]

In February 1964, Harper held a residential conference at Stoke Poges in Buckinghamshire, sensing the need to bring together some of those who had experienced this new life of the Spirit.[11] The majority of those attending were lay Anglicans. A report gives details about the participants:

> They came from different parish Churches and all except two of those present were Anglicans. Apart from ourselves there was one other Minister present with his wife; there was one member of the Episcopal Church of America;[12] one theological student; three architects;[13] one CMS Missionary who was baptised in the Spirit in America on her way home to England on furlough;[14] one missionary recruit, who has since left for Asia and one full-time Church worker.[15] Most of us had never met each other before.[16]

Harper had invited Arthur Wallis to speak at Stoke Poges, but two weeks before the conference Wallis said that he was unable to come. In his place he recommended his friend Campbell McAlpine.[17] Harper knew nothing of McAlpine, and confesses that he was somewhat apprehensive about this man with so Scottish a name.[18]

The conference was felt to be successful beyond all expectations. The few not previously baptized in the Spirit all received.[19] Campbell McAlpine gave 'just the right message'. But for Harper the main impression was of his first experience of charismatic worship integrating use of the spiritual gifts with the ministry of the word and the order of the church.

> For the first time in 8 1/2 years of ordained ministry – and 12 years of Christian experience I saw 1 Cor. 12, 13 and 14 operating exactly as we read in the scriptures. It was thrilling.[20]

As we shall see, the positive experience with McAlpine, whose Brethren background would have been quite foreign to Harper and the other Anglicans, prepared the way for Harper to utilize the teaching experience of several of the men, studied in Section I, who had been baptized in the Spirit but were not Pentecostals.

Towards the end of April 1964, Harper organized a somewhat hectic tour of Britain for Jean Stone, the editor of *Trinity*, and her husband Don.[21] She spoke at two English vicarages, one evangelical and one Anglo-Catholic,[22] and two meetings in the Motherwell area in Scotland.[23] Also, in London, Stone held a press conference at the Savoy Hotel[24] and spoke twice, at Caxton Hall and at the City Temple. These meetings were the first large-scale meetings in Britain on the new movement of the Spirit which were open to the general public. The report sent to recipients of Harper's newsletter recorded:

> At . . . the Caxton Hall Mrs Stone did something which she later confessed she had never done before – she was constrained before speaking to deliver a message from God in tongues, which was interpreted by someone else in the Hall. This was swiftly followed by two further messages from people in the Hall, similarly interpreted. The first concerned God's sovereign work, the second the need of London and in the third the power to meet it was offered. At least three people testified later that for them this was the turning point. God was speaking to them in a personal and direct way and they were baptised in the Spirit very soon afterwards.[25]

Among those baptized in the Spirit at Caxton Hall were Michael Bennett, who later worked for the Fountain Trust,[26] and Trevor Marzetti, later to become a lay leader in the Charismatic renewal

among Anglicans.[27] Marzetti testified that through the baptism in the
Spirit 'the presence of God became a physical and inward reality,
something I had only experienced at conversion before, but which
now became constant in my life'.[28]

In June 1964, Harper arranged another residential conference at
Stoke Poges during a British tour by David du Plessis. Unlike the
February meeting, the June conference was restricted to ministers
and pastors, either baptized in the Spirit or highly sympathetic to
this work of the Spirit. The list of those who accepted the invitation
manifests the expanding range of the nascent movement. This can
be seen more clearly by listing these men according to their ecclesiastical and theological backgrounds:

INDEPENDENTS
Denis Clark	David Lillie
Harry Greenwood[29]	Hugh Thompson

ANGLICANS
(Evangelical)
John Bradberry[30]	David Gardner[32]
Howard Cole	David MacInnes
John Collins	Philip Smith
Donald Eddison[31]	Richard Vick[33]

(Anglo-Catholic)
John Gunstone	Michael Meakin

('Middle-of-the-road')
Reg East	Rex Meakin

METHODIST
Charles Clarke

CHURCH OF SCOTLAND
Gordon Strachan

BAPTIST
Frank Wilson[34]	W. J. James[35]

For many of these men it was their first meeting. Stoke Poges June
1964, was certainly the most representative gathering of leaders and
would-be leaders up to this point, and deepened many participants'
sense of their responsibility for this work that God was doing across
all the churches. In the summer months of 1964, a new momentum

was being felt. Numbers were multiplying.[36] The movement in the Church of England was moving out beyond the evangelical wing.[37]

With the increasing demands on Harper as a reputable Anglican spokesman for the new movement and with his rector taking a position opposing a post-conversion baptism in the Spirit, it is not surprising that Harper began to think of resigning from All Souls to work full-time in this new work of the Spirit. In March 1964, he began his newsletter by announcing:

> Jeanne and I want to share with you the news that we shall be leaving All Souls Church in the summer. This has been a very difficult decision to make. We have been very happy during the six years we have been serving in the Church; but the pressure of this new wider ministry has become so great that we have had to face the necessity of either remaining at All Souls and drastically curtailing this other ministry – or leaving All Souls and devoting all our time to this other ministry which is growing all the time. We have sought to know the will of God, and believe now that He has told us 'Go . . . to the land, that I will show you'. (Genesis 12:1)[38]

Harper left All Souls on 2 July.[39] By this time he saw that his new ministry would require some organizational support, in terms of personnel, finance and expert advice.[40] On 29 September 1964, the Fountain Trust was formed.[41] In his newsletter announcing the plan to set up this Trust, Harper expressed his convictions concerning the relationship of this renewal to the existing churches:

> We feel called to serve every section of the Church, without fear or favour. We are seeing the Holy Spirit moving in unlikely places today, and we rejoice in His power to bring men of different traditions together.[42]

This kind of ecumenical platform was sufficiently flexible to allow for collaboration between committed members of the mainline denominations and independents, including those like Lillie and Wallis who were sceptical of the ability of the churches to do anything other than quench the Spirit. Although the four trustees of the Fountain Trust were all Anglicans,[43] the Advisory Council that was formed came to include leaders from every kind of background.[44]

The Fountain Trust was devised as and functioned strictly as a service agency. It was made clear that one could not join the Fountain Trust, and it did not have branches to which people could belong.

Its aims were later set out in *Renewal* magazine:

1. To encourage Christians of all churches to receive the power of the Holy Spirit and to glorify Christ by manifesting in their lives the fruit and gifts of the same Spirit, so that they may enrich their worship, strengthen their witness and deepen their fellowship.
2. To encourage local churches to experience renewal in the Holy Spirit and to recover the full ministry of the Holy Spirit including that of healing.
3. To encourage Christians to expect and pray for worldwide revival.[45]

When Harper became full-time general secretary of the Fountain Trust it freed him to devote all his energies to making known this move of the Spirit. This he did in three principal ways: writing, travelling, and promotion of conferences and rallies. Harper began his travels in October 1964, and his itinerary indicates many of the places where interest in the renewing work of the Holy Spirit was stirring.[46] Through these travels, Harper met virtually all the ministers who were being baptized in the Spirit.[47]

Harper's first trip beyond the Midlands also took him to Scotland.[48] The formulation of the objectives of the Fountain Trust never specified any geographical limits to its scope. In its first eighteen months, its activities were primarily in England, with a greater thrust in the South, closer to its London base.

In the spring of 1965, Harper and his wife made their first transatlantic crossing, and spent a month in North America.[49] The visit was sponsored by the Full Gospel Businessmen's Fellowship International, and gave Harper the opportunity of meeting more North American leaders, such as Dennis Bennett, Harald Bredesen and Demos Shakarian. In Seattle, Harper had his first experience of speaking in a Roman Catholic setting and meeting Roman Catholics baptized in the Spirit.[50]

In the first conferences and rallies organized under the auspices of the Fountain Trust, Harper drew upon such visitors as David du Plessis[51] and Derek Prince[52] and most importantly a number of the experienced teachers already mentioned in Section I, none of whom were in the ordained ministry of a mainline church tradition. Edgar Trout, Arthur Wallis and Campbell McAlpine all spoke at Fountain

Trust meetings in London in the first six months of the Trust's existence.[53] Cecil Cousen was soon to be a regular speaker at Fountain Trust gatherings, especially the residential conferences.[54]

Harper's writing intensified as he had more time available. A new booklet *Power for the Body of Christ* was published in November 1964, the first new pamphlet under the imprint of the Fountain Trust. The following year saw the publication of a small book, *As at the Beginning*,[55] detailing in popular form the story of the Pentecostal outpouring of the twentieth century from Topeka, Azusa Street and Sunderland early in the century to Van Nuys, Burslem, Gillingham and Langham Place in the early 1960s. This short history was important in making known the story of Sunderland from 1907, in which Alexander Boddy, the Anglican vicar, now appears as a precursor of the Charismatic movement.[56] From late 1964 came two further articles by Harper in the *Church of England Newspaper*.[57]

Another sign of the clear emergence of a recognizable movement of the Holy Spirit was Michael Harper's concern from the first days of the Fountain Trust to keep the bishops informed of what was happening. He obtained permission from the Bishop of London to officiate, now that he was no longer attached to a parish.[58] The Anglican bishops who showed the most interest were Mervyn Stockwood, the Bishop of Southwark, and John Trillo, the Bishop of Bedford.[59] Harper and a small group met with Bishop Stockwood in August 1964 for prayer and discussion, and this led to all Southwark clergy known to have been baptized in the Spirit meeting for a eucharist and luncheon at Bishop's House in December 1964.[60]

The promotional structures of the Fountain Trust were completed at the end of 1965 with the launching of a bi-monthly magazine *Renewal*.[61] The idea of starting a magazine was evidently in the Harpers' minds before the Fountain Trust was conceived.[62] The first newsletter after the Trust's establishment announced that a magazine was in the offing.

> We have now definitely decided not to go ahead with printing TRINITY magazine in this country. There are too many practical difficulties. At the moment we are investigating the possibilities of a much smaller publication which would come out bi-monthly.[63]

With its regular pattern of conferences and its own magazine, the Fountain Trust was now firmly established. The main lines of its contribution to and its role within the Charismatic movement in

Britain were set. With its strong Anglican base, its thrust was primarily towards the encouragement of renewal, particularly parochial-congregational renewal, within the historic Protestant and Reformed churches. However, the Trust was run in a way that sought to maintain the maximum possible links and co-operation with those who were outside the main denominational traditions.

Nineteen

International Ecumenical Vision

Previous chapters have chronicled visits by David du Plessis to Britain between 1959 and 1962.[1] During those years, there was no general awareness among Christians of a new worldwide movement of God's Spirit, and du Plessis' message that God was moving in pentecostal power through 'the denominational Churches'[2] was surprising news to most of his hearers.

By the time of du Plessis' visit to Britain in October 1963, things were beginning to change. News was percolating through evangelical channels concerning St. Mark's, Gillingham, and meetings in the parlour at All Souls, Langham Place. So when invitations were sent out by Michael Harper for a talk to leading ministers and lay people by David du Plessis at the Londoner Hotel on Tuesday 15 October, there was confident expectation of widespread interest and a good attendance. The main problem was to ensure that du Plessis himself knew of the appointment. Eric Houfe had written to du Plessis a year earlier wanting him to speak in London, but only received a reply from Rome, where du Plessis was attending the Second Vatican Council between 28 September and 4 October.[3] Du Plessis told Houfe he would be passing through London in mid-October on his return journey to the USA and on the strength of this information, Harper booked the Londoner Hotel. Contact was made, and du Plessis had an audience of at least 120.[4]

Du Plessis spoke primarily on the baptism in the Holy Spirit, with particular emphasis on Jesus Christ as the baptizer:

> You come to the place where you do absolutely nothing but surrender totally to the Baptizer. That's very simple. That's how you get the Baptism in the Holy Spirit. Total surrender to the Lord Jesus Christ . . . If your intellect hasn't gone under in this process, you're still holding out your intellect against the Spirit. But once you surrender your intellect, the whole being – total surrender to Jesus – then the

> Holy Spirit takes over and at this point he transcends your under-
> standing and you worship in the Spirit in a way you have never
> known before. That's baptism in the Spirit.[5]

However, the talk was liberally sprinkled with anecdotes draw-
ing on du Plessis' unusually wide range of contacts, both internationally and ecumenically. He was both the most travelled of all
those concerned with this movement, and the person with the
widest range of Christian contacts. He had met and talked with
many church leaders, particularly under the auspices of the WCC,
and he was in touch with an astonishingly large number of people
and places, where 'the new Pentecost' was to be found. Within the
USA, no one else, not even Bredesen and Stone for all their promotional activities, even came near du Plessis' range of neo-pentecostal contacts.[6] In Britain, he already knew David R. Smith and Bill
Wood from 1959, and had met Denis Clark at the St. Bride's Institute talk in March 1962.[7] Already in 1963, du Plessis had visited
Colombia, Canada, Holland, Italy and Switzerland before coming
to London, and before his next visit in May 1964, he was to be in
Mexico, Switzerland, Italy, South Africa, France and Germany,
besides the USA.[8] Du Plessis was therefore uniquely placed to
convey a sense of the worldwide character of this charismatic
outpouring.

The Londoner Hotel talk also conveyed a sense of how this move
of the Spirit was touching Christians of many denominations, containing examples of Episcopalian, Lutheran and Reformed ministers being baptized in the Spirit. Du Plessis must have stunned his
largely evangelical audience when he told them of his positive
contacts with Roman Catholics. As he explained with his simple
humour:

> I have very good friends in the Roman Catholic Church. And since
> the Holy Spirit can move in the holy Catholic Church, I can too. Where
> he goes, I can go. He is not at all prepared to leave the Roman Catholic
> Church or any Church in the condition it is.[9]

Du Plessis' unexpected words about Roman Catholics carried
particular weight, because he had just come from Rome, where as
an officially-invited observer he had attended the opening of the
second session of the Second Vatican Council. His hearers knew he
had not just met unrepresentative and deviant Roman Catholics,
but had been meeting bishops and theologians gathered in Rome.

Not only did du Plessis convey a vivid impression of a work of the Spirit touching all continents but he also portrayed it as touching an equally wide range of churches. Nobody else was in a position to be able to do either of these things.

When du Plessis next set foot in Britain, it was mid-May 1964. This time he stayed a full four weeks, and completed an itinerary more comprehensive and taxing than any other prominent speakers from overseas.[10] The names of the places visited include emerging centres of charismatic activity (Burslem, Motherwell, Halesowen, Exeter,[11] Worthing,[12] Farnborough) as well as major cities such as London, Bradford,[13] Bristol,[14] Birmingham, Middlesbrough and Edinburgh. Nearly all these meetings were packed.[15] He addressed Pentecostal groups in London (the SPF) and at Skegness the annual conference of the Elim Pentecostal Church. He was a guest at the General Assembly of the Church of Scotland in Edinburgh, and was entertained by the Inter-Church Relations Committee and the Scottish Churches' Ecumenical Association.[16] He addressed several gatherings in the city, some Church of Scotland, some ecumenical. He spoke in Luton at a meeting of 130 clergy of the St. Albans diocese, at which the Bishop of Bedford presided.[17] In addition, du Plessis spoke at the Stoke Poges Conference, already mentioned, and another LHM Healing Advance.[18]

This tour was itself a unifying force within the emerging charismatic movement. Its organization increased the range of Harper's contacts, and itself gave a much clearer sense of how the movement was arising and developing in many parts of the country.

Du Plessis was in London again in the autumn of 1964 on his return journey to the USA from the third session of the Second Vatican Council. He spoke at Caxton Hall to over 300 people. Harper's advertisement for this talk announced that 'Mr. du Plessis will pray for people after the meeting'.[19] On this visit du Plessis met Edgar Trout for the first time[20] and also 'visited the recently married couple, Mr. and Mrs. Donald Gee'.[21]

In 1965, du Plessis again paid two visits to the British Isles. In May, he spoke at a ministers' meeting at Westminster Chapel,[22] made a quick trip to St. Mark's, Gillingham[23] and returned to Westminster Chapel, where he spoke on 'Jesus as Lamb of God and Baptizer in the Holy Spirit'.[24] In addition, he recorded a television interview and renewed his acquaintance with Bill Wood, Edgar Trout and the Harpers.[25]

November 1965 saw a further longer visit with another extensive tour, mostly to places not visited in the summer of 1964.[26] Of the towns and cities listed, only London, Bradford and Cambridge had been included in the 1964 itinerary. The new places on the 1965 list were mostly in the South; Dartford, Tunbridge Wells, Stanwell, Bexhill, St. Leonards,[27] Rayleigh, Oxford and two suburbs of London, Tufnell Park[28] and Putney. A short trip to the North included Bradford and Otley.[29]

Du Plessis then attended part of the Full Gospel Businessmen's Convention in London to which there was a 'spiritual airlift' of two jet-loads of North Americans baptized in the Spirit.[30] He then spoke at Howard Cole's church at Cogges in Oxfordshire, and spent a day at the Jesuit theological college nearby.[31] Here he was welcomed by Fr. Bernard Leeming, who had met du Plessis at St. Andrews in 1960,[32] and Fr. Robert Murray, who had welcomed him in Rome.[33]

The full scope of du Plessis' activities is revealed in these visits. There is the range of contact; from Pentecostals, through traditional Free Churchmen and Anglicans, to Roman Catholics. There are meetings with church leaders and addresses to official church gatherings. There are open meetings of every size from big city halls to country vicarages. If any category predominated, it would be addresses to groups of ministers.[34] The following chapter will assess further the significance of du Plessis' contribution in examining the agents and factors promoting the conscious emergence of the Charismatic movement in Britain.

Twenty

One Discernible Movement

The three preceding chapters in Section III have all described the stages by which scattered manifestations and leadings of the Holy Spirit across Great Britain came to be recognized and experienced as part of one Charismatic movement. This chapter aims to provide an overview of this process and to evaluate the significance of the various contributory elements and agents.

It has already been remarked that through the efforts of du Plessis and Gee many Pentecostals were aware of a new movement beyond their own ranks before other Christians had any such awareness.[1] However, these Pentecostals often did not grasp the true newness in what was happening, as clearly as Gee and du Plessis. They easily saw the new events as simply an extension of the Pentecostal movement, as they understood it. They were unaware of the trans-confessional and ecumenical character of their own movement in its origins, so they were unable to see the new developments as challenging their narrowed understanding of what it represented. Du Plessis and Gee in their contrasting ways both knew that this 'Pentecost beyond Pentecost' was not simply a numerical expansion of the Pentecostal movement as it had come to be after its first decades. Gee knew more of early Pentecostal history than du Plessis, while du Plessis knew from the content and tone of Wigglesworth's prophecy that the new movement represented something significantly new that was, in some way, a recovery of the original breadth and scope of their own movement.

Gee was little known outside Pentecostal circles. So this sense of God acting in a specific way across all the churches of the world was first conveyed to others by du Plessis. However, before 1963, very few of those touched by this work of the Spirit in Britain had heard du Plessis speak. Of the people mentioned in previous chapters, only David R. Smith, Clark, Wood, Grant and others from the

St. Bride's prayer meeting had heard du Plessis' message.[2] Wood communicated this vision in various LHM Letters, while Grant reported all news of revival in the NPWR mailings. Wood gave more impression than Grant of the rise of a distinctive movement, largely because he focused more on its overall significance. By contrast, Grant recorded and reported particular blessings in detail, without any downplaying of charismatic features. Of the two, Grant's influence was the greater, because his range of contacts was more extensive and because of the solidity of his evangelical reputation. Wood, by contrast, was known only in healing circles, which represented a somewhat smaller constituency than the evangelical revival world of Bill Grant.

However, by the time the first reports appeared in Britain of the charismatic beginnings in North America, very few Christians in the country had got a sense of any new pentecostal outpouring across the world. These reports, and particularly Hughes' editorial in *The Churchman*, reached a Christian public well beyond the revival circles of Grant and the healing circles of Wood. While Grant and Wood communicated their news to a smaller public with a higher potential impact due to their common interests, the reports in the church press reached a wider public with lower potential impact.

Whereas some accounts of the Charismatic movement in Britain suggest that it came from America,[3] the evidence in these chapters indicates this was not the case, although the parallel beginnings in America were mostly earlier in date.[4] However, the news from America evidently did help to convey a sense of an emerging movement that transcended national boundaries, and to promote the coming together in Britain of what previously had been independent or at best intersecting streams of similar experience. The Hughes editorial had spoken in 'movement' terms and had made clear the churchly character of the developments among American Episcopalians. This helped to bring out more clearly for British readers a distinctive feature of the new movement, namely its compatibility with existing denominational loyalty. This indicated something more than a mere extension of Pentecostalism.

While such writings had some effect in creating awareness of a significant new development in the Christian world, they did not of themselves do much to increase knowledge of what was happening in Britain. Indeed, the Hughes editorial gave no indication that any comparable developments were occurring in his own country.

Each year in the early 1960s, there were increasing contacts among the circles growing up in Britain around those whose experiences have already been described. By the beginning of 1963, there were some identifiable clusters within the emerging Charismatic movement; these were partly, theological-denominational and partly geographical. There was the group of those we may call independents, which had a geographical focus in the South-West around Lillie and Wallis. Cousen, Clark and McAlpine also fitted into this category, though their ecclesiologies were not identical. Largely unaware of these independents in their earliest phase, there was the cluster of Anglican evangelicals, developing around Harper and Collins, focused in London and the South-East. Geographically, there was a small nucleus in the Midlands, centred around Philip Smith in Burslem and Charles Clarke in Halesowen. At this point Trout and Wood had little interaction with the other streams.

At the beginning of 1963, there was only one person who was in touch with all these clusters and who knew all the leading figures, and that was Bill Grant.[5] Grant himself belonged to the circle of evangelical Anglicans, who knew him as a helper in NPWR, involved in the production of its newsletter, as well as being editor of the bulletin of APFR. However, he had also attended the Belstone and Mamhead Park Conferences, hosted by Lillie and Wallis, as well as taking part in the conferences of the various denominational revival fellowships. He knew Trout from the visits to Plymouth, where he had lived in lodgings many years earlier. Grant was an indefatigable correspondent, and was in regular correspondence with many of the leaders. He accordingly played a far more significant role in making the early leaders aware of each other and in passing on significant information than would ever be guessed from the published records.

So when Maguire and Christenson visited London in the summer of 1963, and Michael Harper sent out invitations to interested parties, Grant was a major information resource. These two gatherings were the first occasions when interested persons had an opportunity to hear about this work of the Spirit and put any questions they had. Du Plessis' talks in 1960 and 1961 had been respectively at a Faith and Order Conference not open to the public and a residential conference of the LHM. The nearest previous approach had been du Plessis' talk at St. Bride's Institute in March 1962.

Du Plessis' visits contributed more markedly to the same process of making known the existence of this 'neo-pentecostal' or
Charismatic movement. However, he brought not only the basic
conviction of a new work of God's Spirit that he had been preaching for several years, but also up-to-date news from many countries to confirm the reality of his vision. From this point of view, du
Plessis' visits to Britain in October 1963 and the Summer of 1964
were the most important. During the second of these visits, du
Plessis spoke at the second Stoke Poges conference, which had
brought together the most representative group of leaders and
pioneer figures yet to have gathered in the British movement. Such
meetings contributed markedly to the participants' sense of being
part of one new movement of God's Spirit.

That a new movement of the Spirit was emerging was clear by the
time Michael Harper resigned from All Souls, Langham Place and
the Fountain Trust was established. The foundation of the Fountain
Trust specifically to promote and nourish the new movement introduced into its midst a body with a potential to influence its future
direction decisively.

In some respects the Fountain Trust was like its American predecessor, the Blessed Trinity Society: it was a service agency, publishing pamphlets and a magazine, and holding conferences. Like the
Blessed Trinity Society, its basic thrust was towards the Charismatic
renewal in the historic denominations, especially the Anglican communion. However, in other ways the Trust differed from the Blessed
Trinity Society and set a pattern that was later followed in a number
of other English-speaking countries. The Fountain Trust was set up
to serve the Charismatic movement in the nation, whereas given the
size of the USA, the Blessed Trinity Society was confined largely to
California and some neighbouring states. Moreover, with an ordained figure in the leadership, officially licensed by his bishop, the
Fountain Trust acquired an unofficial standing that its American
predecessor never achieved.[6]

The emergence of one Charismatic movement of the Spirit outside the Pentecostal churches and within the major historic denominations represented some degree of fulfilment of the
prophecy of Smith Wigglesworth. Among the instruments used by
God to translate this vision into reality, David du Plessis was given
a quite distinctive role. More than any other leader, du Plessis
contributed to the self-understanding of the new movement and

demonstrated its international character. Through du Plessis' constant preaching of 'Pentecost', he made it clear that the central blessing God was bestowing in this movement was baptism in the Spirit. He was insistent that the blessing being poured out now in the historic churches was the same blessing that had characterized the Pentecostal movement. In this way, and by baptism in the Spirit becoming the customary terminology within the new movement for its core experience of the Lord Jesus Christ and his Spirit, the essential continuity of the new move with the Pentecostal movement was brought out.[7]

Du Plessis' evident commitment to the vision of Holy Spirit renewal of the historic churches ensured that his ministry was never impaired by the mixed feelings experienced by many of the new charismatics towards their Pentecostal brethren. Nobody suspected du Plessis of seeking to detach believers from their church allegiance.

Du Plessis was able to perform this role, first because of his clarity of vision stemming from prayerful appropriation over many years of the Wigglesworth prophecy and his subsequent call. This enabled him to see baptism in the Spirit as the heart of the pentecostal blessing, while recognizing that not everything in the Pentecostal denominations was ideal and to be sought after. He was also able to give this 'Pentecostal' and 'non-Pentecostal' message by virtue of having an impeccable Pentecostal pedigree. Paradoxically, the withdrawal of du Plessis' ministerial credentials in September 1962 by the American Assemblies of God, who disapproved of his ecumenical activities,[8] only served to reinforce the thoroughly representative Pentecostal character of the man who would become known as 'Mr. Pentecost'. In this, du Plessis confounds the received ecumenical wisdom that only a Christian rooted in his own church can play a significant ecumenical role.

In his mission, du Plessis was supported by Donald Gee, whose writings provided intellectual grounds for positions du Plessis arrived at more instinctively. Gee, with his knowledge of Pentecostal history, was able to contrast the reaction of the churches to the early Pentecostal movement in the first decade of the century with the reaction of the same churches to 'the new wave' some five to six decades later.[9] However, Gee's influence on the rise of the Charismatic movement was mostly indirect, being the result of his influence on his fellow Pentecostals.

By the middle of 1964 then, there was a common awareness in Britain of the arrival of this new Charismatic movement. What many participants thought of as its beginning – the visits of Maguire, Christenson and du Plessis with the Spirit-baptism of Michael Harper – were not in fact the origins, but the major instruments by which the previously somewhat scattered streams came visibly and consciously into one movement.

Twenty-One

Further Expansion in Free Church and Independent Circles

The first year of the Fountain Trust (summer 1964 – summer 1965) saw considerable expansion in the new movement, both numerically and in terms of the constituency being renewed. Much of the expansion that occurred among those closely linked to the Fountain Trust has already been indicated.[1] This chapter covers the developments in 1964 and 1965 among some of the Free Church and independent circles, where the thrust towards Charismatic revival was less related to the Fountain Trust, though many of those concerned sought to maintain positive and co-operative relations with Michael Harper. Of particular significance was a marked increase during 1964 among Baptist ministers receiving the baptism in the Spirit.

By mid 1964, the only Baptist minister in England known by the leading figures in the movement to have received the baptism in the Spirit was Frank Wilson.[2] However within a year it was evident that the Baptists were being more affected by this move of the Spirit than any other Free Church in the land.[3]

The initial thrust among Baptists in England[4] came from within the ranks of the Baptist Revival Fellowship, though it happened a year or so after Charles Clarke's influence within the Methodist Revival Fellowship. The BRF held its annual conference late in the year, and it was at the 1964 Conference that the pentecostal issue raised its head.[5] One booked speaker was known to be very anti-pentecostal, but he had to cancel at the last minute. His replacement was David Pawson, minister of Gold Hill Baptist church at Chalfont St. Peter in Buckinghamshire.

In the summer of that year, Pawson had given a Bible study on the person and work of the Holy Spirit to a Baptist ministers' fraternal in the Reading area. He had spoken of the baptism in the Spirit. One of his opponents on this occasion was an old friend,

Harold Owen, minister of a Baptist church in Reading, and also a committee member of the BRF. Pawson recommended Owen to do a Bible study on the Holy Spirit from Genesis to Revelation. This he did, and by the time of the BRF Conference Owen's thinking had begun to change. In the car on the way to High Leigh, colleagues in the BRF told Owen they were in for trouble this year, because several members were now speaking in tongues.[6] On the first evening, many members were engaged in animated conversation about this pente- costal experience. Another committee member, Henry Tyler from Felixstowe, Suffolk, found from the first evening that as he greeted those sitting next to him at meals and said, 'Well, how are you?', he kept getting the response, 'Oh, God has done a wonderful thing for me,' followed by an account of how that person had been baptized in the Spirit.

The next morning, Owen heard Pawson give basically the same Bible study as he had heard several months before, but he noticed a new quality in Pawson himself. Owen said afterwards, 'So, it's happened to you, David', and Pawson said, 'Yes'. Owen was stunned, and told a fellow committee member, 'Give my apologies to the committee but I'm not attending any more sessions today.' Owen locked himself in his room, and sought the Lord in fasting and prayer. Over a period of many hours, Owen experienced the Lord dealing with the barriers in his life. He sensed the Lord saying:

> You are frightened and it's your pride. Because if this were to happen to you, you would lose your name. You would be rejected by the evangelicals you've grown up with, whom you love.

Shattered but peaceful, Owen came downstairs about 8 p.m. The first person he met was Michael Pusey, a younger colleague from the same area west-south-west of London. Pusey had been brought up in the Elim Pentecostal Church, but had drifted away from the practice and preaching of the spiritual gifts. Owen had been acting as an older brother in the ministry to Pusey, and had sought to restrain any pentecostal yearnings. However through a married couple in Basingstoke who had recently received the baptism in the Spirit, Michael and his wife, Margaret, were led back into their pentecostal experience,[7] and he had come to the BRF Conference armed with copies of two of Michael Harper's booklets.[8] Owen now overcame his pride and asked Pusey to pray with him. Pusey confessed that as long as he had known Owen, he had prayed that

God might open Owen's eyes to this reality. Nothing dramatic happened at that moment, but within five minutes of returning to his room, Owen burst out in tongues as he worshipped God.

Later, Owen discovered that at the very same time that he had been seeking the Lord in his room, about half a dozen of his closest friends were being touched by God and being led to the baptism in the Spirit.[9] One of these was Henry Tyler, who was ministered to by Richard Kayes of Liverpool.[10]

It was not long before a group of BRF members from the south of England, all baptized in the Spirit, began to meet informally for fellowship at Spurgeon's Tabernacle in London. In 1965, Pusey moved to Farnborough and Tyler to Ilford. At Basingstoke Pusey was followed by Barney Coombs,[11] a former London policeman, who was baptized in the Spirit while a deacon at East Acton Baptist Church in 1964. Coombs had been brought up in the Brethren, and had first been attracted to pentecostal worship as a teenager in an Elim Church.[12]

To understand the impact of the events within the BRF on British Baptists as a whole, it is necessary to understand more of its background and ethos. The BRF had been formed not long before the outbreak of World War II by a group of London ministers concerned about the low level of spiritual life in the Baptist churches. In the regular polarity among Baptists, between the traditional Baptist emphasis on vigorous congregational independence and an emphasis on the ideals of the Baptists as a denomination focused in the Baptist Union of Great Britain and Ireland, the BRF members tended to come from those on the more evangelical wing with the emphasis on independence.[13] Many of these men were less committed to the Baptist Union than others in the denomination,[14] and so although several senior and respected men in the BRF were baptized in the Spirit, this did not carry the weight among British Baptists as a whole that a comparable development might have had in another denomination. The combination of charismatic and denominational commitment among Baptists was first represented by Douglas McBain, then still in Scotland, and next by Edmund Heddle of Bexhill-on-Sea.[15]

Another milieu where some individuals were being touched in these years was the Salvation Army. The principal charismatic influence on the Salvationists in the London area was John Noble, who lived in the Essex suburbs.[16] Noble's family had been deeply involved in the Salvation Army since the early years of its history, even though he fell away from Christian faith in his late teens and during his national service he had become involved in spiritualist séances. It was the discovery of his bondage to occult powers that persuaded Noble of the reality of the supernatural, and that predisposed him to accept the contemporary availability of the power of the Holy Spirit described in the Acts of the Apostles. It was during his renewed seeking of Christian faith that he was made secretary of the Christian Union at his workplace, Peter Robinson's of Oxford Street. Immediately he met the chaplain to the Oxford Street stores, Michael Harper.

Noble was baptized in the Spirit at the Good Shepherd mission at Bethnal Green in 1961. The location was significant for Noble as the mission was almost on the very spot in Three Colts Lane where William Booth had founded the Salvation Army. He then began to testify and share about his experience of the Spirit at Salvation Army citadels in the East End. With Fred Smith of the Good Shepherd mission, Noble began a prayer meeting for revival in Wanstead, and in early 1964 was closely associated with the series of talks at the Elim Church at Ilford on 'The Work of the Holy Spirit in the Church Today'.[17] From about 1962, Noble was a regular participant in the lunch-hour prayer meetings at St. Bride's.

Cecil Cousen had been one of the speakers in the Ilford series, and this led to his returning to that area for a number of further teaching meetings. At one of these meetings, Cousen prophesied that from that meeting would come forth in that area the fivefold ministry of Ephesians 4. Noble recalls:

> At that time we were thinking more about the gifts of the Spirit in terms of healing, prophecy and tongues than we were about the ministries of Christ. We began to see that God wanted to raise up men to build people together not to build them into another denomination particularly, but to build them into relationships which would function (a) as a value in themselves (relationships to God are an end in themselves) and (b) because of those relationships they could be used by God to expand his kingdom in different ways.

From this time on, Noble emerged increasingly as a leader and teacher in the Essex suburbs of the London Metropolitan area, among fellowships that would later be termed part of the House Church movement'.[18] However, he was always a firm believer in full co-operation with others baptized in the Spirit, and he served on the committee preparing for the FGBMFI Convention in November 1965[19] as well as maintaining his contact with Michael Harper, re-established after the latter's baptism in the Spirit.

Thus around 1964–65, Noble was coming to accept some of the emphases that had for some years been characteristic of David Lillie and Arthur Wallis. By 1965, this 'restoration of the New Testament church' thinking was gaining further ground, aided in particular by the remarkable number of Open Brethren receiving the baptism in the Spirit and having to withdraw from their Brethren assemblies.[20] In April 1965, Lillie and Wallis held the last of their conferences, two and a half years after Mamhead Park. The holding of this conference outside Devon at Herne Bay in Kent represented a conscious policy of no longer appearing as just a group in the South-West.

The Herne Bay conference, which attracted over a hundred invited participants, took as its theme 'The Apostolic Commission'[21]. Several leaders who had not attended any of the Devon conferences were present at Herne Bay, including Campbell McAlpine (now co-convenor with Lillie and Wallis), W. F. P. Burton (the widely respected Pentecostal missionary to Zaire), G. W. North,[22] Norman Meeten (a former Anglican curate from Liverpool),[23] and the Baptist Barney Coombs. At this conference there were clear signs of the coming tension between the Fountain Trust vision of Church renewal and the House Church concept of the restoration of the Church.[24] At the time of the Devon conferences, the Charismatic movement had not yet become visible in the mainline Churches. By 1965, the renewal current was embodied in the Fountain Trust. While both Fountain Trust and 'restoration' people sought to include each other in their activities and gatherings, the ethos of Herne Bay was clearly restorationist and uncongenial to renewal-minded Anglicans. Michael Harper was invited to Herne Bay, but did not attend.[25] Many of the restorationists evidently hoped that 'denominational' Christians would embrace their vision in the light of their experience of the Spirit, and tended to regard their failure to do so as a sign that they placed human respect before the call of the Spirit. This was evidently David Lillie's reading of Michael Harper's history, and was no doubt a major reason for the sudden end to their regular correspondence in October 1964. While a number of the restoration teachers (Lillie, Wallis, Perrins) clearly did not think that it was possible to renew the historic churches, they were not so wedded to *a priori* judgments as to exclude the possibility of true New Testament fellowships arising within historic denominations.[26] Despite these tensions, there were significant figures who felt at home in both settings, for example Campbell McAlpine and Cecil Cousen.[27]

One of the common threads uniting those at the Herne Bay Conference was the conviction that the restoration of the gifts of the Spirit was for the sake of the reconstitution of the church as a vibrant and effective fellowship functioning as the body of Christ. The Herne Bay participants were conscious that people baptized in the Spirit could get sidetracked into seeking spiritual experience rather than God's purpose. They were not content to settle for charismatic prayer groups on the fringe of the church's life. They were calling for fully-committed fellowships (churches) where the whole way of life was submitted to the Lordship of Jesus through the power of the Spirit. Perrins expressed these convictions positively at Herne Bay:

> In all this then, we have a progression. God bringing individuals into Christ to share His fullness, creating these into a body to manifest His fullness. The gifts and graces are given to the body that it might grow into full stature and thus be an expression of the fullness of Christ. This is God's purpose for His Church.

In the meantime, the influence of the house church at[28] South Chard in Somerset was growing,[29] as was the ministry of G. W. North, who moved to the Wirral in 1965. These two networks of influence were however less central to the evolution of the Charismatic movement than the Fountain Trust and the other streams examined in this study.[30]

By 1965, there were in fact a number of charismatic house fellowships in existence in various parts of Britain. Some were based on a theological vision (as that of Wallis in Talaton and of Hardwidge in Exeter[31]) while others had more pragmatic origins, being made up of those baptized in the Spirit seeking deeper fellowship outside existing church structures (as the All for Christ Fellowship in Plymouth led by Edgar Trout and initially that of Dr. Kelly in Glasgow[32]). In the last four years of his life, Edgar Trout had many links with such house fellowships, being much sought after as a teacher and minister of deliverance.[33] The wide range of Trout's contacts underlines the importance of his role as a link between many of these fellowships and the Charismatic movement within the historic churches.

Twenty-Two

Charismatics and Pentecostals

The data adduced so far show a considerable influence by Pentecostals upon the origins of the Charismatic movement in Britain. A fairly high percentage of those in the mainline churches receiving the baptism in the Spirit up to 1963 had either first- or second-hand contact with Pentecostal Christians. The pattern in 1964 and 1965 however shows a definite change.

By 1964, it was clear both to Pentecostals and to charismatics that there was a new movement of the Holy Spirit, in most important ways similar to the original Pentecostal movement, but in some ways different.[1] The charismatics knew that they were not just individuals receiving this pentecostal blessing, but were part of something happening on a wider scale. The Pentecostals also knew that the new development was not just the extensive occurrence of baptism in the Spirit outside the Pentecostal churches, but that the new work was consciously a new movement, beginning to take on its own social characteristics. This situation presented both Pentecostal and charismatic leaders with the need to determine their practical policies with regard to one another.

The evidence suggests that neither side found it easy to work out their proper relationships with the other. There was clearly in the experience of baptism in the Spirit and the accompanying spiritual gifts a significant common foundation, making a claim on a close spiritual kinship, yet each side experienced real hesitations in the way of full co-operation. These hesitations no doubt stemmed from significant differences between the two movements that David Bebbington has spoken of in terms of 'different cultural affinities'.[2]

The Charismatic movement in Britain arose predominantly among the middle class and the more educated. This was clearly true of the movement in the Anglican Church, but it was also true of much of the house church movement.[3] By contrast, British Pentecostalism grew up in a more backstreet working-class world that was neither as upwardly mobile nor as numerically successful as its North American counterparts. All these factors affected the way that British Pentecostals responded and reacted to the Charismatic movement. The Pentecostals reflected more of working-class solidarity, whereas the Charismatics exhibited more individualistic forms of self-expression.[4] Pentecostal preachers from denominational Bible colleges did not easily relate to mainline church clergy with university degrees; this was not only a matter of levels of education, but of different patterns of learning (the Pentecostals at their best were much more experimental and spiritually practical) and of approaches to the Bible. These differences show up for example in the Pentecostal emphasis on physical healing and the Charismatic interest in inner healing; the latter reflects both a more positive correlation between the natural and the supernatural in Anglican thinking (reflected clearly in Agnes Sanford's teaching) and the middle-class appeal of psychology.

From the Charismatic side, leading figures were concerned lest outsiders see it simply as an extension of Pentecostalism. Such an association, it was felt, would impede its spread and acceptance within the historic churches. One Anglican priest-participant writes to Harper, 'We have to be very careful ambassadors and avoid any impression that what goes on is linked with the unwise behaviour of Pentecostalists in the past although their motives were no doubt the highest.'[5]

Early on, Harper had been warned by an American priest to beware of Pentecostals exercising much influence. 'You will find', he was told, 'that as the movement gains impetus in England the Pentecostals will rush in with offers to help. They mean well, and we can learn a great deal from them in private discussions, but NEVER, NEVER, NEVER, have them at prayer meetings where there are sensitive people present.'[6] In fact, the prediction of Pentecostal invasion proved inaccurate, but the warnings evidently had some effect.

It is noticeable, for example, that local Pentecostals were never invited to speak at conferences promoted by the Fountain Trust.[7] This policy was clearly not the imposition of one particular viewpoint; men like Wallis, McAlpine and Cousen, who were in no way committed to the renewal of the historic churches, were frequent and much valued contributors. There was some concern that Pentecostal speakers might urge the newly Spirit-baptized to join their own denomination, and a care that Pentecostal doctrinal statements should not be imposed on the new movement. But as much as anything, there was a conscious determination to have an identity distinct from the Pentecostals. This was reflected in the choice of the term 'Charismatic' to characterize the new movement.[8]

However, this desire to have an identity distinct from the Pentecostals did not imply any reluctance to have fellowship with them. Invitations to speak to Pentecostal gatherings about this spreading work of the Spirit were freely accepted. Both Philip Smith and Michael Harper spoke at the annual General Assemblies of major Pentecostal denominations,[9] and Pentecostal groups featured from time to time among Harper's speaking engagements.[10] When an enterprising Pentecostal, such as Thomas Stevenson, the Elim pastor in Ilford, Essex, ran a series of meetings on this new work of the Spirit, he had no difficulty in finding charismatics willing to speak and testify.[11] In fact, this series was notably successful and was recalled later as a useful example to follow.[12] However, as the Charismatic movement emerged and developed, its further spread became more and more the result of charismatics sharing their witness and enthusiastic faith with others, and less a consequence of other Christians being influenced by Pentecostals. This was a further factor in diminished contacts between the two groups.

The loss of men like Bolt and Forester to the Pentecostals does not seem to have reduced the willingness to have fellowship with the Pentecostals, but at least with the Anglicans, such events seem to have reinforced the determination to have a distinctive identity and style. What is less well known is the fact that some former Pentecostal ministers were ordained into the Anglican ministry, and a few of these retained their pentecostal convictions, which possibly eased in a small way the acceptance of the Charismatic movement among some Anglicans.[13]

That charismatic self-understanding did not exclude the role of the Pentecostals was made particularly clear by Michael Harper's first full book, *As at the Beginning*, published in 1965.[14] This was sub-titled 'The Twentieth Century Pentecostal Revival', and it presented the Charismatic movement as a continuation of the Pentecostal outpouring of 1906–7. Harper is here at pains to point out that the British Pentecostal pioneer, Alexander Boddy, was, and remained, an Anglican priest.[15] Moreover, he records for the first time in print the Wigglesworth prophecy over du Plessis.[16] The thrust of this popular and condensed history is thus to suggest that the Pentecostal revival of the twentieth century is not inherently schismatic and is richer and more significant than what later was called Pentecostalism.

The attitudes on the Pentecostal side towards the charismatics were almost exactly the inverse of those the other way round. Whereas the charismatics tended to keep quiet about their Pentecostal connections, the Pentecostals were continually talking about these charismatic developments. News items on the Charismatic wave appeared regularly in both *Redemption Tidings*[17] and *Elim Evangel*.[18] The latter made more editorial comment,[19] though the former had a number of quotations from or references to the convictions of their foremost spokesman, Donald Gee.[20] A highly positive appraisal of the Charismatic movement was given by the new Administrative Secretary of the Evangelical Alliance and an Elim minister, the Rev. J. Hywel Davies, in a series of four articles published in the *Elim Evangel* in late 1963.[21] A much-respected Pentecostal figure, who fully welcomed the Charismatic movement in the older churches, was Harold Horton, a long-time advocate of the immediate availability of the gift of the Spirit.[22] Horton, by now in his old age, was instrumental in a number of visitors to his flat in Poole, including some Anglican clergy, receiving the 'baptism'[23]

However, while the charismatics were generally willing to enjoy fellowship with any Pentecostals, the Pentecostals were more reluctant to reciprocate. They were fascinated by the new developments, so unexpected and yet corresponding in many ways to their deepest longings. But they were concerned about the full authenticity of this new work. Most evident was their concern about doctrinal orthodoxy. This was not a question of whether charismatics accepted the dominant Pentecostal teaching tying tongues to baptism in the Spirit – the Elim Church had a more flexible position on this in any case – but concerned rather the issues between conservatives and liberals in the churches. The British Pentecostals did not readily accept the full message of David du Plessis, because he made a point of not excluding the World Council of Churches and Rome from the sphere of the Spirit's visitation. An editorial in the *Elim Evangel* in March 1962 had taken du Plessis to task for asserting that Pentecostals have much in common with Roman Catholics and that 'Pentecostals have always denied being Protestant'.[24] Further sentiments of this kind were manifested when the almost universal mourning of the death of Pope John XXIII was filling the media.[25]

However, another concern of the Pentecostals over the authenticity of the Charismatic movement attracted rather less attention. That is their concern for holiness of life, and for moral change. The Pentecostals had traditionally 'tarried' for the baptism in the Spirit with deep heart-searching and persistent seeking, although in many Pentecostal congregations such tarrying was more a memory than an actuality. The charismatics typically prayed over people to receive the baptism in the Spirit, and some charismatics gave the impression of having a transitory experience without much evidence of repentance and deep change of heart. One of the most knowledgeable Pentecostals in Britain believes that this factor was more operative than the doctrinal in the hesitation of many Pentecostals in Britain to welcome unreservedly this new movement.[26]

A somewhat aggressive response came from an Elim pastor George Canty, the energetic public relations officer of the British Pentecostal Fellowship.[27] Canty had not been impressed by a charismatic gathering he had attended, and his tone is evident from the title of his article: 'AND NOW shall we go back to the Church of England?'[28]

The cautious interest that characterized Pentecostal relations with charismatics did not prevent occasional forms of collaboration and consultation. In fact, various Pentecostal leaders co-operated with charismatics on a committee connected with the FGBMFI Convention held in London in November 1965, soon to be mentioned in more detail.[29] Moreover on September 28, 1965 a meeting between Anglican charismatics and an Assemblies of God Consultative Group took place in Bedford. This was favourably reported in *Redemption Tidings*.[30]

By 1965, the relationships between charismatics and Pentecostals were much more casual and occasional than their common experience of the Spirit would seem to have demanded. While this lack of close fellowship is easily understandable given their quite different backgrounds and mentalities, in retrospect it does appear that both sides in their relations with each other were more influenced by fears and anxieties than by prayerful consideration of the implications of being blessed by the same Lord in the same manner. However, the fact that charismatics and Pentecostals could not regard each other as only accidentally related was made clear by two developments in the

period 1964–5, in which Pentecostals again exerted a major influence
on people in the historic churches. The more ostentatious of these two
developments was the Full Gospel Business Men's Convention held
in late November 1965.[31] This convention had already been prepared
for by a prayer conference at Stoke Poges in June 1965, which brought
together a number of leaders in the emerging Charismatic movement
with some Pentecostal spokesmen.[32] For the convention, two jetloads
of Spirit-filled Christians from the United States and Canada flew in
to Heathrow, and most stayed at the London Hilton. A remarkable
number of the pioneer figures in the Charismatic movement in North
America joined this influx. Meetings were held in various famous
settings – the Albert Hall, Church House, Westminster Chapel and
the Metropolitan Tabernacle.

Some British leaders had misgivings about the American style of
the Convention, which was very flamboyant[33] and some were anxious that the evident effort to launch a chapter of the FGBMFI in
Britain should allow for a genuine autonomy which would respect
national characteristics. The holders of such views probably did not
see the FGBMFI Convention as a major event in the Charismatic
movement in Britain.

However, such concerns overlook a number of significant features, a major one being the power of the media in the last half of the
twentieth century. The attention of the church press was caught by
this gathering,[34] as was that of *The Sun* which spoke of 'millionaire
Demos Shakarian . . . dispensing the love of God from his suite at the
London Hilton.'[35] The press interest particularly focused on the
visitors' evangelistic work among the hippies of Soho.[36] The FGBMFI
Convention thus drew the attention of many, especially the Protestant public, to the Charismatic movement in a way that implied
impact and power. Whereas many previous press items had focused
on glossolalia and items like Forester's resignation from Anglican
orders, the FGBMFI Convention reports featured more accurately
the spiritual scope of the new movement, and graphically illustrated
its potential to influence all kinds of people on a wide scale.

The FGBMFI Convention also drew attention to the international
character of the Pentecostal-Charismatic revival.[37] It was also much
the largest gathering associated with the new movement up to that
date.[38] Testimonies in popular language had a more prominent place
in the convention than was customary in British prayer meetings,
and these seem to have added to the Convention's impact.[39]

At a time when the Pentecostals and the charismatics were increasingly looking like distinct and partially parallel groupings, the FGBMFI Convention with its platform combination of mainly Pentecostal laity and mainly charismatic clergy made strongly visible the underlying unity between them.

This impression was furthered when in the week immediately following the convention, the North American visitors dispersed over the country to any local churches willing to receive them. The places visited were spread all over Britain: Oxford, Cambridge, Preston, Exeter, Tiverton, Gloucester, Cheltenham, Porthcawl, Burslem, South Shields, Southampton, St. Leonards and St. Andrew's.[40] One parish particularly impacted was St. Andrew's, Chorleywood in Herts.[41] About thirty young people were converted at St. Andrew's during the visit of Nicky Cruz.[42] Cruz was an ex-drug addict and gang leader converted through the ministry of David Wilkerson, whose story *The Cross and the Switchblade* is the other major Pentecostal influence at this stage on the Charismatic movement in Britain.

The Cross and the Switchblade is the story of David Wilkerson written up by two journalists John and Elizabeth Sherrill.[43] The book tells in highly readable style how Wilkerson, a Pentecostal preacher from a small town in rural Pennsylvania, experienced a divine call to minister to drug addicts and gang members in the slums of New York City. By preaching the gospel in their language and by stressing the power of God in baptism in the Holy Spirit, Wilkerson's ministry led to dramatic results in the transformed lives of many young people.

Unusually, *The Cross and the Switchblade* did not find a British publisher for a number of years.[44] Instead, from mid-1964 copies were imported from the USA in ever-increasing consignments which were rapidly exhausted.[45] Some evangelical bookstores that ordinarily refused to stock Pentecostal literature were led to stock it under the counter.[46]

Soon after its appearance in Britain, *The Cross and the Switchblade* was clearly having an impact beyond any other literature emanating from Pentecostal and charismatic sources. It was recommended in his diocese by the Bishop of Salisbury. At the time of the FGBMFI Convention in November 1965, the *Church of England Newspaper* recognized this impact:

> This book has made an impact upon Anglicans such as few books
> have made in recent years.[47]

The same editorial, though somewhat fastidious in its tone,[48] nevertheless recognized why the book was evoking such a response.

> *The Cross and the Switchblade* shows God at work . . . Here are Chris-
> tians wrestling against evil and lifting others out of bondage and
> hopelessness. It is all so different from the genteel Christianity of the
> suburban church.[49]

Wilkerson's book clearly gave a further impetus to the Charismatic movement in Britain. There are reports of people converted
to Christian faith through reading it[50] and also of it pointing believers towards the baptism in the Spirit.[51] Among those whose initial
interest was aroused by *The Cross and the Switchblade* was Sir
Thomas Lees, the squire of Post Green House in Dorset, later a
prominent centre of Charismatic renewal. It also had a formative
influence on the calling of Nicholas Rivett-Carnac, who from an
aristocratic background came to have a significant inner-city ministry within the Church of England.[52]

The influence of *The Cross and the Switchblade* is important not only
for numerical reasons. It is not a story about the Charismatic movement. It is an account of God's love, mercy and power experienced
in the ministry of a Pentecostal pastor. It demonstrates that what
touches people's lives is not a sound ecclesiology, however desirable
that might be, but a faith-filled proclamation about God, Father, Son
and Holy Spirit.

Twenty-Three

Distinguishing Features of the Origins of The Charismatic Movement in Great Britain

This chapter will examine the distinguishing features and characteristics of the events and experiences that were later seen to have been the first stirrings in Britain of the Charismatic movement. It will therefore be restricted to the period of the origins, during which the movement was in gestation but not yet clearly visible. In the years before there was a common consciousness that these events and their consequences constituted a movement; numerous Christians in Britain beyond the ranks of the Pentecostals were being baptized in the Spirit and were exercising the spiritual gifts of 1 Corinthians 12:8–10. The main streams of influence which contributed to the spread of these experiences have been described in Sections I and II of this study.

The origins and first years of a spontaneous type of movement provide the best opportunity for examining its essential nature. In the initial years, the basic character of these developments is present, before there is much opportunity for infidelity and before deliberate organization begins to influence its shape and direction.

1. EXPERIENCES CHARACTERIZED BY A CHANGED RELATIONSHIP TO GOD

It is important to recognize at the outset that the developments studied here are characterized by a changed relationship of participants to the God, whose being, nature and plan are revealed in the Bible. This is important precisely because the initial defining characteristic of the emerging Charismatic movement is the presence of the spiritual gifts – especially the most unusual and the most specific, namely speaking in tongues, prophecy and gifts of healing. All observers and students of the topic would agree that where none of these

gifts are found, the Charismatic movement is not present. This un-
doubted association of the Charismatic movement with the Corin-
thian charismata could easily lead to the conclusion that the
possession of these gifts is the central feature of the movement. It is,
then, worthy of note that the participants constantly testify that the
primary aspect of accession to the sphere of spiritual gifts is a new
quality in their knowledge and experience of God.[1] This changed
relationship to God is well expressed in the words Richard Trout used
to describe his father's experience: 'He only knew that his spirit was
communing with God in a way more direct, more fundamental, more
basic to his innermost nature, than he had ever thought possible.'[2]

The centrality of a changed relationship to God in the charismatic
experience is further evidenced by the regular association between
receiving the spiritual gifts, and receiving the Holy Spirit. This finds
its most common expression in the concept of baptism in the Spirit,
a point that will be studied further in the following chapter examining the first years of the movement.

In the years prior to the emergence of a clearly-defined movement,
there was no one pattern by which believers came to this changed
relationship to God and the exercise of spiritual gifts. The most
common element was however a personal thirst for more of God.
For several, the pentecostal baptism was the culmination of many
years of persistent spiritual seeking: this is true, for example, of
Clark, Grant, Houfe, Collins, Watson and Clarke. By the time they
received the baptism in the Holy Spirit, most early participants had
come to desire and seek this specific blessing, almost always through
contact with Pentecostal Christians. This was not true of all, however; McAlpine is a clear example of someone who received this
experience without any Pentecostal associations. Some came into a
new experience of God without any exercise of spiritual gifts, but
soon recognized an affinity with pentecostal experience and so
sought the complement of the spiritual gifts. Michael Harper is a
prominent example.

2. CHARACTERISTICS OF CHARISMATIC EXPERIENCE
AT THIS STAGE

In the years before 1963, before it was widely evident that a new and
distinctive movement was arising, there were nonetheless distinc-

tive characteristics in the experience of those Christians being blessed in this way. Throughout this study, it has been assumed that 'charismatic experience' involves manifestation and exercise of the spiritual gifts of 1 Corinthians 12:8–10. In practice, this means tongues, prophecy, healing and miracles, because they are the most visible of these charismata. The place of these gifts in the Charismatic movement will be examined further in the next chapter.

What other characteristics typify the experience of the charismatic pioneers in the period of the origins besides the exercise of spiritual gifts? They are:

a. A new level of awareness of the persons of the Trinity

The changed relationship to God experienced by those baptized in the Spirit was described in a variety of ways, illustrating a greater consciousness of the Trinitarian nature of God.[3] Some spoke of a conscious inflowing of the Spirit of God (Lillie, McAlpine, Bolt, East),[4] with Forester commenting, 'We feel that we know the third person of the Trinity as a person in his own right.'[5] Some had a clear sense of the presence of God and of his glory (Trout, Shaw, Harper, Clarke, David Smith, Marzetti),[6] some of an inner peace and knowledge of God's love (McAlpine, Harper, Amos Edwards, Clarke).[7] There is a particular place in the witnesses for the person of Jesus Christ, with frequent mention being made of a new knowledge and a new love of the Saviour (Bolt, Forester, Grant, Harper, Casebow).[8]

b. A new capacity to praise God

Almost every testimony cites a new ability to praise God. This new capacity to worship was often experienced in terms of a welling up within one's heart and as the work of the indwelling Holy Spirit (Lillie, McAlpine, Trout, David Smith).[9] Sometimes the recipient had a sense of being set free, of release so that what was already within could be freely expressed (Clark).[10]

This aspect of a capacity to praise God is especially associated with receiving the gift of tongues, itself experienced as spontaneous praise. Yet the capacity is clearly wider than the mere ability to speak or sing in tongues. As will be indicated, this new capacity for praise was one of the features indicating most clearly the basic unity in the movement in its initial phases. Witnesses to the gift of tongues as praise testify to the risen Lord Jesus himself being an object of this praise. This is sometimes explicit (Grant, Houfe)[11] but often implicit in references to 'the Lord' (Clark, McAlpine), 'my Lord' (Lillie).[12] Praise of Jesus is closely associated with new knowledge of the Saviour.

This new-found ability to praise God was normally accompanied by a new freedom in physical as well as vocal expression. This physical expression – often with upraised hands, sometimes with notable volume – was evidently experienced as a freeing of the whole personality to worship God.

c. A new capacity for hearing God

Charismatic testimonies regularly include accounts of people baptized in the Spirit hearing God address them. This is particularly marked in the life of Edgar Trout and to a lesser degree in men like Denis Clark, John Hutchison and Cecil Cousen. However almost all indicate, at (and following) baptism in the Spirit, some sense of hearing God, of receiving words, impressions and/or pictures in prayer.

The pioneers of Section I mostly had less hesitation in speaking of hearing God than some of the theologically-trained Anglican clergy who followed them into this blessing. This fact suggests a double-edged influence of theological training in terms of pentecostal experience. Greater intellectual sophistication and knowledge acts as a protection against a naive credulity that accepts every claim to divine communication without any criteria for discernment. However, it often also acts as a barrier in the way of accepting the genuine word of the Lord, when the mind has been influenced by a 'closed system' theology that limits God's action in the world so that it is never more than indirect.

d. New power in own life and in ministry to others

The pentecostal experience has consistently been seen in terms of empowerment by the Holy Spirit. Some began their search for the Holy Spirit through realizing the ineffectiveness of their ministry (Shaw, Casebow, Collins). All who sought more of the Holy Spirit knew that the Spirit comes with the power of God. They knew that the promise of the Father is that the believers will be 'clothed with power from on high' (Luke 24:49).

Some of those baptized in the Spirit first experienced God's power in relation to their own lives, for example in inner healing (Bill Wood, David Smith) or physical healing (Edgar Trout). Others immediately experienced God's power to heal through their ministry (Clark, Hutchison).

But the power of the Spirit evidenced in the origins of the Charismatic movement is not restricted to healing, and can also be seen, for example, in evangelism. Rae Shaw of the Good Shepherd Mission in Bethnal Green testified:

> My own Church has been turned upside down. Instead of table tennis it is the open-air meeting. In two summers we have proclaimed the Gospel to over 6,000 people in East London. Before this blessing the young people would not go into the open air, but now, praise God, there is a hunger for precious souls. 'To God be the glory, great things He has done.'[13]

Some of the credit for emphasizing evangelism as a proper consequence of baptism in the Spirit should go to the Pentecostals. Those directly influenced by the Pentecostals, such as Shaw, were less likely to interpret the main thrust of the movement as simply towards the churches. However, some revival-minded Anglican evangelicals such as those at Gillingham also clearly experienced this baptism as a powerful tool for effective evangelism among the unchurched, though this flowered more in the years following than in the period of the origins.

3. CONTRIBUTORY FACTORS

Several contributory factors used by the Spirit of God in the gestation of the embryonic Charismatic movement can be identified. Among these one can distinguish between 'seeking-factors' and 'finding-factors'. The former are those factors which aroused an interest in, and a thirst for, the pentecostal blessing; the latter are the factors that pointed to the baptism in the Spirit as the blessing sought. The principal seeking-factors are: concern and prayer for revival: experience of God's power in healing: concern for the fullness of the New Testament church.

a. 'Seeking-Factors'

i. Concern and Prayer for Revival

It is evident from the accounts recorded that circles of evangelical Christians praying for revival were among those most affected by the early occurrences of charismatic blessing. Of major importance was the circle gathered around George Ingram in NPWR, which soon made contact with the prayer meeting started by Pentecostal businessmen at St. Bride's Institute in the City of London. This meeting too was primarily seen in terms of prayer for revival, even though the participants saw revival in pentecostal terms. Out of the NPWR circle too came the Nights of Prayer at St. Mark's, Gillingham, which saw the beginnings of pentecostal blessing in that parish. Moreover, the beginnings of the Charismatic movement among Methodists and Baptists in Britain were particularly the fruit of prayer and seeking within the respective denominational revival fellowships. First, some Methodists in the Birmingham area associated with Charles J. Clarke received the baptism in the Spirit, while a year or so later, there were similar blessings within the Baptist Revival Fellowship.

Concern and prayer for revival were evidently a form of preparation for pentecostal blessing. This concern and prayer itself intensified desire for revival and increased the intercessors' openness to receive the forms of revival that God might send. Obviously all such seekers had some criteria for what they would regard as authentic revival from the Spirit of God, as opposed to religious phenomena appearing to come from other sources. While these criteria invariably appealed to the Scriptures, they were in fact based on the Scriptures as understood within particular traditions of exegesis and interpretation. It is a presupposition of Christian faith that the deeper the contact with God in prayer, the more extensive would be the purification of their criteria for authentic revival. This point was of particular significance for those evangelicals who had previously accepted a dispensationalist interpretation of the New Testament, restricting the *charismata pneumatika* to the apostolic age.

Despite such an *a priori* prejudice, those who prayed fervently for revival were best placed to receive such uncovenanted blessing. Such intercession was essentially based on a recognition of humanity's desperate need and our own total insufficiency to meet this need. It was equally based on a faith in God's unlimited power and God's desire to revitalize his people.

Another significant aspect of the associations of prayer for revival is that they encouraged greater knowledge of past revivals. Thus prayer for revival, somewhat paradoxically, at one and the same time promoted the sense of special blessing for this generation and also increased a sense of history, enabling people to locate present events in a wider historical context. As already mentioned, Charles Clarke also provides the clearest example of what is really another contributory factor, namely inspiration through the writings of past spiritual mentors, in his case Samuel Chadwick. Although the knowledge of history encouraged by interest in revival tended to be restricted knowledge of a particular segment of Christian history, namely modern evangelical history, there are signs, as with Clarke, of this interest itself leading to broader horizons including Catholic saints and movements.

The prominence of prayer for revival among the antecedent preparatory factors for the Charismatic movement seems to be far more marked in Great Britain than in other countries. This factor is much less prominent in the origins of the movement in the USA and Canada.

ii. Experience of God's Power in Healing

Another and quite different preparatory factor for pentecostal blessing was the rediscovery of God's power to heal the sick. Here again no one pattern of rediscovery is predominant. Some pioneers discovered God's power to heal in sudden and dramatic ways: with David R. Smith and Clark, it was the experience of being used as an instrument of healing, whereas with Trout it was the experience of being healed. Whereas these pioneers from Section I rediscovered in dramatic ways God's power to heal, some of those mentioned in Section II came to this awareness gradually over a period of years. Wood provides an example of a Christian drawn to divine healing from an early stage in a long life of Christian service. Coming from an Anglo-Catholic sacramental and liturgical background Wood first discovered the power of God to heal through set prayers for the sick, and in particular through the sacrament of anointing. Roy Jeremiah and Roy Parsons were two other Anglicans (the latter distinctly High Church) associated with the London Healing Mission, who came into the baptism in the Spirit following a specialist interest in healing.

David R. Smith and Eric Houfe as evangelicals came to a realization of God's power in healing in a different way. They saw the major role played by healing miracles in the ministry of Jesus, and easily saw a close link between the rediscovery of healing and the significance of healing works of power in the task of evangelization. Yet another approach to the ministry of healing besides the more catholic and the more evangelical is evidenced in the case of Keith Edwards from the Glasgow area. Edwards was led into this area by a concern to relate Christian faith to the modern world of science and medicine and by a recognition of the essential interconnectedness of body and spirit. All these men found that once one discovers the power of God in healing, and recognizes its place in the New Testament, then a significant barrier to acceptance of other works of power mentioned in scripture is removed. Edwards was not alone in seeing the logical connection, one might almost say the exegetical connection, between accepting the contemporaneity of gifts of healing and accepting the present availability of other gifts, such as prophecy and tongues.

However, the more clearly healing is seen to be a work of the Holy Spirit of God, in relation to salvation from sin, the more cautious the healing minister will be in relation to forms of healing, whose power is not evidently holy. This can be seen in Wood's opposition to OSL's tolerance of some forms of healing achieved by spiritualist means.

Unlike prayer for revival, the rediscovery of divine healing as a way into the Charismatic movement is found in a number of countries besides Britain, notably in Holland[14] and in the USA.[15] However, it would seem that some who came into the pentecostal blessing from an interest in healing (rather than from the experience of healing) often saw the Charismatic movement as a more powerful form of healing rather than as a wider and deeper current into which their healing concern had led them.

iii. Concern for the Fullness of the New Testament Church

The quest for the fullness of the New Testament church is not so obvious a contributory factor in the origins of the Charismatic movement in Britain as the two categories of revival and healing. It was nonetheless there in the beginnings, though it is not always easy to determine how much this factor contributed to the rise of the movement and how much it was a consequence of the movement's appearance. It is particularly associated with the person and the thinking of David G. Lillie, and represented the linking of the pentecostal experience with the distinctive Brethren understanding of the church in the New Testament. The concern for the fullness of the apostolic church of the New Testament was in fact the unifying thread in the convening of the Devon Conferences by Lillie and Wallis.

b. 'Finding Factors'

It is clear that, in this period of the origins, the major human instruments used by the Holy Spirit to bring the pioneer figures to the baptism in the Spirit were the Pentecostals. This was true either directly or indirectly of Lillie, Clark, Trout, Bolt, Forester, Grant, Houfe, Strachan, Philip Smith, Shaw and Jeremiah. For relatively few was the initial grace of baptism in the Spirit the result of contact with charismatics or neo-pentecostals, for example, those from the USA. Wood was prayed over by Agnes Sanford, but that was after he had met Gee and read about Wigglesworth. Some received the pentecostal baptism after reading *Trinity* magazine, for example, Casebow, Houfe and East; but only in Casebow's case does it seem to have been unaccompanied by Pentecostal contacts.[16]

The distinctive role of David du Plessis as an instrument of the Spirit of God has already been mentioned. He particularly encouraged the emergence of the Charismatic movement by his preaching of baptism in the Spirit and his accompanying assurance that receiving this blessing did not necessitate leaving one's church.

In seeking to understand how the Charismatic movement in Britain came into being under the impulse of God's Spirit, it is important to hold together what have here been termed the 'seeking' factors and the 'finding' factors. If the latter alone are considered, it is hard to understand why the movement is not simply an extension of Pentecostalism. But if the 'seeking' factors alone are identified, the important influence of the Pentecostals will be ignored and the pentecostal character of the new movement not be clearly acknowledged. The 'seeking' factors all demonstrate a thrust towards a different kind of milieu for the new movement from that of the Pentecostal churches. The revival prayer associations were explicitly praying for revival within the historic churches; this was the case, whether in the denominational fellowships such as MRF and BRF, or in the largely Anglican-led NPWR. Those rediscovering the power of God in healing were mostly committed to doing so within the framework of historic church traditions. The London Healing Mission was integrating healing into an Anglican sacramental context before any of its members were baptized in the Spirit. The Brethren concern for the fullness of the church also demonstrates a thrust distinct from mainline pentecostalism, though it does possess some affinity with lesser Pentecostal groups like the Apostolic Church.[17]

4. ORIGINS OF THE EMBRYONIC MOVEMENT

The evidence adduced indicates both that there was something distinctively new in this emerging movement and that the Pentecostal Christians of the country played an important part in its origins. On the one hand, there is the clear influence of the Pentecostals in their witness to the baptism in the Holy Spirit and the contemporary availability of the spiritual gifts. The majority of the first non-Pentecostals to be baptized in the Spirit heard of the possibility of this blessing from Pentecostal sources. On the other hand, the developments described in Sections I and II were always more than the spread of Pentecostalism. The neo-Pentecostals or charismatics were evidently receiving the same blessing and spiritual endowments as were known to the Pentecostals, but they were not accepting all the features accompanying these graces in the Pentecostal denominations and assemblies.[18] The Pentecostals could not be said to be seeking to encourage the emergence of such a movement. Apart from such unusual and far-sighted figures as du Plessis and Gee, the common Pentecostal reaction in the early 1960s was a mixture of fascination and caution.[19]

It can then be said that the Charismatic movement in Great Britain did not arise from the initiative of any one human founder or from any cluster of human ideas and insights. The diversity in the 'seeking factors' shows too that the movement did not arise from a simultaneous genesis of similar aspirations in different places, as for example many church groups promoting and defending family life have arisen when family life has become seriously destabilized and peace groups spring up when the danger of war is grave. There was no blueprint conceived in a pioneer's mind, which was then communicated to others and actualized among them.[20] Though David du Plessis, more than any other pioneer figure in this history, had a vision of a new pentecostal wave in some way different from the mould of denominational Pentecostalism, the new movement cannot simply be attributed to his influence. It was characteristic of du Plessis' ministry that he regularly described what the Holy Spirit had already done rather than gave a blueprint for the future.

Although the pentecostal experience of baptism in the Spirit was at the heart of the new movement, it was not a common understanding or doctrine of Spirit-baptism that preceded the movement. Rather, the movement existed because a range of people experienced the reality of God in the baptism in the Spirit without prior or subsequent acceptance of the doctrine and ethos of the Pentecostal churches. Moreover, this occurred in an unco-ordinated and humanly haphazard manner. The way in which the new movement emerged up to 1963 can in no way be attributed to human planning.

This conclusion – that the embryonic Charismatic movement in Britain was not the result of any preconceived theory of renewal – is confirmed by the remarkable absence of dominant persons and places in the period of the origins. There is no one person or stream that has a pre-eminence prior to 1963. Some streams are more significant in terms of influence than others, but it would be unfair to single out one of the following to the detriment of the others: Lillie, Wallis and the Devon Conferences; Cecil Cousen and AVF; Edgar Trout; Nights of Prayer for Worldwide Revival. All these influences were operative in the 1950s. Although in 1960 Cousen had a wider ministry than Trout, this gap was to close steadily as Trout's influence extended out beyond south-western England. To single out four major streams is not, however, to reduce the others to insignificance. William Wood and the London Healing Mission were not as influential as the major streams indicated, but it would be a mistake to dismiss their influence as trivial. This mistake could easily be made if significance during the period of the origins were to be estimated solely on the basis of later fame and recognition.

Another aspect of the diversity in the movement's British origins is its trans-confessional character. Not only was there no single dominant leader and planning pioneer, but almost by definition a movement touching such a wide base could not have had such an origin. For even at the preparatory stage treated in Section I, there were Christians from a sufficiently wide range of backgrounds to have made acceptance of a common platform highly unlikely. The strongly Calvinist David R. Smith would not easily have agreed with the more Arminian theology of the Methodist Edgar Trout. The confessional backgrounds in this early phase range from Brethren (Lillie, Wallis, Clark, McAlpine, Hutchison) to Apostolic (Cousen) and Methodist (Trout). But with the spread of the pentecostal experience to Christians more firmly rooted in their Church traditions (Section II), the range of backgrounds widens considerably. Many are evangelical Anglicans (Grant, Houfe, Allen, P. L. C. Smith, Harper, Collins, Watson, MacKenzie). There are a few Methodists (C. J. Clarke, A. Edwards) and the first trickle of Baptists (Frank Wilson, W. J. James).

Of greater potential significance however, is the appearance of pentecostal blessing among Anglicans from non-evangelical backgrounds. The first instance of these comes from an interest in healing with Bill Wood, later to be followed by Roy Parsons. Both these men came from a more sacramental and liturgical churchmanship, as did Michael Meakin and John Gunstone. With the spread of this blessing to the more Catholic wing of the Church of England, something of historic significance has occurred. A movement of spiritual revival has arisen which is no longer identified with one particular type of churchmanship. For the first time since the divisions at the Reformation, a movement of God's Spirit is touching both the evangelical and the Catholic segments of Christendom, not to mention the broad and the liberal. The logic of this thrust was to be more clearly manifest in the subsequent spread of the movement to the Roman Catholic Church. The walls of division are now penetrated and broken, by which Christians for centuries made simultaneous Holy Spirit revival and renewal across all the Christian world practically impossible.

Twenty-Four

Distinguishing Features of the Early Development of the Charismatic Movement in Great Britain

The data presented indicate a progression from a number of distinct though occasionally intersecting streams, within which believers were receiving the baptism in the Spirit, to a stage at which there was a common awareness of these streams having flowed into one recognizable movement of Charismatic revival-renewal. As the evidence presented in Section III shows, this process of growing movement-consciousness was particularly stimulated by the news coming from the USA and by such visitors as Maguire, Christenson and du Plessis. Within this process, the first meetings bringing together the main pioneer figures in Britain were of particular importance, with the Stoke Poges meeting June 1964 having a pre-eminent place. If there is any point where the origins definitively yield to the first years, it would be the Stoke Poges conference, which came just one month before the Fountain Trust was formed. This chapter will now examine the main characteristics of the newly-emerged Charismatic movement. as they can be distilled from the period between June 1964 and December 1965.

1. THE MOVEMENT HAS A DISTINCTIVE SHAPE

From its earliest emergence into public consciousness, the Charismatic movement in Britain possessed certain identifiable characteristics that enabled anyone, whether adherent, critic, or observer, to determine its presence or absence. Undoubtedly, the decisive criterion was whether a person had experienced the exercise of any of the spiritual gifts of 1 Corinthians. However, there were other characteristics associated with the advent of these gifts. which also served to identify 'charismatics'. These were such features as the raising of arms in prayer, the imposition of hands in 'praying over' people, the practice of spontaneous praise and the taking of the Lord's authority in situations of illness, oppression and setback. In fact, the visible distinguishing characteristics of the new movement were primarily new spiritual capabilities: to praise God freely, to speak in God's name, to rebuke evil in the Lord's power, to pray in tongues. To be part of the movement was not simply a matter of picking up a certain style, though no doubt this also happened in later phases; it was having a transforming experience of the Lord that resulted in these new endowments.

That these capabilities, including the exercise of the spiritual gifts, became characteristics of the movement means also that they came to be seen as part of an organic interrelated whole. Whereas individuals here and there aside from the Pentecostals had spoken in tongues before ever this movement was heard of,[1] the rise of the movement was always more than tongues-speaking occurring on a wider scale. The rise of the Charismatic movement was accompanied by the conviction that God was baptizing people in his Holy Spirit and that the whole range of spiritual gifts enumerated by Paul are available to Christians today.

The recognition of the movement's existence represented in fact a combination of two elements: Firstly *a recognition of a core identity in the charismatic experience as it was being received in diverse persons and settings; and, the rise of forms of fellowship and of skeletal organization giving social expression to this identity.*

As the movement was recognized it was seen to be not just a British movement, but one international in character with strong associations with the North American continent. This international character was evidenced not only by special visiting speakers who included Europeans as well as Americans, but also by the coming and going of missionaries touched by this work of the Spirit.[2]

2. THE UNITY OF THE MOVEMENT

One striking feature of these early years is the unity of spirit found among those baptized in the Spirit. When many of the pioneer figures came together for the first time, as some did at Stoke Poges in June 1964, they recognized in each other, whatever their contrasting backgrounds and differences in theology and church government, fundamentally the same revitalizing work of God. Those who received this baptism knew that they had received the same grace. Recipients often spoke in excited terms of this discovery, as for example Charles Clarke:

> In the present worldwide movement of the Spirit, God is taking no notice of the man-made walls of division. He is baptizing with His Spirit, Anglicans, Methodists, Baptists, Lutherans, Roman Catholics, Anglo-Catholics, Plymouth Brethren, Mennonites, Calvinists, Pentecostals, and many other brands of His divided Church. Wherever the anointing comes there is perfect, loving, glorious unity. What God is doing is more important than all our theological arguments. His evident will is what matters.[3]

The claim to perfect unity is no doubt an enthusiastic exaggeration, and indeed Clarke elsewhere stresses the need for constant ongoing growth and purification in the Christian life. But the basis for this enthusiasm was real enough: that a new and genuine level of spiritual fellowship was being experienced, and this fellowship extended well beyond the circles of Christian fellowship that had formerly been enjoyed.

The unity in blessing received was manifested by the participants sharing the new capabilities they did not previously have or exercise. That those baptized in the Spirit could now praise God together in free composition or in tongues; and the fact that they could recognize in each other the same ability to hear the Lord in their inner spirit and to act in his power, showed that their unity in the Spirit was not a matter of mere feelings and joyous emotions. It had an objective basis in themselves and in what they could observably do. This objective basis was most vividly demonstrated in the practice of corporate singing in tongues, when individual worshippers contribute their own 'tongue' and tune to one overall harmony of praise.

Moreover, this new-found unity in the Spirit was not a fresh discovery of graces known previously in separation. These new capabilities were newly received through the baptism in the Spirit. This aspect of gifts newly bestowed by God on people from a variety of traditions highlighted for participants the graced aspect of their new-found unity.

Michael Harper wrote of the Stoke Poges conference: 'There was a great depth of fellowship and unity in the Spirit.'[4] How deep was this fellowship and unity? People hearing about such events at a distance might be sceptical as to the real depth of the shared encounter. Obviously the fellowship at such a conference did not possess the depth that only comes with time in committed relationships. But what Harper was evidently affirming was the depth of the level at which the encounter occurred. That is to say, the grace of baptism in the Spirit touches a believer in the depths of the human spirit, and the new capabilities received arise from the depths of the person's being.

Enjoying this newly-received spiritual unity did not result in immediate dissolution of conflicting doctrines and theologies. Bill Wood was one of the signatories to a statement of British, Australian and New Zealand brethren at a seminar in the USA, that stated:

> The meeting together of Methodist, Lutheran, Presbyterian, Baptist, Reformed Churches, Disciples, Mennonites and Pentecostals in Holy-Spirit inspired unity has given cause for joy in all our hearts. We recognise that complete doctrinal agreement and unity in practice is not for us on this earth but we have found a place in the Baptism of the Holy Spirit where barriers are lowered and fellowship in Christ realised.[5]

Indeed it was one of the remarkable features that impressed the early participants that people holding quite divergent theologies could be brought into such a tangible unity. This is particularly evident in the fellowship and correspondence between David Lillie, who saw all denominational organization as spiritually irrelevant, and the solidly Anglican Michael Harper. While it is true that Lillie hoped that Harper and others in the historic churches would be won over to his view of 'the rediscovery of the True Church of the New Testament,'[6] nonetheless the strong awareness of shared blessing and of divine providence bridging abysses of human making dominated these early exchanges. Thus Lillie writes in October 1964: 'We must keep together – for surely the Lord brought us together!'[7]

The sense of wonder at this new-found spiritual unity did not lead all beneficiaries immediately into a denigration of doctrine and a hostility to all theology, although obviously such sentiments can be found among some of the less mature and less measured in utterance. Several were aware that what they were experiencing would challenge many received theologies and religious assumptions. Clarke wrote of the movement of the Spirit having 'serious implications' saying:

> The more I read my New Testament. the more I am amazed at the strange way we all ignore some most serious elements of its teaching. We have blind spots. Some truth we see. Some we do not see. Protestant Evangelical readers of the Bible see the truths they are taught to see. Sometimes we get a hunch that the Book is showing us a rather different image from what we are seeing – but we easily reject the hunch and see just the traditional teaching.[8]

The exciting newly-found unity of spirit was not then seen simply as 'unity on the cheap'. Rather the unity was experienced as real, but the grace of which this unity was an expression was recognized by the more far-sighted as having costly implications.

3. THE CENTRALITY OF BAPTISM IN THE SPIRIT

Although it was clear from the start in Britain as elsewhere that the spiritual gifts were phenomenologically distinguishing characteristics of the Charismatic movement, it was also evident that participants did not see those gifts as its heart or foundational reality. The evidence is constant from an early date that the central distinguishing feature of this movement was baptism in the Spirit. This is what united them.

The centrality of baptism in the Spirit within the Charismatic movement can be seen clearly from the impact of *The Cross and the Switchblade*. In Wilkerson's book, the emphasis is on God's power, an efficacious love that changes lives, however spoiled and broken. Not much is said about tongues, and the baptism in the Spirit is identified as the crucial factor.[9] As the young gang-members and drug addicts of New York City turn to God and come to the baptism in the Spirit, they come to a knowledge of Jesus, and a communication with their heavenly Father, as well as experiencing a release from old enslaving patterns by the power of the Spirit. The major impact of Wilkerson's book was to demonstrate that 'these things still happen today', the wonders of salvation, of healing and deliverance described in the Scriptures. It communicated the sense of a

God who loved broken and alienated humanity so much that he sent
his son Jesus Christ who defeated the power of evil through his own
death on the cross. It presented the risen Lord Jesus as alive, active
and powerful, the Son of God who communicates with his creatures,
whom he loves. These were the convictions that Wilkerson knew to
be associated with the baptism in the Spirit that attracted readers and
led them to desire the same in their own lives.

The centrality of baptism in the Spirit for participants was also
shown in the energy with which participants repudiated the label-
ling of the whole phenomenon as a 'tongues movement'. Not surprisingly, the phenomenon of speaking in tongues was a particular
focus of media interest, and press reports included such captions as
'Tongues' "Movement Grows." '[10] Tongues' Vicar Resigns[11] and
'Tongues in Loughborough.'[12] The *Church Times* reported that Harper was resigning his position at All Souls, Langham Place, 'to
devote his time and energies to furthering the understanding and
practice of glossolalia throughout the English Churches.[13]. Various
protests against this misunderstanding were made.[14] John Gravelle
of Toddington, Bedfordshire, made the point: 'To call it a "tongues"
movement, however, seems to be misleading. As I understand it the
movement's chief concern is not "tongues" but "renewal" '[15].

The tendency to focus on the apparently extraordinary and to
identify the movement in terms of glossolalia alone was also com-
bated in a book that in fact began as a study of the tongues phenomenon. Written by an American Episcopalian, John Sherrill, *They Speak
with Other Tongues* was published in 1964 and was soon made
available in Britain.[16] In this book, Sherrill recalls how a charismatic
leader likened the relationship of tongues and the full life of one
baptized in the Spirit to a Gothic chapel with a bright red door.

> Tongues . . . are like that door. As long as you stand outside your
> attention is going to be riveted there and you're not going to be able
> to see anything else. Once you go through, however, you are sur-
> rounded by the thousand wonders of light and sound and form that
> the architect intended. You look around and that door isn't even red
> on the inside. It's there. It's to be used. But it has taken its proper place
> in the design of the whole Church.[17]

The same conviction is evident in Cecil Cousen's protest about
imposition of hands for baptism in the Spirit without prior evidence
of conversion in conviction of sin, repentance and faith. Speaking in

tongues may follow, but no life-changing experience. Baptism in the Spirit, he insists, is much more than speaking in tongues.[18] Again the implication is clear: baptism in the Spirit is the heart of this work of God.

4. THE UNDERSTANDING OF BAPTISM IN THE SPIRIT

How participants in the Charismatic movement in Britain first understood their being baptized in the Spirit depended to some extent on how they came into this experience. The majority came to know of this possibility by meeting, hearing or reading about other Christians who had already received. Initially those whose testimonies so touched others were almost all Pentecostals,[19] but as the new movement spread, the predominant witness was from outside Pentecostal ranks by those newly-baptized in the Spirit.[20] W. B. Grant is one who described the effects of this baptism he saw in the lives of others and then wanted for himself. Writing about the group of men where he first met people who had been baptized in the Spirit, Grant wrote: 'We soon noticed that there was something unusual about a number of these men . . . their secret was they had received a personal pentecost.'[21] Grant then longed for this transforming experience. This majority category consisted then of those who were led to seek the baptism in the Spirit through personal witness. Those who were led to seek and receive the baptism in the Spirit in this way did not begin with a clear-cut understanding of the nature and purpose of this transforming grace. For them, the baptism in the Spirit connoted a rich complex of blessings which flooded in on them and included a new closeness to and love for Jesus Christ, a new joy and peace, a new capacity to praise God, new desire to read the Scriptures, a power for ministry and witness, a confidence in God.

A few people came into this Holy Spirit experience without any prior contacts with Pentecostals or charismatics. Michael Harper and Ellita Howell Williams are examples of Christians who had such an experience of the Lord initially without any manifestation of spiritual gifts, but who on hearing and reading of Pentecostal and neo-pentecostal witnesses of 'the baptism' knew that this was what they too had received. Their subsequent reception of the gift of tongues was then experienced as a further freeing and opening up to God along the line already begun. Molly MacKenzie and Elspeth Shaw are examples of believers who were sovereignly baptized in the Spirit and received one or more spiritual gifts apparently without any prior information or teaching concerning such a possibility. For these individuals, the search for understanding of what they had received began from scratch following such unexpected blessing. Michael Harper wrote of that phase:

> We had little idea then how to explain to ourselves, let alone others, what God had done for us. At once we turned to our Bibles with new interest, and were amazed at what we found. We realised that we had stumbled on lost treasure. That hidden in the Scriptures was a promise for Christians – the baptism in the Holy Spirit, which a compound of ignorance and prejudice had hidden from us for all those years.[22]

There do not appear to have been any significant instances in Britain of the pattern experienced in the Irvingite movement in the previous century, namely of arriving at the convictions concerning the present availability of spiritual gifts exclusively from the study of Scripture and without having heard of any contemporary instances of their presence and exercise.[23] However, it was possible for people, particularly ministers, to become aware of baptism in the Spirit with spiritual gifts through reading or hearing more theological or exegetical presentations either for or against this new phenomenon.[24] These would have been the only people whose initial understanding of baptism in the Spirit would have been more coloured by theological definitions and distinctions than by the content of personal witnesses.

It was both inevitable and necessary that the more descriptive accounts of baptism in the Spirit found in witnesses and testimonies should be complemented by more theological approaches concerned to understand more clearly the nature of this gift from God. The predominance of evangelicals among the first charismatics in Britain, and the vehement opposition of many fellow-evangelicals, led to the first formulations concerning baptism in the Spirit being apologetic in nature. They sought to defend, from the New Testament, a post-regeneration reception of the Holy Spirit appropriately accompanied by a visible manifestation such as the gift of tongues.[25] The position that such evangelicals sought to defend was in fact the classical Pentecostal definition of baptism in the Spirit as 'empowerment for ministry', but modified by loosening the ties between tongues and 'the baptism'. There was also a greater concern to locate the baptism in the Spirit within the frame-work of Christian initiation.[27] The first charismatics were thus in some way 'de-doctrinalizing' the Pentecostal teaching, though their indebtedness to Pentecostal predecessors was probably greater than they realized.[28]

The teaching that baptism in the Spirit is essentially empower-ment for ministry was embraced by two of the major teachers within the nascent movement, Cecil Cousen and Michael Harper. It appeals almost exclusively to the writings of Luke, to the end of Luke 24 and the Acts of the Apostles.[29] It reflects the characteristic evangelical concern to anchor a teaching in the New Testament, but this scrip-tural interpretation does not seem to have been preceded by a careful analysis of the components of the experience. The quasi-definition of baptism in the Spirit in terms of empowerment for ministry does not in fact do justice to all the data described in countless testimonies. In particular, it makes no reference to the element that is so central in many testimonies, namely a new level of knowledge of Jesus Christ,[30] and some awareness of the love of the Father and the distinctiveness of the Holy Spirit.[31]

The aspect of baptism in the Spirit as producing a new depth of relationship to Jesus Christ and through him to the Father is also confirmed by other elements regularly mentioned in testimonies. One is the language of surrender, in which recipients describe how the breakthrough occurred as they yielded in faith, including yield-ing their tongues, not to an impersonal force but to a personal God.[32] Yielding to God changes the relationship to God. Another is the almost universal experience of those who speak in tongues that this gift is one of praise. The constant association of reception of tongues with baptism in the Spirit, which Pentecostals and charismatics regularly make but have difficulty in explaining theologically, dem-onstrates that this baptism is first concerned with the candidate's relationship to God, for the visible sign of reception of tongues (whether regarded as *a sine qua non* or in a more *de facto* manner) is the only gift among the list in 1 Corinthians 12:8–10 that concerns relation with God rather than with humans.[33]

To assert that the baptism in the Spirit first concerns the be-liever's relationship with God, and that the important conse-quences for ministry flow from this, is not to appeal to experience rather than to the word of God. It is to demonstrate that the baptism in the Spirit as described by recipients responds to the full meaning of the Spirit-baptism terminology used in the New Testament. In fact, it is a mistake to limit the meaning of 'baptized in the Spirit' in Luke-Acts to empowerment for ministry,[34] for in these books the Holy Spirit is presented as 'the promise of the Father'[35] who brings about the fulfilment of all that God has promised for his people.[36] This understanding of the Spirit's coming is most clearly developed in the Johannine writings, in which the person and work of the Holy Spirit is closely tied to the person and work of the Second Person of the Trinity. Charles Clarke showed an evident awareness of this when he alluded to John 16:14[37] in describing his baptism in the Spirit:

> What happened to me on that early February morning was verse one of chapter one in a new life in the Spirit in which I am but a novice. I have entered into the first form of the school of Christ with the Holy Spirit as my tutor, who is taking the things of Christ and showing them to me.[38]

In the gospel of John, the Spirit is the one who bears witness to Jesus (15:26), a teaching confirmed in the first letter of John (1 John 4:2; 5:7).[39] C. K. Barrett remarks that: 'John's thought about Jesus is . . . not so much functional as essential; what Jesus does arises out of what he is'.[40] This more essential account of the role of the Spirit in John was evidently the fruit of a long life of prayerful reflection and contemplation on the life and ministry of Jesus.[41] The first accounts of baptism in the Spirit reflect the more kerygmatic view of the synoptic gospels; they witness to the visible effects of the Spirit's coming in relation to the life and teaching of Jesus. Just as John penetrated the heart of the meaning of the coming of the Holy Spirit upon the primitive church, so an adequate account of baptism in the Spirit needs to penetrate to the heart of its meaning in the believer's changed relationship to Jesus Christ.

This perspective of the Fourth Gospel reinforces what is indicated elsewhere in the New Testament:[42] that there is no coming of the Holy Spirit in the New Covenant that is not also a manifestation of Jesus Christ.[43] Any separation of Jesus and the Spirit tends towards a depersonalization of the Spirit, and opens the door to an absorption in spiritual power separated from the quest for union with God. It is indeed possible that John the evangelist had seen, maybe in some Gnostic circles, the results of such a separation leading to an exaltation of spiritual power in itself.

The evidence then points to the conclusion that a more comprehensive understanding of baptism in the Spirit is needed that attributes primary place to the personal transformation resulting from a theophanic experience of the triune God. This experience has a 'downward' revelatory dimension, an 'upward' worship dimension and an 'outward' service element that includes, but is not restricted to, evangelism. In this wider perspective, empowerment for ministry is a consequence of a changed relationship to Jesus, the Spirit and the Father.[44]

5. IMPORTANCE OF THE CHARISMATA

The data thus present an evident paradox. On the one hand, participants maintain that the baptism in the Spirit, not the gifts of the Spirit. is the movement's foundation-experience. On the other hand, no matter how many people claimed to be baptized in the Spirit, if there were no expectation or manifestation of the spiritual gifts, then there would be no Charismatic movement in the sense here being studied. Moreover, charismatics consistently expected baptism in the Spirit to be accompanied or followed by speaking in tongues even if the majority refused to accept the common Pentecostal position that ties baptism in the Spirit to speaking in tongues.

No systematic theological explanation of the relationship between baptism in the Spirit and the spiritual gifts had been advanced by 1965. However, here and there in the writings there are significant pointers. For example, Cecil Cousen sees glossolalia as a living symbol of the work of the Holy Spirit in the Christian. He writes, 'For men to speak as the Holy Ghost gives utterance is a fitting symbol . . . to signify that divine treasure has come to abide in earthen vessels.[45] He later explains this further:

> Speaking in tongues is a perfect illustration of the nature of the whole purpose of the enduement of power from on high. The glossolalia is an ideal symbol of the communion of the Holy Ghost (2 Cor. 13, 14). The word 'communion' carries with it the thought of 'partnership' . . . . How does the partnership work? How does it work in the matter of glossolalia? That is a perfect symbol. In the glossolalia I do two things, or one thing in two stages: I yield a member of my human body, my tongue, to the Holy Ghost for His use. Then, when the tongue is completely yielded to His control I speak; I do the speaking.[46]

That the spiritual gifts symbolize the relationship between God and humans in the Spirit-filled body of Christ can help to explain why these gifts are both vitally important and yet are not the central reality of the Charismatic movement. As actions involving the yielding or surrender of the spirit to God, they symbolize the revelatory and soteriological activity of God working in and through believing human persons.

It has already been remarked that an ability to hear God is a characteristic of the Charismatic movement. The immediate consequence of that capacity is the ability to speak in God's name. The prophet, the person who speaks for God, is first a seer (or hearer). He has to see and hear before he can speak.[47] The spiritual gift of prophecy then symbolizes and concentrates the wider Christian experience of being enabled to hear God, and then to act and speak with divine authority and power. The gift illustrates in concentrated form an element that is essential to full Christian life. The gift by itself is not the most important thing. But what it represents is essential. The very appearance of the gift thus points to something essential to full Christian life that was widely lacking in the life of the churches. Some commentators remarked on the significance of the movement's first years coinciding with the appearance of John Robinson's *Honest to God* and the widespread debate it set off.[48] While some are declaring the impossibility or grave difficulties in the way of modern people believing in miracles and the supernatural, others are proclaiming that the same range of wonders described in the New Testament narratives is occurring today.

6. THE SCOPE AND PURPOSE OF THE MOVEMENT

The scope and purpose of the Charismatic movement as it was manifested in Britain in its origins and first years can be considered in two main ways: (a) by an examination and assessment of the understanding of its scope and purpose found among the participants at that time and (b) by a comparison between this movement and other movements in Christian history.

a. The Initial Self-Understanding within the Movement

Because the origins of the Charismatic movement in Britain lay in similar events rather than in any common theory or vision, an understanding of the scope and purpose of the movement was not given automatically with the basic experience of baptism in the Spirit. Lives were being changed, often dramatically, as people were being baptized in the Spirit, but the scope and purpose of the overall movement of the Spirit had still to be sought out and discovered. So the period of the first years (1964–5) following the clear emergence of a distinctive new movement was the time when the question of its meaning and significance was first being addressed.

A first observation must be that those making public their reflections on the movement's scope and purpose saw it as God's work, and thus they saw themselves as discovering God's purpose through prayer and reflection, both on Scripture and on their contemporary experience. They were not conferring a significance on the movement, but they were discovering the purpose that was already inscribed in the events being experienced. However, these men who wrote and spoke about God's purpose in this movement of the Spirit were all in ministering and teaching roles, the demands of which increased as the movement spread. Their reflections thus tended to be brief and condensed, appearing in editorials and conference talks, rather than in any form of extended and detailed analysis.

How did the first British interpreters of the Charismatic movement understand this work of the Holy Spirit? Hardly any understood it in the Pentecostal framework of the 'Latter Rain' implying a comparative inactivity of the Holy Spirit between the pristine rain of Pentecost and the latter rain of a twentieth-century Pentecost.[49] Those already praying fervently for revival who received the baptism in the Spirit naturally saw the beginnings of the Charismatic movement as the first signs of a new revival.[50] However, the fact that this work of God did not have a visibly explosive effect on society – and after a few years was still restricted to a relatively small number of people – led many to reinterpret the movement in terms of preparation for spiritual revival in the nation (in Edgar Trout's phrase, 'laying the sticks for revival').[51]

This largely evangelical expectation concerning revival was however in some quarters accompanied by a more corporate concern for the church. This relating of the reception of the Holy Spirit to the building of the body of Christ was found in two particular forms. One in the circles associated with David Lillie and Arthur Wallis asserted that this outpouring of the Spirit was for the sake of restoring afresh the New Testament church of Christ. While these men adopted a very low view of the redeemability of the historic churches, they clearly had a high estimate of the significance of the new movement.[52] The other milieu in which this new move of the Spirit was interpreted in terms of the church was predominantly Anglican, and found its principal spokesman in Michael Harper. It was to become a linking point with the first Anglo-Catholics baptized in the Spirit and was from the start firmly supported by the spokesmen and writers of a more Catholic tendency such as John Gunstone.

For an evangelical like Harper, discovery of the importance of the church as the body of Christ was an exciting new dimension brought with this new movement[53] and seems to have come first from the experience of vital Spirit-led worship.[54] Reflection on the Pauline teaching on the spiritual gifts also reinforced this understanding of their being given for the building of the body of Christ. This church-relatedness of the movement found particular expression in the term *renewal*, which soon came to be used to describe this all-embracing scope of the Spirit's work.[55] Michael Harper wrote in an introduction to a booklet that appeared in May 1964:

> It is the renewal of the Church that God is principly [*sic*] concerned about – not that of the gifts. The gifts are for the building up of the Church – in order that it may become once more a powerful and influential force in the world. It is the recovery of New Testament Church life which is our greatest need today.[56]

This same breadth of perspective is shown again in Harper' announcement of the formation of the Fountain Trust.[57] The elevation of the term 'renewal' to titular status, indicated for example by the choice of this term to designate the Fountain Trust's bi-monthly magazine, ensured that the objective of corporate renewal of all dimensions of the church's life through the Holy Spirit would be kept before participants.

The difference of vision for the future of the church, between the Lillie-Wallis circle (summed up in the term *Restoration*), and those primarily looking to Harper and the Fountain Trust for leadership (finding their vision better expressed by the term *Renewal*), was fundamentally a difference in received ecclesiology. The vision of the church shared by Lillie and Wallis[58] was rooted in the ecclesiology of the Plymouth Brethren, with the new power and life brought by the Holy Spirit and the spiritual gifts being seen as the means by which this vision would be realised.[59] The ecclesiology of Harper and his colleagues was less uniform and less focused than that of Lillie and Wallis, but in the early stages of the movement it represented an evangelical view of the church enriched by a new sense of the church as the body of Christ; yet strongly supported among the Anglican majority by traditional loyalties to the Church of England and its historic role in the life of the nation. It was not easy to see how these two visions could be reconciled.

What conclusions can be reasonably drawn by those examining the evidence some thirty years later? The characteristics of the Charismatic movement in its British origins do confirm the judgement that the grace of God being received in baptism in the Spirit concerns the basic realities of the Christian life. The characteristics of a new quality of relationship with Jesus Christ and his Father through the Spirit, of new capabilities to praise God from this new fullness within, of a new directness of communication between the believers and their Lord, of new power in evangelism and service, all these belong to the heart and essence of the life of the church. These cannot be regarded as tangential blessings. These are indeed the consequences of the Spirit's advent of which one reads in the New Testament: knowledge of Jesus and his salvation (John 16:8–15); exuberant praise of God (Acts 2:4, 11, 47; Ephesians 5:19); direct communication with God (Acts 2:18) and new power in evangelism and service (Acts, *passim*).

However, the years being studied were the very beginnings of the Charismatic movement as a recognizable force within the churches of Great Britain. Hence the conclusions are necessarily judgements concerning potential, based on the evident characteristics of the movement's beginnings, rather than judgements concerning long-term accomplishment. At this stage, the impact of Christians receiving the baptism in the Spirit is more evident in individual testimonies than in whole parishes and local communities, although there are places such as Gillingham, Chorleywood and some house fellowships where signs of more corporate renewal can be seen. But at this stage, what is evident is that the new depth of relationship to Jesus Christ conferred through baptism in the Spirit points to the movement's remarkable potential to revitalize Christian life.

b. Comparisons with other Christian Movements

Summing up some of the characteristic features of the Charismatic movement in Britain, it can be said that it had a distinctive shape that was associated with the rediscovery of the spiritual gifts of 1 Corinthians 12:8–10, that it nonetheless found its centre in the spiritual event of baptism in the Spirit, and that its range of occurrence was not restricted to particular Christian churches or traditions. All these points are significant when comparison is made with other movements of the Spirit in Christian history.

The first two characteristics of charismata and baptism in the Spirit are found equally in the Pentecostal movement, but this earlier movement did not touch many parts of the Christian world and it soon became a cluster of new denominations. Moreover, the charismatic vision of the outpouring of the Holy Spirit and the spiritual gifts for the sake of the renewal of the entire body of Christ represented one major contrast from the earlier Pentecostal movement. The first generation of Pentecostals did not think in terms of the body of Christ, for they were convinced that the return of the Lord was so imminent that there was no time to think in terms of church renewal.[60]

Comparison of the Charismatic movement with other Christian movements of revival and renewal indicates that both in Britain and elsewhere it represented an unusual combination of characteristics. Movements of evangelical revival, whether of the more spontaneous form like the Welsh Revival of 1904–6 or of the more humanly-led form like the work of Wesley and Whitefield, have ordinarily been characterized by the preaching and realization of gospel truths already acknowledged in theory;[61] that is, in Cardinal Newman's terms, they represent a transition from an assent that is notional to one that is real.[62] They have not ordinarily been accompanied by the appearance and teaching of elements that are effectively new in relation to the recipients and their immediate tradition. The spiritual gifts and their association with the reality of baptism in the Spirit do in fact represent such a new element. This element of newness reinforces the degree of the challenge posed to the churches by this movement. For either the newness is evidence of the movement's suspect character (the reaction of the more unsympathetic evangelicals) or, if recognized as authentic and a recovery of something clearly present in the New Testament, it points to the movement having a high degree of importance.

Movements calling for the recovery and restoration of long-neglected elements in church life are however not unknown, especially in recent Christian history. The liturgical movement contains many elements of such a restorative character, and has issued in clear elements of restoration of long-defunct institutions and practices such as the catechumenate and eucharistic concelebration.[63] However, movements such as the liturgical movement have only very limited likeness to the Charismatic movement. These other restoration movements were all ideas-movements in which the key-ideas of the movement first existed in the minds of pioneers before any acts of restoration occurred. In the Charismatic movement, the forgotten gifts appeared without any such vision or campaign.[64] Moreover, ideas-movements tend to appear and flourish mainly in the tradition of the pioneers. By contrast, the Charismatic movement as an event-movement can never be said to have belonged to or characterized any one church tradition more than another.[65] Hence when people have said 'the gifts are for the sake of the church' and 'the movement is to renew the church', there is an essential ambiguity attaching to the term 'church' in the case of a movement inherently transcending denominational divisions. It is not then surprising that charismatics have seen this outpouring of the Spirit as aimed at a renewal of the entire church of Christ, and as a force capable of breaking down the longest-standing ecclesiastical barriers.

Lastly, the Charismatic movement that has crossed denominational lines shows significant differences from previous patterns in the Ecumenical movement. Unlike the Ecumenical movement, the Charismatic movement has not arisen from any vision or desire for organic unity among separated Christians. For most charismatics, their interest in Christian unity is the result of a spiritual unity already received in baptism in the Spirit. The unity in the Charismatic movement is a by-product, albeit a highly significant by-product, of the Lord's action in baptism in the Spirit. It is an illustration of the truth of the gospel words, 'Seek first the kingdom of God and his righteousness, and all these things will be added unto you' (Mt. 6:33). The ecumenical movement – concerned with the restoration of unity among all Christians[66] – has begun from a situation of separation, one might say from experiencing the sin of division. Ecumenical dialogue has then sought to determine what is held in common between the churches (at the level of professed faith, teaching and public worship), and what are the grounds for the patterns of diver-

gence between them. From this theological starting-point of perceived grounds for partial unity and partial disunity, the ecumenical
encounter seeks to actualize the unity, whilst dialogue and research
aim to extend the grounds for unity and diminish those for disunity
through deeper penetration of the gospel and of the core-concerns
of each tradition. While the ecumenical movement has included
many efforts to promote spiritual renewal it is nonetheless working
on a linear model, from lesser communion to greater communion.
By contrast, the Charismatic movement starts from a position of
unity in a shared experience of the Triune God and of fellowship in
the worshipping body of Christ. The Charismatic movement is an
action of the Holy Spirit which has a totality in its beginning. In
baptism in the Spirit a full spiritual communion is given. However,
its consequences then have to be worked out in all the dimensions
of life: personal, moral, social, theological, ecumenical.[67]

This study suggests that there is a direct connection between the
nature of the grace bestowed in baptism in the Spirit and the unity
resulting therefrom among Christians from a wide variety of theological, spiritual and cultural backgrounds. This link implies a corollary, namely that fidelity to the grace of baptism in the Spirit
includes a commitment to and consolidation of this unity. The
coexistence of different visions grounded in conflicting ecclesiologies is at one and the same time a potential threat to the unity of the
movement and an invitation to overcome and transcend the divisions inherited from the past. That which has made unity possible
between Christians from such a wide range of backgrounds – namely
the life and power of the Holy Spirit – must possess the potential to
preserve and deepen this unity.

In other words, the continuation and development of the movement in faithfulness to its central inspiration would be just as marvellous and unpredictable a grace of the Holy Spirit as its origins.
The pioneers and initial leaders of the Charismatic movement in
Britain did see the hand of God in their new-found fellowship,
though more amongst themselves than between themselves and the
Pentecostals. But they did not seem to have had a clear sense of the
imperative to continue in that fellowship and to see that such con-
tinuance required common commitment to build on what united
them. There is no suggestion that they were determined to seek in
common prayer ways to find God's way, beyond the doctrinal and
theological oppositions of the past.

This analysis points to the need for a common understanding of the significance of this work of the Holy Spirit. The unusual character of the Charismatic movement as a breath of the Spirit transcending many historic confessional and theological barriers necessitates a corresponding grace of understanding. In brief, a shared grace of new life calls for a shared grace of understanding that new life. By the nature of the wounds inflicted by division and mutual opposition, the understanding of the gospel is fragmented. By the nature of separation and division, the reigning theology[58] of the churches before such a grace of the Spirit is inadequate to the task of this understanding. Interpretations totally within the received categories of divided traditions cannot be shared.

So when the unexpected occurs, and Christians from a wide variety of separated traditions experience the same work of God that flows out in the capacity to hear, praise and serve God together, they should expect a corresponding grace from God for this newly-bestowed spiritual reality to be understood through the grace of the Spirit. This is the only way in which the necessary theological understanding of the movement will not reduce its God-given significance.

The comparisons with other movements help to indicate some of the reasons why the Charismatic movement has been in effect the first widespread grass-roots movement of this ecumenical century. It has concerned relationship with God, knowledge of Jesus and the reality of the Holy Spirit, rather than ideas about God. The fellowship experienced between participants has not been primarily kinship of ideas, but knowledge of lives being touched by God in the same way.

c Conclusions

The analysis of the distinctive features of the Charismatic movements in Britain in it origins and first years enables the following conclusions to be drawn:

1. *The central reality of the movement is the spiritual transformation known as baptism in the Spirit.* It was the shared experience of this reality that brought about the unity among those baptized in the Spirit.

2. *The heart or meaning of baptism in the Spirit is the believer's changed relationship to Jesus Christ, brings a personal revealed knowledge of Jesus*

Christ as Saviour and Lord. This transformation commonly makes the doctrine of the Trinity a living reality to the charismatic Christian. The other blessings coming with baptisms in the Spirit such as new power in praise, evangelism and ministry are consequences of the new relationship to Jesus Christ.

3.   *The grace of baptism in the Spirit is the same among Pentecostals and charistmatics.* The differences between the Pentecostal movement and the Charismatic movement are not in the nature of the grace being bestowed, but in the context of its reception and in the framework within which it is understood.

4.   *While there was a genuine communion in the Spirit between the Spirit-baptized, there was not a common understanding of the movement and of its purpose in God's sight.* The possibility of a common understanding was dependent on the participants being willing to allow their received theologies, especially their ecclesiologies, to be challenged and expanded in common fidelity to the grace of baptism in the Spirit and in parallel fidelity to the work of God at the heart of each tradition.

5.   *The importance of the baptism in the Spirit for the life of the churches is demonstrated by the centrality of its constituent elements and its consequences for the life of the Christian and the life of the Christian community.* The comparison with other movements in the churches reinforces the unusual character of the Charismatic movement.

6.   *The combination of recall to the gospel message concerning Jesus Christ, and the power of his cross and resurrection of rediscovery of long-forgotten spiritual gifts and of unprecedented ecumenical dissemination all point to the Charismatic movement being a movement of God the Holy Spirit offering the Christian people an unprecedented opportunity for the renewal of the life of the whole body of Christ.*

Twenty-Five

A Comparison with North America

This study indicates that the Charismatic movement in Great Britain was in its origins and early development more indigenous than is commonly supposed. There were influences from and links with the North American continent, but these were not constitutive elements of the movement in Britain. Readers of the British story will naturally be interested to know the points of similarity and difference between the origins of the same movement of the Spirit in North America. As there is no comprehensive study of the Charismatic movement in North America,[1] it is necessary to outline the major features in its gestation and development before making detailed comparisons with the corresponding period in Great Britain.

As in Britain, there were many strands of pentecostal blessing outside the Pentecostal churches before the Christian public became aware of the genesis of any new movement of the Spirit. The making public of pentecostal phenomena within a historic church tradition in the USA first occurred among the Episcopalians in 1960. This resulted from two factors: first, Dennis Bennett's announcement to his parishioners in Van Nuys, California, that he and a number of people in his parish had received 'the fullness of the Holy Spirit' accompanied by the gift of tongues; and secondly one of those parishioners, Jean Stone, notifying *Newsweek* and *Time* magazines both of which that summer published stories of Bennett's announcement and subsequent resignation.[2] Many later commentators recognize that the events at Van Nuys made visible a trend that had been gathering momentum through the 1950s, but were not able to give much detail of the precursors and pioneers.[3]

STIRRINGS BEFORE 1960

The most widely-recognized influences prior to 1960 favouring the
occurrence of baptism in the Spirit with the spiritual gifts beyond the
ranks of the Pentecostals were David du Plessis and the Full Gospel
Business Men's Fellowship International.[4] In fact, though du Plessis
sensed his call to an ecumenical witness to 'Pentecost' from the early
1950s, his itinerant ministry preaching the baptism in the Spirit to
Christians of all denominations did not begin on any significant scale
in the 1950s.[5] There was a definite acceleration of tempo in du Plessis
ecumenical outreach in 1959, but it would appear that his major
influence as a Pentecostal witness to other Christians was more a
result than a cause of the Van Nuys publicity in 1960. What is true is
that du Plessis' convictions were clearly being formed throughout
the 1950s and that his visits to church leaders and institutions beyond
Pentecostal ranks began in the 1950s and mushroomed around
1958–9.[6]

FGBMFI was undoubtedly a major influence in bringing many
people from other Christian traditions to receive the baptism in the
Spirit. Formed by the successful Californian dairy-farmer, Demos
Shakarian, in 1951, but only really developing from 1953, FGBMFI
was a lay organization initially made up of Pentecostal business men
with the aim of evangelizing and witnessing to non-Pentecostals. By
means principally of prayer breakfasts (a distinctively American
tradition) and conventions across the North American continent,
aided by their monthly magazine *Voice* (begun in 1953), the Full
Gospel businessmen reached and won over many men, including
ministers, in the mainline denominations.[7]

From a fairly early date FGBMFI established close links with
many of the more prominent healing revivalists, such as Oral
Roberts, William Branham, Jack Coe, Gordon Lindsay and Tommy
Hicks. Historian David Harrell has done most to highlight the influence of these healing evangelists on the rise of the Charismatic
movement in the United States.[8] These independent preachers often
became unofficial promoters of new FGBMFI chapters during their
healing campaigns.[9]

Neither FGBMFI nor the healing evangelists made much effort to
integrate into Pentecostal churches those baptized in the Spirit
through their influence. In this indirect sense they contributed to the
rise of Spirit-baptized Christians in non-Pentecostal denominations

and assemblies. However, they cannot be said to have had any vision of the historic churches being renewed in the Spirit.

Probably the person who contributed most to the spread of baptism in the Spirit with spiritual gifts among those firmly committed to their own church tradition was Agnes Sanford. Wife of an Episcopalian priest, Edgar Sanford (died 1960), her interest in divine healing had been aroused initially when she was healed of mental depression through the laying on of hands in prayer. When her first book on this subject, *The Healing Light*, was published in 1947, Agnes Sanford already had many years of experience in the ministry of healing. Around 1953 or 1954, she experienced the strong inner working of the Spirit when two friends laid hands on her to receive the Holy Spirit and shortly afterwards she received the gift of tongues.[10]

From this time on, Agnes Sanford frequently spoke in private, to those to whom she was ministering, of the baptism in the Spirit and the spiritual gifts.[11] The scope for such ministry was further increased when in 1955 the Sanfords began what they called a 'School of Pastoral Care', week-long conferences for those involved in healing (ministers, doctors and nurses) where they spoke of 'the power of the Holy Spirit working in men and women to the healing of their physical, mental, social and spiritual ills'.[12]

Agnes Sanford was also active in the Order of St. Luke, a organization promoting the healing ministry in the Christian churches.[13] Many clergy subsequently active in the Charismatic movement received their introduction to the healing power of the Spirit of God during OSL conferences or through OSL contacts. Of these, one of the first to be baptized in the Spirit was Richard Winkler, rector of Trinity Episcopal Church, Wheaton, Illinois. Winkler was baptized in the Spirit on 26 April, 1956, at a meeting in Chicago conducted by the Assemblies of God evangelist, John Stiles,[14] and not long after began what was almost certainly the first pentecostal-type prayer-meeting among Episcopalians in the United States.[15] Another Episcopalian priest-member of OSL baptized in the Spirit not long after Winkler was Paul Kratzig of Texas.[16] These developments among Episcopalians were a good two years before the beginnings of charismatic activity in the parish of the Holy Spirit, Monterey Park, California, through which Dennis Bennett came to know of the possibility of baptism in the Spirit.[17]

Another mainline denominational pastor to come into the pentecostal experience in the mid-1950s was James Brown, pastor of

Upper Octorara Presbyterian church in Parkesburg, Pennsylvania.[18] Though his initial experience was not linked with the Full Gospel businessmen, Brown subsequently made contact with FGBMFI and became one of their regular speakers in the late 1950s and early 1960s. Brown also began a pentecostal-type prayer-meeting in his church, which became a point of attraction for many enquirers as the movement spread and became better-known.

While Winkler and Brown developed what would later be known as charismatic prayer-meetings in traditional Protestant surroundings, two other Protestant ministers baptized in the Spirit exercised a more itinerant ministry and influence. These were Harald Bredesen, trained as a Lutheran, but then inducted as minister of a Dutch Reformed church in Mount Vernon, New York, and Tommy Tyson, a United Methodist minister from North Carolina. Bredesen's baptism in the Spirit was as far back as the mid-1940s at a Pentecostal camp meeting following a visit to Glad Tidings Tabernacle in New York City.[19] Tyson was baptized in the Spirit around 1951 when without an knowledge of spiritual gifts he responded during a talk on Acts 2 to an inward voice saying 'Well, do you want a ministry or do you want to be baptized with the Holy Ghost?'[20]

Another instrument or at least an occasion for the spreading of pentecostal blessings among non-Pentecostal Christians was Camps Farthest Out (CFO), founded by Glenn Clark in the 1930s. The leading figures in CFO all taught and practised divine healing through prayer,[21] and some clearly knew God's word in prophecy well before the rise of the Charismatic movement.[22] However, these gifts were experienced and understood, not in the framework of baptism in the Spirit, but in the context of creativity of spirit helping Christians to a fuller realization of their human potential. CFO were thus week-long camps for the fuller flowering of human talents and gifts in a Christian environment of faith, with much scope being given to those leading the particular gathering. In fact, various Spirit-baptized speakers, such as Bredesen, became regular CFO leaders[23] and several witnesses speak of receiving the baptism in the Spirit while at CFO camps.[24]

Another instrument for the spread of pentecostal blessing outside the Pentecostal churches was the evangelical monthly *Christian Life*. Early in the 1950s, its editor, Robert Walker, was baptized in the Spirit. He soon began to make place in the columns of his magazine for items about a fuller life in the Spirit, though never using explicitly Pentecostal terminology. An article by Myrddin Lewis in 1953 entitled 'Are we Missing Something?' with implicit references to a pentecostal experience sparked a considerable correspondence and response.[25] Several figures prominent in American Evangelicalism responded to Lewis' challenge.[26] From 1959, *Christian Life* regularly featured articles on congregations experiencing awakening through a pentecostal-type outpouring of the Spirit.[27] Another influential figure whose name occurs quite frequently in *Christian Life* is Henrietta C. Mears, from Hollywood Presbyterian Church, California who was a well-known Christian educator and popularizer of the Scriptures. Mears' biographers give indications that she received the baptism in the Spirit around this time.[28]

IN THE WAKE OF VAN NUYS

What then changed with the developments at Van Nuys, California involving the resignation of Dennis Bennett? As has been mentioned, this was the first 'neo-Pentecostal'[29] occurrence to receive national media attention. In April 1960, Bennett made a public announcement concerning his baptism in the Spirit and his speaking in tongues, followed by his resignation as rector; almost immediately the Episcopal bishop of Los Angeles issued a pastoral letter banning speaking in tongues at any events under official church auspices.[30] The national publicity in *Newsweek* and *Time* followed some months later in mid-summer. Mention in the church press only followed the item in *Newsweek*[31]. Not only was Bennett's the first public announcement by an ordained minister of a historic church tradition that he spoke in tongues, but it was also the first clear statement that this experience of the Holy Spirit was wholly compatible with the church heritage, and that the recipient intended to remain in that church tradition.[32]

However, had Jean Stone, wife of a Lockheed executive, not been one of Bennett's parishioners, it is doubtful whether his gesture would have had much significance. Not only did Stone contact the Los Angeles offices of *Time* and *Newsweek*,[33] but she was the prime mover in the launching of the Blessed Trinity Society in 1961. Initially formed as a prayer society, BTS soon became the first agency promoting the baptism in the Holy Spirit with the spiritual gifts in a context of commitment to historic church traditions. BTS influence was principally among Episcopalians, only two of its seven directors not belonging to the Episcopal Church (Harald Bredesen and David du Plessis). They published several pamphlets,[34] and *Trinity* magazine from 1961 to 1966, under the editorship of Jean Stone.

With the advent of BTS and *Trinity* magazine, there was now a alternative and potential rival to FGBMFI and *Voice*. Both were promoting baptism in the Spirit and the spiritual gifts, both gave prominence to witness and testimony-type articles, both were run by lay Christians and both were centred in California. However, their methods were different. *Trinity* was more glossy, hinting at more culture, whereas *Voice* was more snappy, pocket-sized and direct. Also their attitudes to the churches were different, though both were distinctively lay and populist (theology was never a major preoccupation of *Trinity* despite the Episcopalian influence). While *Voice* included both Pentecostal and charismatic items, *Trinity* made no place for merely Pentecostal news, though it did nothing to repudiate Pentecostal terminology and connections.[35] Moreover, while both were based in California, FGBMFI and *Voice* achieved a more national distribution than BTS and *Trinity*. This was primarily because FGBMFI established local branches (known as chapters) and held regular conventions in widely-dispersed locations, whereas BTS did not establish local units. The events sponsored by Jean Stone (generally with Harald Bredesen) did not extend far beyond the Rockies.[36]

Stone and Bredesen also have the distinction of coining the term 'charismatic' to denote the new movement of the Holy Spirit within the older churches. At the end of an article 'Return to the Charismata' published at Pentecost 1962, Bredesen says that we call this movement 'the charismatic revival'.[37] The following year saw a major escalation in Christian press comment on the new movement, almost invariably treating it as a glossolalia phenomenon,[38] and among the more significant articles was one by the editor of the evangelical monthly *Eternity*, Russell Hitt, entitled 'The New Pentecostalism'.[39] Hitt wrote:

> One of the most amazing religious movements of the day is the sudden sweep of Pentecostalism into the main line denominations of U.S. Protestantism. Not following the patterns of the older Pente-costalism, it might better be described as neo-Pentecostalism.[40]

This first adoption of the phrase 'neo-Pentecostalism' forced upon those who did not like it the need to adopt an alternative label. So, in a response to Hitt, published partially in *Eternity* and fully in *Trinity*,[41] Stone and Bredesen stated:

> First, the title, 'Neo-Pentecostalism' could be misleading. We have made too many mistakes of our own to bear the added onus of mistakes we have not made, but thanks to the help of our Pentecostal friends have avoided. We prefer the title, 'The charismatic renewal in the historic churches'.[42]

It appears from the subsequent explanation that the designation 'charismatic renewal' is preferred because the movement is seen as restoring the full range of the gifts of the Spirit and not simply as a tongues' movement.[43] This setting-aside of Pentecostal terminology is not surprising. when it is remembered that the early literature from BTS, in contrast to *Voice*, makes hardly any reference to Pentecostal antecedents.

After the publication of this response, 'charismatic renewal' is evidently the accepted terminology for the leaders of BTS. The only mentions of 'charismatic revival' in *Trinity* from that time occur in quotations from other journals. At this stage, there is no considered discussion of the term 'renewal', which seems to have been more instinctive for Episcopalians than the more evangelical term 'revival'.

These changes in designation soon acquired *droit de cité*, particularly through their adoption by FGBMFI and *Voice*.[44] By contrast the term 'neo-Pentecostalism' is rarely used in popular parlance and is most used in more academic and objective studies of the new movement.[45]

Among the factors making this movement of the Holy Spirit much more widely known was the book *They Speak with Other Tongues* by John L. Sherrill, published in 1964. Sherrill, an Episcopalian and a journalist, began to investigate the phenomenon of speaking in tongues. What began as a journalistic investigation became a personal discovery. The book possessed the winning combination of an exciting personal awakening and the telling of the story of the wider movement through interviews, stirring and gathering the thoughts and memories of many participants. Almost all those who played a significant part in the early years of the Charismatic movement in the USA find some mention in Sherrill's book.[46] *They Speak with Other*

Tongues with its instant popularity conveyed to participants both a stronger sense of the unity and the scope of the new movement and helped to commend and lead others into the baptism in the Spirit. It was also important for its holding together of the Pentecostal and neo-Pentecostal waves, within one overall vision.

OPPOSITION WITHIN THE CHURCHES

The first official opposition by any church authority to the new movement was the reaction of Bishop Bloy of Los Angeles to the outbreak at Van Nuys. However, this achieved minimal publicity. In general, the reaction of Episcopalians to these new developments was remarkably open, as is witnessed by the coverage in the Episcopalian weekly *The Living Church*,[47] and the less hasty response of the Bishop of Chicago to the group under Winkler in Wheaton, Illinois.[48] The later furore over glossolalia in San Francisco seems to have owed more to the strong feelings of Bishop Pike than to any widely-felt antipathy among Episcopalians.[49]

One place where a charismatic outbreak occasioned some controversy was in the Anglican diocese of Caledonia in British Columbia, Canada. An Anglican Franciscan priest from that diocese, Norman Scovell, was baptized in the Spirit during a visit to Van Nuys in 1961,[50] and word of his experience led to a group of clergy from several denominations meeting in the Cathedral in Prince Rupert. One of those who received the baptism in the Spirit on that occasion was George Pattison, the Anglican[51] Dean. Opposition to Pattison developed over the following months so that late in 1962 he offered his resignation.[52]

However, a more general unease about the spread of pentecostal phenomena in their ranks seems to have characterized American Lutherans. While some Lutherans from Bethany Church in Minneapolis were baptized in the Spirit in the 1950s,[53] the first Lutheran pastor to become publicly identified as a leader in the new movement was Larry Christenson of San Pedro, California. Christenson had been active in OSL, though his immediate stimulus to seek the baptism in the Spirit was from a Pentecostal.[54] Baptized in the Spirit in August 1961, Christenson at this point had had no contact with BTS nearby. David du Plessis, aware of the suddenness with which Bennett had told his congregation and then resigned at Van Nuys, advised Christenson to tell his wife and church superintendent but to be careful about any public announcement to the whole congregation. So it was not until Pentecost 1962 that Christenson told the people. This led to a year of tension culminating in the parish council asking Christenson to resign. At the end of May 1963, he did so, but a congregational meeting two weeks later refused, by a clear majority, to accept his resignation.[55] Several of the dissenting members left over the following months, but after that Trinity Lutheran Church in San Pedro experienced no marked tension over being both Lutheran and (partially) charismatic. Even more than any Episcopalians until this time, Christenson sought explicitly to demonstrate the compatibility of Charismatic renewal with confessional convictions.

More endemic tension among Lutherans concerning anything pentecostal surfaced in connection with the ministry of Herbert Mjorud, an official evangelist in the American Lutheran Church. Mjorud was baptized in the Spirit in early 1962 following a visit to Dennis Bennett's church in Seattle,[56] and he immediately became an ardent apostle for the pentecostal baptism in the Spirit. Through his preaching, several pastors later prominent in Lutheran charismatic renewal received this pentecostal blessing.[57]

As Mjorud was preaching a distinctively Pentecostal message while conducting missions for Lutheran congregations, it was not surprising that he aroused the opposition of many pastors. Their complaints led the ALC to appoint a Committee on Spiritual Gifts to deal specifically with healing and glossolalia. When Mjorud's appointment as church evangelist came up for renewal in June 1963, the church authorities were clearly unhappy with his ministry and reappointed him only for one year with the requirement that he 'cease promoting glossolalia in the church'.[58] Soon after, the Committee on Spiritual Gifts reported to the ALC Commission on Evangelism, recognizing that speaking in tongues was a spiritual gift attested in Scripture, but was not there seen as normative for salvation.

Their report, made available for pastors and people, was a call for tolerance, restraint and sound instruction. Promotion of glossolalia was however deplored, and specific forms of promotion (envisaging Mjorud's ministry) were stated to be unacceptable.[59] In July 1964, the Council of the ALC decided not to renew Mjorud's appointment because he had continued to promote glossolalia in his evangelistic work.[60]

However, the suspicion of charismatic enthusiasm among Lutheran authorities does seem to have represented something characteristic of their tradition rather than personal and transient factors. Consistently, Lutheran charismatics have had to defend themselves against charges of being *schwärmerei*, the term used in the 16th century to stigmatize those appealing to experience of the Spirit against the gospel as preached by Luther.[61] While the more moderate ALC averted further tensions over charismatic pastors by their official statements, trouble was soon stirring among the more conservative Missouri Synod Lutherans. The first case of outright conflict occurred in 1965 when the Rev. C. Donald Pfotenhauer, pastor of Way of the Cross church in Minneapolis, Minnesota, was suspended by his district president because of his 'wrong concept with regard to the work of the Holy Spirit'.[62] Unlike previous cases of controversy between charismatics and church authorities, the focal point of contention was not glossolalia. The stated issue was whether God can and does speak to believers today other than through the text of the Scriptures. This question arose in acute form because at a full congregational meeting with local church officials present, a woman member spoke a prophetic word:

> What will you gain with your pointing fingers? . . . Did you come with kindness or did you come with deliberate malice? Search your hearts at this moment and say, 'Am I here for the good of Christ and his Word, or am I here to destroy that which I do not understand?'[63]

While objection was made to the speaker having usurped male prerogatives and having passed judgement on district officials, the more theological issue of how God speaks today was identified as crucial. The Lutheran Church – Missouri Synod then and subsequently came down squarely for a rejection of any contemporary words from the Lord. An official Synod statement stated:

> Lutherans have always believed that through the Word and sacraments the Holy Spirit bestows on the believer all the blessings and spiritual gifts that are ours in Christ. The view that God gives His Holy Spint apart from the 'external word' is rejected by the Confessions as 'enthusiasm'.[64]

Another tradition in which some opposition to the charismatic movement was experienced was the Presbyterian. No major difficulties seem to have arisen in the late 1950s or the early 1960s in connection with James Brown in Pennsylvania or with other Presbyterian pastors baptized in the Spirit.[65] California again was particularly affected, and San Francisco saw the first FGBMFI chapter sponsored by a mainline church congregation.[66] It was only in 1964 that, at the instigation of the Presbytery of Central Texas, the Presbyterian Church in the United States set up a committee to study the phenomenon of glossolalia.[67] Although the subsequent development of this initiative goes beyond the period covered in this study, it is clear that some Presbyterian ministers were under suspicion and investigation for their charismatic involvement by the end of 1965, for one of the stated reasons for establishing the Charismatic Communion for Spirit-filled Presbyterian pastors the following year was to help ministers suffering such tensions.[68]

COMPARISONS WITH GREAT BRITAIN

Some similarities in the patterns described are immediately evident. In both nations, there was an extension of pentecostal blessing and phenomena beyond the Pentecostal churches before there was a clear combination of commitment to baptism in the Spirit and to denominational or confessional traditions. That is also to say that baptism in the Spirit was being received quite extensively outside the Pentecostal churches, before any reflective theory of renewal of the historic churches through pentecostal blessing was formulated.

Prominent among the factors preparing Christians for this baptism in the Spirit is the rediscovery of the ministry of healing both in Britain and in the United States. The combined influence of Agnes Sanford and the network of OSL (although OSL was never in favour, and later came out against it) led many who had found the power of God in healing on to baptism in the Spirit and the full range of spiritual gifts.

However, the influence of associations of prayer for revival so evident in Britain does not have an obvious parallel in North America. No doubt this reflects a somewhat more optimistic evaluation of spiritual prospects among Americans than among Britons. In both cases, the influence of Pentecostals is evident, though in the United States there were influential networks of lay or independent Pentecostals not aligned with Pentecostal denominations (both FGBMFI and the healing evangelists). Both these fostered effective pentecos-

tal evangelism without suggesting affiliation with Pentecostal
churches. For this reason, the influence of Pentecostals on the spread
of the Charismatic movement has been more acknowledged in
America than in Britain.

The healing evangelists were no doubt more instrumental in the
genesis of the Charismatic renewal in the USA than has been commonly recognized,[69] and this was on a much larger scale than their
counterparts such as Peter Scothern in Britain. This not only reflects
the traditions of enormous tent-meetings in America, but also the
ready availability of more ample facilities on the North American
continent.

The contribution from those Camps Farthest Out which were led
by Spirit-filled teachers in the USA does not have an exact parallel
in Britain. Though there were occasional CFOs in Britain, these were
more residential conferences and lacked the camp associations of
residential conferences away from people's home environment as a
common and congenial setting for exposure to and reception of this
work of the Holy Spirit. The British parallels to CFO would then be
EDH Conventions and LHM Healing Advances. At such gatherings
individual Christians feel free to face the new challenge, without
predetermining their stance upon their return to their home church.

What has virtually no parallel in North America is the incidence
and influence of Plymouth Brethren being baptized in the Spirit. In
fact, the only country besides the United Kingdom where the Brethren were a significant factor appears to have been New Zealand.[70]
While there were some people in the USA seeing the recovery of the
charismata in terms of the restoration of the New Testament Church
(as for example John Myers in California with his quarterly *A Voice
in the Wilderness*), the non-denominationalism among some charismatics in the States was notably less doctrinal and more pragmatic
than its counterpart in Britain. That is to say, there was a good deal
of non-denominationalism but very little anti-denominationalism in
the movement in North America.

As in Britain, there were those like Ron and June Armstrong in
Canada who came into this pentecostal experience without direct
contact with Pentecostals or charismatics and who only after this
event learned of the existence of a Charismatic movement in the
churches. Ron, an Anglican priest later prominent in the movement
in Ontario, received the baptism in the Spirit during a leave of
absence from his parish in order to counter a dissatisfaction with his

ministry through an extended period of personal prayer and Bible study.[71]

A number of obvious contrasts between American and British origins and early development reflect the strongly contrasting geography of the two countries. The regular coming together of leaders was more difficult in the USA than in Britain owing to the sheer size of the country.[72] For the same reason the movement in the States appeared more amorphous and less cohesive than its counterpart in the British Isles.

In both countries. the movement spread throughout the Protestant denominations. If the spread is wider in the United States, that is simply due to the greater number of churches in America, a result both of ethnic diversity and of native enterprise. In particular, the strong presence of Lutheranism in some parts of the United States added a dimension not found in the movement in Britain. The Lutheran sense of confessional identity and loyalty led both to some of the tensions already described and to a stronger impulse to reflect theologically on the pentecostal experience in the light of Scripture.

Another difference from Britain was the more liturgical and sacramental emphasis of the majority of Episcopalian priests baptized in the Spirit. This combination was thus present from an earlier stage of the American movement than in Britain. Further, in the USA there were isolated cases of Roman Catholics being baptized in the Spirit by the end of 1965,[73] before the corporate beginnings of the Catholic Charismatic movement in early 1967.

Whereas in Britain, there were no statements from either local or national church leaders or bodies on the emerging movement at this time (the first were in fact in 1973),[74] there were statements by individual Episcopalian dioceses and by several national bodies in the USA between 1962 and 1965.[75] The significance of this contrast is not immediately easy to discern. It does not mean that there was no opposition to the Charismatic movement in Britain.[76] It seems likely that there was less controversy within parishes and local congregations in Britain than in North America, but the Americans have recourse to legal proceedings far more readily than the British. It may also reflect a somewhat wider impact of the new movement on the North American continent.

Overall the process whereby a relatively disparate set of local outbreaks and individual blessings came to be perceived and experienced as one nation-wide and indeed worldwide move of the Spirit of God was less clear-cut than in Britain. Again geography was a major reason. But so was the absence of any one organ or platform associating all the major figures and centres in the movement. While there were obvious differences of theology and convictions between participants in Britain, there were times when they came together in the early years, and there were publications which brought together contributions from a range of sources. This was not true to the same degree in the United States. However, although the overall unity of the movement was to that extent less visible in America, it was still evident to any serious observer such as John Sherrill that the basic characteristics of the movement were the same, whether one was faced by liturgical Episcopalians or folk closer to the heady atmosphere of the healing revivalists.

BASIC SIGNIFICANCE

When, however, questions are asked concerning the essential meaning and significance of the Charismatic movement in the British Isles and on the North American continent, what is immediately striking is the basic similarity in the first-hand witnesses. What was happening to people on both sides of the Atlantic was evidently the same. Though limitations of space prevent this supplement from including the details of participants' personal testimonies from the USA and Canada, there is abundant evidence of the same characteristics associated with the baptism in the Spirit: a new level of awareness of the persons of the Trinity, a new level of knowledge and love for Jesus Christ, a new capacity to praise God and to hear his voice, and a new power in people's lives, both for their own transformation and in ministry to others.[77] That the same work of the Spirit of God was happening across oceans and national boundaries was evidenced by the mutual acceptance of preachers and witnesses crossing the Atlantic in both directions[78] and by the regular inclusion of material from the other side in the first charismaticperiodicals and publications.[79]

As in Britain, American charismatics were just as adamant that this was not simply a 'tongues movement', but that its heart lay in the baptism in the Spirit.[80] Here too can be found what at first sight is paradoxical: that the charismata re regarded as intrinsic to this work of God, but 'the baptism' is its distinguishing inner reality. The

American data confirm the judgement that the grace of God in baptism in the Spirit concerns the basic realities of the Christian life.

The way sin which this movement of the Spirit arose in North America are just as diverse and humanly unco-ordinated as in Britain. Indeed, the denominational range affected was wider in America, reflecting the greater diversity of American churches. The indications that this movement's unplanned and diverse origins manifest its providential character apply with equal force in America as in Britain. There too its unprecedented denominational spread is a sign of its extraordinary ecumenical potential. The differences between the movement across the Atlantic thus concern more the incidental differences in the receiving agents and milieux, rather than any significant variation in the gift being bestowed.

Appendix I

Letters of Donald Gee to Benedict Heron

19th June 1960

Dear Mr. Heron,

It has given me very great joy to receive your kind letter of June 11. I have often thought of our afternoon of fellowship last winter, and have been touched at the thought of you going to the trouble to make the long journey to Henley especially to make this possible.

I am more convinced than ever of the essential unity of those truly in Christ Jesus, even when members of communions as utterly diverse as Roman Catholic and Pentecostal. This is really an amazing thing, perhaps more of a 'miracle' than some of the things we mutually call 'miracles'.

You have enriched my own spiritual life very much by this gesture of love and fellowship. In the Pentecostal Movement I am trying to inculcate a bigger vision in many ways, and I am sure that the atmosphere is changing in that direction. In both the Roman Catholic and the Pentecostal Groups there are extremists which we must both deplore. I fear there are some among us who almost equate 'Protestant' with 'Christian', and there is almost as much ignorance and prejudice where the Orthodox Churches are concerned. It is my privilege to teach Church History to the students here, and so I have some golden opportunities to inculcate a more balanced view. But my need of carefulness has to be as great as your own, and I know you will treat this letter with the same great discretion that I accord to yours.

I read the pamphlet about the Abbé Paul Couturier that you kindly left with me with great appreciation. Such are true Saints of THE CHURCH.

I would like you to attend a really good Penetecostal meeting, but I fear there are many that I hesitate to commend to such as yourself because of their weaknesses. And yet the Holy Spirit is greater than our fears, and if He leads you I am sure all will be well. I love our *good* Pentecostal meetings when the manifestations of the Holy Spirit are in evidence, and sometimes to me they seem like a page taken out of the N.T. There are some Pentecostal meetings in Belgium, but I have not visited them personally. Let us believe that the Lord will open this for you in His Own best time and way.

There is a constant temptation to imitation when we profess belief in the present miraculous. Some sincerely confuse the psychic. Also I think we need to be careful in our definitions. Among Pentecostals the term 'supernatural' is used much too loosely. In many it just means the spectacular. We need to see the grace and power of God at work in ways not so immediately spectacular. How good if and when we can mutually come together to talk about these things. For the glory of God.

I hope you will feel free to keep in touch with me, and please accept again my assurance of how deeply I value this fellowship in Christ;

Very sincerely yours,
DONALD GEE

January 5, 1961.

Dear Brother in Christ,

Your card of greetings for the New Year, and your expression of best wishes and prayers, gave me deep joy.

I assure you that this fellowship across the gap of our denominations does touch my heart. I am sure it pleases our one Lord and is in His will for us both.

May I most sincerely reciprocate your greetings and good wishes for the New Year, and at all times.

I send no formal cards, and so I am sure you will accept this little letter.

Very sincerely yours,
DONALD GEE Principal.

October 9, 1963

Benedict M. Heron,
Monastère du Christ Roi,
Gelrode, Belgium.

Dear Brother in Christ,

It has been very kind of you to write to me, and enclose a copy of your short article on Christian Unity and Love. One cannot but endorse such scriptural sentiments and suggestions for prayer. I do not think many of our Pentecostal people would agree with Point 10, indeed I fear that many do not regard Roman Catholics as being saved. I am glad that others take a better view.

Unity as between individuals (and I am happy that we can include ourselves) seems a blessed present possibility and I am sure should be cherished by all possible means.

I am distressed that the usual official Protestant attitude in so many quarters seems to be that anything said by Catholics is suspect, and is not to be taken at its face value. All is regarded as propaganda to put Protestants off their guard and so ease the road for their return to Rome, rather than a brotherly conversation as equals in seeking truth. To build up confidence will be a long, hard road, and at present the end is not at all in sight. Personal and private contacts are the only way. One of the main objections by the Pentecostal Churches to the W.C.C. is that it is a subtle tendency Romewards.

Meanwhile I have received a most interesting and enthusiastic letter from my friend David J. du Plessis from ROME, where he was served with a special ticket that gave him a seat near the throne of St. Peter for the great opening of the 2nd. assembly of the 2nd Vatican Ecumenical Council. He was evidently deeply impressed and he personally believes that the Holy Spirit is moving among both Catholics and Protestants for what he calls a spiritual "Springtime". I expect him to see me in London next week, when I have no doubt he will have more to say.

With my kind wishes in Christ,
Yours sincerely,
DONALD GEE
Kenley.

August 24, 1964.

Benedict M. Heron,
Monastère du Christ Roi,
Gelrode – Poste Betekom,
Belgium.

Dear Brother Heron,

Just now I am in the midst of the dislocation of my office at Kenley consequent on moving, but I do want to send this line of appreciation for the E.C.Q. containing your article on the Abbé Couturier, which I have read with deep interest. He was surely a saint of God.

It still seems almost impossible to make any progress in Christian unity except on the lines of correspondence such as ours. For that reason I wish to cherish it and thank you for writing. Fundamentally the unity of the Spirit is personal and not denominational.

There is so much prejudice and fear among the circles with which I mix where Rome is concerned that everything is viewed with suspicion. Any new attitude is not believed. Of course as a Protestant I have my own difficulties of a theological nature. Recently I was in France for the holiday connected with the assumption of the Virgin Mary. It is difficult for me to understand how intelligent people can accept such a dogma. But there it is!

I am retiring from my position as Principal of Kenley on the 31st. inst. after thirteen very happy and full years. I am going into a small maisonette at Lindfield, Sussex after marrying again to a Pentecostal widow of Edinburgh. But dreams of a quiet life are already filled with many calls for spoken and written service. God's will be done. I am unworthy of all the kind wishes now expressed. My address after Oct. 4 will be 49b Pelham Road, Lindfield.

With kind wishes in Christ, our Redeemer,
DONALD GEE

Appendix II

Correspondence recalling Alexander Boddy and the Anglican element in the origins of the Pentecostal movement in Britain

Letter from Revd. A. F. Kitching[1] **to Revd. Michael Harper**

Combe Down Vicarage
Bath

29.10.63.

Dear Sir,

I was much interested in your article in the CEN of Oct. 25th. But I must find fault with the title!! This is not exactly a "new thing". Before World War II was in touch with this movement. I stayed for a few days with the vicar of an Anglican Church in Sunderland by name Boddy who was a leader among the local Pentecostalists. I knew his son very well and he himself was an excellent man with no lack of balance or sensationalism. At their meetings I heard 'speaking in tongues' followed by interpretation by someone else; I believe they had gifts of healing too. I lost touch with the family during the war and since then I have heard practically nothing of the movement. I look forward to your second title next week . . .

Yours faithfully,
A. F. KITCHING

Letters from Cuthbert A. Gray to Revd. Philip Smith

Rehoboth,
Helions Bumpstead,
Haverhill, Suffolk.

16.2.64

Dear brother Smith,

At last I have got your name etc. from "A of G" publishing house. I write to ask if you are in Cambridge or this district any time if you will permit me to meet you. I know your friend Pastor Knowles of Saffron Walden.

I was born in Rushmere Vicarage in 1894 and have many Anglican friends. I knew Rev. Alex A. Boddy of All Saints, Monkwearmouth, Sunderland.

I have been sending copies of your article to friends. Bro. Knowles told me you would probably be coming to Cambridge soon and perhaps to Saffron Walden.

Looking forward to meeting you in the will of God.
CUTHBERT GRAY

P.S. Of course we should be pleased if you called here. Allow me to introduce you to a friend in Cambridge. Dr. Basil Atkinson, 24 Newton Road, was with me in Wakefield Prison 1917–18.[2]

Helions Bumpstead,
Haverhill, Suffolk.

25.4.64.

Dear brother Philip,

Greetings from your brother – Cuthbert Gray. You remember I told you I knew Rev. A. A. Boddy. He did not resign his living as a C of E clergyman neither did he as far as I am aware discontinue baptizing infants. Yet God was pleased to bless this man and make his preaching and writings a blessing to very many. I was one. I wish I possessed all his Roker tracts . . .

Dominus Jesus Christus cum spiritu tuo,
CUTHBERT GRAY

Appendix III

The Ecclesiology of the Plymouth Brethren as background to the stream of the Charismatic movement associated with D. G. Lillie and A. Wallis.

This appendix fills out with more detail the assertions made in the main text of this study[1] concerning the influence of Brethren convictions regarding the church on the stream in British charismatic origins manifested in the Devon conferences at Exmouth (1958), Belstone (1961) and Mamhead Park (1962) and associated with the leadership of David G. Lillie and Arthur Wallis. The fact that these men, along with many other Christians,[2] were repudiated by the Brethren following their baptism in the Spirit does not reduce in any way the nature and life of the church, which they brought with them from Brethren assemblies into the new fellowships that they formed.

To speak of 'Brethren ecclesiology' in this way is not to imply the existence of one clear-cut theology of the church among all the Brethren. Rather, it is to refer to a cluster of characteristics that typify the Brethren, whether among the branch, known as the Exclusives and stemming from John Nelson Darby, or those (now the majority) known as the Open Brethren who trace their lineage back to such men as George Muller, Henry Craik, Anthony Norris Groves and Robert Chapman. In particular, it is to uncover the continuing impact of the Brethren movement's original inspiration in the late 1820s and 1830s prior to the numerous schisms which have troubled their history.

Characteristic Brethren positions concerning the church

Right from the first gatherings of the future Brethren in Dublin in the late 1820s, there was an anguished concern about the state of the churches and the evident gap between their lifelessness and the church of power described in the Acts of the Apostles. Rowdon has written:

> The conviction was shared very widely among Brethren that the existing state of the church was not to be dismissed as of little consequence, but should be brought into the full light of day and confessed as sin.[3]

Darby called it the great duty of all Christians to recognize the ruin of the church.[4] Together with this distress over the disastrous state of the churches, there was among the first Brethren a strong drive to understand the true nature and characteristics of the church as found in the New Testament. Thus Darby's first pamphlet, published in 1828, was entitled *Considerations on the Nature and Unity of the Church of Christ*.[5]

This concern differentiated the Brethren from other evangelical Christians of the day, and led a prominent historian of the movement to describe Darby's group, the Exclusive Brethren, as 'High Churchmen of the most pronounced type'.[6]. All the Brethren of whatever branch[7] regarded it as of vital importance to understand correctly the nature of the church and to be visibly part thereof. For all Brethren likewise, the regular observance of the 'breaking of bread' was central to their worship.[8] To these more 'High Church' characteristics, which differentiated them all from other evangelicals, the Exclusive Brethren came to add an absolute separation from all who did not share their own convictions and obey their own discipline.

Whether their attitude was refusal of all fellowship with those not of their own party (the Exclusives) or one of welcoming all true believers in Jesus Christ (the Open Brethren), there was unanimity in the Brethren's rejection of the existing churches. For them 'denomination' was always a pejorative term, and they ordinarily refused to use the term 'church' when talking about what they dismissively referred to as 'denominational systems'. As with other issues, it was Darby who provided the most systematic theological argument for this rejection of the historic churches and for the corollary that all effort to renew them was in vain. Using his theory of dispensations'[9] by which he understood 'a certain state of things established by the authority of God, during a given period,'[10] Darby maintained that the dispensation of the church was finished. It was pointless then to try to restore what God had doomed to destruction for the sin of apostasy.

The Brethren originally rejected both 'special ministry' and 'special membership', though both principles have become somewhat mitigated over the course of time. By 'special ministry' they meant all forms of ordination which set believers apart for ministry and thereby created a division between an ordained clergy and an unordained laity. They energetically repudiated the prevailing model of the 'one-man' pastorate with one minister, who alone is expected to fulfil every form of ministry. In this, they regarded the patterns of congregational ministry among Free Churchmen as no better and no more scriptural than the ordained priesthood of the Anglican and Roman Catholic Churches.

The Brethren emphasized instead the priesthood of all believers, within which leadership would be provided by a team of men, later acquiring the label of elders. But, as Rowdon comments, 'they disapproved of the democratic principles of church government in the major dissenting bodies'[11]. Groves, we are told, 'found many allusions in Scriptures to "many bishops in one church", but not a single reference to "one bishop over many churches" '[12]

By 'special membership' the Brethren meant membership of an assembly or a denomination that ipso *facto* meant non-membership of other bodies containing true Christian believers. This position was early expressed by Edward Cronin, who was evidently upbraided for taking communion within a range of dissenting bodies in Dublin:

> I was then informed that I could no longer be allowed to break bread with any of them without special membership with some of them. That was the starting point with me. With the strong impression on my soul, though with little intelligence about it, that the Church of God was one, and that all that believed were members of that one body, I firmly refused special membership.[13]

In this, the early Brethren took up a different position from other proponents of 'the gathered church', such as the Congregationalists and the Baptists. The difference reflects not only the Brethren's greater concern about the nature of the church, but also their awareness of the 'one body' transcending the local assembly.[14] In the original conception, Brethren coming from other assemblies had as much right to participate as the regular attenders from that locality. This rejection of 'special membership' was another expres-

sion of their abhorrence of denominationalism, which was embodied in each denomination having its own list of members.

An Ecumenical Vision among the early Brethren?

In the origins of the Brethren, there was clearly a protest both
against the worldliness and corruption of the churches, and against
the narrowness of outlook, influence and fellowship stemming
from the mutual recrimination and exclusion involved in denominational division. The rejection of 'special membership' of any one
denomination or local assembly, on the grounds that it produced
separation from other members of the one body of Christ, does in
fact represent a radical kind of ecumenical vision. Although this
dimension of the original Brethren vision became somewhat
dimmed, especially among the Exclusives, it has never been entirely forgotten and its spirit can be seen in the works of some
recent Brethren historians[15].

The most consistent critic of denominational-type narrowness
among the early Brethren was Anthony Norris Groves (1795–1853).
Though he spent most of his adult life as a missionary, first in
Baghdad and then in India, Groves was not altogether without
influence on the Brethren in the United Kingdom, particularly as
he was an assiduous correspondent and as his brother-in-law,
George Muller, was a major figure among those who became
known as 'the Open Brethren'. Groves was consistent in his opposition to all restrictions associated with denominational divisions,
other than those between the converted and the unconverted. He
was a firm proponent of the view that what unites Christian believers is infinitely more significant than what divides them. He explains in 1834:

> If my Lord should say to me, in any congregation of the almost
> unnumbered sections of the Church, 'What dost thou here?' I would
> reply, 'Seeing Thou wert here to save and sanctify, I felt it safe to be
> with Thee.' If He again said, as perhaps He may among most of us,
> 'Didst thou not see abominations here, an admixture of that which
> was unscriptural, and in some points error, at least in your judgment?'
> my answer would be, 'Yea, Lord, but I dared not call that place unholy
> where Thou wert present to bless, nor by refusing communion in
> worship reject those as unholy whom Thou hadst by Thy saving
> power evidently sanctified and set apart for Thine own.'[16]

Groves was soon protesting to Darby against the latter's increasing tendency to witness against error rather than to witness for truth, and asserted that complete separation from all that is tainted with evil also involves rejection of all that is good in such an association.[17] The uniqueness of Groves' position was the thoroughness with which he implemented the principle that no barriers to communion be placed from his own side. Let others do what they would, he would not reject fellowship and communion with any who sincerely professed the faith of Christ. As he wrote in the *Memoirs* assembled by his second wife:

> If I am hindered from intimacy with many, it is because they have, of their own will, annexed terms that I cannot comply with. I believe they do it conscientiously, though, I think, wrongly; but I feel no heart-division from them on this account. I rejoice in all the Lord's goodness has vouchsafed to them, and show my love and oneness with them, as fully and as often as I can, publicly and privately owning all the congregations of the faithful in the land, 'but none of their systems.'[18]

The influence of Brethren ecclesiology on David G. Lillie and Arthur Wallis

The dominant characteristics of Brethren thinking about the church can be seen very clearly in the programme of the Devon conferences organized by David Lillie and Arthur Wallis.[19] First of all, the title-themes of the conferences at Exmouth (1958) and Belstone (1961), respectively 'The Church of Jesus Christ: its purity, power, pattern and programme in the context of to-day', and 'The Divine Purpose in the Institution of the Church: an enquiry' accurately reflect the characteristic Brethren concern about the church, its nature and its purpose. Secondly, both Lillie and Wallis, as well as other former Brethren in the Charismatic movement, regard the historic churches as irrelevant to God's plan for the church today.[20] Here too, can be found the greater place attributed to the breaking of bread in worship than is the case among evangelicals generally.[21] The Brethren rejection of special ordained ministry and the 'one-man' pastorate is quite clearly presented,[22] as well as the firm denial that their assemblies constitute a new denomination.[23] The position adopted by Wallis on the possibility of genuine fellowships of the Spirit within, though accidentally within, historic denominations is identical with what Coad has written of the Brethren:

> The truly independent congregation is not concerned with denomi-
> nation, or with ecclesiastical politics, for it is free to recognize every
> congregation (whatever its label or church affiliation) as a fellow
> 'household church' of the one great Church of Christ, when it sees in
> that congregation the evidences of the presence of Christ.[24]

The ecumenical character of the Charismatic movement, bringing Christians into new fellowship from a wide variety of backgrounds naturally elicited in the hearts of many of these
ex-Brethren the ecumenical aspirations of Anthony Norris Groves.
What is important for a proper understanding of their contribution
and its evolution is the recognition that for all their protests against
tradition, they too represent a tradition, that which was embodied
in modern times most clearly in the Open Brethren.[25] To affirm that
the Lillie-Wallis stream in the origins of the Charismatic movement
in Britain represents a development within a tradition is neither to
dismiss completely their view of this tradition as a deeper penetration of the New Testament nor is it to deny an element of development in the impact of baptism in the Spirit and the pentecostal
experience of spiritual gifts upon this understanding of the
church.[26]

Appendix IV

Further Reflections on the Relationship between Renewal and Restoration

The language of 'Renewal' has been used by those within the Charismatic movement who see this new impulse of the Holy Spirit as a
grace for the spiritual renewal and revitalization of their own
Churches. This conviction and hope led to the widespread use of the
phrase 'Charismatic Renewal'. The language of 'Restoration' was
taken up by the groupings initially known as the 'House Church
movement' and more recently as 'the new Churches'. For them, the
word "renewal" was insufficiently radical; Charismatic Renewal
was seen by Restorationists as an attempt to put new wine into old
wineskins. For them, the outpouring of the Holy Spirit required new
wineskins, and the formation of new churches based on a new
foundation, often seen as the fivefold ministry of Ephesians 4:11.
This vision was expressed in the term 'restoration'; the planting of
new local churches with patterns of trans-local ministry and fellowship represented for them a restoration of the Church according to
the pattern of the New Testament.

These two concepts of Renewal and Restoration have thus been
in some tension with one another. The tension has focused on the
'Stay In – Come Out' issue and the status of the denominations in
God's sight. The issue was never whether members of mainline
denominations could be vehicles of the Holy Spirit; that was always
recognized even by the most ardent opponents of 'denominationalism'. Neither was the issue whether the Holy Spirit could be at work
corporately in denominational congregations; house church leaders
generally recognized that the Holy Spirit could renew and reshape
a local denominational assembly, though they anticipated difficulties. The focal point of difference was the theology of the Church,
and whether or not the denominations are renewable as denominations. The Renewalists said Yes, the Restorationists said No. Where

local denominational congregations accepted the work of the Holy Spirit corporately as a congregation, the possibility of the realization of God's purpose for them in the eyes of the Restorationists depended on their ability and willingness to sit light to the requirements of the denomination.

Everybody tends to read history through their own particular optic. Accounts of the origins of this movement of the Spirit seen in terms of Charismatic Renewal tend to focus on those strands that were committed to the vision of the baptism in the Spirit contributing to the renewal of the historic Churches. These accounts would typically emphasize the role of Dennis Bennett in the United States and of Michael Harper in Great Britain. The accounts of the Restorationist currents tend to pick out the Lillie-Wallis strand in Britain and the Fort Lauderdale grouping in the United States. Sometimes, especially in the tensions of the mid- to late 1970s, the impression was given that Renewal and Restoration were really quite separate currents from the beginning.

The data provided in this book indicate that there was one overall movement of the Holy Spirit, commonly known as the Charismatic movement, within which there were a range of theological positions, including a number of conflicting theologies of the Church. The basis of there being one movement despite the different theologies is that the movement was constituted by the occurrence of an event, that of baptism in the Spirit, that in an important sense transcended the theologies of the recipients. Thus, as was stated in Chapter Twenty-Four, the charismatic movement has been primarily an event-movement rather than an ideas-movement. It was the recognition that fundamentally the same event had occurred to the others that made possible the fellowship and association of those with differing theological and doctrinal convictions, for example Arthur Wallis's long association with the Fountain Trust.

If the identity of the Charismatic movement is a consequence of the foundational event of baptism in the Spirit, why should it be considered as separate and distinct from the Pentecostal movement that is likewise grounded in the same spiritual event? My argument does require the affirmation of a fundamental affinity between the Pentecostal and the Charismatic movements. In my judgment, the only reason for affirming a distinction between the two lies in the fact that Pentecostalism had by the 1950s largely lost its character as an event-based movement of the Spirit, and had become a cluster of new denominations. As soon as becoming a Pentecostal meant more than being baptized in the Spirit, with signs following, whether it meant joining a Pentecostal denomination or subscribing to a particular doctrinal position, the way was open for a new movement to emerge, participation in which was constituted simply by being baptized in the Spirit. Seen from this angle, the Charismatic movement represents a recurrence of the Pentecostal experience without the additions of Pentecostalism.

The view that the Charismatic movement, as the Pentecostal movement before it, is an 'event-movement' rather than an ideas-movement does not mean that the event of baptism in the Spirit is devoid of any theological content, a kind of generic spiritual experience into which any doctrinal content can be inserted. It is rather that the encounter with and deeper surrender to the Lordship of Jesus Christ that is the heart of baptism in the Spirit both presupposes the preaching of a basic message about Jesus and transcends particular formulations. The paradigm is the event of Pentecost and the coming of the Holy Spirit upon the nascent (Jewish) Church; here there was a framework of faith concerning Jesus as Messiah and an event that transcended prior expectations and formulations. The Church's doctrine of the Holy Spirit was to be worked out over centuries in the light of this and subsequent experience. Obviously there are differences between the origins of the Church and subsequent patterns of revival and renewal. But what is common to both is a form of sovereign intervention of God whose transcendent 'direct' character challenges previous formulations and expectations. This is particularly evident from the ecumenical character of the Charismatic movement that challenges the adequacy of formulations and expectations shaped by separated Church traditions in isolation from one another.

The data provided indicate that people from all kinds of Christian background were being baptized in the Spirit. Some brought with them highly developed frameworks of doctrine and worship, others less. The former especially were faced with the challenge of how to evaluate their received ideas and practice, especially their theology and their worship, in the light of their new Charismatic experience, which itself contained a revelatory-cognitional element. The two main frameworks that participants brought with them were represented by the terms **Renewal** and **Restoration**. The renewalists brought with them their denominational convictions; in the case of

Anglicans from a Higher Church background (and later with Roman Catholics) the framework was one of a high ecclesiology linked to sacramental-liturgical theology and practice. Many of the restorationists brought with them convictions about the importance of the Church understood in an 'anti-denominational' way that came from the Brethren. The experience of the Spirit and the discovery of the spiritual gifts, whose validity in the post-apostolic age had been denied by the Brethren, opened most of these brothers to the ministry-gifts of Ephesians 4:11.

The history of the Charismatic movement in Britain illustrates both the fundamental identity of the foundational experience of the Spirit and the tensions caused by conflicting theological and doctrinal convictions. As the emphasis is placed on the doctrines at issue, to that degree the unity and identity of the overall movement is threatened; the period between 1972 with the rise of the house church currents and the mid-1980s saw heightened tension between the advocates of Renewal and the advocates of Restoration. From the mid-1980s, this tension began to decrease, first perhaps through the influence of John Wimber, who was acceptable in both house church and Anglican circles. The fellowship and collaboration between the new churches, as they were by now being called, and Anglicans really mushroomed with the arrival of the 'Toronto blessing' in the summer of 1994. Here we have another instance of believers with different doctrinal and theological positions being brought together by a common acceptance of a new current of blessing and life. The extraordinary diffusion of the Alpha course, an Anglican product from Holy Trinity, Brompton, among a wide range of churches, has further defused the tensions between Renewal and Restoration.

In Britain, the basic unity in the Spirit of Charismatic Christians was significantly underpinned by the Charismatic Leaders Conference, an annual gathering of leaders from all backgrounds, but in which the house church contribution has been strong. The bonds of fellowship and friendship established in this Conference, possibly stronger than in other countries, may have made possible the new degree of fellowship and collaboration that came with the 'Toronto blessing'. The greater closeness between many mainline Church Charismatics and the new Church people in Britain in the mid-1990s is in this view a confirmation of the original coherence of the Charismatic movement as a common experience of the Spirit.

However, the observation that emphasis on doctrine accentuates tensions and divisions is not to be understood as a devaluation of doctrine. Just as the Charismatic event-experience is not content-free, but includes a core knowledge of Jesus Christ and his mission, so the elemental unity of the Spirit experienced by Charismatic Christians is not based on mere emotion, but on a commonly-experienced encounter with the Lord. Most Christians would agree that doctrine is essential to Christian faith. The true challenge posed by the Charismatic movement is not a jettisoning of doctrine, but the subordination of all other doctrines to the heart of the Christian revelation in Jesus Christ. The tension-level between Renewalists and Restorationists rises, not when either side believes in conscience something different from the other side, but when that difference is made more important than the central realities of Christian faith experienced together in the baptism in the Holy Spirit. This distortion occurs whenever fellowship is weakened or broken off because the others do not accept our doctrinal distinctives or when these distinctives are presented to the others as requirements for basic authenticity of Christian faith.

Notes

Abbreviations in citations refer to the bibliographies that follow.

Preface

1 A few exceptions: Brian R. Ross, *Donald Gee. In Search of a Church, Sectarian in Transition.* Martin Robinson, *Two Winds Blowing,* (on A. A. Boddy and M. Harper). The book edited by W. J. Hollenweger to be entitled *Pentecostal Research in Europe; Problems, Promises and People* with research by Sandidge, MacRobert, Gerloff, van der Laan and others, listed in the original edition of this book, was never published.
2 On the relation between the official ecumenical movement and the Charismatic Movement, see A. Bittlinger (ed)., *The Church is Charismatic. The World Council of Churches and the Charismatic Renewal,* Geneva, WCC, 1981 (in particular an overview by the General Secretary, Philip Potter).
3 See pp. 123, 141–2, in this volume. On du Plessis see the dissertation by Martin Robinson entitled *To the Ends of the Earth – the Pilgrimage of an Ecumenical Pentecostal, David J. du Plessis, 1905–87.*
4 In this volume pp.
5 See the documentation by Kilian McDonnell, *Presence, Power, Praise,* 3 vols.
6 See the discussion on D. Wilkerson, *The Cross and the Switchblade,* in this volume, pp. 145–9.

Chapter 1

1 For information on the Azusa Street revival, see *Like as of Fire* (a reprint of the earliest issues of *The Apostolic Faith,* collected by Fred T. Corum, n.p., 1981); Douglas J. Nelson *For Such a Time as This: The Story of Bishop William J. Seymour, A Search for Pentecostal-Charismatic Roots,* Frank Bartleman *Azusa Street.*

2 For the influence of Parham's visit to Zion City, see Edith L. Blumhofer 'The Christian Catholic Church and the Apostolic Faith: A Study in the 1906 Pentecostal Revival' in Cecil M. Robeck, Jr. (ed.) *Charismatic Experiences in History.*

3 Few detailed studies have been made of the early Pentecostal pioneers who remained in their churches of origin. On Revd. Alexander A. Boddy see Martin Robinson *Two Winds Blowing*; on Cecil Polhill see P. Hocken 'Pentecostal Layman' *Pneuma* 10 (1988), 116–140. No studies exist on Revd. Thomas E. Hackett (Church of Ireland), Archdeacon Robert Phair (Anglican Church of Canada). Of the continental Europeans mentioned by W. J. Hollenweger in *The Holy Spirit*, (ed. D. Kirkpatrick), 215, only the Germans K. Ecke, C. O. Voget and J. Paul belonged to the earliest period of the Pentecostal movement.

4 The information given in this chapter is based on David du Plessis (as told to Bob Slosser)*A Man Called Mr. Pentecost; The Spirit Bade Me Go,* and two interviews.

5 Wigglesworth was seventy-six at this time, not 'nearly seventy' as stated in *A Man Called Mr. Pentecost*, 2. Wigglesworth's life is treated in Stanley Frodsham *Smith Wigglesworth, Apostle of Faith.* Two other memoirs are W. Hacking *Smith Wigglesworth Remembered*, and Albert Hibbert *Smith Wigglesworth, the Secret of His Power.*

6 The version of Wigglesworth's prophecy given here is a composite message put together on the basis of several accounts of it given by David du Plessis. The oldest versions in print are: (1) a very short extract in World Pentecostal Conference 1952 Souvenir Brochure, 2; this only refers to du Plessis leaving 'Jerusalem' and going to the uttermost parts of the earth, and does not mention any revival beyond the Pentecostal Churches; (2) in 'Du Plessis Speaking . . .' in AVF July–Sept. 1964, 13; (3) in Michael Harper *As at the Beginning*, 51–2 (1965). More recent versions are in (4) *A Man Called Mr. Pentecost*, 2–3 (1977); (5) An interview with du Plessis (1982); (6) Letter from D. du Plessis to Jimmy Swaggart, Jan. 30, 1983, 2. The criteria used in assembling this composite version were: (1) what was in the earliest versions but not in the later is included as probably authentic (thus the references to Jerusalem and the uttermost parts of the earth are included from 1952 and 1965, even though they don't fit easily into the flow); (2) Ideas common to almost all versions (i.e. all except 1952) are included, but the wording chosen has eliminated unlikely terminology (e.g. the term 'renewal' used in an interview and the Swaggart letter but which was not part of du Plessis' and Wigglesworth's language in 1936 is not used); (3) Details unlikely to be the product of imagination have been retained (thus the reference to the 'fields of people' which du Plessis particularly emphasized in an interview is included, as he recalled being puzzled by this phrase, not

having then experienced enormous rallies in open-air fields and stadia. Likewise the reference to remaining faithful and humble is included, as it evidently made a particular impression on du Plessis, whose subsequent life impressed many people by its single-minded fidelity to God's call and by his refusal to build a spiritual following and monuments to his own achievements; (4) details more likely to belong to later periods are omitted, as the command to go to church leaders (in 1982 and 1983 placed in the original prophecy but in 1977 during du Plessis' convalescence in 1948–9).

7 This was at High Leigh, Herts in June 1961 (see Chapter Nine, 53).

8 It was in January 1952 that du Plessis visited the National Council of Churches office and that of the International Missionary Council in New York City. These ecumenical contacts referred du Plessis to Dr. John A. Mackay at Princeton, who opened many further ecumenical doors for his new Pentecostal friend. See Robert R. Curlee and Mary Ruth Isaac-Curlee 'Bridging the Gap: John A. Mackay, Presbyterians and the Charismatic Movement' *American Presbyterians* 72/3 (Fall 1994) 145–6.

9 M. Harper *As at the Beginning*, 52–3. The accuracy of this incident was confirmed by du Plessis. Charles S. Price was a Congregational minister from California, who was baptized in the Spirit in 1922 and exercised a pentecostal-type Full Gospel ministry, though still a Congregational minister, until his death in 1946. Both Harper (*As at the Beginning* 52) and Shakarian (*The Happiest People on Earth*, 83) tell of Price having words or visions about a future pentecostal movement of the Spirit.

10 Du Plessis shared the prophecy with Ware, an Assemblies of God pastor in Lausanne, Switzerland during the winter of 1946–7. Ware had also been the recipient of a Wigglesworth prophecy, and it was Ware's sharing of this with du Plessis that led him to share in return. Wigglesworth was instrumental in healing Ware of a speech impediment at the age of sixteen, at which time Wigglesworth prophesied concerning Ware's future.

11 In one interview, du Plessis thought he had informed Gee of the Wigglesworth prophecy at the Paris Conference of 1949. This was in reply to a direct question. Later, he stated categorically it was at Memphis, without being questioned. This seems more likely in view of their evidently warm relationship, confirmed by Gee's proposing du Plessis as secretary for the proposed PWC.

12 Both the Harper and Slosser versions include the 'after Wigglesworth's death' dictum in the 1936 conversation immediately after the major prophecy was given. Du Plessis assured the author that this occurred around 1946, shortly before Wigglesworth's death.

13 *A Man called Mr. Pentecost*, 157.

14 Ibid., 158. See criterion no. 4 in note 6 above.

15 Ibid., 158.

16 As yet there is no authoritative account of the origins of the Charismatic movement worldwide: the fullest information is probably in Peter Hocken's article on the 'Charismatic Movement' in *Dictionary of the Pentecostal and Charismatic Movements,* currently being revised for a second edition. Detailed studies of particular countries will have to precede any comprehensive survey at a world-level. One recent example treating the charismatic origins in Holland as part of the history of the Dutch Pentecostal movement is *Pinksteren in beweging* by two brothers, Cees and Paul van der Laan. The fullest account for the USA is in the doctoral dissertation of James T. Connelly (see Chapter Twenty-Five, note 1). Al Reimers' book *God's Country* has very extensive details on Canadian origins, almost entirely in witness form. A booklet, edited by Robert L. Bruce entitled *Streams of Renewal,* published by the Uniting Church Board of Mission in 1991, has much data concerning Australia, but without any overall synthesis.

17 E.g. Denis Clark (in Europe especially Scandinavia), Campbell McAlpine (in Europe and particularly in New Zealand) and Michael Harper.

18 Visitors from the USA are mentioned in Chapter Seventeen.

19 'this same blessing' (Slosser, 2) 'You will bring the message of Pentecost to all churches' (Harper, 51), 'this is going to be a Pentecostal move of the Spirit' (interview).

Chapter 2

1 Besides the interviews with Cousen, information for this chapter was also based on Jeanne Hinton 'Church with a lift' RN 22, 20–23.

2 Such prophecy was not unusual in the Apostolic Church, in which the attempt was made to integrate prophecy into the constitution of their Church. In their Constitution for the British Isles, the section on Prophets speaks of 'Prophets set apart for International work'. Among their specified responsibilities are 'Major matters connected with the work of the Missionary Committee' and among their duties 'To attend the General Council Meetings,' from *The Apostolic Church: its Principles and Practices,* 151.

3 On the Latter Rain movement, see Richard Riss 'The Latter Rain Movement of 1948' PN 4/1 (1982) 32–5, and William W. Menzies *Anointed to Serve,* 321–5.

4 This was in contrast to the customary Pentecostal tarrying for this baptism, based on Acts 1. In fact some early Pentecostals did lay on hands in prayer for baptism in the Spirit (see note 15 to Chapter Nine).

5 The atmosphere of these days is well conveyed in B. G. Evans 'Latter Rain Falls' V Dec. 1951, 5–6.

6 The first issue appeared in Dec. 1953.

7 The first issue of AVF is dated Mar. 1957.

8 P. C. Rhodes 'This New Move' AVF Oct.–Dec. 1957, 3–5.

9 Ibid., 3.

10 This utterance led Cousen's mother to produce from her handbag a piece of paper bearing an almost identical prophetic message spoken to Cousen in 1926.

11 AVF Mar. 1957, 2.

12 AVF July–Sept. 1957, 2.

13 Exmouth, 56. On the Exmouth Conference see Chapter Three, 15–17.

14 Description in each issue on page 2.

15 'Some aspect of truth is made real to a particular group of people. Birds of a feather then naturally flock together and before long the truth is crystallized into a doctrine, which in no time becomes the main point of a code of beliefs. Men have pulled in their skirts, lest they should be contaminated of course, and drawn a ring round themselves. That henceforth is the narrow way and anyone who strays from its legal interpretation is anathema. Dogmatic doctrines always divide . . .' AVF Jan.–Mar. 1959, 1–2.

16 See editorial in AVF Jan.–Mar. 1961, 1–2, 4.

17 As e.g. at Exmouth in 1958 (see Chapter Three, 15–17) and at High Leigh in 1960 (AVF Apr.–June 1961, 9). In his High Leigh talk, Cousen says the name given to this experience does not matter (AVF Jan.–Mar. 1961, 10).

18 This is treated more fully in Chapter Four, 23–4.

19 See Chapter Seventeen.

20 AVF Jan.–Mar. 1961, 1.

21 There were of course various magazines put out by independent Pentecostal preachers. For the distinction between charismatics and independent Pentecostals, see Chapter Seven, 39.

22 It was 7,000 in 1969 (RN 22, Aug.–Sept. 1969, 22) and came out quarterly until its discontinuance in 1977.

23 For further information on North, see Joyce V. Thurman *New Wineskins*. 30–34, 67–9.

24 For a comment on North's teaching on baptism in the Spirit see note 43 to Chapter Twenty-Four.

25 North's articles in AVF began with 'Heaven-Now!' in Oct.–Dec. 1962, 9–11, but were discontinued in 1966 due to a concern about North's unusual teaching on the new birth.

Chapter 3

1 Information relating to David Lillie, Arthur Wallis and the Devon Conferences is based principally upon interviews with both men, on the three Conference reports, Exmouth, Belstone and Mamhead, on A. Wallis 'Springs of Restoration' RS July–Aug. 1980, 21–4; Sept.–Oct. 1980, 6–9; and on Jonathan Wallis's biography of his father *Arthur Wallis – Radical Christian*, published since the first edition of this study.

2 Jackman left the Elim assembly in Exeter for reasons very similar to those for which Jeffreys not many years later separated himself from the denomination he had founded. See A. W. Edsor *George Jeffreys Man of God*, 83; D. W. Cartwright *The Great Evangelists*, 138–59.

3 Burton was co-founder of the Congo Evangelistic Mission. His story is told in Harold Womersley *William F. P. Burton Congo Pioneer*.

4 Lillie recalls: 'The elders approached me and said in view of the views which you hold about tongues . . . we are afraid that we can no longer allow you to teach at Sunday school or take any active part in the ministry of the fellowship. You are entitled to come, you may break the bread but you are not to take any active part in the ministry.'

5 Lillie agreed with Jackman that all born-again believers were baptized in the Holy Spirit, but regarded a subsequent 'infilling' as normative for New Testament believers. This is a largely terminological difference from the typical Pentecostal formulation.

6 The meaning of this phrase is discussed later in Chapter Seven, 39.

7 Lang was therefore different from other Brethren in accepting in theory the contemporary availability of the spiritual gifts of 1 Cor. 12:8–10. Lang had written two pamphlets critical of the Pentecostal movement, *The Modern Gift of Tongues: Whence is it?* and *The Earlier Years of the Modern Tongues Movement*.

8 Although Cousen used the term 'Restoration' of Dean House in Bradford, that meant in effect the overcoming of formalism and the recovery of the power of the Holy Spirit through faith. For him it did not have the same weight it had for Lillie, for whom restoration always means restoration of the New Testament church. However, Cousen was evidently influenced by the Exmouth Conference of 1958, as his next editorial in AVF proclaims: ' "Restoration" is God's message for this day.' (July–Sept. 1958, 1).

9 On Purse and the church at South Chard, see J. V. Thurman *New Wineskins*, 34–5, 71–3.

10 In the early days of Chard, the worship there was much influenced by Henri's Glory Meetings (this judgment of Lillie is also found in A. Wallis 'Springs of Restoration' RS July–Aug. 1980, 23). On Henri Staples and his 'Glory Meetings' see note 13 to Chapter Four.

11 Lillie's recollection agrees with Jonathan Wallis in dating this meeting to 1952 (J. Wallis, op. cit., 105). Arthur Wallis had stated 1951 in RS July–Aug. 1980, 22. Lillie had cycled over to the Wallis home at Talaton to see G. H. Lang, who was visiting.

12 See J. Wallis op. cit., 57.

13 The additional data on the day conferences at Countess Wear was provided by David Lillie in a letter to the author, dated 13 April, 1996.

14 Wallis has written: 'David had come to his own clear convictions about the church, and God used him to temper the fires of my revivalism with the N.T. Church vision. I also saw that without a widespread restoration of the power and gifts of the Spirit to make it come true, the vision would always remain a vision.' (RS July–Aug. 1980, 22).

15 It was at one of the Countess Wear conventions in the mid-1950s that Wallis first heard tongues, interpretation and prophecy, and had 'an instinctive witness that they were genuine' (ibid., 23); see J. Wallis, op. cit., 107.

16 Parkyns had left the Apostolic Church about the same time as Cousen, and was in close contact with the Dean House Christian Fellowship. He was a regular contributor to AVF from its inception. By the early 1960s, Parkyns had become a missionary in Nigeria.

17 Lillie recalls being impressed by Cousen having 'a little touch of dignity . . . At this stage I hadn't come across people of his calibre . . . who were moving in so-called charismatic or Pentecostal circles.'

18 See J. Wallis, op. cit., 127.

19 Exmouth, 4.

20 From convening letter, Exmouth, 6.

21 The report on the Exmouth Conference was published privately by D. G. Lillie and ran to 92 pages. Papers given at Exmouth were also reprinted, in whole or in part, in AVF: July–Sept. 1958, 3–5; Oct.–Dec. 1958, 8–9; Jan.–Mar. 1959, 11–14; Apr.–June 1959, 16.

22 Exmouth, 5. Evidently Cecil Cousen was seen as such a man, taught of the Spirit.

23 Wallis writes that 'He (Parkyns) and Cecil brought to those early conventions a charismatic dimension that would otherwise have been lacking' (art. cit. in RS July–Aug. 1980, 23). Another ex-Apostolic present at Exmouth was H. David Edwards, who had pioneered a fellowship in Pontypridd, South Wales on similar lines to Dean House in Bradford.

24 Perrins had been recommended to visit G. H. Lang by the principal at the South Wales Bible College, where he was studying. Lang referred him to Lillie, and he was immediately invited to Exmouth. Perrins moved from the Anglican Church in Wales to the Baptists to the Brethren as his convictions grew concerning believer's baptism and the

pattern of church order he saw in the New Testament. The Brethren had problems with Perrins' testimony to the baptism and gifts of the Spirit, and in 1967 he became a leader of an independent house fellowship in the Cardiff area. See G. Perrins 'Joined Together' *Fulness* 7, and P. Hocken 'The Prophetic Ministry of Graham Perrins' RN 226, Mar. 1995, 36–8. On Perrins' baptism in the Spirit, see Chapter Six, note 2.

25 Forster gave one of the talks, on the Pattern and the Programme in the Epistles, but it is not printed in the conference report. He does not appear to have been present at Belstone, but gave a teaching at Mamhead Park in 1962, entitled 'Bring Back the King!' (Mamhead, 30–34). Much later, Forster became a significant leader in the Charismatic movement, but in the period covered in this study and for some time afterwards, he had serious reservations hindering any identification with it; see Anthony O'Sullivan 'Roger Forster and the Ichthus Christian Fellowship: The Development of a Charismatic Missiology' PN 16/2 (1994) 252–9. Brian Hewitt outlines Forster's later relationship with the House Church movement (*Doing a New Thing?* 112–16).

26 Exmouth, 50–62.
27 Ibid., 56.
28 Ibid., 59–60.
29 Ibid., 60.
30 The published report on the Belstone Conference, held 27–30 September, 1961, runs to 64 pages. Some of the papers were also published, in whole or in part, in AVF: Jan.–Mar. 1962, 6–10; Apr.–June 1962, 6–8, 10–12, 15.
31 Those present included P. H. P. Gutteridge, who belonged to a small group of Pentecostal Churches, and F. A. Pride, the organizer of the Abinger evangelical weeks in Surrey, and later, following his baptism in the Spirit, promoter of the Capel Bible Week.
32 Rae A. Shaw, born in 1912, became superintendent of the Bethnal Green mission in 1947. After a close friend received the pentecostal baptism early in 1949, Shaw began to re-read those passages of Scripture that had been a closed book to him, especially 1 Cor. 12 and 14. He began to hunger for this experience himself and was baptized in the Spirit on 17 September, 1959 at a Workers' Christian Fellowship meeting in the City at which a Pentecostal pastor was ministering. The Good Shepherd mission soon became a dynamic centre for evangelism. It was some while before the trustees of the mission realized what had happened. When they did, Shaw resigned. From 1967–70 he was an accredited minister within the AoG in Great Britain and Ireland. The basic details of Shaw's witness are included in a booklet *I Received the Holy Spirit*, 10–13.
33 Belstone, 3.

34 Ibid., 31.
35 Ibid., 32. Wallis expounds in the same talk his understanding of the self-sufficiency and the completeness of each local church (25–7).
36 Ibid., 32.
37 Among those present from a Brethren background with no prior sympathy for the Pentecostal movement were Stanley Dipple, Wyndham Mathieson, Ralph Shallis, T. G. Tester and William Ward.
38 Belstone, 58.
39 The Mamhead Park report states 'The conference held at Belstone, Devon in the previous autumn gave great cause for encouragement in that a number present experienced a real anointing of the Holy Spirit, and others had the desire for this awakened or quickened' (Mamhead, 3).
40 Lillie had seen the article on glossolalia in Illinois by J. Ralph Deppen in CEN Apr. 28. 1961 (see Chapter Seventeen 107–8). See Belstone, 41–2 and D. G. Lillie 'Panorama' AVF Jan.–Mar. 1965, 6–8.
41 The report of the Mamhead Park conference held 26–29 September 1962, was again published privately by D. G. Lillie (88 pages). Some of the papers were also printed, in whole or in part, in AVF: Jan.–Mar. 1963, 8–10, 13; Apr.–June 1963, 6–11; July–Sept. 1963, 8–11; Oct.–Dec. 1963, 8–11.
42 RS July–Aug. 1980, 23. Bryn Jones had been baptised in the Spirit at Aberaman Assembly of God in South Wales in 1957 at the age of 17. After a time as a student at Swansea Bible College, in 1961 he began evangelistic work in Cornwall with his college friend Bob Hyslop, campaigning particularly in Methodist chapels and hired halls. In 1962–3, Jones worked with Operation Mobilisation in France for nine months, before leaving in 1963 for Guyana with Philip Mohabir. On Jones's early ministry see Joyce V. Thurman *New Wineskins*, 24–7, the interview by Terry Brooks 'Trained in the School of God' RS May–June, 1980, 5–7, Brian Hewitt *Doing a New Thing?* 7–34, and another interview, this time by Wesley Richards 'Everything you ever wanted to know about Bryn Jones, but were afraid to ask' RS Mar.–Apr. 1989, 28–33.
43 Mamhead, 41–52. This talk was published in AVF under the title 'If any man thirst' Apr.–June 1963, 6–9; July–Sept. 1963, 8–10.
44 Ibid., 41.
45 Ibid., 53–9.
46 Ibid., 55.
47 Mamhead, 27–9. This was also printed under the title 'Very Much Overlooked . . .' in AVF July–Sept. 1963, 11, 10.
48 Quoted, ibid., 29.
49 Ibid., 29.

50 The six-page report entitled 'Questionnaire Findings' summarizes the replies of over fifty out of seventy participants in the Mamhead Park Conference.

51 QF 4.

52 'God awakened me at Barry on the morning of October 4th at about 3 a.m., filled me with the Spirit, with the manifestations mentioned in Acts 19:6.' (letter from A. Wallis to W. B. Grant dated Nov. 1, 1962). This happened during a visit to the home of Graham and Sylvia Perrins (J. Wallis, op. cit., 144–5).

53 The closing of the Brethren doors to Wallis during his tour of New Zealand is described in detail in J. Wallis, op. cit., 150–173.

54 See Chapter Twenty-One, 136. The original intention had been to have the fourth Conference in April 1964, but it was delayed due to Wallis' prolonged stay in New Zealand (see letters D. Lillie to M. Harper. Nov. 15, 1963 and Jan. 6, 1964). Wallis was absent from Britain from March 1963 until November 1964 (RS Sept.–Oct. 1980, 7; see also J. Wallis, op. cit., 150, 179–180).

55 See Mamhead, 3.

Chapter 4

1 See Chapter Fourteen. There was also a third David Smith in the early days of the Charismatic movement who was a director of Smith and Philips in Witney, Oxfordshire.

2 Information on David R. Smith is from an interview and various issues of EDHN as well as the sources cited in subsequent footnotes.

3 The tutor was Howard Belben, subsequently principal of Cliff College for many years, and later a convinced participant in the Charismatic movement.

4 The date '1885' is given by Smith in *Divine Healing*, 8–9. At that meeting the term 'Divine Healing' was deliberately chosen in preference to 'Spiritual Healing' and 'Faith Healing', a choice Smith emphatically endorsed.

5 Eileen F. M. Thomson *It's a Wonderful New Life! The Don Double Story*, 30.

6 Mid-Week Message. 1979. Series on 'Dynamic Evangelicalism', no 1, 1.

7 Ibid., 1.

8 The main outline of Double's life and ministry is given in Thomson's book. In 1961 Double began his pentecostal-style full-time ministry reaching out beyond Pentecostal circles, and at the same time he also started to publish an occasional magazine *Ripened Grain*. An interesting aspect of Double's early ministry is his sense of God's call to minister in the small towns and villages of Britain:

'When God spoke to me and called me some years ago, He spoke very clearly, and told me that I was to take the message of "this gospel of the Kingdom" for mind, soul and body to the under-privileged people in the villages and very small towns of Great Britain. This by the grace of God I have attempted to do and every time we have gone to the villages and small towns we have had a successful ministry, many souls saved, many bodies healed, for which we give Him all the glory. I confess that many times I have been tempted to hold crusades in larger towns and cities, because of the easiness of getting a crowd together, but to God be the glory, His grace has been sufficient, God allows me to take rallies or week-ends in the bigger places. but not crusades. Jesus in His earthly ministry never neglected the villages as so many of the evangelists with the deliverance ministry seem to do today, but I count it a privilege to be chosen of God to have a small part in His plan of taking the gospel to every creature. We see in Luke 8 v 1 that Jesus went throughout every city and village. His plan hasn't changed, He still wants everyone to know of His redeeming love. Although it has meant sacrifice and a financial burden because of minis-trying [sic] to smaller numbers, offerings are small, it has been a tremen-dous privilege and blessing to watch the country folk proving the power of God just as those in the big cities.' (RG Summer 1963, 4).

9   Thomson, op. cit., 9–11. Scothern's ministry, based on Mansfield, Notts emphasized the miraculous and supernatural, and is documented in a magazine entitled *Deliverance*, which began publication in 1952.

10   Thomson, op. cit., 32. This description accurately reflects Smith's lan-guage of 'being filled with the Spirit' rather than 'being baptized with/in the Spirit'.

11   Thomson, op. cit., 35–6.

12   Vic Ramsey, then a Methodist, had been baptized in the Spirit in a Pentecostal church during his national service in 1952. He was ordained to the ministry in a free evangelical church, with Pentecostal connec-tions, in 1954. He pioneered the AoG work in Thetford and Swaffham before moving to Yarmouth by 1956. After a spell as staff evangelist for the Elim Church in Suffolk, he went into independent pentecostal-style ministry by 1959.

13   Henri and Connie Staples held 'Glory Meetings' in various parts of England. For many years Staples ran a multiple-store business in Newark. Effectively driven out of the Newark Assembly of God when he began his own preaching, Henri started to hold regular revival meetings to spread 'the glory'. From the late 1950s, he also produced a regular magazine known as *Henri's Glory News*. In effect an inde-pendent Pentecostal, Henri was disturbed by the lack of fire in most Pentecostal assemblies. The 'Glory Meetings' became known for their noise and exuberance. Though disapproved by many, who sensed a

lack solid biblical teaching, Henri's Glory Meetings certainly reached many working-class people as well as youth, not touched by more conventional ministries. Charles Clarke gives a sympathetic account of a 'Glory Meeting' with Henri and Connie at Southend in Q Oct. 1963, 16–19.

14 'Being filled with the Holy Spirit is a clear-cut experience quite separate from conversion.' (David and Doreen Smith, *The Holy Spirit and You*, 16).

15 Smith already disagreed with Osborn's views and practice, though he was involved in some 'After-Meetings' following Osborn's campaign in Holland in 1958.

16 The 'Some Light' Series included the following titles by David and Doreen Smith or by David Smith alone: *A New You*; *The Return of Jesus Christ, Fasting, The Holy Spirit and You, True Prosperity* and *Disease and Deliverance*. The Smiths also produced a leaflet on *Divine Healing and Evangelical Truth*. Later titles by David R. Smith include *Divine Healing* and *Queer Christians*. The last-named was later retitled *Extremism* because of the changing connotation of the original.

17 Smith was in the Congregational ministry from 1959 until 1974, when he was finally accepted as a Baptist.

18 Grant had met Smith some months earlier at the newly-formed Congregational Evangelical Revival Fellowship.

19 'This is a very special moment. We are gathered for the opening meeting of an important Convention. This is the first time for 75 years that there has been a company of people from many denominations, under a truly evangelical basis of faith, assembling for the purposes of teaching and studying the subject of Divine Healing. In our small way, we are making an addition to Church history!' D. R. Smith (ed.) *Be Thou Made Whole*, (Messages from the EDH Convention of September 1960) 7. This passage was omitted from the second booklet of the same title, published in 1965, that gathered addresses from several EDH Conventions.

20 Smith wrote in a letter to the author: 'As I look back on my life, I think that the emphasis has been on "teaching" mixed with evangelism and prayer.'

21 This address is printed under the title 'Power from on High' in AVF Jan.–Mar. 1961, 10–14 and Apr.–June 1961, 9. This address was not printed in either version of *Be Thou Made Whole*, presumably because it makes very few references to healing. There is no evidence from High Leigh of disagreement over the Spirit-baptism issue. Cousen printed an item by David R. Smith and a High Leigh address of W. H. Fullerton in AVF (Jan.–Mar. 1961, 5–6) and Cousen's addresses more directly concerned with healing are included in *Be Thou Made Whole*. A state-

ment on Divine Healing formulated at High Leigh by the convening committee was published both in AVF (Oct.–Dec. 1960, 13, 12) and in *Be Thou Made Whole*, 1st edition, 5–6. (There are minor differences between these two texts). A third version of this statement appeared in *Be Thou Made Whole*, revised version, under the heading 'Doctrinal Statement of the Evangelical Divine Healing Convention', 74–5.

22 See Chapter Eleven, 72.

23 E.g. Marjorie Stockman later with LHM.

24 The bulletin, initially called the EDH News, began quarterly in January 1961. Later the Word 'Fellowship' was added after EDH, and the issues were no longer numbered.

25 Part of Allen's address is given in AVF July–Sept. 1962, 10–12.

26 Stephen Wyatt, in his youth a student at Cliff College, was baptized in the Spirit through the ministry of Harry Greenwood (see note 13 to Chapter Six). At this time he was pastor of an independent evangelical chapel in Bournemouth. In his old age, Wyatt recalled this as being 'about 1960' but his letter to LF in 1963 suggests it had not yet occurred (Apr. 4, 1963, 329).

27 Letter of W. B. Grant to P. L. C. & N. Smith, Aug. 13, 1963.

Chapter 5

1 The information on Campbell McAlpine comes from letters and an interview. McAlpine's witness is printed anonymously as testimony No. 7 in D. G. Lillie *Tongues under Fire*, 55–6.

2 Cited in P. Hocken 'The Generous Spirit of Campbell McAlpine' RN 219, Aug. 1994, 34.

3 Information given in obituary in IAN Feb. 1, 1982, 1. See also the obituary in RN 98, Apr.–May 1982, 11. Clark's anonymous witness is printed as testimony No. 2 in D. G. Lillie, op. cit., 50.

4 Lillie, op. cit., 50.

5 Lillie, op. cit., 55. There is another reference to McAlpine's baptism in the Spirit in RS Nov.–Dec. 1979, 13. McAlpine's reception of tongues was in mid-1955.

6 'Campbell McAlpine left for New Zealand on June 18th.' (Circular Letter from Denis Clark, July 3, 1959, 1).

7 Lillie, op. cit., 50.

8 See Chapter Three, 17 and note 32.

9 Smith was also an active participant in the Fleet Street prayer meetings, described in Chapter Ten, 56–8. He was known as 'Alarm Bell' Smith, because he ran a firm making burglar alarms for business premises.

10 Clark is reported to have responded 'I already speak six'.

11 Lillie, op. cit., 50. His wife recalls that Clark began to speak in tongues on the top of a bus.

12 Stanley Jebb in RN 98, Apr.–May 1982, 11.

13 The issue of Feb. 1, 1961, states that 'it is ten months since the prayer letter last appeared', so it was certainly sent out by April 1960. *Greetings* appeared twice yearly between 1960 and 1970, generally in February and August. In 1971 it was re-named *Views*, becoming *Views News Reviews* in 1972.

14 4 Feb. 5 Mar. 23 Apr.–mid-May; 11 Oct. 19 Nov. [?](G 1 Feb. 1961 and Aug. 1961).

15 G Aug. 1961, 2. Clark's teaching on the baptism in the Holy Spirit was included in a small book *You Were Asking*, 15–22.

16 RT 25 Aug. 1961, 16. A briefer description by Clark himself appeared in G Aug. 1961, 4. See also Ken Terhoven 'Repercussions of the Matlock Project' LF 26 Sept. 1963, 980, 986. It does not seem that anything lasting developed in Matlock following this crusade, although Beth Clark recalls that several people blessed on that evening were drawn into various forms of dedicated Christian service (but see also Chapter Ten, 61, for Richard Bolt's ministry in Matlock).

17 E.g. the witness of Maureen Woodfall, ministered to by Clark at Bury St. Edmunds in April 1963 (Q Oct. 1963, 8–9); letter of Tony & Janet Nash of Farnborough to P. L. C. & N. Smith, 7 Dec. 1963.

18 On Farnborough, see Chapter Fifteen, 96–7.

19 Clark and Wallis jointly launched the work *Intercessors for Britain* in 1969 (RN 25, Feb.–Mar. 1970, 18–19), after Clark had a vision for Intercessors for the Nations in Copenhagen in 1968 (IAN 1 Feb. 1982, 1).

20 Peter Lyne recalls Michael Harper giving a talk on this occasion. The second Week was more public at the Greenhills Baptist Youth Centre in Worthing, when McAlpine joined Clark (see J. Wallis, op. cit., 181).

21 On McAlpine's later role, see Chapter Eighteen, 115–6, 119.

Chapter 6

1 Information on Trout is based on an unpublished and unfinished manuscript by his son Richard entitled *Strength Out of Weakness: The Christian Life of Edgar Trout*, as well as on interviews with, and letters from, Richard Trout.

2 Trout had met Lillie and Wallis by 1961. That summer, Lillie organised a house party at Heatree House at Manaton on Dartmoor, at which the Trouts joined the Lillie and the Wallis families among others for a holiday together. Jonathan Wallis records Trout's role in Graham Perrins' initiation into the realm of spiritual gifts that took place during this week (op. cit., 132 – 3).

3 Obituaries of Edgar Trout are found in RN 15, June–July 1968, 3–4, 22–3. Cecil Cousen wrote of him: 'Edgar had learnt more than anyone I have ever met, to know the Lord, His mind and His will.' (ibid., 22).

4 Edgar John Trout was born on 28 September 1912 (Trout, op. cit., 2). The date 1913 given in RN 15, 22 is in error.

5 Trout, 26.

6 Ibid., 35–37.

7 Trout served on the Central Executive of Toc-H from 1948 to 1953 (ibid., 54).

8 The Revd. Charles De Cerjat (ibid., 101). Trout mentions this episode in a taped talk, 'Gifts of Healings', printed in AVF Jan.–Mar. 1967, 13–16.

9 Ibid., 101–2: see also E. W. Tattersall in MR Apr. 11, 1957, 1. Another account of Trout's healing is in LHML 49, Summer 1965, 1.

10 The first time in his childhood, and the second time of a duodenal ulcer in 1953 (ibid., 102).

11 Ibid., 112–13. The mission ran from 14 to 28 October (details on printed leaflet).

12 Details are from Trout, 116–117.

13 From the mid-1960s, Greenwood was associated with the House Church network of Sid Purse based at South Chard in Somerset.

14 There was however a very positive series of six articles on the Bath Street mission in *The Methodist Recorder* in 1957, running from April 11 to May 23, weekly but with a gap on May 16.

15 Trout, op. cit., 150.

16 Ibid., 150.

17 The 'Gloryland' meetings were linked with the ministry of Henri Staples (see note 13 to Chapter Four).

18 Trout, op. cit., 155.

19 Hutchison, a native of Scotland, was by this time around forty years of age. Following the Brethren's disapproval of his healing activities, he joined Upton Vale Baptist Church in the Torbay area. On Hutchison, see also P. Hocken 'The Charismatic Brother from Devon' RN 213, Feb. 1994, 40–2.

20 Hutchison found himself used in the healing of others immediately after the experience of the Lord that he recognized as his baptism in the Spirit. He came into the gift of tongues in 1959 at Trout's home.

21 Trout, op. cit., untyped section.

22 AVF Jan.–Mar. 1967, 14–15.

23 This superintendent was the Revd. John Barker, a prominent officer in the MRF, on which see Chapter Twelve.

24 Fourteen people attended this first conference.

25　E.g. in the life of Don Double in Eileen F. M. Thomson *It's a Wonderful New Life*, 60–2, 82–5, 92–3; of Faith Lees of Post Green in Faith Lees *Love is Our Home*, 64–6; of Frank Wilson in Frank Wilson *House of New Beginnings*, 10, 15–16, of Arthur Wallis in RS Sept.–Oct. 1980, 7.

26　RN 8, Apr.–May 1967, 19.

27　From talk given at Presbyterian Church of Wales summer school on divine healing at Aberystwyth in July 1965 ('Revival-Word of Testimony', 34).

28　See Chapter Eleven.

Chapter 7

1　Of the leading figures described, only Wallis and Clark had not received the gift of tongues by the end of the decade. However, Clark had experience of other spiritual gifts from 1954 and Wallis fully endorsed the authentic character of these gifts and their normality for the life of the church.

2　E.g. Peter Scothern, Don Double, and from the end of the 1950s Vic Ramsey, of those mentioned in this Section. Henri Staples could also qualify as an independent Pentecostal, although his 'Glory' message distinguished him from others in this category.

3　See Chapter Three, 17.

4　See A. Wallis *In The Day of Thy Power*, 57–96.

5　Trout was introduced to members of the Houses of Parliament Christian Fellowship and exercised some ministry in the homes of the aristocracy (see 'Revival' Word of Testimony, 32). NPWR had begun prayer meetings for revival at Westminster in conjunction with the secretary of this Fellowship shortly before the start of their meeting at St. Bride's, on which see Chapters Ten, 56–8 and Eleven, 71.

6　See Appendix III.

7　One Anglican, Barry Kissell, knew Trout for some time before discovering he was a Methodist.

8　See Chapters Eleven, Twelve and Sixteen.

9　AVF Oct.–Dec. 1961, 1.

Chapter 8

1　The phrase seems to have been first used by du Plessis, who published a small pamphlet under this title in late 1960 (see also the quotation by Wood in Chapter Nine, 52 and note 23). *The Spirit Bade Me Go* is a revised and expanded version of *Pentecost Outside 'Pentecost'*, but omits significant reports on du Plessis' travels and meetings from 1959 and 1960.

2   The most comprehensive study of Gee is the unpublished dissertation of Brian R. Ross *Donald Gee: In Search of a Church: Sectarian in Transition*. The most available study is Richard Massey *Another Springtime. The Life of Donald Gee, Pentecostal Leader and Teacher*. See also John Carter *Donald Gee – Pentecostal Statesman*, the chapter by Colin Whittaker on Gee in *Seven Pentecostal Pioneers*, Lois Gott's essay 'Donald Gee: The Apostle of Balance' in Paul Elbert (ed.) *Essays on Apostolic Themes* and Peter Hocken's paper 'Donald Gee: Pentecostal Ecumenist?'

3   David du Plessis subsequently served as secretary to the third PWC in London (1952) and the fifth in Toronto (1958). (D. J. du Plessis *Pentecost Outside 'Pentecost'*, 30).

4   D. J. du Plessis *The Spirit Bade Me Go*, 13.

5   Mackay had seen the expansion of the Pentecostal movement at first hand during his years as a missionary in Peru (1916–33).

6   See Robert R. Curlee and Mary Ruth Isaac-Curlee 'Bridging the Gap: John A. Mackay, Presbyterians, and the Charismatic Movement' *American Presbyterians* 72/3 1994, esp. 145–7. Mackay was responsible for all du Plessis's major ecumenical invitations of the 1950s: to the meetings of the International Missionary Council, not at that time integrated into though having a close association with the WCC, at Willingen, Germany (1952) and Accra, Ghana (1958); to the Second Assembly of the WCC at Evanston, Illinois in 1954; to international Presbyterian-Reformed meetings in the USA (1954) and in Sao Paolo, Brazil (1959). A statement of Pentecostal leaders submitted by du Plessis to the International Missionary Council at Willingen, Germany in 1952 is printed in *Missions under the Cross* (ed. N. Goodall), 245–50. Du Plessis was also invited to address a group of ecumenical leaders in the USA in 1956 (*The Spirit Bade Me Go*, 15–16).

7   Gee was a member of the Executive Council from 1925 and of the missionary Council from 1926. (Alfred F. Missen *The Sound of a Going*, 38). He was chairman of the executive on several occasions. He was principal of the AoG Bible College at Kenley, Surrey from 1951–64 (ibid., 38).

8   Although the first PWC was only held in 1947 (at Zurich), the idea was certainly mooted before the outbreak of World War II. Gee is on record as having suggested the idea to the Swedish leader Lewi Pethrus in 1938 (John Carter *Donald Gee – Pentecostal Statesman*, 91), while du Plessis recalls Gee having proposed him as secretary for the PWC at Memphis, Tennessee in 1937 (*The Spirit Bade Me Go*, 101). Gee served on the advisory Council for the World Pentecostal Fellowship from its inception until his death in 1966 (Carter, *op. cit.*, 115).

9   Gee was named as editor at the first PWC at Zurich in 1947. Nothing indicates more clearly the esteem in which Gee was already held by his

Pentecostal brethren than the recommendation of the Swedish leader Lewi Pethrus: 'He enjoys the general confidence of the Pentecostal people in the whole world. He knows the Pentecostal Movement all over the world better than most of us, and he is a man with a vision and a deep spiritual knowledge of the Pentecostal Movement.' (Carter, op. cit., 48).

10 It was this gift and reputation that initially produced the invitations from almost all parts of the world, and his resulting travels which then gave him such a wide knowledge of the worldwide Pentecostal movement.

11 Originally published in 1941 under the title *The Pentecostal Movement*, it was subsequently revised and updated in 1949 and 1967. *Wind and Flame* is the title of the final version published posthumously.

12 'Are we too 'Movement' Conscious? P 2, Dec. 1947. (Where no page references are given to Gee's articles in P, the references are to editorials appearing on the inside of the back cover.).

13 ' "Tongues" and Truth' P 25, Sept. 1953. The same conclusion is at least implicit in an earlier editorial in which Gee addressing a Methodist wrote: 'That does not necessarily mean that we wish you to leave your denominations and join ours. That must be determined by the amount of freedom you find in your present connection, and might find in ours, to let God have all His way in your heart and life.' ('Thank-you, Brother, but -'[?] P 8, June 1949).

14 'Billy Graham in London' P 27, Mar. 1954.

15 This was the revival of which David R. Smith heard (see Chapter Four, 22). Gee makes another reference to pentecostal experience in WEC in 'Renewed Opposition' P 42, Dec. 1957.

16 These three citations are from 'Orientation for 1960' P 50, Dec. 1959.

17 The December 1959 editorial instanced several promising omens, including the openness of the *British Weekly* to publish Pentecostal items. There was however no mention of any pentecostal phenomena outside Pentecostal circles in Britain.

18 The beginnings of the Charismatic movement in Holland among Dutch Reformed pastors can be traced back to the early to mid-1950s. Their magazine *Vuur* began in March 1957 (C. & P. N. van der Laan *Pinksteren in Beweging*, 135). Gee visited Holland in early 1961 and wrote 'There are two streams of the Pentecostal revival in Holland. We can conveniently call them the "old" and the "new". Indeed this distinction is generally recognized and accepted.' ('What I found in Holland' P 56, June–Aug. 1961, 3).

19 It was at this conference that du Plessis first met David R. Smith and William Wood.

20 T. H. Stevenson 'From my Diary' EE 23 Jan. 1960, 59.

21 Du Plessis also met Donald Gee, Dr. Norman Goodall of the International Missionary Council and John Lawrence. the editor of *Frontier*. Details of these days are in *Pentecost Outside 'Pentecost'*, 9–10.

22 Gee attended two sessions and regretted he was unable to stay throughout the conference ('Contact is not Compromise' P 53, Sept.–Nov. 1960).

23 An incident involving Ramsey and du Plessis at St. Andrews is related in *A Man Called Mr. Pentecost*, 200–201.

24 The Catholic contact at St. Andrews was the Jesuit Father Bernard Leeming (*A Man Called Mr. Pentecost*, 201).

25 See Chapter Seventeen.

26 'There are large numbers of ministers within the National Councils and the World Council that are enjoying the same glorious Pentecostal experience that the Pentecostals have, and yet they are still loyal to their own confessions and have not been disfellowshipped by their brethren. I personally know many Lutheran, Reformed, Episcopalian, Methodist and Baptist ministers who are "filled with the Holy Spirit . . . speaking in other tongues as the Spirit [gives] them utterance." ' (*The Spirit Bade Me Go*, 33). An abridged version of this address was also published in P 53, Sept.–Nov. 1960 (back cover).

27 *The Spirit Bade Me Go*, 33.

28 *Pentecost Outside 'Pentecost'*, 19.

29 E.g. in P 54, 3; 56, 2; 57, 9; 58, 8; 59, 3.

30 Redemption Tidings, the organ of the AoG, had three such reports in 1960:

i. 'On Thursday, February 5th, 1959, eight members of a local Methodist Church baptized in the Holy Ghost and speaking with other tongues were politely shown the door. That same evening, they decided to form a Pentecostal Church. After holding cottage meetings for some months a Hall became available in October, since when the Lord has poured His blessings out. Many members of surrounding Methodist Churches, having come under their influence, have been baptized in the Holy Ghost.' (Feb. 26, 1960, 15). This report came from Congleton in Cheshire.

ii. The issue of Aug. 19, 1960, 7–8 reports how the pentecostal blessing came to a Yorkshire congregation of a small Methodist denomination, the Wesleyan Reform Union. The story traces the beginnings of this blessing to a visit of two evangelists to Wombwell in 1953, and gradually a number of members were baptized in the Spirit through the mid-1950s, leading to their holding a prayer meeting with 'the Inspirational Gifts' each Thursday night. 'In early 1958 we linked ourselves with believers in a neighbouring church . . . even though we received opposition from other churches in our circuit at first, it was not long before the Lord had wondrously moved this opposition, and the right to freedom of worship in our churches established.'

iii. The issue of Oct. 28, 1960, 11 mentions how two elders of a Congregational chapel in a Leicestershire village, Stanton-under-Barden, were baptized in the Spirit following a visit to a campaign of Divine Healing held in Leicester by an American Evangelist, A. C. Valdez. There followed 'a re-awakening in their chapel. At once a campaign was conducted in the village and Christians came from other denominations to be filled with the Holy Spirit.'

31 P 50, Dec. 1959.

32 Benedict Heron's relationship with Donald Gee was first made public in David Allen 'That They May be One' RT July 16, 1981, 6–7.

33 Gee's letters to Heron are printed as Appendix I to this study.

34 Letter dated 19 June 1960.

35 This judgment is also confirmed by Gee's article 'The New Pentecost' PE 1/1, 11–13, in which he comments on du Plessis' contact with Fr. Daniel O'Hanlon, SJ in California and on O'Hanlon's article 'The Pentecostals and Pope John's "New Pentecost"' in A May 4, 1963, 634–6.

36 P 56, June–Aug. 1961.

Chapter 9

1 CCD 1980–2, 1124.

2 LHML 44, Christmas 1963, 20–1.

3 LHML 36, Easter 1961, 6.

4 Wood later wrote: 'The Mission has prospered since April 1949, when the Revd. John Maillard provided the opportunity. Six of us, as intercessors, started offering to pray for the sick and providing regular healing Services.' (LHML 25, Summer 1957, 2).

5 The LHM Constitution requires that the Warden be an Anglican priest (LHML 45, Easter 1964, 1). Some non-Anglicans have been associated with LHM and for a while in 1963–4 Wood had a Baptist assistant. Speakers at LHM Healing Advances were drawn from many Church traditions.

6 Hickson (1861–1933) published a magazine called *The Healer* from 1908. The most accessible work for information on Hickson's ministry is his own book *Heal the Sick*. A series of addresses given by Hickson was also published under the title *Behold the Bridegroom Cometh*.

7 LHML 35, Christmas 1960, 5.

8 LHML 45, Easter 1964, 2. McAlister was a Presbyterian who later became a Pentecostal.

9   Cliffe was the author of *Lessons in Successful Living*, a revision of *Lessons in Living*, and *Let Go and Let God*.

10 LHML 17, Christmas 1954, 1.

11 Sunderland, Los Angeles, India and Chile all refer to the beginnings of the Pentecostal movement. Los Angeles refers particularly to Azusa Street, India to Pandita Ramabai's homes at Mukti and Chile to events in the Methodist Episcopal Church in Valparaiso.

12 Wood's dates are one year out. The Pentecostal events at Sunderland began in 1907. Wood mentioned Sunderland again in LHML 29, Christmas 1958, 2. For other contemporary awareness of Boddy's role, see also Appendix II.

13 LHML 18, Easter 1955, 1.

14 Wood refers to Frodsham's book in LHML 23, Christmas 1956, 8.

15 Wigglesworth was baptized in the Spirit at Sunderland in 1907, after Mrs Mary Boddy had laid hands on him for this purpose.

16 Wood told a story from one Wigglesworth meeting in LHML 23, Christmas 1956, 6–7.

17 Gee was accompanied by John Woodhead (LHML 40, Summer 1962, 11). Gee's paper was included in the published report on the Conference.

18 LHML 23, Christmas 1956, 5–8. 'The International Order of Saint Luke the Physician' to give it its full title, an outgrowth of the Fellowship of St. Luke that had begun in 1932, was founded by the Revd. John Gayner Banks and his wife Ethel Tulloch Banks in 1947 and incorporated as a non-profit corporation in California in 1953. Information given *passim* in *Sharing*, OSL's monthly journal. Though open to Christians of any denomination, it always had a strong Episcopalian component.

19 On Sanford, see Chapter Twenty-Five, .

20 Wood later wrote: 'Not until 1958, when a prayer group ministered in tongues and with the laying-on of hands, was the babe within the man comforted and released, and the power of the Holy Spirit replaced the energy running to waste through the wounds of jealousy.' (LHML 44, Christmas 1963, 20).

21 For example, Pasteur Forget of the French Reformed Church and some clergy in Holland.

22 LHML 35, Christmas 1960, 7.

23 LHML 35, 7.

24 LHML 35, 6 and LHML 36, Easter 1961, 4. Du Plessis also spoke at the AoG General Conference at Prestatyn on this visit (P 57, Sept.–Nov 1961, 9).

25 'A Pentecostal in Ecumenical Circles' in *The Spirit Bade Me Go*, 9–20.

26 For an indirect reference in 1952, see note 6 to Chapter One.

27 LHML 37, Autumn 1961, 1. Du Plessis reported that this Healing Advance was attended by one hundred and fifty Anglicans (P 57, Sept. – Nov. 1961, 9).

28 E.g. LHML 39, Easter 1962, 7 and 40, Summer 1962, 10–11.

29 Wood was in California from 23–25 May 1962 (LHML 39, Easter 1962, 1).

30 LHML 43, 3.

31 See Chapter Nineteen, 122–3.

32 DdPN Oct. 1963, 2.

33 Wood was inducted as a member of OSL in 1950 (LHML 7, July 1951, 5) and was in turn chaplain for London and then Warden at large for Europe.

34 OSL in Britain was legally constituted in 1961 under the title 'The Order of St. Luke the Physician in the United Kingdom Ltd.' (LHML 36, Easter 1961, 13).

35 The resolution approved included the following stipulations: '(1) Be it resolved that in all meetings and conferences of the . . . Order . . . the members shall proclaim, teach and practise only such things as are related to Spiritual Healing, sacramental acts, prayer, and Christian living, as set forth in the OSL Manual. They shall not by word or action use the OSL to exploit or promote their own particular philosophies, doctrines, and practices, which would include spiritualism, glossolalia (commonly called speaking in tongues) and prophecy . . . (2) Be it further resolved that during . . . conferences the leaders and speakers shall publicly discuss and answer only such subjects and questions as are related to the purposes, principles, and practices of The International Order of Saint Luke The Physician. (3) Be it further resolved that any member . . . who uses his OSL identity, or permits it to be used, to promote teachings or practices not related to the purposes of the OSL, shall be liable to reprimand . . . and if their warning is disregarded, his membership in the O.S.L. may be canceled.' (Statement issued on OSL paper undated; references to the meeting of 9 Sept. 1963, at which these resolutions were passed are in *Sharing*, Nov. 1963, 10,13).

36 Wood protested vigorously against some infiltration of spiritualism into OSL in the USA. (Missioner's Message in LHML 53, Christmas 1966, 1–2).

37 Wood writes in Monthly Message No. 142, Jan. 1967: 'My hopes that the Order of St. Luke in the United Kingdom might some day inherit the Mission must be deferred, as I have been expelled from the International Order.' (LHML 54, Easter 1967, 2).

38 On CFO, see Chapter Twenty-Five, .

39 See note 21 to Chapter Twenty-Five.

40 'In the past few years your National Advisory Council Ring has been asked by local Camp Council Rings, by the individual leaders and campers alike, as to the place "speaking in tongues" should have in the CFO programme . . . "Speaking in tongues" we recognize as a genuine gift of the Spirit. We acknowledge it as an aid to private devotions, and that it can be a sign to unbelievers. All we would question is its appropriateness as an integral part of the particular purposes that are peculiar to the CFO programme.' (LHML 44, Christmas 1963, 11).

41 Cole was baptized in the Spirit at a FGBMFI Convention in Zurich at Pentecost 1963.

42 LHML 50, Christmas 1965, 2.

43 The Revd. F. Roy Jeremiah (see Chapter Ten, 58).

44 Parsons was to speak at a Fountain Trust meeting in London in September 1965 (MHN 14, Aug. 1965, 1) and became a trustee of LHM by 1967 (LHML 56, Christmas 1967, 2). St. Martin's, Ludgate Hill was to become a temporary office for the Fountain Trust from September 1966 to December 1968 (MHN 21, Oct. 1966, 1; MHN 30, Dec. 1968, 1).

45 Agnes Sanford was the most prominent example of this pattern in the USA.

46 See Chapter Four.

47 E.g. under the headings 'Baptism of the Holy Spirit and Healing' (LHML 43, Summer 1963, 11), 'Let's be Frank' (LHML 45, Easter 1964, 1–3) and 'Jesus at Work in this Decade' (LHML 52, Summer 1966, 7–8). See also 'Message from the Missioner' (LHML 49, Summer 1965, 1–2).

48 LHML 43, 11.

49 The speakers included Edgar Trout on his first appearance at a Healing Advance. The previous year Trout ministered at the LHM chapel, an occasion when David du Plessis was present. 'Edgar Trout of Plymouth was wonderful in his ministry on exorcism at the London Healing Mission where Brother Bill Wood and many ministers were gathered.' (DdPN, Dec. 1964, 2).

50 LHML 49, 2.

Chapter 10

1 It is difficult to determine the exact date. One participant thought it was 1959, but this is certainly too late as the Nights of Prayer Tuesday meeting (see Chapter Eleven, 71) which certainly started after the Pentecostal meeting, began in late 1958. Grant's recollection that 'for some years a lunch-hour prayer meeting for business men had been held in the same room on a different day of the week' ('God broke through my barrier' Q July–Sept. 1965, 11) suggests an origin prior to 1957 or 1958, but this does not accord with the memories of other

participants. The most accessible account of the St Bride's lunch-hour meeting is in Chapter 14 of Andy Milliken's book, *From the Kwai to the Kingdom*, entitled 'Renewal in Fleet Street' 119–127.

2 St. Bride's Institute had no connection other than proximity to St. Bride's Church. The Institute, which stands on the south-east side of the Church on Bride Lane, was run by the Greater London Council.

3 See Milliken, op. cit., 120.

4 Grant, art. cit., 11.

5 Down ran a gentlemen's outfitter business in London's West End and in this capacity had met Cecil Cousen during the latter's business days prior to 1949.

6 On Birkenshaw, see Milliken, op. cit., 120–1.

7 See note 32 to Chapter Three and note 9 to Chapter Five.

8 Milliken was in advertising and later established his own advertising and PR consultancy firm (see Milliken, op. cit., 82–103). In 1965, Milliken was involved in organising the publicity for the FGBMFI Convention in London (see Chapter Twenty-Two, 143–4) that led to subsequent involvement with the Full Gospel Business Men in Britain.

9 Art. cit., 11.

10 Grant, art. cit., 11.

11 This is described more fully in Chapter Eleven, 69–71.

12 F. R. Jeremiah, *Divine Healing: the Way of It*, 17.

13 Ibid., 17.

14 On Ramsey, see note 12 to Chapter Four. He had been invited to the St. Bride's meeting by du Plessis. By now, Ramsey was no longer associated with any Pentecostal denomination, and in 1964 was led from itinerant evangelistic ministry into starting the New Life Foundation, a work for the rehabilitation of drug addicts through the power of the Holy Spirit (Jeanne Hinton 'Soho break-in' RN 23, 11, 13–16). Nicholas Rivett-Carnac (see Chapter Twenty-Two, 145) was baptized in the Spirit through the ministry of Vic Ramsey (Jenny Cooke *Upon this Rock*, 38–9, 45).

15 This white South African is not to be confused with another (black) nurse from South Africa, Peggy Mabali, who accompanied Jeremiah to this meeting. Mabali was associated with the LHM and was at that time Warden of the Isle of Wight Healing Home at Ventnor (LHML 38, Christmas 1961, 16).

16 Anne White was an Episcopalian and wife of an officer in the US Navy, stationed for some years in London. Like Agnes Sanford, she was led into charismatic experience from a background of healing ministry. At the time of du Plessis' visit to St. Bride's Institute, Mrs. White was not long experienced in the charismatic realm.

17 Jeremiah, op. cit., 18.
18 As Warden of Kearsney Homes of Healing in Natal (LHML 45, Easter 1964, 20).
19 LHML 48, Easter 1965, 1.
20 LHML 56, Christmas 1967, 2.
21 The date was November 7 (letter C. Cousen to M. Harper 3 Nov. 1963). It was on this occasion that Cousen first met Harper.
22 Richard Bolt 'Out for Ordination – Received the Baptism' RT 16 Sept. 16, 1960, 5.
23 'Clutching at a Straw?' interview of David Gosling with Richard Bolt, CEN 15 May 1964, 7.
24 Art. cit., RT, 5.
25 Ibid., 5.
26 Pastor George Rutherford.
27 Ibid., 6.
28 This information is from Christopher Squire and a letter of Bernard Bateson to Bill Grant dated May 26, 1959, as well as Bolt, art. cit. in note 22. An article entitled 'Students' Pentecostal Fellowship' in EE 26 Aug. 1961, 539 and RT 11 Aug. 1961, 17 sees the groups formed by Bolt for 'Pentecostal fellowship' as the origin of SPF.
29 Letter from Revd. T. Anscombe, the Principal, dated 2 December, 1959.
30 David R. P. Foot was in partnership with Noel Davson, who became one of the trustees of the Fountain Trust. Their office was in Buckingham Street just off the Strand.
31 'Just in time to give a testimony at the Conference' art. cit., in note 22, 6.
32 'Students' Pentecostal Fellowship' EE 26 Aug. 1961, 539 (also in RT 11 Aug. 1961, 17).
33 The Assemblies of God paper announced in November 1959 that 'Brother Richard Bolt has accepted the pastorate of the Full Gospel Mission, Straight Road, Lexden, Colchester.' (RT Nov. 20, 1959, 13).
34 A letter from Ralph Jarrett, the organiser of the house party, to Richard Bolt dated 21 April 1960 states: 'I was sorry that there is the division between you and the [Crusaders'] Union and all the more I feel indebted to you coming amongst us in the way that you did and for showing deference to the Union's position in spite of your strong convictions and barriers that have been erected.'
35 Extract from a letter from J. R. Adkins to the president of the Christian Union at Southampton University, (undated, but from contents evidently in 1965) complaining of the president's unsigned circular letter attacking the ministry of Bolt which it implied was the work of Satan.
36 Arts. cit., in EE and RT.
37 Arts. cit., in EE and RT.

38 Arts. cit., in EE and RT.
39 One of the Oxford members, David Petts, a student at Brasenose College, who later became an AoG minister and a Travelling Secretary for the SPF, had earlier written an article 'Pentecost at Oxford University' in RT 27 May 1960, 12–13. Petts and his fiancée, at that time both Baptists, were baptized in the Spirit on 8 September 1959, following contact with Pentecostals. Petts 'witnessed to the men in the College Christian Union and last term the leader of that group, an Anglican, was baptized in the Holy Spirit' (art. cit., 13). Petts' group became the Oxford branch of the SPF on its formation.
40 E.g. Petts at Oxford.
41 RT 16 Mar. 1962, 4.
42 Leaflet, undated, entitled Students Pentecostal Fellowship. It was evidently published not earlier than late 1963, as Bolt's address is given as Tunbridge Wells, where he moved in 1963 (RT Dec. 6, 1963, 16).
43 *The Pentecostal*, of which only four issues were ever issued, Vol. 1, Nos. 1–4.
44 PE Vol. 1/1, 3.
45 Art. cit., 4.
46 The Revd. John Lefroy.
47 Bill Grant estimated the number as perhaps a dozen young people.
48 D. R. P. Foot 'London meetings conducted by Richard Bolt' P 69, 16. The dates were Dec. 2 – 7, 1963 and March 2 – 11, 1964 (information from printed leaflets).
49 Dr. Adams continued to hold meetings in her home after joining Bolt's Church, and quite a number received the baptism in the Spirit through her influence.
50 The story of Forester and charismatic beginnings in Beckenham is found particularly in an interview 'Vicar of Beckenham receives baptism in the Holy Spirit' RV Nov. 1963, 6 and in G. H. Forester 'The Revival of the Charismata in an English Parish . . .' PE Vol. 1/2, Spring 1964, 9–11. Further details can be found in a signed message from Forester entitled 'Baptism in the Holy Spirit at Beckenham' (sent as an enclosure with MHN 2, Mar. 1964) and G. H. Forester 'A Vicar is led into Pentecostal Pastures' RT Feb. 26, 1965, 9–10.
51 Art. cit., RV, 6.
52 Art. cit., PE, 9.
53 Date from art. cit., PE, 9 and mention of Pentecostal friends from art. cit., RV, 6.
54 Details in art. cit., PE, 10.
55 Date in art. cit., PE, 10 (confirmed by postcard from M. Harper to P. L. C. & N. Smith 16 Sept. 16 1963); mention of Bolt in art. cit., RV, 6.
56 Art. cit., RV, 6.

57 Art. cit., RV, 6.

58 Forester wrote to Harper 'Since last time we spoke together another 3 have received the Spirit here and also two friends from Bromley Parish Church (all five through Richard Bolt's ministry).' (letter dated Oct. 3).

59 The letter of 3 Oct. 1963 also states: 'Am holding a public instruction on the Baptism in the Holy Spirit next Tuesday evening.'

60 Selwyn Hughes had been a probationer minister at the Elim Church in Colchester (RT 21 Aug. 1959, 18) and in 1962 had formed the London Revival Crusade with offices in Oxford Street. Its name was changed to 'Crusade for World Revival' in March 1964, reflecting the extended range of Hughes' ministry (RV Mar. 1964, 2). By late 1963, Hughes was holding regular meetings of a pentecostal character on Saturday evenings in Denison House on Vauxhall Bridge Road.

61 Although the first issue of RV was dated January 1963, regular monthly publication only began at the end of that year. RV had a decidedly Pentecostal flavour as can be seen from part of Hughes' editorial in November 1963: 'The deadness and drabness of formal religion has been invaded in many quarters by a tide of the Spirit of God that has lifted worship and devotion into a higher plane. Thousands of people in all Denominations have received the Baptism of the Holy Spirit according to Acts 2, verse 4. Hundreds more have received healing from Christ in a miraculous manner. In this year four of the world's leading Full Gospel Evangelists have visited this country.' (ibid., 2).

62 Ibid., 6.

63 CEN 15 Nov. 1963, 1.

64 Among the Spirit-baptized Anglican clergy who wrote to CEN were Philip Smith of Burslem (Dec. 13, 18) and Charles May of Woking (Nov. 22, 6 and Dec. 6, 6). Another letter was from a former Pentecostal minister now an Anglican priest, Harry Fisher of Attenborough, Notts (Dec. 6, 6). Fisher wrote that 'The Pentecostal Movement, which was (in this country at least) intended to function within the framework of the historic Churches, and not as an independent "sect," can, in spite of localised extravagances, fairly claim that the Pentecostal phenomena are evidence of a renewed work of the Holy Spirit, and as such are Scriptural, apostolic and historic.'

65 A four-page mimeographed report, enclosed with MHN 2, Mar. 1964.

66 MHN 2, 2.

67 See report, 3.

68 Ibid., 4.

69 Ibid., 4.

70 'Tongues' "Vicar Resigns" ' CEN Dec. 11, 1964, 1. Forester in fact moved to Bradford to work with Cecil Cousen at Dean House Fellowship in early 1965 (MHN 11, Apr. 1965, 2) but later joined the AoG,

becoming pastor in Deal, Kent.

71 Ibid. Forester gives this argument in fuller detail in a letter to his friends dated Christmas 1964.

72 CEN Dec. 11, 1964, 1.

73 See Chapter Thirteen, 86–7.

74 The basic facts in this story, though without mentioning Ron Bailey's name, are given in an article by the Rector, Revd. Philip Smith, which was published in several places (see note 93). M. Harper's account in *As at the Beginning*, 80–1, somewhat telescopes the events, and regards Smith's baptism in the Spirit as the beginning in Burslem. Smith was aged 40 in 1962 (CCD, 1980–2, 948).

75 Additional details to the sources in note 74 were given by Philip Smith. See also M. Harper, op. cit., 80.

76 Written account by B. Sillitoe dated 5 Oct. 1962.

77 Art. cit., in note 93. Sillitoe was baptized in the Spirit in Britain on 1 January 1963. Later he wrote an article in RN 7, Feb.–Mar. 1967, on 'New Power in Africa prison ministry' 22.

78 Art. cit., in note 93. Garner was twenty-five years old (letter P. L. C. Smith to Russell Mills, 17 June 1963).

79 On the influence of Hughes' editorial, see Chapter Seventeen, 109–11.

80 P. L. C. Smith 'Glossolalia – a phenomenon rather unusual in contemporary Anglicanism' T Whitsuntide 1964, 30–31.

81 Arts. cit., in notes 80 and 93.

82 Letter of N. Smith to M. & J. Harper, 6 Feb. 1963.

83 Some thirteen or fourteen of the young people at St. John's had received the baptism by February 1963 (letter N. Smith to M. & J. Harper, 6 Feb. 1963).

84 Letter of M. Harper to P. L. C. Smith dated 29 Jan. 1963. On Gillingham see Chapter Fourteen.

85 This is a reference to Fr. Francis Maguire, an American Episcopalian, whose visit to Britain is described in Chapter Seventeen, 111–12.

86 Q Oct. 1963, 7. Edwards moved to Brierley Hill, also in Staffs, a few months later. He was an active member of the MRF.

87 Letter from J. Bradberry to P. L. C. & N. Smith dated 5 Nov. 1963.

88 Information from Smith and art. cit. in note 93.

89 Letter of Jack Evans to G. & M. Ingram of the NPWR dated 3 May 1963.

90 Postscript to art. cit. in note 93.

91 Smith spoke for example at the Eric Hutchings Crusade in Bristol in June 1963 (letter P. L. C. Smith to Russell Mills, 17 June 1963), and at a Conference at Holmes Chapel organized by the Sandbach Congregational Church led by Revd. James Grimshaw in November 1963 (letter of J. Grimshaw to P. L. C. Smith, 14 Nov. 1963). Grimshaw had been baptized in the Spirit by this time.

92 RT Oct. 25, 1963, 5–6.
93 It was also published under the same title in Q Oct. 1963, 3–6, and EE
    9 Nov. 1963, 707–708, in EC under the title 'Tongues in a Church of
    England Parish' Nov. 22, 1963, 10, and in T and M under the title 'A
    New Work' (T Septuagesima 1964, 26–27; M July–Sept. 1964, 76–78). It
    was also translated into German for the Pentecostal magazine *Der
    Leuchter*. Jean Stone, the editor of *Trinity*, was less respectful of the
    author's anonymity, and stated 'Mr. Smith is Rector of St. John's
    Church of England, Burslem Parish Church.' (T art. cit., 26).
94 RT reported increased sales for that issue (letter A. Linford to P. L. C.
    Smith 27 Nov. 1963).
95 E.g. at Hanley Assembly in November 1963 (RT 6 Dec. 1963, 14) and at
    the AoG Conference in Clacton in May 1964 (RT 12 June 1964, 3–4).

Chapter 11

1   An account of the origin of NPWR can be found in Carol Acworth 'The
    nights of prayer and how they started' RN 13, Feb.–Mar. 1968, 4–6.
2   More information on Ingram's life can be found in obituaries following
    his death in September 1969 at the age of eighty-eight. See e.g. RPFN
    Nov.–Dec. 1969, 1 and 'George Ingram: A life lived with God' RN 24,
    Dec. 1969–Jan. 1970, 19–20.
3   RPFN Nov.–Dec. 1969, 1; RN 24, 20.
4   Acworth, art. cit., 4–5.
5   RPFN Nov.–Dec. 1969, 1.
6   The British Israelites, never a separate denomination, believed that the
    British people were the descendants of the lost tribes of Israel and as
    such were heirs to the specific blessings of the Old Covenant.
7   He had also compiled a booklet *We have a Guardian*, instancing divine
    interventions in British history.
8   See J. Edwin Orr *The Fervent Prayer*, Chapters Seven to Nine, and Eifion
    Evans *When He is Come* (reprinted under the title *Revival Comes to Wales*).
9   Grant drove George Ingram to Westminster Chapel each Sunday morn-
    ing to hear these sermons.
10 See note 1 to Chapter Ten.
11 See Chapter Ten, 56–8.
12 Houfe states that 'he refused to open his mouth to receive the gift of
    tongues which he received two years later when he opened his mouth
    and received this gift' (letter to author). See also art. in T Christmastide
    1962–3, 27.
13 The first meeting for members of APFR took place in the Church
    Parlour at Langham Place on 11 July 1960 (APFRQB 3 July 1960, 10).
    The APFR meetings then took place on average three times a year. By

the beginning of 1961, APFR had a membership of nearly six hundred including 'some from overseas'. (APFRQB 6 Apr 1961, 10).

62–3 See Chapter Ten, 76.

15 Prebendary Kerr was the President, and George Ingram the Chairman. There was then considerable overlap between the officers of the APFR and the organizers of NPWR. David Foot (see note 30 to Chapter 10) was treasurer, and continued so throughout the seven-year history of APFR, despite his becoming a Pentecostal.

16 APFRQB 2, 6–10.

17 Ingram wrote two small books on this topic called *Life and Life Abundant* and *The Fullness of the Holy Spirit*.

18 Harper recalls this occasion in *None Can Guess*, 42, but gives a later date. The earlier date was confirmed by Houfe's personal diary.

19 It is worth mentioning that All Souls, Langham Place had very close connections with the medical profession. Harley Street, the centre of British medical practice, was close by, and John Stott, the rector, was the son of the distinguished surgeon, Sir Arnold Stott. Healing services of intercession were however held occasionally at All Souls, though without any imposition of hands.

20 Harper, op. cit., 38.

21 See Chapter Ten, 58.

22 W. B. Grant 'God broke through my barrier' Q July–Sept. 1965, 11.

23 E. Houfe, 'An Act of Faith' T Christmastide 1962–63, 27.

24 Harper, op. cit., 44–45.

25 Houfe, art. cit., 27.

26 Grant, art. cit., 12–13. These dates are confirmed by a postcard sent by Grant to P. L. C. Smith dated 30 Aug. 1963.

27 Harper, op. cit., 20–30.

28 M. Harper 'An Anglican Priest and the Holy Spirit' T Whitsuntide 1964, 27 (reprinted in Q Oct.–Dec. 1965, 16).

29 The Revd. John Lefroy.

30 On 13 November according to Harper, op. cit., 44.

31 The influence of *Trinity* magazine in Britain is examined in Chapter Seventeen, 108–9.

32 Op. cit., 40–41.

33 This was true of men like David Lillie, Edgar Trout, William Wood, and Philip Smith even though they did not subscribe to the whole Pentecostal world-view.

34 E.g. David R. Smith, Campbell McAlpine.

35 See Chapter Three. Trout's passion for revival came after his baptism in the Spirit (see Chapter Six, 36).

36 'A New Work of the Holy Spirit – Are We Ready?' was the title given to the reprint of Dr. Philip Hughes' editorial in *The Churchman*, which

was widely distributed about this time (see Chapter Seventeen, 109–11).

37 E.g. 'The Church at Ephesus,' APFRQB 13, 2–4; 'The Promise of the Father' APFRQB 14, 5–6. Also letters to P. L. C. Smith, dated 29 Jan and 13 Feb. 1963.

38 Letter from D. M. Lloyd-Jones to M. Harper, 5 Apr. 1963.

39 Date from diary of Michael Harper. On Collins and Watson, see Chapter Fourteen. Saunders and Sansom (*David Watson*, 71) mention only one meeting with Lloyd-Jones, and add David MacInnes to the group of Anglicans visiting Lloyd-Jones.

40 Letter D. M. Lloyd-Jones to M. Harper, 11 Apr. 1963. Lloyd-Jones seems to have been more encouraging about the Charismatic movement in private than in public. An address at the Evangelical Library in 1964 dealt rather negatively with 'a recrudescence of interest in gifts of the Holy Spirit'. which led David Lillie to some correspondence with Lloyd-Jones (see letters of D. Lillie to M. Harper dated 23 Aug. 1964; 28 Aug. 1964; 24 Sept. 1964). Harper recalls Lloyd-Jones always being most encouraging to him in his ministry and endeavours (see M. Harper 'Raising standards' RN 37, Feb.–Mar. 1972, 34). The explanation for this apparent contrast of public and private attitudes is probably that Lloyd-Jones was strongly aware of the danger of people being more interested in gifts and in 'experiences' than in God and the Lord Jesus Christ (see his Foreword to E. Evans *The Welsh Revival of 1904*, 5–6), but that he wished to encourage those in whom he saw the work of the Spirit and an awareness of these dangers.

41 'I think it is urgent for those who are baptised with the Spirit to have fellowship' (letter M. Harper to P. L. C. & N. Smith, 28 May 1963).

42 Ibid., 28 May 1963.

43 'We need to pray that we are preserved from the trouble that came with the last outpouring at Sunderland, when those who had received were forced out of the Church.' (letter M. Harper to P. L. C. & N. Smith. 3 July 1963).

44 Ibid., 3 July 1963.

45 The Harpers were staying in Herts with Ben Allen, who drove them over to Cambridge (letter M. Harper to P. L. C. Smith 1 Aug. 1963).

46 Harper, op. cit., 54–5. On Christenson's visit see Chapter Seventeen, 112.

47 A letter of Jeanne Harper to Norah Smith dated 4 August 1963 says in relation to tongues 'Michael and I are confident now, as we go ahead in faith, that we shall exercise what He has now given to us both in a very small degree.'

48 Peppiatt's baptism in the Spirit is described by Harper, op. cit., 58. The visiting Pentecostal was Ted Whitesell.

49 Frank Maguire (see Chapter Seventeen, 111–12) and David du Plessis (see Chapter Nineteen, 122–3).
50 Tuesday, 7 January 1964 (CEN 10 Jan. 1964, 1). See also CH 10 Jan. 1964, 1, 12 and M. Saward 'The Holy Spirit in the Life of the Church' LF 16 Jan. 1964, 60.
51 Stott's talk was entitled 'The Individual Christian and the Fullness of the Holy Spirit' (CEN 10 Jan. 1964, 1). See note 32 to Chapter Seventeen.

Chapter 12

1 Information concerning Charles J. Clarke is mostly taken from 'Dominies Diary' in Q, from his witness in RN 1 Jan. 1966, 14–15 and RN 2, Mar.–Apr. 1966, 12–13, and from three interviews.
2 Q Apr. 1963, 3.
3 The union of three separate denominations within the Wesleyan Methodist tradition to form the Methodist Church of Great Britain had taken place only a few years previously in 1932.
4 Samuel Chadwick was born in Burnley, Lancs in 1860. He was superintendent of Oxford Place Chapel in Leeds from 1894–1907, and then spent the rest of his life (the years of World War I apart) at Cliff College, a Methodist lay training school in Derbyshire. From 1919 until his death in 1932, Chadwick was principal at Cliff. See Norman G. Dunning *Samuel Chadwick*; Charles Clarke *Pioneers of Revival*, 43–8; David H. Howarth *How Great a Flame*.
5 One such instance is reported by Chadwick:

> 'We prayed for him; took the Gospel to where he was likely to be found; and our Lazarus came. A man whose brutality and wickedness was a by-word, signed the pledge and gave his heart to God. It was talked of as a miracle. It was discussed in every barber's shop and public-house in the district. Lazarus was converted! We hadn't long to wait for the crowd. The largest building in the valley would not hold the people who came, not to hear me preach, oh dear no! precious little they cared for preaching; nor to see Jesus, but that they might see Lazarus whom He had raised from the dead. Never shall I forget the glorious work that followed! Hundreds of great, big, rough fellows were converted, and many godless women turned unto the Lord.' (Dunning, op. cit., 53).

6 This interest was not widely known in his lifetime and it is not mentioned in Dunning's biography. Evidently Chadwick began to read the works of Cardinal Newman about the time of Newman's death in 1890. One morning a week of his private devotions was set aside for intercession for the Roman Catholic Church, though he confessed, 'I don't know how God will do it.' This concern, surely a work of the Holy

244 *Streams of Renewal*

Spirit, must have been virtually unique among Free Churchmen of Chadwick's day. When Dr. Leslie Davison, then President of the Methodist Conference in Britain, met Pope John XXIII in 1963, the Pope said to Davison, 'Now tell me all you know about your man Samuel Chadwick.' (See John W. Harley 'Samuel Chadwick and Roman Catholics' D 21, Oct. 1977, 19 and David H. Howarth *How Great a Flame*, 34–5).

7 *The Way to Pentecost*, 40–3.

8 Ibid., 36.

9 The best account of the development from Wesley's teaching on entire sanctification through later Holiness teaching on baptism of the Holy Spirit for sanctification to the Pentecostal emphasis on baptism in the Holy Spirit with signs following for empowerment is found in Donald Dayton's *Theological Roots of Pentecostalism*.

10 E.g. 'The Lord and Healer still gives to men the gift of healing by His Spirit; and the gift works quite apart from medical knowledge of the use of drugs or herbs. Miracles are the gift of the Spirit, and the age of miracles is not past.' (ibid., 105).

11 'The Gift of Tongues comes last on the list, and is first in controversy. There is a gift of Tongues that is given for the perfecting of the saints and the building up of the Body of Christ. It means more than a gift for acquiring an unknown language, and it is certainly no substitute for such learning. A careful study of the New Testament places the gift among the enduements of the Church, and specially safeguards it against abuse, (ibid., 105–106).

12 David R. Smith, who was a student at Cliff College, knew Chadwick's widow, who still lived on the estate, and who was sure that Chadwick never spoke in tongues.

13 Another Methodist minister led to the baptism in the Spirit through Chadwick's writings was Kenneth McDougall, then (1966) of St. John's Methodist Church, Glasgow ('The Baptism of the Holy Spirit: A Methodist Minister's Testimony' SR Jan. 1967, 10–14, reprinted as 'New World of Reality' RN 9, June–July 1967, 4–8). McDougall became a Baptist minister within a few years.

14 Clarke was at Endike Hall from 1943–8.

15 Q Oct. 1961, 4. David Ruddock was assistant to Clarke at Endike Hall. He was a Methodist who was baptized in the Spirit under George Jeffreys, but after a spell as a Pentecostal, he rejoined the Methodists. hoping to bring the Pentecostal blessing back into Methodism. In this, his hopes were not realized.

16 In fact Clarke 'was not impressed by Pentecostalists generally and believed the Movement to be 'off-centre'' (Q July–Sept. 1964, 3).

17 Clarke produced abundant material on revival, much of it originally spoken addresses. See for example: *Resurgence* (36 pp. mimeographed,

no date but evidently 1956 from reference to Hebrides revival being 'about seven years ago' [15]: *The Pattern of Revival*, (37 pp., 1964); *Four Steps to Blessing for Service* (6 pp. printed, no date but reprinted from RN). *Pioneers of Revival* (71 pp., 1971) and *WorldWide Revival* (12 pp. printed, no date but reprinted from D).

18 From leaflet 'Christian Resurgence' written around December 1961.

19 The prayer meeting at Halesowen was called the 'Halesowen Resurgence Group' (see issues of Q in 1962–63).

20 Q July 1963, 21.

21 Chadwick is mentioned regularly in Clarke's writings e.g. TT Autumn 1957, 9: Winter 1957, 28–9; Q Apr. 1963, 3; July–Sept. 1964, 2–3; RN 2, Mar.–Apr. 1966, 12.

22 Q Apr.–June 1964, 2. See also RN 2, 12.

23 The MRF was formed in January 1952 and was formally approved as a Methodist body by Conference in 1955 (SR Apr. 1965, 1–2).

24 Q changed to a slightly larger and improved format with the January 1963 issue, which was however undated. The last issue as a separate magazine was that for October–December 1965 after which it merged with RN, Clarke writing a regular column under the title 'Quest'.

25 *The Torch* was Clarke's church magazine while he was minister in Cowes, Isle of Wight (1956–61). It ran from Summer 1957 until Winter 1961.

26 SR was a quarterly publication first issued as 'The Quarterly News Letter of the Methodist Revival Fellowship' becoming *Sound of Revival* in 1958.

27 Clarke probably did not know much about du Plessis at this time as his name was spelled 'du Plessey'.

28 Q Jan. 1962, 13.

29 Q Jan. 1962, 13.

30 Clarke wrote in a later account that after his arrival in Halesowen: 'God gave me young friends who had been baptized into the Holy Spirit, pentecostal fashion.' (Q Apr.–June 1964, 2–3).

31 RN 2, Mar.–Apr. 1966, 13.

32 Q Jan. 1963, 14–15.

33 Q Jan. 1963, 16. This date is also suggested by the fact that T is first mentioned in this issue of Q. It is unlikely Clarke would have delayed this news had he known of it before the October 1962 issue was completed.

34 Grant also sent Clarke a copy of APFRQB (letter of Trevor Pearson to W. B. Grant dated 11 Oct. 1962).

35 Q Jan. 1963, 12. This issue has several pages on the news from the USA (8–12).

36 RN 2, Mar.–Apr. 1966, 12–13. See also Q Apr.–June 1964, 3.

37 Q Apr. 1963, 3.
38 Entry for 30 January Q Apr. 1963, 17. Clarke later dates this experience to February 1963 (Q July–Sept. 1964, 4 where Clarke adds 'I cannot remember when I first praised in tongues').
39 Among other Methodists baptized in the Spirit in the early years of the Charismatic movement were some in a group led by R. V. Dinner, a lay preacher from Launceston, Cornwall (see letter from 'R.D.' in RV Dec. 1963, 7 and letter in CH 20 Aug. 1965, 10) and a group in Newquay, Cornwall visited by Edgar Trout.
40 On 9 February 1963. The week-end was at Eastwood Grange, Ashover (details Q Apr. 1963, 9–13).
41 Miss Milly Banks of Edgbaston, whose witness is in Q Apr. 1963, 11–12.
42 Q Apr. 1963, 21. This meeting was led by Amos Edwards of Stoke-on-Trent, who was soon to receive through the ministry of Philip Smith (see Chapter Ten, 67).
43 Q July 1963, 10.
44 AVF July–Sept. 1963, 4–5. The extracts are from Q Apr. 1963, 3–4, 20–2, 6–7, 14–15.
45 SR Jan. 1964, 4–7.
46 The first possibility was based on the view that miracles normally authenticate particular revelation, and would mean that the present outbreak was a sign of the rediscovery of neglected previous revelation. The second possibility appealed to the view that such gifts should be the norm for the church of every generation (ibid., 4). Lamb also raised the possibility that the restoration of these gifts was a sign of the Last Days, the 'Latter Rain' view (ibid., 5).
47 Derrick Mallen of Halesowen reported that 'Seven or eight of us received the baptism of the Holy Spirit and the gift of tongues as a sign.' (Q Jan. 1964, 16). This was confirmed by John Bagshawe of Sheffield (ibid., 17).
48 For Pawson, see Chapter Twenty-One, 132–3. Reference to his address at Swanwick is in SR Jan. 1965, 3 and Q Jan.–Mar. 1965, 4–5, 14.
49 See Chapter Fourteen on Gillingham. Reference to Collins' address at Swanwick is in SR Jan. 1965, 3 and Q Jan.–Mar. 1965, 6–7.
50 The new MRF Chairman, Robin Catlin, noted apropos of the Charismatic movement that 'The evangelical world seems to be quite sharply divided in its reactions to these reports, and this seems likely to be true within our own Fellowship.' (SR Jan. 1966, 4). Catlin evidently sought to be open to this movement being a work of the Holy Spirit, while preserving the right of MRF members to participate or not to participate.
51 E.g. a reprint of an article of Michael Harper from APFRQB 18, 'What is Hindering Revival?' and the anonymous testimony of Kenneth McDougall (see note 13 above).

52 The Clarkes moved to Ely, Cambridgeshire in September 1964.
53 Pat Baker was the married name of the Pat Nixon mentioned on page 81. She was responsible for producing the Birmingham District MRF Prayer Letter, which came out twice yearly.
54 They were married by Michael Harper at All Souls, Langham Place on 11 June 1964 (Q July–Sept. 1964, 12). Clarke had first met Harper in August 1963 on the occasion of Christenson's visit. Mary Collins had known Harper somewhat longer.
55 Mary Clarke's witness 'His Love Overflows' is reprinted in RN 17, Oct.–Nov. 1968, 19–22. See also 'He is Not Bound' Q Oct.–Dec. 1964, 7–10. Mary Collins had first heard of the baptism in the Spirit through the LHM, of which she had been an intercessor since 1958.
56 See note 24 above.
57 In September 1968, Clarke started a *Newsletter for Methodists interested in Charismatic Renewal*, and four years later merged this into *Dunamis*.
58 Clarke wrote three series on historic personalities in RN. The first on 'Pioneers of Revival' appeared in 1969–71 (RN 22–31), later published by the Fountain Trust as *Pioneers of Revival*, the second immediately followed as 'Men of Prayer' (RN 32–39, 41), while the third was entitled 'Portraits of Preachers' (RN 42–8, 50–1).
59 Teresa of Avila is mentioned in Q Oct. 1963, 17. Brother Lawrence and the Curé d'Ars were included in the series on 'Men of Prayer' (RN 33, June–July 1971, 20–2; RN 37, Feb.–Mar. 1972, 20–4). John Chrysostom was also included among the preachers, RN 44, Apr.–May 1973, 31–3. Brother Lawrence is also mentioned in Q July–Sept. 1965, 5, 7.
60 *Newsletter for Methodists*, July 1969, 2–3.

Chapter 13

1 Grant met Ross at the EDH Convention at Herne Bay in 1962.
2 See Chapter Five.
3 J. V. Thurman, *New Wineskins*, 32.
4 MHN 7, Dec. 1964, 2.
5 Kelly subsequently became associated with the work of G. W. North (see Thurman. op. cit..[?] 32–3).
6 The details in this paragraph are taken from Gordon Strachan 'My Story' PE 1/3, 1964, 11–12.
7 Strachan, art. cit., 12.
8 Casebow was minister of St. Margaret's Parish in Motherwell (T Whitsuntide 1965, 17). Casebow's struggles at this time are recounted in M. Harper *As at the Beginning*, 82–4.
9 Brian Casebow 'The Baptism of the Holy Spirit Transforms a Church of Scotland Minister' RV Dec. 1963, 6.

10   Art. cit. in RV 6. See also Brian Casebow 'The Joy of His Presence' T
     Christmastide 1962–3, 40–1.
11   Strachan, art. cit., 12.
12   Casebow, art. cit., 6.
13   Strachan, art. cit., 12.
14   Casebow, art. cit., 6.
15   The name of the village is given in an article 'Revival Blessings at
     Eastwood, Derbys' in RT Aug. 3, 1962, 7. The report refers anony-
     mously to a Church of Scotland minister receiving.
16   Strachan, art. cit., 12.
17   This item was reprinted in T Septuagesima 1964, 30.
18   EE 9 May 1964, 293.
19   McBain was then minister of Wishaw Baptist Church.
20   Details from an interview with McBain.
21   Report on the Visit of Mr. & Mrs. Don Stone, 1 (circulated with MHN
     3 May 1964).
22   Peddie's experience and message are described in his book *The Forgot-
     ten Talent*.
23   Op. cit., 102–3.
24   Op. cit., 104–8, 127.
25   Now known as the Gorbals Parish Church.
26   *Christian Life* magazine, published from Wheaton, Illinois, edited by
     Robert Walker, began publishing articles on this topic from the mid-
     1950s. It is one of the least known among the formative influences
     behind the Charismatic movement in the United States. See Chapter
     Twenty-Five, .
27   Burnett's witness is entitled 'This is the Baptism of the Spirit – What
     Else?' in LW Aug. 1965, 13–14. He answered a critic in a further article
     'The Baptism of the Holy Spirit' LW Oct. 1965, 27.
28   Art. cit., Aug. 1965, 14.

Chapter 14

1   Information on the events in Gillingham is drawn from interviews with
    John Collins, David MacInnes, David Smith and W B. Grant, as well as
    the sources cited in subsequent footnotes.
2   At St. Helen's, Bishopsgate.
3   An account of life at St. Mark's during this time period can be found in
    Teddy Saunders and Hugh Sansom *David Watson*, Ch. 6 'St Mark's,
    Gillingham', 46–58.
4   David MacInnes writes about this growth in David Watson in his
    contribution, entitled 'A Personal View' to Edward England (ed.) *David
    Watson: A Portrait by his Friends*, 14–38; for this point see pages 28–9.

5 Holy Sepulchre. Cambridge, known as 'The Round Church'.
6 An item in Q Apr. 1963, 7 probably forwarded to Clarke from Grant, reported In the early hours the pentecostal fire fell upon them and filled them full of God and joy. About fifty persons were filled with the Spirit.' The discrepancy between the figure of thirty (Collins) and fifty (in Q) is probably accounted for by the fact that not all the participants were present for the full eight hours. The Smiths, mentioned below, split the night, with David taking the first half, and Jean the second.
7 An anonymous report on the aftermath of the first Gillingham Night of Prayer, by 'A Vicar of an English Parish' was published under the title 'A Breath of Renewal' in APFRQB 14, 2–4.
8 Operation Mobilization is an evangelistic organization. founded by an American, George Verwer. While not encouraging charismatic experience, OM did not refuse or expel workers who received it, as e.g. Bryn Jones (see note 42 to Chapter Three).
9 Collins was the author of the report mentioned in note 7 above.
10 Q Apr. 1965, 7.
11 Letter to W. B. Grant, Sept. 23, 1963.
12 On Ridgelands, see Chapter Fifteen, 97–8.
13 Letter of Molly Heath to P. L. C. & N. Smith, dated 18 Sept. 1963.
14 Letter of M. & J. Harper to P. L. C. & N. Smith, 13 Feb. 1964, 2.
15 The house party was from 8 August 29–September 1964 (letter T. C. White to M. & J. Harper, Oct. 22, 1963).
16 M. Harper *None Can Guess*, 89–91. The letter from J. Collins quoted by Harper is dated 24 Sept. 1964.
17 On Walker's weekend at Gillingham, see Tom Walker *Renew Us By Your Spirit*, 32–40.
18 Walker, op. cit., 41.
19 Watson describes his experience in his autobiographical book *You Are My God*, 64. He told Michael Harper of his first taste of tongues in a letter dated 7 Oct. 1963.
20 Saunders and Sansom, op. cit., 82.
21 Ibid., 80.
22 Watson's difficulties are described in a letter of M. Harper to P. L. C. Smith. 12 Mar. 1964.
23 See Chapter Ten, 63–5.

Chapter 15

1 Details in this paragraph are taken from letters to the author from Miss Ellita Howell Williams and a letter of Miss Williams to Michael Harper dated 9 Feb. 1963.

2 Letter to Harper cited in note 1. Clark's first visit was probably in late 1962, as the letter of 9 February suggests that some weeks have passed since the visit.

3 See Chapter Fourteen, 91. Sillitoe went straight from the all-night prayer vigil to Farnborough on February 2, and two days later wrote to Harper telling him of Miss Williams' and Canon Hutchinson's search.

4 20 February (letter Miss Williams to M. Harper, 13 Feb. 1963).

5 Letter D. G. Clark to M. & J. Harper, 29 June 1963.

6 Sillitoe, who spent the weekend August 30–September 1 in Farnborough, reports that seven from the parish church had received the baptism in the Spirit with the sign of tongues, all in varied ways and without any laying-on of hands (letter B. Sillitoe to P. L. C. Smith, Sept. 1, 1963). Three weeks later the number has risen to ten (letter B. Sillitoe to W. B. Grant, 23 Sept. 1963).

7 These details from letter of Sillitoe to P. L. C. Smith, 1 Sept. 1963. Pastor Joseph Smith was a veteran Elim pastor with personal links to the early days of the Pentecostal movement.

8 On Greenwood, see also Chapter Six, 34 and note 13. Love's meeting with Greenwood is mentioned in a letter from Tony & Janet Nash to Philip & Norah Smith, 7 Dec. 1963. Osborn's meetings in Birmingham were from 7–9 October 1963 (LHML 43, 11).

9 The contrast between the more sober style of Clark and the more flamboyant style of Greenwood is evident from the letters of the Nashes. 'We know that the Lord has sent us a number of people, first the prayer-sowers, then those who sowed by the Word, e.g. Dennis Clarke [sic] from Worthing, then dear Harry who sowed mightily but also reaped' (letter cited in note 8). An earlier letter reports numerous dramatic healings through Greenwood's ministry, detailing a deaf ear, a deformed toe, a slipped disc, asthma, mongolism and hay fever (letter undated from Nashes to Smiths, to which Smith replied on 3 Dec. 1963).

10 May 23 (CPL 10 Jan. 1964, 2) and 22–26 July 1964 (CPL 15 Apr. 1964, 2).

11 CPL 15 Apr. 1964, 2.

12 17 May (see Chapter Nineteen, 124). About twenty people were baptized in the Spirit on that day (MHN 4, 10 July 1964, 2). Campbell McAlpine also visited Farnborough for a week-end at the end of November 1964 (letter cited in note 13).

13 Five were immersed on that day, Bob & Norah Love, Susan Love, their daughter, who by then was working for Don Double, and two young people (letter from the Loves to Michael Harper. dated 'Mon 30th', in fact 30 November 1964, datable by other references in the letter).

14 Letter cited in note 13.

15 Miss Williams also moved to Exeter with the Loves.

16 See also Chapter Twenty-One, 133–4.

17 Details on Mrs. MacKenzie and Ridgelands Bible College are from an interview with Mrs MacKenzie, unless otherwise indicated. See also P. Hocken 'The Unquenched Spirit in Molly MacKenzie RN 218, July 1994, 32–4.

18 One of these was Helen Guttery from Stourbridge, Worcs, who then developed contacts with St. Mark's, Gillingham (see letter of Molly Heath to P. L. C. & N. Smith, 18 Sept. 1963).

19 David MacInnes' wife, Clare, was one who was baptized in the Spirit while a student at Ridgelands after another student recounted her experience of being thus blessed at a meeting outside the College. The evidence points to this being in the first half of 1964.

20 The events of this week-end are briefly narrated as 'hot news' in a letter of Leslie Sutton to M. & J. Harper dated 15 July 1964.

21 Mrs. MacKenzie's description.

22 MHN 8 Jan. 1965, 2.

23 Martin Peppiatt was an early contributor to *Renewal*, writing 'The Christian's relation to Christ and the Spirit at conversion' RN 4, Aug.– Sept. 1966, 4–6.

24 Letter M. Peppiatt to M. Harper, 4 Feb. 1964.

25 Letter M. Peppiatt to M. & J. Harper, 6 June 1964.

26 Another college in the South of England where several students were baptized in the Spirit in 1963 and 1964 was Wye College, Ashford, Kent. This is described in John Dean 'A Wonderful Work of the Holy Spirit at Wye College, Kent, England' in PE 1/4, 1965, 10–12. John Dean was evidently in touch with Frank Wilson, a local Baptist minister, on whom see note 34 to Chapter Eighteen.

27 The story of Lee Abbey and of Sutton's role in its founding is told by Richard More *Growing in Faith: The Lee Abbey Story*. An earlier account Jack C. Winslow's *The Lee Abbey Story* is highly reticent in relation to the identity of the founders. Further details can be found in an obituary 'Great Adventure: Leslie Sutton 1894–1968' in RN 15, June–July 1968, 23–4.

28 RN 15, 24, and letter of L. Sutton to M. Harper, 7 June 1963.

29 Letter dated 10 June 1963.

30 Letter dated 6 July 1963.

31 Sutton spoke at both places in the first week of June 1963 (letter to M. Harper, 7 June 1963) and speaks regularly of both places and of Forester and Hutchinson in subsequent letters.

32 See Chapter Six, 36 and letter of L. Sutton to M. Harper, 15 July 1964.

33 Interestingly the British Pentecostal pioneer Cecil Polhill of Howbury Hall, Bedford, was a CIM missionary and remained on the CIM Council until his death.

34 Letter K. Macnair to M. Harper, 20 Dec. 1963.
35 Ibid. Harper had mentioned Newbigin's book in his CEN article of Oct. 25, 1963 (see Chapter Eighteen, 114).
36 Letter to M. Harper, Whit Sunday 1964.
37 30 May-6 June and 6–13 June (ibid).
38 R. More *Growing in Faith*, 148–9. D. Coomes refers to the beginnings of the movement at Lee Abbey in RN 49, Feb.–Mar. 1974, 15.
39 A group of young couples and two of the chaplains, Kristeen Macnair and Michael Vickers, came together to seek a deeper understanding of the work and role of the Holy Spirit. They ended by laying hands on each other at the end of the holiday. R. More (op. cit., 152) dates this event in 1963, while Barry Kissell whose account is otherwise less reliable places it in 1964 (*Springtime in the Church*, 52). Other data in this section are from a conversation with John Perry and letters of J. Perry to M. Harper unless otherwise stated.
40 18 Nov. 2 Dec. and 16 Dec. 1964 (MHN 6 Nov. 1964, 2 and *Prayer Bulletin* I, Dec. 1964, 1).
41 Harper states four visits (*None Can Guess*, 87). Kissell wrongly indicates two (*Springtime in the Church*, 51, 53), though he is correct in saying the original invitation was for two dates (letters J. Perry to M. Harper 22 & 31. Oct: 1964).
42 M. Harper, *None Can Guess*, 87.
43 Ibid., 87.
44 Visits of Trout are mentioned in Kissell. op. cit., 33–4, 55.
45 See Chapter Twenty-Two, 148.
46 Gravelle's witness is printed under the title 'Pentecost Sunday 1964' in T Whitsuntide 1965, 20–1. He was baptized in the Spirit a week after the Larry Christenson meeting at Langham Place, i.e. in the first week of September 1963.
47 Letter M. Meakin to Jean Stone, 25 Apr. 1964.
48 Letter J. Gravelle to M. Harper, 17 Nov. 1963.
49 Rex Meakin 'The Work of the Holy Spirit in a Midland Parish' T Whitsuntide 1965, 22–3 (see also note 1 to Chapter Twenty-Four).
50 Dunstone's witness is in RN 2, Mar.–Apr. 1966, 14–15.
51 Moore was baptized in the Spirit in the early summer of 1964 (letter of D. Watson to M. Harper, July 9, 1964). Moore reported to Harper on a Clergy Conference at Keble College, Oxford at which Dr. Michael Ramsey, the Archbishop of Canterbury, remarked that 'in a Church in which the Holy Spirit dwelt he would expect speaking in tongues' but urged those who had the gift 'to think as little about it as did St. Paul' (letter L. Moore to M. Harper, 26 Sept. 1964).
52 Letter of R. East to M. Harper, 27 Apr. 1964. The date 'early 1963' given in the two books mentioned in note 52 is thus incorrect.

53 J. Gunstone *Greater Things Than These*, 11 and *The Beginnings at What-combe*, 12.
54 See J. Gunstone *A People for His Praise* and *Pentecostal Anglicans*. Gunstone has related his liturgical and Anglo-Catholic interests to the work of the Spirit in 'The Spirit and the Lord's Supper' TR 10, Oct. 1978, 29–32 and 'After Seven Score Years and Ten: Celebrating the Oxford Movement' TR 24, July 1983, 18–26.

Chapter 16

1 David R. Smith and Edgar Trout were slightly different cases, for reasons given in Chapter Seven. Neither however could be said to have sought to relate the pentecostal blessing to an existing church tradition.
2 Du Plessis, Gee and Bolt have been mentioned in Section II, because of their influence, direct (du Plessis, Bolt) or indirect (Gee), on the emergence of pentecostal patterns of blessing within the historic churches of Britain.
3 See Chapter Seven, 42–3.
4 On *The Churchman* editorial, see Chapter Seventeen, 109–11.
5 See for example articles of M. Harper (see note 4 to Chapter Eighteen) and references in notes 63–4 to Chapter Ten.
6 See items in LF for 27 Sept 1962, 800; 14 Feb. 1963, 150; 7 Mar. 1963, 222, 227; 21 Mar. 1963, 275, 284; 28 Mar. 1963, 294, 296; 4 Apr. 1963, 323, 329; 11 Apr. 1963, 357–358; 18 Apr. 1963, 371–372, 380; 25 Apr. 1963, 402.
7 Several issues of EC in late 1963 made reference to the gift of tongues (e.g. 4 Oct. 8; 1 Nov. 9; 15 Nov. 9; 22 Nov. 10 [?](art. of P. L. C. Smith. see note 93 to Chapter Ten); 6 Dec. 15). A series of three critical articles in EC on 'Modern Pentecostalism' by Revd. R. Bell of Kirkdale, Liverpool (20 Dec. 3; 27 Dec. 3, 5; and 3 Jan. 1964, 3) then triggered further correspondence.
8 See the articles by J. Hywel Davies in CR Jan. 1964, 16–17, 23 and Feb. 1964, 12–13, 32.
9 On the IVF, see Chapter Fourteen, 103.
10 An undated letter from David M. Hughes to Harper (but evidently before Harper left All Souls, Langham Place in July 1964) reports several at Oak Hill being 'blessed'.
11 CEN 10 Jan. 1964, 1.
12 CT 10 Jan. 1964, 1, 24.
13 It seems that the charismatic experience at The People's Church in Everton, Liverpool, under Richard Kayes had probably begun by this time and the Anglican Norman Meeten had received this blessing (see Chapter Twenty-One, 134, 136).

14 The beginnings in South Wales were particularly associated with people outside the historic churches, such as Graham Perrins of Cardiff (see note 24 to Chapter Three). A conference was held at Rhoose near Barry in June 1963 on lines similar to those of Belstone and Mamhead Park (letter A. Wallis to M. Harper, 19 Mar. 1963).
15 An Anglican priest from Devon, baptized in the Spirit by 1963, and in touch with Wallis, was Ian Barclay, curate at Cullompton (letter A. Wallis to M. Harper, 9 Feb. 1963).

Chapter 17

1 See Chapter Twenty-Five 181.
2 See Chapter Twenty-Five 177, 181.
3 CEN Apr. 28, 1961, 13–14.
4 See Chapter Twenty-Five 184.
5 The Commission's report with appendices is published in Kilian McDonnell *Presence, Power, Praise*, I, 10–20.
6 CEN 28 Apr. 1961, 10.
7 'Readiness to learn from other Christians and an avoidance of cast-iron attitudes should be the marks of Anglicanism east or west.' (art. cit., 10). A similar position had been taken in an editorial in LC 'Pentecostal Voices', July 17, 1960, 9.
8 Belstone, 41–42 and Chapter Three, 18 and note 40.
9 Both Smith and Grant kept cuttings of this article.
10 CEN 4 Aug. 1961, 7.
11 CEN 8 Sept. 1961, 9. Bennett is described here as 'Vicar of St. Luke's Episcopal Church, Washington, D.C.' whereas he was in fact at St. Luke's, Seattle in the state of Washington.
12 Ronald A. Ward 'Tongues in Canada' CEN Dec. 21, 1962, 5.
13 On *Trinity* magazine, see Chapter Twenty-Five, .
14 Connelly, op. cit., 75.
15 These copies had certainly arrived by August 1962, as Houfe was reading T on 27 August (see Chapter Eleven, 73) and Clarke seems to have received his copy on September 7 (see Chapter Twelve, 82).
16 Q Jan. 1963, 10.
17 Q Apr. 1963, 2.
18 The first issue of Q, advertising T as available from Clarke's address, is July 1963, 24. T first mentions Clarke as agent in the issue for Trinitytide, 1963.
19 M. Harper, *None Can Guess* 46–7.
20 B. Casebow. 'The Joy of His Presence', 40–1.
21 See note 93 to Chapter Ten.
22 CEN arts. of 25 October 1963 and 1 November 1963 (see note 4 to Chapter Eighteen), both reprinted in T Septuagesima 1964, 28–9.

23 For example, the following issue of T for Whitsuntide 1964 has articles by M. Harper 'An Anglican Priest and the Holy Spirit', 26–8 and by P. L. C. Smith 'Glossolalia – a phenomenon rather unusual in contemporary Anglicanism', 30–31.

24 The information in this paragraph was provided by Clarke.

25 Hughes had already published a positive account of the pentecostal Episopalians under the heading of 'Review of Current Religious Thought' in CTO, 11 May 1962, 63, for which he was the British Editorial Associate. Douglas McBain recalls first hearing of the movement through this short article.

26 Art. cit., 63.

27 C Sept. 1962, 131.

28 C Sept. 1962, 133.

29 The reprint was entitled 'A New Work of the Holy Spirit – Are We Ready?'

30 Clark sent the leaflet with his Prayer Letter of 12 July 1963 and Wood with LHML 43.

31 'The largest attendance ever known at the Islington Clerical Conference held last Tuesday packed the Assembly Hall at Church House, Westminster, occupied the Press seats and the gangways and overflowed into Partridge Hall, while late-comers were unable to obtain a seat in either hall. The Scripture Union served a record number of over 450 buffet lunches in the Central Hall.' (CEN Jan. 10, 1964, 1). See also note 50 to Chapter Eleven.

32 An expanded version of Stott's talk was published by the IVP in July 1964 as a pamphlet under the title 'The Baptism and Fullness of the Holy Spirit'.

33 Lillie first heard of Harper from a friend in Sussex, who had met Harper at a house party near Bognor. The meeting at Harper's flat coincided with the only weekend for many years that Lillie had to be in London on business.

34 Lillie circulated a hundred copies of the July–Aug. 1962 issue of AVW to his friends.

35 E.g. 'I Will Pour Out of My Spirit' AVW July–Aug. 1961, 8–10 and George Forester's circular from MHN reprinted under the title 'This Current Revival' AVW Apr.–June 1964, 24–27, 23.

36 AVW reprinted some items of the Pentecostal pioneer Frank Bartleman, e.g. AVW Nov.–Dec. 1962, 1–3, 28–32 and Oct.–Dec. 1963, 16–24. The latter is introduced with the comment: 'From the pen of Mr. Bartleman himself we read here how it all began – catching much of the depth and significance which has been so largely lost in what has become known as Pentecostalism.' (16–17).

37 D. Bennett, *Nine O'Clock in the Morning*, 1–6, 16–25.

38   See M. Harper, *None Can Guess*, 57.
39   M. Harper, *As at the Beginning*, 85.
40   Ibid., 85.
41   This was arranged by Charles Clarke and took place on Friday 3 May (Q Apr. 1963, 15 and July 1963, 8).
42   This information was provided by Harper personally.
43   M. Harper *None Can Guess*, 57. On Christenson, see Chapter Twenty-Five, .
44   From invitation dated 'August 1963' marked 'Confidential' and signed by Michael Harper (in possession of Revd. Philip Smith). The clergy meeting was held in the Parlour at All Souls, Langham Place (introduction to tape of talk).
45   There is a brief written account of Maguire's message in Q, where Clarke began his report 'He told how the Episcopalian Revival began in his own Church' (July 1963, 8). Amos Edwards mimeographed a two-page summary from notes he took of Maguire's talk (copy in possession of author).
46   Details that follow are taken from a tape in possession of Revd. Michael Harper.
47   M. Harper, *None Can Guess*, 59–60. The first printing of *Speaking in Tongues, A Gift for the Body of Christ* in the autumn of 1963 sold out before the setting up of the Fountain Trust, which then reprinted this pamphlet. The first edition was advertised in LHML 45, Easter 1964.
48   M. Harper, *None Can Guess*, 58.
49   On Sanford, see Chapter Twenty-Five, .
50   Bromley on August 11–13 and Reigate on August 14 (LHML 43, Summer 1965, 1).
51   Agnes Sanford returned to England in June 1964 (see Chapter Fifteen, 100).
52   The vicar of St. John's, Bromley, F. Noel Palmer, who had been a member of OSL and interested in the healing ministry for some years, was baptized in the Spirit on 11 October 1963 after hands were laid on him by Mary Collins, the future wife of Charles J. Clarke. He wrote an article replying to John Stott's criticisms, 'Two-Stage Experience?' (CEN Jan. 17, 1964, 5).
53   Chapter Twenty-Five, .

Chapter 18

1   Letter of M. Harper to P. L. C. & N. Smith, 28 May 1963.
2   Letter of M. Harper to P. L. C. & N. Smith, 16 Aug. 1963. This letter mentions Howard Cole, David Gardner (see note 31 below) and George Forester of St. Paul's Beckenham, as being available for this meeting.
3   Letter of M. Harper to P. L. C. & N. Smith, 6 Sept. 1963.

4 'A New Thing' CEN Oct. 25, 1963, 7 and ' "Word Only" Preaching' CEN 1 Nov. 1963, 7.

5 Newbigin's Pentecostal stream obviously includes the Pentecostal Christians of the twentieth century but also extends to all those whose conviction is that 'the Christian life is a matter of the experienced power and presence of the Holy Spirit today' (*The Household of God*, 87).

6 See Chapter Nineteen, 122–3.

7 Among those who received on this occasion were the Revd. Charles May, then a curate in Woking and later Vicar of St. Luke's, Hackney, and Diana Collins, wife of John Collins of Gillingham.

8 Letter of M. Harper to P. L. C. & N. Smith, Feb. 13, 1964.

9 MHN 1, Jan. 1964, 2.

10 E.g. advertising two meetings sponsored by Bill Wood playing tapes of Oral Roberts (MHN 1, Jan. 1964, 2).

11 M. Harper *None Can Guess*, 74. The date, February 12, is given in a two-page report 'Stoke Poges Prayer Conference 1964', circulated with MHN 2, Mar. 1964. This was reprinted in P 68, June–Aug. 1964, 5.

12 Mrs. Anne White (*None Can Guess*, 75).

13 These included Eric Houfe and Geoffrey Gould.

14 Katherine Cox, who had been baptized in the Spirit, while visiting Dennis Bennett's parish in Seattle. She wrote about Stoke Poges 'there were 27 the first day and 22 the second' (letter to Norah Smith, Feb. 26, 1964).

15 Miss E. Howell Williams from Farnborough (see Chapter Fifteen, 96, 98).

16 SPR, 1.

17 Although Wallis and McAlpine had got to know each other in Britain around 1957–58, their friendship deepened during Wallis' visit to New Zealand. In February 1964, Wallis was still in New Zealand, whence McAlpine had recently returned.

18 See *None Can Guess*, 75.

19 SPR, 1. Katherine Cox says there were five such people (letter to N. Smith, Feb. 26, 1964).

20 All these details are from SPR, 1.

21 Information from MHN 3, May 1964, 1 and accompanying report 'The Visit of Mr. and Mrs. Don Stone'. Bill Grant was first asked to arrange this tour but referred Mrs. Stone to Harper.

22 The evangelical vicarage was Burslem (see Chapter Ten, 65–8) and the anglo-catholic Woburn Sands (see Chapter Fifteen, 101).

23 See Chapter Thirteen, 87–88.

24 Seventeen representatives of the Christian press attended (see report by T. W. Walker in EE 20 June 1964, 387). Another account is in EC 19 June 1964, 5.

25 'The Visit of Mr. and Mrs. Don Stone', 2. Mrs. Stone's message was interpreted by Brian Sephton, a minister of the Apostolic Church see the appreciation by Michael Harper in RN 252, May 1997, 9.

26 See M. Bennett 'A Question of Freedom' RN 50, Apr.–May 1974, 15–16.

27 Trevor Marzetti, for a time administrative secretary of Vic Ramsey's New Life Foundation, later became editor of *Anglicans for Renewal*.

28 T. J. Marzetti 'Headed for the Hard Road' RN 51, June–July 1974, 13.

29 Hugh Thompson is another ex-member of the Brethren, whose testimony is given in D. G. Lillie's *Tongues under Fire* (testimony no. 4, 52). Thompson was baptized in the Spirit at a conference near Basingstoke in April 1964, after seeking counsel and prayer from Campbell McAlpine, one of the speakers. He has been part of the New Covenant network under Bryn Jones for many years.

30 See Chapter Ten, 67.

31 David Gardner, travelling chaplain for the Boys' Covenanter Union from 1960 until 1978, was much exercised about national revival.

32 Donald Eddison, another former curate of All Souls, Langham Place (1951–53), began seeking the baptism in the Spirit following David du Plessis' address at the Londoner Hotel in October, 1963. He received it within a month (letter D. Eddison to M. Harper, 5 Nov. 1963). Eddison became vicar of St. John's, Tunbridge Wells, in 1965.

33 Richard Vick, vicar of St. Paul's, Westcliff-on-Sea, Essex, stated that he had received the baptism in the Spirit in 1958. By late 1964 he had between six and twelve people in his parish who spoke in tongues. These details are from an article 'Baptism Issue Explodes' CEN Dec. 18, 1964, 1.

34 Frank Wilson was at this time minister of Willesborough Baptist Church, Ashford, Kent. His involvement in the Charismatic movement was linked to a visit of Edgar Trout to the Ashford area, when Trout gave Wilson a word about a future ministry to broken lives that God would give him (F. Wilson *House of New Beginnings*, 10). Wilson served as an unofficial assistant to Harper at the Fountain Trust in the first quarter of 1965 (MHN 7, Dec. 1964, 2; MHN 11, Apr. 1965, 2), and then went into full-time ministry to drug addicts.

35 James was minister of Gresham Baptist Church in the Balham-Brixton area of South London, after having been a deacon at Westminster Chapel for many years. He was still seeking the baptism in the Spirit at this time.

36 Harper wrote in MHN 3, May 1964, 1, that 'This newsletter will be going to four times the number of people the first one went to – an indication of the great interest in the movement of the Holy Spirit in this country.' The same letter mentions three follow-up meetings arranged in London for June as 'so many Christians have in the last months been baptized in the Spirit' (MHN 3, May 1964, 2).

37 Harper's first article in the more High Church weekly, *The Church Times*, was published at this time, 'Modern "Speakers in Tongues" ' CT May 15, 1964, 11, 13.

38 MHN 2 Mar. 1964, 1. See also *None Can Guess*, 62.

39 MHN 4, July 10, 1964, 1.

40 On the genesis of the Fountain Trust see MHN 4 July 9, 1964 and *None Can Guess*, 63.

41 The first idea had been to call it the Watergate Trust (*None Can Guess*, 63–4).

42 MHN 4, 9 July 1964, 2.

43 The first trustees were Eric Houfe, Bill Grant, Geoffrey Gould (see note 13 above) and Noel Davson, an accountant (see note 30 to Chapter Ten). The trustees were picked solely on the basis of professional competence and their support for this work of the Spirit, and not on denominational grounds.

44 The members of the Advisory Council in the early years of the Fountain Trust included Arthur Wallis, Cecil Cousen, Charles Clarke and Campbell McAlpine.

45 RN 21, June–July 1969, 2–3.

46 Harper's autumn itinerary in 1964 included a number of places where the Charismatic movement early surfaced in Anglican parishes, e.g. Cheltenham, Gillingham, Loughborough and Chorleywood (see MHN 5, Oct. 1964; MHN 6, Nov. 1964). The beginnings in Cheltenham were associated with John Baker, curate at St. Mark's and Bob Paget, curate at St. Aidan's.

47 Harper visited Goldhill Baptist Church in Chalfont St. Peter in October 1964 and the Gresham Baptist Church, Brixton in November. He had also recently met Douglas McBain of Wishaw, Scotland. On the Baptist developments, see also Chapter Twenty-One, 132–4.

48 MHN 7, Dec. 1964, 2.

49 This trip is described by Harper in *None Can Guess*, 93–6 and in a two-page summary 'North American Diary' and extracts from letters sent to recipients of MHN.

50 Entry for May 13 in 'North American Diary'. This was almost two years before the main beginnings of the Charismatic movement among Roman Catholics in the USA.

51 Du Plessis spoke in London on 10 November 1964 (MHN 6, Nov. 1964, 1).

52 Derek Prince spoke in London on 23 November 1964 (MHN 6, Nov. 1964, 1).

53 Edgar Trout spoke at the City Temple on 26 October 1964 (MHN 5, Oct. 1964, 1), Campbell McAlpine also at the City Temple on 28 December 1964 (MHN 7, Dec. 1964, 1), Arthur Wallis at the Westminster Chapel

on 25 January 1965 (MHN 8, Jan. 1965, 1). At the following London meeting on 1 April 1965, again at Westminster Chapel, the speakers were Wallis and McAlpine (MHN 10, Mar. 1965, 1). Wallis and McAlpine spoke at the first Fountain Trust January Conference at High Leigh, January 22–24, 1965 (Q Apr. 1965, 3–4). Many of the early tapes marketed by the Fountain Trust were the tapes from these talks. Trout also conducted a seminar for ministers in November 1964 on ministry to the mentally sick and deliverance from demonic powers (MHN 5, Oct. 1964, 1, 4).

54 As at High Leigh in January 1966 (see RN 2, Mar.–Apr. 1966, 9–11).

55 *As at the Beginning* was reprinted in the USA by the Society of Stephen (Altadena, California) in 1994. The Society of Stephen is directed by Rick and Jean (Stone) Willans.

56 From 1963, Harper began to read about the Pentecostal movement, and read of Boddy in Gee's book *The Pentecostal Movement* (later *Wind and Flame*). There were in fact some people still alive who recalled the Pentecostal ministry of Boddy with gratitude. Letters from two of these men are printed in Appendix II.

57 'Change in Climate' CEN Dec. 11, 1964, 14 and 'First edify, then evangelize' CEN Dec. 24, 1964, 2.

58 Letter of Bishop Stopford to M. Harper, Sept. 25, 1964.

59 See Chapter Nineteen, 24.

60 Letters of Bishop Stockwood to M. Harper, 5 Oct. 1964 and 28 Oct. 1964.

61 The first issue was dated January 1966.

62 See undated letter of Jeanne Harper to Norah Smith from autumn 1963. Norah Smith's reply is dated November 11, 1963.

63 MHN 5, Oct. 1964, 2.

Chapter 19

1 July 1959 to Glasgow (see Chapter Four, 23 and Chapter Eight, 47); January 1960 to London (see Chapter Eight, 47); August 1960 to St. Andrews (see Chapter Eight, 47–8); June 1961 to High Leigh (see Chapter Nine, 52–53) and March 1962 to London (see Chapter Ten, 57–78).

2 This Pentecostal phrase was regularly used by du Plessis.

3 Dates from DdPN, Oct. 1963, 2.

4 Details about the invitation and attendance were given by Eric Houfe, who recalled three hundred invitations being sent out with a hundred and twenty present. Harper's figures are '150 invitations with about 150 present' (*None Can Guess*, 59).

5 From tape of talk.

6 Du Plessis' range of contacts on his almost incessant travels can be seen from his newsletters.

7   P 61, Sept.–Nov. 1962, 7.

8   Details from DdPN.

9   From tape of talk.

10 Du Plessis' itinerary was published with MHN 3, May 1964. Confirmation that he did speak in these places is in MHN 4, 10 July 1964, 2–3.

11 Meeting organized by David Lillie.

12 Meeting organized by Denis Clark.

13 Extracts from the Bradford talk are given in AVF July–Sept. 1964, 13–15. These include the first version of the Wigglesworth prophecy to appear in print (see note 6 to Chapter One).

14 The meeting in Bristol was attended by a number of the staff and members of the Anglican Theological Colleges (MHN 4, 10 July 1964, 3).

15 Ibid., 2.

16 Du Plessis' visit to Edinburgh is described in G. Strachan 'The Pentecostalists raise some disturbing questions' LW July 1964, 219 (reprinted in slightly abbreviated form in P 69, Sept.–Nov. 1964, 8).

17 MHN 4, 2.

18 Du Plessis' visit to the 1961 LHM Healing Advance is mentioned in Chapter Nine, 52–53. The 1964 Healing Advance is briefly reported in LHML 46, Summer 1964, 4.

19 MHN 6, Nov. 1964, 1. Du Plessis reported: 'About 30 presented themselves for the baptism in the Holy Spirit and Jesus graciously baptized about half of them in a beautiful quiet and reverent meeting.' (DdPN Dec. 1964, 2).

20 This was at the LHM. See note 49 to Chapter Nine.

21 DdPN Dec. 1964, 2. Donald Gee married Mrs. Jean Coombe on 3 October 1964 (John Carter *Donald Gee – Pentecostal Statesman*, 97). Du Plessis made a point of visiting Gee on his British visits (see also DdPN June 1965, 2).

22 This talk was evidently on 21 May the day before the public sessions in the same church (DdPN June 1965, 2).

23 DdPN June 1965, 2.

24 MHN 11, Apr. 1965, 1 and MHN 12, June 1965, 1.

25 DdPN June 1965, 2.

26 Places visited are listed in DdPN Feb. 1966, 2.

27 The focal point of the Charismatic movement in the Hastings-Bexhill-St.Leonards area by 1965 was the St. Leonards Baptist Church. Frank Wilson tells Harper of 'a young and intellectual Baptist minister in Bexhill' being baptized in the Spirit in October 1964 (letter dated Oct. 13, 1964). This was David Jones, assistant at Beulah Baptist Church. Tom Walker, then curate in an Anglican parish in St. Leonards, reports of a local Baptist Church 'where the young people were even speaking

in tongues' (*Renew Us By Your Spirit*, 12). This was Chapel Park Road Baptist Church in St. Leonards, whose minister, Gordon Hunt, had already been baptized in the Spirit. The meeting at St. Leonards, mentioned in Chapter Twenty-Two, was in this church (RN 2, Mar.–Apr. 1966, 6–7). The then moderator of the Kent and Sussex Baptist Association, Edmund Heddle, of Bexhill, was baptized in the Spirit in 1965, receiving the laying on of hands in February and the gift of tongues in November.

28 The Anglican vicar in Tufnell Park, Bob Marsh, had been baptized in the Spirit in February 1964 following the witness of his sister-in-law, Katherine Cox (see note 14 to Chapter Eighteen). The testimony of Marsh and his wife is in RN 7, Feb.–Mar. 1967, 5–6.

29 The movement began in the Anglican parish in Otley, Yorks when several lay people were baptized in the Spirit in late 1964 and early 1965. Evidently there was some contact with Pastor G. W. North of Bradford. One of the curates, Harry Cooke, and his wife received the baptism in the Spirit around this time (letters of H. Cooke to M. Harper, 4 Feb. 1965 and 21 July 1965).

30 On the FGBMFI London Convention, see Chapter Twenty-Two, 143–4.

31 DdPN Feb. 1966, 2.

32 See Chapter Eight, 47 and *A Man Called Mr. Pentecost*, 201–4.

33 *A Man Called Mr. Pentecost*, 207–208.

34 As, e.g. October 1963 at the Londoner Hotel, at Bradford, Motherwell, Edinburgh, Birmingham, Luton, Stoke Poges and London in May–June 1964, and Westminster Chapel in May 1965.

Chapter 20

1 See Chapter Eight, 44.

2 David R. Smith, though admiring du Plessis, did not share his vision (see Chapter Four).

3 This is implied in Michael Harper's *As at the Beginning*, where two chapters on the USA are followed by one on Britain entitled 'Atlantic Crossing'.

4 See Chapter Twenty-Five, .

5 Of Grant's close friends, Ben Allen more than Eric Houfe shared the contacts with the independents, and with Grant attended the Belstone and Mamhead Park Conferences (see Chapter Three, 17). However, Allen was not a focal point for organization and information to the same degree as Grant, and his contribution was diminished by his recurring ill-health.

6 On the Blessed Trinity Society, see J. T. Connelly *Neo-Pentecostalism*, 74–90 and Chapter Twenty-Five, .

7 Central to du Plessis' preaching was the message that Jesus Christ is the baptizer in the Holy Spirit. A characteristic point is made by du Plessis: 'One theologian said, why do you not use the word "infilling"? The reason is that I am not talking about what happens to the candidate; I am talking about what Jesus does.' (AVF July–Sept. 1964, 14). A pamphlet of du Plessis on this topic *Jesus Christ the Baptizer in the Holy Spirit* received wide circulation (and was sent by Wood to all subscribers to LHML with issue no 49, Summer 1965). It was also published in PE 1/3, 1964, 8–11.

8 *A Man Called Mr. Pentecost*, 195–8.

9 'There are encouraging signs, for which we can be thankful, that greater tolerance is being manifested than was the case at the beginning of this century.' (D. Gee 'At the Crossroads' P 56, June–Aug. 1961).

Chapter 21

1 E.g. at Burslem, Gillingham, Chorleywood, Woburn Sands and Loughborough.

2 See note 34 to Chapter Eighteen.

3 A young Baptist from Holland Road Baptist Church in Hove, Terry Virgo, later a prominent leader in the House Church movement, was touched by a friend's witness to seek the baptism in the Spirit. This he received at Peniel Chapel in Kennington in 1962. His minister at Holland Road, Rev. E. G. Rudman, encouraged Terry to share this witness and lead young people in the congregation to the baptism. This led to a new evangelistic enthusiasm among those young people, many of whom began to take part in regular open air evangelistic meetings on Brighton seafront. Within a year Terry had left his secular employment to take on a faith venture of full-time evangelism. In 1965 he moved to London to attend London Bible College and also on Sunday mornings regularly to attend the pioneering charismatic church led by Richard Bolt in Buckingham Street.

4 These comments do not apply to Scotland.

5 Information on the BRF and on the events at the 1964 Conference was provided by Harold Owen and Henry Tyler, unless otherwise stated.

6 Among these were Arthur Neil of Burnham-on-Sea, Somerset; Michael Pusey of Basingstoke; Richard Kayes of Everton, Liverpool; and Leslie Moxham of South Norwood, London.

7 Information from 'A Tale of Two Churches' F 7, 7–8, which contains elements of Pusey's witness.

8 Letter from M. Pusey to M. Harper, 27 Nov. 1964.

9 Prayer Bulletin I from the Fountain Trust dated December 1964 gives praise for a 'a number of Baptist Ministers who have entered recently into the blessing of the Holy Spirit'.

10 Kayes, minister of the People's Church, Everton, Liverpool, prayed for Tyler in an unusual way, praying first and primarily for the whole body of Christ, and only at the end, almost 'as a postscript', specifically for Tyler.

11 Accounts of the impact of the Holy Spirit in the congregation at Basingstoke nearly all ignore the role of Pusey, and attribute all the charismatic dimension to the period of Coombs' ministry.

12 Valentine Cunningham 'Alive in the Spirit' RN 35, Oct.–Nov. 1971, 32–3.

13 These details are taken from a booklet published by the BRF in 1964, entitled *Liberty in the Lord*, which gives a good idea of dominant concerns in its membership.

14 The fact that many of the main charismatic figures from the BRF later left the Baptist Union does not therefore have the same significance as secession by ministers with previously strong denominational allegiance.

15 On Heddle, see note 27 to Chapter Nineteen.

16 Noble provided the information about himself. Some further background is in 'I.D.' F 23, 18–19.

17 See note 8 to Chapter Twenty-Two.

18 Noble was later part of the network of house church leaders that produced*Fulness* magazine.

19 See Chapter Twenty-Two, 143–4.

20 Besides Lillie, Wallis, Clark, McAlpine, Purse, Perrins, Hutchison and Coombs, whose Brethren backgrounds have already been mentioned, other ex-Brethren in the Charismatic movement included Hugh Thompson (see note 29 to Chapter Eighteen), Jack Hardwidge (see note 30 below), Alan Pavey (for a time a colleague of Hardwidge), David Mansell (later a house church leader) and David Tomlinson (baptized in the Spirit at one of G. W. North's meetings in Liverpool in 1965 and also later a house church leader, RS Nov.–Dec. 1978, 6).

21 The Conference was held from 5–9 April 1965 (MHN 10, Mar. 1965, 2). Some of the talks were subsequently published in AVF, those of Wallis in July–Sept. 1965, 10–14 and Oct.–Dec. 1965, 3–7, of Cousen in Jan.–Mar. 1966, 3–7, of Perrins in Jan.–Mar. 1966, 12–13, 15, and Apr.–June 1966, 14–16 and of Roger Forster in Apr.–June 1966, 6–9.

22 On North, see Chapter Two.

23 Norman Meeten, curate at St. Saviour's, Liverpool from 1961–64, was baptized in the Spirit in May 1963 (letter M. Peppiatt to M. & J. Harper, 18 Apr. 1964). He was one of the trustees of The Longcroft, the home on the Wirral where G. W. North moved in 1965.

24 The fullest information on the house churches in Britain is in Andrew Walker *Restoring the Kingdom* and J. V. Thurman *New Wineskins*. See

also Derek Williams 'Denominations – the End of the Road?' CR Jan.
1981, 22–6; W. J. Hollenweger 'The House Church Movement in Great
Britain' ET Nov. 1980, 45–47; Brian Hewitt *Doing a New Thing?*

25 Harper originally accepted the invitation but later withdrew.

26 This position is indicated in an article by Wallis 'The church in the
house' RN 52, Aug.–Sept. 1974, 14–16, where he wrote: 'Our only
loyalty is to Christ, and then to the local church where He wants us to
be, of whatever sort it may be. But denominational loyalty (as distinct
from loyalty to a local church that may happen to be denominational)
only weakens the unity of the body as a whole' (16). This Brethren-type
understanding of the church is further studied in Appendix III.

27 Many years later, in his retirement at Scarborough, Cousen became
more critical of restorationist views and became active in the Anglican
Church.

28 AVF Jan.–Mar. 1966, 13.

29 On Chard and its leader, Sid Purse, see notes 9 and 10 to Chapter Three.
Harry Greenwood moved to the Chard Fellowship in the mid-1960s.

30 This lesser influence on the movement as a whole was partly due to
their own lack of involvement (though North had more such contacts
than Purse) and was partly due to aspects of their teaching being
regarded with suspicion by other Christians (see Thurman, op. cit.,
68–9, 72).

31 Hardwidge was the leader of a fellowship that broke off from the
Plymouth Brethren, and was distinct from the other house fellowships
and churches of a charismatic nature growing in the Exeter area, as that
of David Lillie at Countess Wear (see Chapter Three) and Bob Love (see
Chapter Fifteen, 97).

32 See Chapter Thirteen, 85.

33 Trout is known to have been in contact with the house fellowships in
Glasgow (Dr. Kelly); Middlesbrough (led by the Hintons); Gosport,
Hants (led by Ted Kent); Burford, Oxfordshire (led by Eddie Horner);
Blackhorse, Bristol (led by Peter Lyne); Maidstone, Kent (led by the
Mutimers) and Swindon, Wilts (led by Dr. Cullis).

Chapter 22

1 See Chapters Twenty-Three and Twenty-Four.

2 D. W. Bebbington *Evangelicalism in Modern Britain: A History from the
1730s to the 1980s*, 232.

3 The Brethren whose contribution to the beginnings of the house church
movement has been noted were a particularly middle-class body, with
strong representation among lawyers and teachers. The least middle-
class sector was probably the circle associated with Bryn Jones, which

may explain the lesser involvement of his grouping in later pan-Charismatic patterns of association.

4 Bebbington says of the Charismatics that: 'The traditional, the institutional, the bureaucratic were rejected for the sake of individual self-expression and idealised community.' (*Op. cit.*, 233).

5 Letter dated 5 June 1964.

6 Letter of F. Maguire to M. Harper, 10 Sept. 1963.

7 The only Pentecostal speakers sponsored by the Fountain Trust were David du Plessis, who was seen as the unique ecumenical Pentecostal, and Derek Prince, for some years principal of a Pentecostal college in Kenya, who as an Old Etonian and former Cambridge Fellow was not exactly a typical Pentecostal preacher.

8 Harper was here following the terminology introduced by Bredesen and Stone in the USA (see Chapter Twenty-Five).

9 Smith spoke at the AoG Conference in Clacton in May 1964 and Harper attended the Elim Conference at Skegness the following month with du Plessis (EE 17 June 1964, 410–411).

10 E.g. SPF on 27 November 1964 (MHN 6, Nov. 1964, 2) and the Elim Central Church, Clapham on 6 March 1965 (MHN 9, Feb. 1965, 2) and at Farnborough Pentecostal Church on 7 May 1966 (MHN 18, Feb. 1966, 2). He also spoke to a city-wide gathering at the Elim Church in Bristol on 16 October 1964 (MHN 5, Oct. 1964, 4).

11 Harper, Cousen and Bolt were among the speakers. A report on this series was published by T. H. Stevenson under the title 'The Work of the Holy Spirit in the Church Today' in EE Apr. 18, 1964, 244–5 (reprinted in P 68, June–Aug. 1964, 4).

12 See MHN 4, 10 July 1964, 1.

13 One ex-Elim Anglican priest, Arthur Jackson of Stone, Staffs helped a number of former Pentecostal ministers to join and adjust to the Church of England. Jackson 'did retain his Pentecostal convictions but they were not pronounced', according to Desmond Cartwright. Kenneth Matthew, a former Elim minister, ordained deacon in the Church of England in 1964 and priest in 1965, was one of the speakers at Southwark Cathedral in November 1965 on 'The Twentieth Century charismatic renewal' sponsored by the Fountain Trust (MHN 16, Oct. 1965, 2). See also the reference to Harry Fisher, also ex-Elim, in note 64 to Chapter Ten.

14 Edward England hails the courage of Leonard Cutts of Hodder and Stoughton, a publishing company with a high reputation among evangelicals, in publishing *As at the Beginning* (E. England *An Unfading Vision*, 58).

15 Harper writes of Boddy and Polhill, the two Anglican pioneers in the Pentecostal movement 'They were determined to keep the movement

in the churches – while the churches seemed equally determined to keep it out.' (*As at the Beginning*, 45).

16 51–3.

17 E.g. RT 17 May 1963, 16; 10 Apr. 1964, 6, 9; 6 Nov. 1964, 7.

18 E.g. EE 6 July 1963, 426–7; 10 Aug. 1963, 508; 9 May 1964, 293; 16 May 1964, 311; 20 June 1964, 387–8; 7 Nov. 1964, 710; 21 Nov. 1964, 742.

19 E.g. EE 15 Apr. 1961, 226; 14 July 1962, 434; 9 Mar. 1963, 146; 20 Apr. 1963, 242; 9 Nov. 1963, 706; 16 May 1964, 306.

20 E.g. RT 5 Apr. 1963, 13–14; 21 Feb. 1964, 12–15; 29 May 1964, 5–6; 4 Dec. 1964, 5–7.

21 J. Hywel Davies 'The Penetration of a New Pentecost' EE Nov. 9, 1963, 712–3; 23 Nov 1963, 744–6; 30 Nov. 1963, 760–762; 14 Dec. 1963, 792–3. See also the two articles by Davies in CR, cited in note 8 to Chapter Sixteen.

22 'It is exciting to hear reports from many quarters of the incursion of blessed Pentecost into Anglican and the various popular denominations.' (Letter of Harold Horton to Richard Bolt, November 25, 1963). Horton was a strong encourager of Bolt's ministry. Horton was the author of well-known booklets *Receiving without Tarrying* and *The Baptism in the Holy Spirit*.

23 See ' "You will before you leave" – Profile of Harold Horton' RN 7, Feb.–Mar. 1967, 16–18. Horton died on 1 January 1969 ('Death of Harold Horton' RN 19, Feb.–Mar. 1969, 20).

24 EE 10 Mar. 1962, 146.

25 EE 29 June 1963, 402.

26 Desmond Cartwright of the Elim Church.

27 Canty had earlier objected with vigour to the articles by Revd. R. Bell in EC, on which see note 7 to Chapter Sixteen (EC 17 Jan. 1964, 10).

28 M Oct.–Dec. 1964, 98–9. See also M. Robinson *Two Winds Blowing*, 143–4.

29 The Convention was organized by an independent English committee, working in close touch with the FGBMFI (MHN 13, July 1965, 2). Among those serving on the committee were Alfred Missen, general secretary of the AoG in Great Britain and Ireland; Percy Brooke of the United Apostolic Faith Church; Michael Harper; John Noble.

30 RT 29 Oct. 1965, 20. This meeting was arranged on the initiative of Douglas Quy, the AoG pastor in Bedford.

31 The Convention took place from 24–27 November. The names of the speakers are given in the Convention brochure. A report can be found in RN 1, Jan. 1966, 4–10. There is an editorial 'Tongues Speak' in RT Dec. 10,1965, 2.

32 This conference was on 19–20 June (MHN 12, June 1965, 2). Participants tend to remember this conference for a difference of scriptural interpre-

tation between Percy Brooke (see note 29 above) and Edgar Trout. In
the ensuing debate, Brooke was supported by Arthur Wallis. Some
recollections mistakenly associate this discussion with the 1964 Stoke
Poges conference for leaders, at which none of these three men were
present.

33 The report in *Renewal* was anxious to point out that 'The "package deal"
fortnight cost each American a little more than it costs a Briton to spend
a fortnight in the Holy Land.' (RN 1, Jan. 1966, 4).

34 The CEN had items by Honor Gilbert, an article ' "Cross and Switchblade" man comes to town' (26 Nov. 1965, 1) and a report 'Full Gospel
men in Church House' (3 Dec. 1965, 16), as well as the editorial cited in
note 48. See also Douglas Smith 'The Spirit Level' BW 2 Dec. 1965, 3;
'Full Gospel in London' CH 3 Dec. 1965, 5; A. Morgan Derham 'Talking
Point' CH 10 Dec. 1965, 2; Pat Robertson 'Even the Beatniks Listened'
CL Feb. 1966, 14–15.

35 24 Nov. 1965, 3.

36 See RN 1, Jan. 1966, 5.

37 Besides the Americans and Canadians, there were also some visitors
from the European Continent.

38 See RN 1, Jan. 1966, 8.

39 See RN 1, Jan. 1966, 6–8.

40 See RN 1, Jan. 1966, 8, 10; RN 2, Mar.–Apr. 1966, 5–7. Burslem is not
mentioned in these lists, but was visited by Revd. Gordon Scovell and
Ralph Wilkerson.

41 See Chapter Fifteen, 100–101.

42 RN reported 'We have just heard of about thirty converted in an
Anglican Church visited by Nicky Cruz.' (1, Jan. 1966, 8). This was
Chorleywood (B. Kissell *Springtime in the Church*, 54–5).

43 John Sherrill also wrote about the Pentecostal outpouring of the Spirit
in a book *They Speak with Other Tongues*, which did not have as great an
impact in Britain as in the USA see Chapter Twenty-Five.

44 For various reasons, the first British version of *The Cross and the Switchblade* was in hardback.

45 References in MHN 5, Oct. 1964, 2; 'completely sold out' (MHN 6, Nov.
1964, 2); 'plenty . . . in stock' (MHN 7, Dec. 1964, 3); 'fresh supplies . . .
expected' (MHN 8, Jan. 1965, 2); 'stocks again' (MHN 9, Feb. 1965, 2).

46 E.g. the Scripture Union bookshop in London's West End of which
Edward England was then manager.

47 CEN 3 Dec. 1965, 8.

48 The editorial speaks of *The Cross and the Switchblade* being 'crudely
written for crude tastes', a judgment that confuses popularity with
crudity.

49 Ibid.

50 E.g. a girl mentioned by E. Houfe in 'Victorious Victoria' T Whitsuntide 1965, 19.

51 E.g. Jeanne Hinton, one-time staff member of the Fountain Trust and later editor of TR magazine (*Towards Renewal*) and *Grassroots* (see GR Jan.–Feb. 1982, 1); and Donald Bridge, a Baptist minister (D. Bridge & D. Phypers *More Than Tongues Can Tell*, 18). Letters to M. Harper also mention the book's impact, e.g. 'Just before I left college at half term *The Cross and the Switchblade* was going the rounds again; also at the C of E training college in the close at Salisbury. It is always received with joy.' (letter of Jane & John Leonard, 17 June 1965). See also letter of A Rowley of Gillingham, 26 Nov 1964.

52 Jenny Cooke *Upon this Rock*, 37.

Chapter 23

1   See e.g. the testimonies of Lillie, Clark, McAlpine, Bolt, Amos Edwards, Grant, Harper, Clarke and David Smith.

2   R. Trout *Strength Out of Weakness*, 155.

3   Of the witnesses that follow, all except Lillie, David Smith and Trout come from personal accounts close to the initial experience. Richard Trout's account of his father's experience was based on Edgar Trout's personal diaries not seen by this author.

4   Page references above are 12, 27, 59, 102 respectively.

5   RV Nov. 1963, 6.

6   Page references apart from Shaw: 35, 74, 82, 92, 116–17; Shaw in *I Received the Holy Spirit*, 12.

7   Page references: 27, 74, 67, 82.

8   Page references: 59, 63, 74, 74, 86.

9   Page references: 12, 27, 35, 92.

10 Page reference: 44.

11 References: 74, E. Houfe's 'An Act of Faith' T Christmastide 1962–63, 27.

12 Page references: 28, 27, 12.

13 *I Received the Holy Spirit*, 13.

14 P. N. & C. van der Laan *Pinksteren in beweging*, 133.

15 See Chapter Twenty-Five.

16 Casebow had however an indirect association with Pentecostals through Gordon Strachan and Bill McLean (see Chapter Thirteen, 86).

17 The affinity lies in the Apostolic Church's restoration of New Testament ministries from Eph 4:11 as part of church order. However, the Apostolics did not have the same emphasis on the completeness of the local Church and on depth of fellowship as the Brethren.

18 This was evident, for example, in the 'de-doctrinalizing' tendency

mentioned in Chapter Twenty-Four, 166. It is also seen in some disso-
ciation from aspects of Pentecostal 'culture', as their fundamentalistic
reading of Scripture and their 'God or Satan' approach to spiritual
causality.

19 See Chapter Twenty-Two, 140–1.
20 This judgment necessitates some qualification of Wallis' statement
concerning the late 1950s and early 1960s: 'In the movement of the Spirit
at this time there were 3 commingling streams. There was a revival
emphasis, a NT church emphasis, and a Pentecostal emphasis.' (RS
July–Aug. 1980, 23). This is an accurate delineation of emphases among
those being brought into the Charismatic movement in its origins, but
this movement of the Spirit did not come about as a result of the
intermingling of ideas, which is what the 'emphasis' language tends to
imply.

Chapter 24

1 This was true for example of Rex Meakin, the rector of Loughborough,
who had spoken in tongues since before World War II. See also R.
Meakin 'The Work of the Holy Spirit in a Midland Parish' T Whitsuntide 1965, 23.
2 E.g. Katherine Cox of the CMS (see note 14 to Chapter Eighteen);
Godfrey Dawkins, a missionary in Maseno, Kenya (see MHN 15, Sept.
1965, 1) and John Kitts of Nairobi, Kenya (see Q July–Sept. 1965, 14–15).
3 Q Jan.–Mar. 1965, 10.
4 MHN 4, July 10, 1964, 3.
5 Report on Seminar at Oral Roberts University, Tulsa, Oklahoma, Nov.
11–22, 1963 in LHML 45, Easter 1964, 15.
6 Letter of D. Lillie to M. Harper, 24 Jan. 1963.
7 Letter of D. Lillie to M. Harper, 1 Oct. 1964.
8 Q July–Sept. 1964, 6.
9 *The Cross and the Switchblade*, 193.
10 CEN Feb, 21, 1964, 1 and heading over subsequent correspondence, 28
Feb. 1964, 6 and 6 Mar. 1964, 6.
11 CEN Dec. 11, 1964, 1 and heading over correspondence in Dec. 18, 1964,
6.
12 CEN 10 Sept. 1965, 1.
13 CT May 8, 1964, 3.
14 E.g. M. Harper in 'Something is Happening' APFRQB 16, Winter 1964,
3 and 'The Accusers' RN 4, Aug.–Sept. 1966, 3; Mrs. J. Crees in CEN 18
Dec. 1964, 6. See also G. Strachan in CR July 1964, 30.
15 CEN 28 Feb. 1964, 6.
16 It was published in England by Hodder and Stoughton in 1965.

17 John L. Sherrill *They Speak with Other Tongues*, 114–15.
18 AVF July–Sept. 1965, 1–2, 5.
19 This was the case with those who influenced Lillie, Grant, Houfe, Ron Bailey, Shaw, McLean, Sillitoe.
20 E.g. Harper's witness at Gillingham, the influence of American visitors such as Maguire, Christenson and Stone and the many people influenced by Edgar Trout.
21 Q July–Sept. 1965, 11.
22 *Power for the Body of Christ*, 7 (Revised introduction written in 1969). Harper is here describing his Farnham experience in September 1962, before he heard of the gift of tongues from Houfe and *Trinity* magazine.
23 Edward Irving arrived at such a conclusion. and it was only among those influenced by his preaching that the spiritual gifts then came into exercise (see C. Gordon Strachan *The Pentecostal Theology of Edward Irving*, 55–60).
24 The Islington conference of January 1964 with John Stott's negative stance towards the new move is a prominent example (see Chapter Eleven, 77).
25 As e.g. M. Harper *Power for the Body of Christ*, 13–15; *As at the Beginning*, 97–104.
26 The Declaration of Faith of the AoG of Great Britain and Ireland states: 'We believe . . . in the baptism in the Holy Spirit with the initial evidence of speaking in tongues' (quoted in W. J. Hollenweger, *The Pentecostals*, 520). The doctrine of the American AoG is the same, but formulated in slightly greater detail (see Hollenweger, op. cit., 515).
27 This is evident in Harper's writings as, e.g. MHN 1, Jan, 1964, 1 and *As at the Beginning*, 97–8.
28 This 'de-doctrinalizing' was also manifest in the charismatics generally being quite unaware of the official Pentecostal distinction between speaking in tongues as the 'initial evidence' of baptism in the Spirit and speaking in tongues as an ongoing spiritual gift. One consequence of this is that charismatics use the gift of tongues in personal prayer much more than Pentecostals.
29 Especially Lk. 24:49; Acts 1:8; 10:38. This emphasis is found in C. Cousen 'Power from on High' AVF Jan.–Mar. 1961, 10–14; M. Harper MHN 1, Jan. 1964, 1; *Power for the Body of Christ*, passim; *As at the Beginning*, 103, 122.
30 Rex Meakin, while teaching the purpose of baptism in the Spirit as the power to witness, recognizes other effects, e.g. 'While the Baptism in the Spirit is not primarily intended for the building up of Christian character it has this most blessed result that it brings us into much closer fellowship with Jesus and makes us more Christ-centred.' (*Power for Service*, 3).

31 Bryn Jones remarked that 'The baptism with the Spirit will bring us into a greater awareness of each member of the Godhead.' ('Pentecostal Casualties' AVF July–Sept. 1966, 16).

32 See the words of du Plessis (Chapter Nineteen, 122–3).

33 See 1 Cor. 14:2.

34 'They, (the Pentecostals) and by no means only they, are . . . wrong in making Pentecost only and primarily an experience of empowering. On the contrary, the Baptism in the Spirit, as always, is primarily initiatory, and only secondarily an empowering.' (J. D. G. Dunn *Baptism in the Holy Spirit*, 54).

35 Acts 1:4 (see also Lk. 24:49; Acts 2:33, 39; 26, 6).

36 'L'affirmation centrale concerne la présence de la Promesse, de l'Esprit, et celui-ci est répandu par le Christ exalté. Cette réalité, ce fait d'expérience chrétienne, c'est l'accomplissement de tout ce que Dieu a juré de faire pour son peuple.' (F. Martin 'Le Baptême dans l'Esprit' NRT Jan.–Feb. 1984, 35).

37 'He will glorify me, for he will take what is mine and declare it to you.'

38 RN 2, Mar.–Apr. 1966, 13 (see also Q July–Sept. 1965, 3–5).

39 See also Rev. 19:10. On the mutual relationship of the roles of Jesus and the Spirit in 1 Jn. 5:6 see F. Martin, art. cit., 40 and I. de la Potterie *La Vérité dans Saint Jean*, I, 315–28.

40 C. K. Barrett *The Gospel according to St. John*, 45 (see also W. G. Kummel *The Theology of the New Testament*, 314).

41 See Barrett, op. cit., 53; A. Wikenhauser *New Testament Introduction*, 301–2.

42 E.g. 1 Cor. 12:3; Eph. 1:17; Tit. 3:4–7.

43 This concern not to separate the Spirit from the person of Jesus has been a central thrust in the teaching of G. W. North on the baptism in the Spirit (see G. W. North *One Baptism*, 69, 103–5, 112–120). Thus, for example: ' "At that day (Pentecost) ye shall know that I am in My Father and ye in me and I in you". This was the dearest wish in Jesus' heart for them; it is by far the most important thing that takes place in the Baptism in/of/with the Spirit.' (op. cit., 103). This reflects the strong Holiness background and orientation of North's teaching.

44 This distinction between the meaning and the purpose of the baptism in the Spirit can be made with regard to the early Pentecostals between their initial witness to and the subsequent doctrinal formulation of baptism in the Spirit; see P. Hocken 'Jesus Christ and the Gifts of the Holy Spirit' PN Spring 1983, 1–16.

45 AVF Apr.–June 1964, 2.

46 Ibid., 3.

47 'It is curious that the prophets are said not only to have heard Yahweh's word, but to have seen it. The prophetic revelations are regarded as

visions, even when nothing is "seen" in our sense. The prophetic words of Amos are something that he had seen (i.1.).' (J. Lindblom *Prophecy in Ancient Israel*, 121).

48 E.g. M. Harper *As at the Beginning*, 95–6 and in RN 7, Feb.–Mar. 1967, 3.

49 C. J. Clarke stated in his first enthusiastic report on the news of Charismatic revival from America 'These are the days of the Latter Rain foretold in Scripture' (Q. Jan. 1963, 13), but this did not remain a part of Clarke's normal presentation. Other references are in Q July–Sept. 1964, 2 and W. B. Grant in APFRQB 17, Summer 1964, 7.

50 E.g. Grant, Houfe, Clarke, Wallis, Collins. Edgar Trout's passion for revival came mostly after his baptism in the Spirit.

51 The evolution in Harper's thinking on this point is described by M. Robinson *Two Winds Blowing*, 148–150.

52 See Appendix III.

53 See M. Harper ' "Word Only" preaching' CEN 1 Nov. 1963, 7.

54 See SPR 1–2.

55 See M. Harper *Prophecy; a Gift for the Body of Christ*, 5; MHN 4, 9 July 1964, 1; 10 July 1964, 1.

56 *Prophecy – a Gift for the Body of Christ*, 5.

57 MHN 4, 9 July 1964.

58 It should be noted that Wallis' views later developed further beyond the Brethren ecclesiology by his acceptance and advocacy of apostles exercising an authority over local churches. (See A. Wallis *The Radical Christian*, 183 and 'Apostles Today? Why Not!' RS Nov.–Dec. 1981, 2–5). 59
See Appendix III.

60 W. J. Hollenweger *The Pentecostals*, 415–16.

61 See A. Skevington Wood *Baptized with Fire*, 102–111.

62 J. H. Newman *The Grammar of Assent*, 89–97.

63 See Vatican Council II, Constitution on the Liturgy *Sacrosanctum Concilium*, paras. 57, 64. Louis Bouyer *Liturgical Piety*, 38–69); T. A. Vismans 'Concelebration' in *Liturgy in Development* (ed. L. Alting von Geusau), 97–122.

64 The inclusion of a paragraph on charismata in Vatican Council II's Constitution on the Church (*Lumen Gentium*, 12) did not entail any such vision, though this section later served as hierarchical backing for the reappearance of the spiritual gifts of 1 Cor. 12:8–10.

65 The de-doctrinalizing tendency in the Charismatic movement vis-à-vis classical Pentecostalism is then a condition for the movement to touch the range of traditions that it has. A doctrinalizing tendency such as occurred in the transition from 'Pentecostal movement' to 'Pentecostalism' would then be a misfortune for the Charismatic movement, but

awareness of this danger should not obscure the need for the search for common understanding.

66 See Vatican Council II decree *Unitatis Redintegratio*, 1. Other definitions of the ecumenical movement include 'the dynamic concern for the unity and renewal of the Church and of all things in Jesus Christ' (T. F. Torrance *Theology in Reconciliation*, 15), 'the movement among the Christian churches for the recovery of their visible and institutional unity' (B. Till *The Churches Search for Unity*, 15) and 'Christian Interchange and the quest for Christian universality' (B. Lambert *Ecumenism*, 30).

67 This is to affirm existentially of baptism in the Spirit what is theoretically affirmed by Catholic theology about the sacrament of Baptism, namely that a total work occurs in the recipient, which then has to be worked out in all areas and facets of life.

68 By the 'reigning theology' is meant current understandings of the Christian faith. To say that the reigning theology is inadequate to the task of understanding this ecumenical reality is to state that current understanding without deeper penetration of the objects of faith is unable to accomplish this task. Such deeper penetration will necessitate a closer study of those periods and places within the various Christian traditions, which witness to such spiritual realities later forgotten or misunderstood. This comment is then directed at the limitations of contemporary understanding – whether conservative-traditionalist or liberal-radical – and is enhancing rather than reducing the importance of the data of Christian tradition.

Chapter 25

1 The fullest study is the unpublished doctoral dissertation of James T. Connelly *Neo-Pentecostalism: The Charismatic Revival in the Mainline Protestant and Roman Catholic Churches in the United States, 1960–1971* (submitted to the University of Chicago in 1977). However, Connelly's research was restricted to the background to official church statements on the Charismatic movement, and thus has no mention of developments in churches that made no statements in that period (such as the Baptist and the Methodist churches). Among the published works, the revised edition of Richard Quebedeaux's study entitled *The New Charismatics II* is the most comprehensive, but Quebedeaux's information on developments prior to 1960 is scanty.

2 'Rector and a Rumpus', *Newsweek*, 4 July 1960, 77; 'Speaking in Tongues', *Time*, 15 Aug. 1960, 53, 55.

3 Michael Harper *As at the Beginning*; Charles Hummel *Fire in the Fireplace*, 43–5 (U.S.), 34–6 (U.K.); Rex Davis *Locusts and Wild Honey*, 26; Richard Quebedeaux, *The New Charismatics II*, 59.

4 E.g. R. Quebedeaux op. cit., 59–60; W. J. Hollenweger *The Pentecostals*, 6–7; R. Davis, op. cit., 26.

5 This point has become clearer through Martin Robinson's doctoral dissertation on David du Plessis: *To the Ends of the Earth – the Pilgrimage of an Ecumenical Pentecostal, David J. du Plessis 1905–1987.*

6 The Brief Life Sketch of David J. du Plessis on the inside of the back-cover of *Pentecost outside 'Pentecost'* has nothing for 1955–57, one non-Pentecostal item for 1958, and five for 1959. See also D. J. du Plessis *A Man Called Mr. Pentecost*, 193.

7 By the mid-1960s FGBMFI had established 300 chapters and had about 100,000 members. (D. E. Harrell *All Things are Possible*, 147).

8 *All Things are Possible*, especially 138–149.

9 Ibid., 147.

10 Agnes Sanford *Sealed Orders*, 217–222.

11 Connelly has described how Mrs. Sanford introduced many clergy privately to baptism in the Spirit and glossolalia, especially at the Schools for Pastoral Care. 'Since these clergymen in turn introduced others in their congregations and among their friends to these experiences, Agnes Sanford was one of the people most responsible for making current in the historic Protestant denominations the concept of a baptism in the Spirit and the practice of glossolalia. Although she always cautioned those whom she introduced to these experiences to be wary of speaking about them to others, her counsel was not always followed.' (Connelly, op. cit., 183).

12 Quoted by Connelly, op. cit., 179, from a description written by Agnes Sanford.

13 Martin Marty termed OSL in 1957 'the most prominent focus for spiritual healing in orthodox non-Roman Christianity. A non-monastic order. it appeals to all church people who recognize in themselves a calling to participate in the ministry of health.' (Martin E. Marty 'Healing Ministry – Historic Church', *The Christian Century*, 28 Aug. 1957, 1010).

14 Connelly, op. cit., 57. K. McDonnell has a slightly different account in *Presence, Power, Praise*, I, 10, that confirms Connelly's data.

15 On the events at Wheaton, see J. T. Connelly, op. cit., 56–70. For further information on the development of the charismatic prayer meeting at Trinity Episcopal, see P. Hocken 'Charismatic Rector Fulfilled His Call' RN 214, Mar. 1994, 39. There is also a chapter on Richard Winkler in Emily Gardiner Neal *God Can Heal You Now*, 145–9.

16 Kratzig who was active in OSL was the young Texan priest referred to in Dennis Bennett *Nine O'Clock in the Morning*, 33.

17 A married couple in Holy Spirit parish, John and Joan Baker, were baptized in the Spirit in the spring or early summer of 1959. Their vicar,

Frank Maguire, then sought the advice of Dennis Bennett, leading to both Maguire and Bennett being baptized in the Spirit the following November.

18 On Brown, see Connelly, op. cit., 342–346; James H. Brown 'Signs, Wonders and Miracles' in *Presbyterians and the Baptism of the Holy Spirit* (FGBMFI) 6–8. 'Every Christian must become a Pentecostal', *Voice*, Sept. 1959, 7–8.

19 H. Bredesen *Yes, Lord*, 51–60. Bredesen dated this as 1946 at the Kansas City Conference in 1977 (Interview in the *Kansas City Star*, 24 July 1977, 26A).

20 Thomas Tyson 'Fulfillment of the New Birth', T Septuagesima 1964, 22–23.

21 See Glenn Clark *How to Find Health through Prayer* (1940), *Be Thou Made Whole* (1953); Starr Daily, *Release* (1945), 135–152; *Recovery* (1948). Clark also influenced John Gayner Banks, the founder of OSL, and was a friend of the Sanfords (Clark's son, Miles, married Sanford's daughter, Virginia).

22 See Glenn Clark *Collaborating with Eternity* (1948), 16, 26.

23 These included Agnes Sanford (e.g. in 1959, 1964), Tommy Tyson (in 1963, 1964), Francis Whiting, a Baptist (1964).

24 E.g. Don Basham *Face Up with a Miracle*, 54–66; Fr. William Sherwood T Trinitytide 1961, 9; 'Church of Christ Minister', T Trinitytide 1962, 53; John B. Covey T Eastertide 1963, 45.

25 M. Lewis 'Are we Missing Something?' CL April 1953, 28–29.

26 Responses included: wrong emphasis (Carl F. H. Henry); worthwhile (Robert A. Cook, Harold J. Ockenga, V. Raymond Edman); 'amen' (J. Roswell Flower).

27 Harald Bredesen 'Discovery at Hillside', January 1959, 16–18 Clifford H. Richmond 'This Church Found the God of Power', July 1959, 14–15; W. Wessman 'Transformation at Vine', Sept. 1961, 16–19; Marvin Buck 'This is What Happened When the Holy Spirit Came to a Methodist Church', Jan. 1962, 34–6.

28 Ethel May Baldwin and David V. Benson *Henrietta Mears and how she did it!*, 236, 275–6 (pointing to an experience of the Spirit's power 'not unlike the experience of the disciples at Pentecost' in 1947 and implying exercise of 'spiritual gifts' by 1957, possibly earlier).

29 This term was only coined in 1963, (art. cit., in note 39).

30 The pastoral letter dated four days after Bennett's announcement was only addressed to the parishioners of St. Mark's. Two days earlier, Bennett had sent them a letter explaining his resignation 'My dear people . . .', T Christmastide 1961–62, 6–7.

31 'Closely Guarded Secret', *The Living Church*, July 10, 1960, 5; 'Pentecostal Voices' LC 17 July 1960, 9.

32 'What I am standing for is to be found within the Episcopal Church: no one needs to leave the Episcopal Church in order to have the fullness of the Spirit. But it is important that the Spirit be allowed to work freely in the Episcopal Church, and it is to this that I bear witness, and will continue to bear witness'. D. Bennett art. cit., in note 30, 7.

33 See Jean Stone Willans *The Acts of the Green Apples*, 43–4.

34 These were published before *Trinity* magazine began.

35 The first issue of *Trinity* reprinted an article on baptism in the Spirit from *Elbethel*, a Pentecostal magazine (T Trinitytide 1961, 10–12).

36 Stone and Bredesen organized conferences called 'Christian Advances'. In 1962 and 1963, Christian Advances were held in a number of Californian cities, in Portland and Eugene (Oregon) and in Great Falls (Montana). See Connelly, op. cit., 81–2.

37 Harald Bredesen 'Return to the Charismata' T Whitsuntide 1962, 22–3, 45 (this ref. on 45).

38 The following periodicals published articles on glossolalia in 1963: The Church Herald, Moody Monthly, Brethren Missionary Herald, Presbyterian Life, Christianity Today, The Lutheran Witness, The Mennonite, The Covenant Companion, Christian Advocate, The Sunday School Times. The Lutheran Standard had preceded these with an article on speaking in tongues in September 1962.

39 Russell T. Hitt 'The New Pentecostalism: An Appraisal' E July 1963, 10–16.

40 Art. cit., 10.

41 'The Charismatic Renewal in the Historic Churches' T Trinitytide 1963, 28–35.

42 Art. cit., 29.

43 See H. Bredesen, art. cit. in note 37.

44 The first use of the term 'charismatic' occurs in *Voice* in December 1963, and the new FGBMFI magazine *View*, which appeared in 1964, was advertised as 'a quarterly journal interpreting the WorldWide Charismatic Renewal' (on title page of first issue). At the same time *Voice* began to publicize 'charismatic seminars' aimed at ministers within the historic churches.

45 E.g. John A. Mackay *Ecumenics: the Science of the Church Universal*, 198; James N. Lapsley and John H. Simpson 'Speaking in Tongues: Infantile Babble or Song of the Self?' *Pastoral Psychology*, Sept. 1964, 16–24; 'Speaking in Tongues' *Princeton Seminary Bulletin*, Feb. 1965, 318; Donald Bloesch, 'The Charismatic Revival' *Religion in Life*, Summer 1966, 364–380.

46 Besides those mentioned in this survey, Catherine Marshall is one of those who plays a significant part in Sherrill's story.

47 Thus, besides the references in note 31, 'Questions Remain' LC Jan. 1,

1961, 1, an issue that also carried Dennis Bennett's 'Speaking in Tongues', 12–13.

48 The report of the Bishop of Chicago's Commission is printed in McDonnell *Presence, Power, Praise*, I., 10–20.

49 Bishop Pike issued a pastoral letter on Glossolalia on the same date as the Study Commission he appointed reported. Both documents are printed in McDonnell. op. cit., but the pastoral (96–104) is much more negative than the commission's report (71–95).

50 Norman Scovell's witness 'Baptized with the Holy Ghost: The Testimony of a Franciscan Friar' is in T Eastertide 1962, 2–4.

51 Pattison's witness 'An Anglican Dean and the Holy Spirit' is in T Trinitytide 1963, 2–5.

52 *The Caledonia Diocesan Times*, Nov. 1962, 1.

53 These were led by two pastors in the Bethany Fellowship, Theodore Hegre and Harold Brokke. See T. Hegre 'Lutheran Minister Tells of Pentecostal Experience' *Voice* Oct. 1957, 22–24; Vernon M. Blikstad 'Spiritual Renaissance' CL May 1964, 31–33.

54 Christenson's witness 'A Lutheran Pastor Speaks' is in T Whitsuntide 1962, 32–35. See also L. Christenson *The Charismatic Renewal Among Lutherans*, 25–31.

55 Connelly, op. cit., 205, 207.

56 Connelly, ibid., 191–3. See also Herbert Mjorud *Dare to Believe*, 92–8; A. Herbert Mjorud 'A Lawyer Convinced' *Acts*, I/4, 1968, 31–5.

57 E.g. Morris Vaagenes and George Voeks.

58 Mjorud *Dare to Believe*, 114–17 and *Reports and Actions of the Second General Convention of the American Lutheran Church* held at Columbus, Ohio, 21–27 Oct. 1964, 122–3.

59 This report is printed in McDonnell, op. cit., 57–63 (the deploring of forms of glossolalia-promotion is in para. 7, 60).

60 Mjorud, op. cit., 118–123; Connelly, op. cit., 220.

61 See the articles of Theodore Jungkuntz. The most thorough study examining both Luther's attitude to the *schwärmerei* and the Charismatic renewal among Lutherans is by Carter Lindberg *The Third Reformation?*

62 Letter from Rev. E. H. Stahlke, district president, 9 Mar. 1965, quoted by Connelly, op. cit., 225.

63 Quoted by Connelly, ibid., 233 from E. Jorstad *Bold in the Spirit*, 67–8. The fullest account of the Pfotenhauer controversy is in an unpublished thesis by Conrad J. Christianson, Jr. *Sola Scriptura? Traditions in Conflict, Lutheranism and Pentecostalism* (Lutheran Theological Seminary, Gettysburg, Pennsylvania).

64 Extract from 'The Charismatic Movement and Lutheran Theology', 1972, McDonnell, op. cit., 357.

65 Other Presbyterian ministers baptized in the Spirit were Paul Morris, of Hillside Presbyterian Church, Jamaica, New York in 1957 (see *Presbyterians and the Baptism of the Holy Spirit*, 10–13); Ivan Gamble of Prince Rupert, B. C., Canada in 1961 (T Christmastide 1961–62, 40–41); Robert C. Whitaker of Chandler, Arizona in 1962 (Connelly, op. cit., 350).

66 *Voice*, May 1962, 35.

67 See McDonnell, op. cit., 131.

68 See *Newsletter of the Charismatic Communion of Presbyterian Ministers*, No. 3, July 1967, 1 and No. 4, Nov. 1967, 1.

69 David Harrell maintains that the Charismatic movement grew out of the healing revival (a position expounded most lucidly in his article 'The origins and evolution of the charismatic revival, 1945–1980' RHE, 1984, 287–98). The difficulty with this more socio-historical thesis is that it does not take adequate account of theological factors, in particular the rise of a vision of renewed churches. It also pays insufficient attention to the other pre-1960 currents mentioned in this chapter. Harrell's studies are however an important corrective to the widespread view that the Charismatic movement in the USA appeared from nowhere, so to speak, with Dennis Bennett in 1960. In particular they serve to highlight a less reputable contributory current that some charismatics might wish to de-emphasize.

70 See Peter J. Lineham. 'Tongues Must Cease: the Brethren and the Charismatic Movement in New Zealand', *Christian Brethren Review*, Journal No. 34. Nov. 1983, 7–52.

71 See Al Reimers *God's Country*, 54.

72 The one major meeting of US leaders was in September 1962 near Columbus, Ohio convened by David du Plessis, aided by Dean John Weaver of St. Paul's Episcopal Cathedral, Detroit. See DdPN Oct. 1962, 1–2.

73 Thus Barbara Shlemon, later known for her healing ministry, was baptized in the Spirit at Trinity Episcopal Church, Wheaton, Illinois in March 1965 (questionnaire filled out for Connelly, in Holy Cross Archives, Notre Dame, South Bend, Indiana), and a nun in Grand Forks, North Dakota in 1966 (see R. D. Wead *Catholic Charismatics Are They For Real?*, 109). See also Chapter Eighteen, and note 50.

74 These were from the Church of Scotland and from the Methodist Church.

75 The U.S. national statements were from the Christian and Missionary Alliance (1963), the Lutheran Church in America (on 'Anointing and Healing' in 1962), the American Lutheran Church (1963, 1964 and 1965), and the Presbyterian Church in the United States (1965). All these statements are in McDonnell, op. cit.

76 The opposition in Britain was strong among leading evangelicals following the Islington Conference of January 1964 (see Chapter Eleven, 77).

77 That baptism in the Spirit involves at its heart a deeper knowledge of Jesus is shown for example in such witnesses as Dennis Bennett *Nine O'Clock in the Morning*, 23; L. Christenson *The Charismatic Renewal Among Lutherans*, 30; W. T. Sherwood (T Trinitytide 1961, 9); G. Otis (T Septuagesima 1964, 4).

78 Besides the Americans visiting Britain, Michael Harper visited the United States in 1965 (M. Harper *None Can Guess*, 93–6).

79 *Trinity* in particular published a large number of British witnesses.

80 See Jean Stone and Harald Bredesen, art. cit., in note 41, 29.

Appendix II

1 Albert Ford Kitching was born in 1883, and was ordained priest in the Church of England in later life in 1948 (CCD, 1980–82, 576).

2 Cuthbert Gray was evidently one of the Pentecostals imprisoned for conscientious objection during World War I. Donald Gee reports how the Wakefield Assembly of God had its source among the Pentecostal conscientious objectors imprisoned in Wakefield gaol (*These Men I Knew*, 77).

Appendix III

1 For example in Chapters Three, *passim*; Chapter Seven, 42; Chapter Twenty-One, 136; Chapter Twenty-Three, 154 and Chapter Twenty-Four, 171.

2 E.g., those listed in note 19 to Chapter Twenty-One.

3 H. H. Rowdon *The Origins of the Brethren 1825–1850*, 269.

4 This was particularly expressed in his leaflet *Reflections on the Ruined Condition of the Church, and on the Efforts Making by Churchmen and Dissenters to Restore It to its Primitive Order* (1841), on which see F. R Coad *A History of the Brethren Movement*, 126.

5 See W. B. Neatby *A History of the Plymouth Brethren*, 18, 30–2.

6 W. B. Neatby op. cit., 199.

7 The divisions among the Brethren were primarily among the Exclusives and these are detailed by Napoleon Noel in *The History of the Brethren*.

8 See F. R. Coad, op. cit., 271, 276.

9 Darby was the theologian behind the whole dispensationalist strand that later spread over much of the Protestant evangelical world far beyond the confines of the Brethren, and which exercised its greatest influence through the footnotes in the Scofield Bible.

10 Quoted by Rowdon, op. cit., 281.

11 Op. cit., 276.

12 *On the Liberty of Ministry* 67 (quoted by Rowdon, op.cit., 274).

13 Quoted by Neatby, op. cit., 19.

14 This position is expressed clearly by Noel: 'as long as Christians are content to be "members of churches" (concerning which nothing is said in the Scriptures), all of which being viewed as distinct one from another, they cannot be meeting as members of the body of Christ . . . For, since all believers are members of the One Body of Christ, and the assembly of believers in any one place is the expression of "the body" (1 Cor. xii. 27); any ground of meeting which does not admit all the members of the body simply as members of Christ (excepting those under Scriptural discipline) is not the ground of the Church of God.' (N. Noel *The History of the Brethren*, I, 72).

15 E.g., in Rowdon's Appendix 1 entitled 'The Ecumenical Perspective' (op. cit., 267–300) and F. R. Coad in his chapter 'Unity and its Expression' (op. cit., 275–282).

16 *Memoir of the late Anthony Norris Groves*, 535.

17 This was in 1836.

18 *Memoir of the late Anthony Norris Groves*, 446.

19 See Chapter Three, 15–20.

20 See letter entitled 'Renewal in historic churches' by D. G. Lillie in RN 5, Oct.–Nov. 1966, 7–8.

21 See Mamhead, 87.

22 See Wallis in Belstone, 27, 29–30.

23 See Wallis in Belstone, 27 and Lillie in Mamhead, 14.

24 F. R. Coad. op. cit., 287.

25 E. H. Broadbent's book *The Pilgrim Church* maintains that the characteristic Brethren teachings and convictions had many historic precedents among Christian groups regarded by the dominant churches as heretical.

26 Lillie's convictions have been further expounded in *Beyond Charisma*.

Bibliography

Books and booklets directly relating to the history of the Charismatic movement in Britain or North America up to 1965

The Charismatic Movement in the Church of England (CIO Publishing, London, 1981).

I Received the Holy Spirit (BPF, London, n.d.).

Liberty in the Lord (BRF, London, 1964).

The Church of Jesus Christ: Its Purity, Power, Pattern and Programme in the Context of To-Day, the report of a conference held at Exmouth May 1958 (published privately n.p.).

The Divine Purpose in the Institution of the Church: an Enquiry, the report of a conference held at Belstone, near Okehampton, Sept. 1961 (published privately. n.p.).

The Present Ministry of the Holy Spirit, relative to Personal Need, Corporate Function and Gospel Witness, the report of a conference held at Mamhead Park, near Exeter, Sept. 1962 (published privately, n.p.).

World Pentecostal Conference 1952 *Souvenir Brochure* (BPF, London, 1952).

Angel, Gervais, *Delusion or Dynamite? Reflections on a quarter-century of charismatic renewal* (MARC, Eastbourne, 1989).

Bebbington, D. W., *Evangelicalism in Modern Britain: A History from the 1730s to the 1980s* (Unwin Hyman, London, 1989).

Bennett, Dennis J., *Nine O'Clock in the Morning* (Logos International, Plainfield, New Jersey, 1970).

Bridge, Donald and Phypers, David, *More than Tongues Can Tell* (Hodder and Stoughton, London, 1982).

Carter, John, *Donald Gee,- Pentecostal Statesman* (AoG Publishing House, Nottingham, 1975).

Christenson, Larry, *Speaking in Tongues. A Gift for the Body of Christ (Published first by M. Harper, later by the Fountain Trust, London, 1963).*

Clark, Denis G., *If You Ask Me* (The Victory Press, Eastbourne, 1971). *You Were Asking* (The Victory Press, Eastbourne, 1972).

Clarke, Charles J., *The Pattern of Revival* (The Epworth Press, London, 1964). *Four Steps to Blessing for Service* (n.p., n.d.). *Pioneers of Revival* (The Fountain Trust, London, 1971). *World-Wide Revival* (n.p., n.d.).

Connelly, James, T. *Neo-Pentecostalism: The Charismatic Revival in the Main-line Protestant and Roman Catholic Churches in the United States 1960–1971* (Unpublished dissertation, University of Chicago, 1977).

Cooke, Jenny, *Upon This Rock* (Hodder and Stoughton, London, 1989).

Coombs, Barney, *No Other Way* (Harvestime Publications distributed from Basingstoke, 1972).

Du Plessis, David J., *Pentecost Outside 'Pentecost'* (Published by author, n.p., n.d.). *The Spirit Bade Me Go* (Published by author, Oakland, California. 1963). *A Man Called Mr. Pentecost*: as told to Bob Slosser (Logos International, Plainfield, New Jersey, 1977).

England, Edward, *An Unfading Vision* (Hodder and Stoughton, London, 1982).*The Spirit of Renewal* (Kingsway Publications, Eastbourne, 1982). ed. *David Watson – A Portrait by his Friends* (Highland Books, Crowborough, 1985).

Foot, David R. P., *Divine Healing in the Scriptures* (Henry E. Walter, Worthing. 1967).

Garratt, Dale (comp.), *The Profile of the Pioneer* (Earthmovers, Auckland, New Zealand, 1993).

Gee, Donald, *Wind and Flame* (AoG Publishing House, London, 1967).

Gunstone, John, *Greater Things than These* (The Faith Press, Leighton Buzzard, 1974). *The Beginnings at Whatcombe* (Hodder and Stoughton, London, 1976). *Pentecostal Anglicans* (Hodder and Stoughton, London, 1982).

Harper, Michael, *Prophecy A Gift for the Body of Christ* (The Fountain Trust. London 1964). *Power for the Body of Christ* (The Fountain Trust, London, 1964). *As at the Beginning* (Hodder and Stoughton, London, 1965). *None Can Guess* (Hodder and Stoughton, London, 1971).

Hewitt, Brian, *Doing a New Thing?* (Hodder and Stoughton, London, 1995).

Hinton, Jeanne R. (ed), *Renewal, an Emerging Pattern* (Celebration Publishing, Lytchett Minster, 1980).

Hollenweger, W. J., *The Pentecostals* (SCM Press, London, 1972).

Ingram, George S., *Life and Life Abundant* (Christian Literature Crusade, London. n.d.). *The Fulness of the Holy Spirit* (Christian Literature Crusade, London, 6th impression 1957).

Jeremiah, F. Roy, *Divine Healing: the Way of It* (Lakeland, London, 1974).

Kissell, Barry, *Springtime in the Church* (Hodder and Stoughton, London, 1976).

Lees, Faith (with Hinton, Jeanne), *Love is Our Home* (Hodder and Stoughton, London, 1978).

Lees, Tom, *Another Man* (Hodder and Stoughton, London, 1980).

Lillie, David G., *Tongues Under Fire* (The Fountain Trust, London, 1966).-

Beyond Charisma (The Paternoster Press, Exeter, 1981).

Massey, Richard, *Another Springtime. The Life of Donald Gee, Pentecostal Leader and Teacher* (Highland Books, Guildford, 1992).

McDonnell, Kilian, *Presence, Power, Praise*: Vol. 1 (The Liturgical Press, Collegeville, Minnesota. 1980).

Meakin, Rex, *Power for Service* (Gateway Outreach, Witney, n.d.).

Milliken, Andy, *From the Kwai to the Kingdom* (Marshalls, Basingstoke, 1985).

Missen, Alfred F. (AoG Publishing House, Nottingham, 1973).

More, Richard, *Growing in Faith, The Lee Abbey Story* (Hodder and Stoughton, London, 1982)

North, G. W., *One Baptism* (Published privately, Exeter, 1978).

Quebedeaux, Richard, *The New Charismatics* (Doubleday, New York, 1976).*The New Charismatics II* (Harper and Row, San Francisco, 1983).

Reimers, Al, *God's Country* (G. R. Welch, Toronto, 1979).

Robinson, Martin, *Two Winds Blowing* (Christian Renewal Trust, Leicester, 1986). *To the Ends of the Earth – the Pilgrimage of an Ecumenical Pentecostal, David J. du Plessis, 1905–1987* (Unpublished dissertation, University of Birmingham, 1987).

Ross, Brian R., *Donald Gee. In Search of a Church, Sectarian in Transition*, (Unpublished dissertation. Knox College, Toronto, 1974).

Sanford, Agnes, *Sealed Orders* (Logos International, Plainfield, New Jersey, 1972).

Saunders, Teddy and Sansom, Hugh, *David Watson: A Biography* (Hodder and Stoughton, London, 1992).

Scothern, Peter, *Thirty Years of Miracles* (Voice of Deliverance, Mansfield, n.d.).

Shakarian, Demos, *The Happiest People on Earth* (Logos International, Plainfield, New Jersey, 1975).

Sherrill, John L., *They Speak with Other Tongues* (Hodder and Stoughton, London, 1965).

Smith, David R., *Fasting* (Rushworth Literature Enterprise, Braughing, Herts, 1961). *Divine Healing* (Rushworth Literature Enterprise, Braughing, Herts, 1965). *Queer Christians* (Rushworth Literature Enterprise, Braughing, Herts, 1967).

Smith, David R. (ed), *Be Thou Made Whole*: Messages from 1st EDH Convention (n.p., 1961). *Be Thou Made Whole* (Rushworth Literature Enterprise, n.p., revised edition, 1965).

Smith, David R. and Doreen, *Divine Healing and Evangelical Truth* (Published by authors, Ipswich, n.d.). *A New You* (M.B. Publications, Braughing, Herts, n.d.). *Disease and Deliverance* (M.B. Publications, Braughing, Herts, n.d.). *The Holy Spirit and You* (Braughing, Herts, n.d.). *The Return of Jesus Christ* (M.B. Publications, Braughing, Herts, n.d.). *True Prosperity* (M.B. Publications, Braughing, Herts, n.d.).

Stott, John, *The Baptism and Fullness of the Holy Spirit* (IVP, London, 1964).

Strachan, C. Gordon, *The Pentecostal Theology of Edward Irving* (Darton, Longman and Todd, London, 1973).

Thomson. Eileen F. M., *It's a Wonderful New Life! The Don Double Story* (Kingsway Publications, Eastbourne, 1981).

Thurman, Joyce V., *New Wineskins: A Study of the House Church Movement* (Peter Lang, Frankfurt/Bern. 1982).

Trout, Richard, *Strength out of Weakness. The Christian Life of Edgar Trout* (Unpublished and unfinished manuscript).

Walker, Andrew, *Restoring the Kingdom* (Hodder and Stoughton, London, 1985). *Restoring the Kingdom* (Hodder and Stoughton, London, rev. edns. 1988 & 1989).

Walker, Tom, *Renew Us By Your Spirit* (Hodder and Stoughton, London, 1982).

Wallis, Arthur, *In the Day of Thy Power* (Christian Literature Crusade, London, 1956). *The Radical Christian* (Kingsway Publications, Eastbourne, 1981).

Wallis, Jonathan, *Arthur Wallis: Radical Christian* (Kingsway Publications, Eastbourne, 1991).

Watson, David, *Towards Tomorrow's Church* (Falcon Books, London, 1965).*You Are My God* (Hodder and Stoughton, London, 1983).

Wilkerson, David, *The Cross and the Switchblade* (Bernard Gels Associates, New York, 1963).

Willans, Jean Stone, *The Acts of the Green Apples* (Society of Stephen, Altadena, California. 1973).

Wilson, Frank, *House of New Beginnings* (Lakeland, London, 1977).

Other Books and Booklets of Background Relevance

Liberty in the Lord (BRF, London, 1964).

The Apostolic Church: Its Principles and Practices (Apostolic Publications, Penygroes, 1937).

The Growth and Progress of the Church of God (Conference of Brethren at Swanwick, Sept. 1958, n.p., n.d.).

The New Testament Church in the Present Day (Conference of Brethren at High Leigh, Hoddesdon, Sept. 1954. n.p., n.d.).

Bartleman, Frank, *Azusa Street* (Logos International, Plainfield, New Jersey, 1980).

Bax, Josephine, *The Good Wine: Spiritual Renewal in the Church of England* (Church House Publishing, London, 1986).

Broadbent, E. H., *The Pilgrim Church* (Pickering and Inglis, London, 1931).

Cartwright, Desmond W., *The Great Evangelists* (Marshall Pickering, Basingstoke, 1986).

Chadwick, Samuel, *The Way to Pentecost* (Hodder and Stoughton, London, 1932).

Clark, Glenn, *A Man's Reach* (Harper and Brothers, New York, 1949).

Cliffe, Albert, *Lessons in Successful Living* (Prentice-Hall, New York, 1953). *Let Go and Let God* (Prentice-Hall, New York. 1951).

Coad, F. Roy, *A History of the Brethren Movement* (The Paternoster Press, Exeter, 1976).

Corum, Fred, *Like As of Fire* (n.p., 1981).

Dayton, Donald W., *Theological Roots of Pentecostalism* (Francis Asbury Press, Grand Rapids, Michigan, 1987 and Scarecrow Press, Metuchen, N. J., 1987).

Dunn, James D. G., *Baptism in the Holy Spirit* (SCM Press, London, 1970). *Jesus and the Spirit* (SCM Press, London, 1975).

Dunning, Norman G., *Samuel Chadwick* (Hodder and Stoughton, London, 1934).

Edsor, Albert W., *George Jeffreys Man of God* (Ludgate Press, London, 1964).

Elbert, Paul, *Essays on Apostolic Themes* (Hendrickson, Peabody, Mass., 1985).

Evans, Eifion, *The Welsh Revival of 1904* (Evangelical Press of Wales, Bridgend, 1969). With Foreword by D. M. Lloyd-Jones. *Revival Comes to Wales* (Evangelical Press of Wales, Bridgend, 1979).

Frodsham, Stanley H., *Smith Wigglesworth Apostle of Faith* (Gospel Publishing House, Springfield, Missouri, 1948).

Gee, Donald, *These Men I Knew* (AoG Publishing House, Nottingham, 1980).

Goodall, Norman (ed), *Missions under the Cross* (Edinburgh House Press, London, 1953).

Grant, W. B., *We have a Guardian* (The Covenant Publishing Co., London, 1952).

Groves, Mrs., *Memoir of the late Anthony Norris Groves* (James Nisbet, Bristol, 1857).

Hacking, W., *Smith Wigglesworth Remembered* (Harrison House, Tulsa, Oklahoma, 1981).

Hibbert, Albert, *Smith Wigglesworth, the Secret of His Power* (Harrison House, Tulsa, Oklahoma, 1982).

Hickson, James Moore, *Heal the Sick* (Methuen, London. 1924). *Behold the Bridegroom Cometh* (Methuen, London, 1937).

Hollenweger, Walter J. (ed.), *Die Pfingstkirchen* (Evangelisches Verlagswerk, Stuttgart, 1971).

Howarth, David H., *How Great a Flame* (Moorley's Bible and Bookshop, Ilkeston, 1983).

Kirkpatrick, Dow (ed.), *The Holy Spirit* (Tidings, Nashville, Tennessee, 1973).

Lang, George H., *The Modern Gift of Tongues; whence is it?* (Published privately, London, 1913). *The Earlier Years of the Modern Tongues Movement* (Published privately, London, 1958).

Martin, David and Mullen, Peter (ed.), *Strange Gifts? A Guide to Charismatic Renewal* (Basil Blackwell, Oxford, 1984).

Menzies, William W., *Anointed to Serve* (Gospel Publishing House, Springfield, Missouri, 1971).

Neal, Emily Gardiner, *God Can Heal You Now* (Prentice-Hall, Englewood Cliffs, NJ, 1958).

Neatby, W. Blair, *A History of the Plymouth Brethren* (Hodder and Stoughton, London, 1901).

Nelson, Douglas J., *For Such a Time as This: the Story of Bishop William J. Seymour, a Search for Pentecostal-Charismatic Roots* (Unpublished dissertation, University of Birmingham, 1981).

Newbigin, Lesslie, *The Household of God* (SCM Press, London, 1952).

Noel, Napoleon, *The History of the Brethren* (W. F. Knapp, Denver, Colorado, 2 vols., 1936).

Orr, J. Edwin, *The Fervent Prayer* (Moody Press, Chicago, 1974).

Peddie, J. Cameron, *The Forgotten Talent* (Oldbourne, London, 1961).

Robeck, Cecil M. Jr. (ed.), *Charismatic Experiences in History* (Hendrickson, Peabody Mass., 1985).

Rowdon, Harold H., *The Origins of the Brethren 1825–1850* (Pickering and Inglis, London, 1967).

Spittler, Russell P. (ed.), *Perspectives on the New Pentecostalism* (Baker Book House, Grand Rapids, Michigan, 1976).

Van der Laan, Cees and Paul, *Pinksteren in Beweging* (J. H. Kok, Kampen, 1982).

Winslow, Jack, *The Lee Abbey Story* (Lutterworth Press, London, 1956).

Womersley, Harold, *William F. P. Burton Congo Pioneer* (Victory Press, Eastbourne, 1973).

Wright, Nigel, *The Radical Kingdom* (Kingsway Publications, Eastbourne, 1986).

Articles relating directly to the history of the Charismatic movement in Britain or North America up to 1965

Acworth, Carol, 'David Wilkerson at the Albert Hall' RN 6, Dec. 1966–Jan. 1967, 5–7.

'The nights of prayer and how they started' RN 13, Feb.–Mar. 1968, 4–6.

Allen, Ben 'The Whole Gospel of Making Men Whole' in *Be Thou Made Whole*, 1st edn., 24–7.

'Faith and the Prayer of Faith' in *Be Thou Made Whole*, 1st edn., 35–7.

'Revival in the New Testament and the Prayer Book' APFRQB 4, Oct. 1960, 3–5.

'Seasons of Refreshing: Further New Testament Authority' APFRQB 9, Jan. 1962, 2–4.

'Principalities and Powers' AVF July–Sept. 1962, 10–12.

'Very Much Overlooked' AVF July–Sept. 1963, 11, 10 (also printed in APFRQB 16, Winter 1964, 7–9 and under the title 'The Gift of the Spirit in his two phases' in Mamhead, 27–29.

'Regeneration and Baptism in the Holy Spirit' T Whitsuntide 1965, 48–51.

Allen, David, 'That They May be One' RT July 16, 1981, 6–7.

Baggarley, J., 'Veteran Pentecostal Missionary addresses University Students' P 69, Sept.–Nov. 1964, 5.

Baker, Pat, 'Copy of Report to MRF Committee' Q Apr. 1963, 12–13.

Barham, E. Lawrence, 'Grace Abounding' LF Mar. 7, 1963, 227.

Bell, R., 'Modern Pentecostalism' EC Dec. 20, 1963, 3; Dec. 27, 1963, 3, 5; Jan. 3.1964, 3.

Bennett, Dennis J., 'Tongues and Healing' CEN Sept. 8, 1961, 9.

Bennett, Michael, 'A Question of Freedom' RN 50, Apr.–May 1974, 15–16.

Bolt, Richard, 'Out for Ordination – Received the Baptism' RT Sept. 16, 1960. 5–6.

'The Baptism in the Holy Ghost' RT Jan. 26. 1962, 5–6.

'The Gift of the Holy Ghost' PE 1/1, 22–24.

'Clutching at a Straw?' (interview by David Gosling), CEN May 15, 1964, 7.

'Paul's Quiet Time' PE 1/3 (1964), 30–32.

'New Testament Worship' PE 1/4 (1965), 29–31.

Bredesen, Harald, 'Return to the Charismata' T Whitsuntide 1962, 22–23, 45.

Bredesen, Harald with Stone, Jean, 'The Charismatic Renewal in the Historic Churches' T Trinitytide 1963, 28–35.

Brooke, Percy, 'B.P.F. Annual Meetings' RT Nov. 6, 1964, 7–8.

Brooks, Terry, 'Trained in The School of God: A Profile of Bryn Jones' RS May–June 1980, 5–7.

Buckley, W. H., 'The New Outreach of the Holy Spirit' RT 10 Apr. 1964, 9.

Burnett, John B., 'This is the Baptism of the Spirit – What Else?' LW Aug 1965, 13–14.

'The Baptism of the Holy Spirit' LW Oct. 1965, 27.

Canty, George, 'AND NOW – Shall we go back to the Church of England?' M Oct.–Dec. 1964, 98–99.

Casebow, Brian, 'The Joy of His Presence' T Christmastide 1962–63, 40–41.

'The Baptism of the Holy Spirit Transforms a Church of Scotland Minister' RV Dec. 1963, 6.

'Gifts of Healing' T Whitsuntide 1965, 16–17.

'This Extraordinary and Exciting Life in the Spirit' RN 10, Aug.–Sept. 1967, 4–5.

Clarke, Charles J., 'Dominie's Diary': TT Autumn 1957, 10–17; TT Winter 1957, 16–27; TT Spring 1958, 16–20; TT Autumn 1958, 12–21; TT Winter 1959, 18–26; Q Jan. 1962, 11–15; Q July 1962, 12–16; Q Oct. 1962, 13–19; Q Jan. 1963, 14–20; Q Apr. 1963, 16–22; Q July 1963, 5–11; Q Oct. 1963, 15–19; Q Jan. 1964, 23–7; Q July–Sept. 1964, 9–10; Q Oct.–Dec. 1964, 14–16.

'Birmingham Road Pulpit' TT Winter 1957. 28–30.

'My Quest' Q Oct. 1961, 3–6.

'Praying Together for Revival' SR Oct. 1962, 5–8.

'Commentary on Resurgence News' Q Jan. 1963, 12–13.

'Pastoral Letter': Q Apr. 1963, 2–4; Q July 1963, 2–4; Q Oct. 1963, 2; Q Jan. 1964, 2–3; Q Apr.–June 1964, 2–3; Q July–Sept. 1964, 2–8; Q Oct.–Dec. 1964, 2–6; Q Jan.–Mar. 1965, 2–13; Q Apr.–June 1965, 2–9; Q July–Sept. 1965, 2–10; Q Oct.–Dec. 1965, 2–3.

'Wait for the Promise' Q July 1963, 12–18.

'The Quest' AVF July–Sept. 1963,–5.

'The Pattern of Revival' AVF Jan.–Mar. 1964, 11–14, 16; AVF Apr.–June 1964, 5–7; AVF July–Sept. 1964, 9–12.

'The Pattern of Revival' RV Mar. 1964, 4–5.

'The Essential Secret of Revival' Q July–Sept. 1964, 17–19.

'Quest' RN 1 Jan. 1966, 14–15; RN 2 Mar.–Apr. 1966, 12–13.

'Men of Prayer': 'John Hyde' RN 32, Apr.–May 1971, 9–10, 12–13; 'Brother Lawrence' RN 33, June–July 1971, 20–22; 'Rees Howells' RN 34, Aug.–Sept. 1971, 22–25; 'John Oxtoby' RN 35, Oct.–Nov. 1971, 26–27, 29; 'George Muller' RN 36, Dec. 1971–Jan. 1972, 31–33, 36; 'The Curé d'Ars' RN 37, Feb.–Mar. 1972, 20–24; 'J. O. Fraser' RN 38, Apr.–May, 1972, 16–18; 'Sadhu Sundar Singh' RN 39, June–July 1972, 20–22; 'David Brainerd' RN 41, Oct.–Nov. 1972, 68.

'Portraits of Preachers': 'John Knox' RN 42, Dec. 1972–Jan. 1973, 15–17; 'Charles Haddon Spurgeon' RN 43, Feb.–Mar. 1973, 15–17; 'John Chrysostom' RN 44, Apr.–May 1973, 31–33; 'William Edwin Sangster' RN 45, June–July 1973, 41–43; 'Gipsy Smith' RN 46, Aug.–Sept. 1973, 37–39; 'Dwight L. Moody' RN 47, Oct.–Nov. 1973, 26–29; 'John Sung' RN 48, Dec. 1973–Jan. 1974, 20–23; 'Edward Irving' RN 50, Apr.–May 1974, 23–26; 'Watchman Nee' RN 51, June–July 1974, 22–25.

Clarke, Mary E., 'He is not Bound' Q Oct.–Dec. 1964, 7–10.

'His Love Overflows' RN 17, Oct.–Nov. 1968, 19–22.

Collins, John ('A Vicar of an English Parish') 'A Breath of Renewal' APFRQB 14, Apr. 1963, 2–4.

Collins, Mary E. (later Clarke), 'This is the Secret!' Q Apr.–June 1964, 4–9.

Coomes, David, 'Not so Quiet on the South-West Front' RN 49, Feb.–Mar. 1974, 14–15.

Cope, Bernard, 'I.D.' F 23, 18–19.

Cousen, Cecil, 'The Power of the Church' Exmouth, 50–62.

'Signs and Wonders' AVF Oct.–Dec. 1960, 8–12.

'Divine Healing in Isaiah 53' in *Be Thou Made Whole*, 1st Edn., 12–19.

'Divine Healing – A Parallel to Regeneration' in *Be Thou Made Whole*, 1st edn., 28–34.

'Come down out of the Ship' in *Be Thou Made Whole*, 1st edn., 49–52.

'Current Comments': AVF Jan.–Mar. 1961, 1–2, 4; AVF Apr.–June 1961, 1–2; AVF Oct.–Dec. 1961. 1–4, 10; AVF July–Sept. 1962, 1–2, 15; AVF Oct.–Dec. 1962, 1–2, 16; AVF Jan.–Mar. 1963, 1–6; AVF July–Sept, 1963, 1–3, 15; AVF Jan.–Mar. 1964, 1–5; AVF Apr.–June 1964, 1–4; AVF July–Sept. 1964, 1–2; AVF Oct.–Dec. 1964, 1–2; AVF Jan.–Mar. 1965, 1–2; AVF Apr.–June 1965, 1–6, 9; AVF July–Sept. 1965, 1–2, 5; AVF July–Sept. 1966, 1–5.

'Power from on high' AVF Jan.–Mar. 1961, 10–14; AVF Apr.–June 1961, 12–15, 9.

'The Church in the Acts' Belstone, 45–58.

'Deliverance' AVF July–Sept. 1962, 4–6.

'The Pioneer of Kingdom Authority' AVF July–Sept. 1962, 13–15.

'The Holy Spirit and the Personal Need of the Believer' Mamhead, 41–52.

'Gateway to Revival' AVF Oct.–Dec. 1962, 5–8.

'Wholeness – Preach it all!' in *Be Thou Made Whole*, 2nd edn., 41–51.

'Apostles' AVF Jan.–Mar. 1966, 3–7.

'With Christ . . . A man of God' RN 15, June–July 1968, 22–23.

Cunningham, Valentine, 'Alive in the Spirit' RN 35, Oct.–Nov. 1971, 32–33.

Curlee, Robert R. and Mary Ruth Isaac, 'Bridging the Gap: John A. Mackay, Presbyterians and the Charismatic Movement' *American Presbyterian*, 72/3 (Fall 1994) 141–156.

Davies, J. Hywel, 'The Penetration of a New Pentecost – U.S.A.' EE 9 Nov. 1963. 712–713.

'The Penetration of a New Pentecost – Britain' EE 23 Nov. 1963, 744–6.

'The Penetration of a New Pentecost – For Believers Everywhere' EE 30 Nov. 1963, 760–2.

'The Penetration of a New Pentecost – its significance to Pentecostal people' EE Dec. 14, 1963, 792–793.

'The New Pentecostalism In the United States' CR Jan. 1964, 16–17, 23.

'The New Pentecostalism in Britain' CR Feb. 1964, 12–13, 32.

Dean, John, 'A Wonderful Work of the Holy Spirit at Wye College, Kent, England' PE 1/4, 1965, 10–12.

Deppen, J. Ralph, 'Glossolalia – a phenomenon rather unusual in contemporary Anglicanism' CEN Apr. 28, 1961, 13–14.

Derham, A. Morgan, 'To Another . . . Tongues' CR Sept. 1964, 20–1.

'Talking Point' CH July 2, 1965, 2; July 9, 1965, 2; Dec. 10, 1965, 2.

Dunstone, Bob 'I had little to offer' RN 2, Mar.–Apr. 1966, 14–15.

Du Plessis, David, 'Are we going back to the Churches?' P 34, Dec. 1955.

'Pentecostal Revival and Revolution, 1947–1957' P 41, Sept. 1957.
'The WorldWide Pentecostal Movement' P 53, Sept.–Nov. 1960, 18 (abridged version of paper given to Faith and Order Commission Conference in Aug. 1960).
'New Wave of Pentecostal Blessing Continues' P 57, Sept.–Nov. 1961, 9.
'The 'Changed Climate' towards the Pentecostal Testimony' P 58, Dec. 1961–Feb. 1962, 8–9.
'Hundreds of Ministers "Receiving" ' P 64, June–Aug. 1963.
'God is Moving by His Spirit' RV Nov. 1963, 3.
'What is the Baptism in the Holy Spirit?' RV Apr. 1964, 3.
'Du Plessis Speaking . . .' AVF July–Sept. 1964, 13–15.
'Du Plessis Still Speaking . . .' AVF Oct.–Dec. 1964, 8–9.
'Jesus Christ – the Baptiser' PE 1/3, 1964, 8–11.
Letter to Evangelist Jimmy Swaggart, 30 Jan. 1983.
Eddison, John, ' "Tongues" ' CEN 22 Jan. 1965, 8.
Edwards, Amos, 'Notes taken at the visit of Father Francis Maquire [sic] to Warley Woods Methodist Church' mimeographed privately, 1963.
'Anointed in the Rectory!' Q Oct. 1963, 6–7.
Evans, B. G., 'Latter Rain Falls' V Dec. 1951, 5–6.
Fennell, Dennis and Maillard, John, 'Message from the Co-Trustees, LHML 48, Easter 1965, 1.
Ferm, Robert O., 'Talking Point' CH 24 Sept. 1965, 2.
Fleming, Michael, 'The Changing Attitude to Pentecost' EE Sept. 9, 1961, 563.
Foot, David R. P., 'London Meetings Conducted by Richard Bolt' P 69, Sept.–Nov. 1964, 16.
Forester, George H., 'Vicar of Beckenham Receives Baptism in the Holy Spirit' RV Nov. 1963, 6.
'Baptism in the Holy Spirit at Beckenham' (4-page report sent with MHN 2, Mar. 1964), also reprinted as 'This Current Revival' AVW Apr.–June 1964, 24–7, 23.
'The Revival of the Charismata in an English Parish . . .' PE 1/2, Spring 1964, 9–11.
'A Vicar is Led into Pentecostal Pastures' RT 26 Feb. 1965, 9–10.
'Power Releasing Worship' AVF July–Sept. 1965, 15–16.
Forster, Roger 'Apostolic Churches' AVF Apr.–June 1966, 6–9.
Gee, Donald, 'Are we too 'Movement' Conscious?' P 2, Dec. 1947.
'Thank-You, Brother, but -'[?] P 8, June 1949.
' "Tongues" and Truth' P 25, Sept. 1953.
'Billy Graham in London' P 27, Mar. 1954.
'Renewed Opposition' P 42. Dec. 1957.
'Orientation for 1960' P 50, Dec. 1959.
'Institutions Cannot Love' P 51, Mar. 1960.

'Another Springtime' RT June 24. 1960, 10–12; 1 July 1960, 3–5.
'Contact is not Compromise' P 53. Sept.–Nov. 1960.
'Pentecost and the World' P 54, Dec. 1960–Feb. 1961.
'What I Found in Holland' P 56, June–Aug. 1961, 3.
'At the Crossroads' P 56, June–Aug. 1961.
'What Manner of Spirit?' P 57, Sept.–Nov. 1961.
'To Our New Pentecostal Friends' P 58, Dec. 1961–Feb. 1962.
'Pentecostals at New Delhi' P 59, Mar.–May 1962.
'World Presbyterian Alliance to Emphasize the Spirit' P 60, June–Aug. 1962 (inside front cover).
'Don't Spill the Wine' P 61, Sept.–Nov. 1962.
'Pentecostal Theology' M Jan. 1963, 21–23.
'For Theological Students – and Others' P 63, Mar.–May, 1963.
'Donald Gee in Springfield and New York' RT Apr. 5, 1963, 13–14.
'Those who have not spoken in Tongues' P 64, June–Aug. 1963.
'Experience and Theology' P 65, Sept.–Nov. 1963.
'The "New Pentecost" ' PE 1/1, 11–13.
'Wheat, Tares and "Tongues" ' P 66, Dec. 1963–Feb. 1964.
'The "Old" and "New" Pentecostal Movements' M Jan.–Mar. 1964, 14–16.
'The Pentecostal Churches and the World Council of Churches' P 67, Mar.–May 1964.
'Ecumenical Pentecostalism' P 68, June–Aug. 1964.
'Remote or Realistic?' P 68, June–Aug. 1964.
'Divisiveness' P 69, Sept.–Nov. 1964.
'The Indwelling Spirit' PE 1/3, 1964, 16–18.
Gilbert, Honor, ' "Cross and Switchblade" man comes to town' CEN 26 Nov. 1965,1.
'Full Gospel men in Church House' CEN Dec. 3, 1965, 16.
Gorton, Gladys, 'Women's column: a missionary's testimony' EE 16 May 1964, 311.
Graham, Billy, 'Spiritual Expectancy and Revival' APFRQB 12, Oct. 1962, 3–5.
'Something is Happening' RV Nov. 1963, 1, 8.
Grant, W. B., 'The Second Evangelical Awakening in Britain' APFRQB 2, Apr. 1960, 6–10.
'When God Sends Revival I – The Church' APFRQB 5, Jan. 1960, 8–10.
'When God Sends Revival II – The People' APFRQB 6, Apr. 1961, 5–7.
'Revival and Manpower' APFRQB 7, July 1961, 6–8.
'A Spiritual Resurrection' APFRQB 8, Oct. 1961, 6–9.
'John Wesley's Pentecostal Experience' APFRQB 9, Jan. 1962, 7–11.
'Conviction of Sin' APFRQB 10, Apr. 1962, 7–9.
'Beginning!' APFRQB 17, Summer 1964, 5–7.

'God broke through my barrier' Q July–Sept. 1965, 11–13.

'George Skinner Ingram . . .' RPFN Nov.–Dec. 1969, 1.

Gravelle, John, 'Pentecost Sunday 1964' T Whitsuntide 1965, 20–21.

Green, L. W., 'The 1964 Elim Conference in Skegness' EE June 27, 1964, 408–410.

Hacking, W. 'Five Glorious Days' RT May 22, 1964, 9–10.

Harley, John W., 'Samuel Chadwick and Roman Catholics' D 21, Oct. 1977, 19.

Harper, Michael 'New Testament Revival . . . The Church at Ephesus' APFRQB 13, Jan. 1963, 2–4.

'The Promise of the Father' APFRQB 14, Apr. 1963, 5–6.

'Is History Repeating Itself?' APFRQB 15, Summer 1963, 9.

'A New Thing' CEN 25 Oct. 1963, 7.

' "Word Only" Preaching' CEN Nov. 1, 1963, 7.

'Something is Happening' APFRQB 16, Winter 1964, 2–6.

'Modern "Speakers in Tongues" ' CT May 15, 1964, 11, 13.

'An Anglican Priest and the Holy Spirit' T Whitsuntide 1964, 26–28.

'Pure Oil' APFRQB 17, Summer 1964, 2–4.

'Michael Harper Reports' Q July–Sept. 1964, 12.

'Change in Climate' CEN Dec. 11, 1964, 14.

'First edify, then evangelize' CEN 24 Dec. 1964, 2.

'It is Good to *Know* but better to *Have!*' Q Oct.–Dec. 1965, 14–17.

'What is Hindering Revival' APFRQB 18, Winter 1965, 8–11 (reprinted in SR July 1965, 5–6).

'Roland Allen in the Light of a Modern Movement' *View* 1965, No. 2, 33–6, 39.

'After Five Years – the New Pentecostalism' CR Oct. 1965, 16–17.

'The Signs of the Times' APFRQB 19, Spring 1966, 2–5.

'Time for Action' RN 1, Jan 1966, 2–3.

'The strife of tongues' RN 2, Mar.–Apr. 1966, 2–3.

'The accusers' RN 4, Aug.–Sept. 1966, 2–3.

'Is Rome changing?' RN 5, Oct.–Nov. 1966, 2–3.

'The plus' RN 6, Dec. 1966–Jan. 1967, 2–4.

'Where do we go from here?' RN 7, Feb.–Mar. 1967, 2–4.

'Good News!' RN 9, June–July 1967, 2–3.

'Nights of prayer' RN 13, Feb.–Mar. 1968, 2.

'Ministry of encouragement' RN 19, Feb.–Mar. 1969, 2–4.

'Raising Standards' RN 37, Feb.–Mar. 1972, 34–5.

Hinton, Jeanne 'Revived not redundant' RN 21, June–July 1969, 17–20.

'Church with a lift' RN 22, Aug.–Sept. 1969, 20–3.

'Soho break-in' RN 23, Oct.–Nov. 1969, 11, 13–16.

'Full Circle' GR Jan.–Feb. 1982, 1–2.

Hitt, Russell T., 'The New Pentecostalism: An Appraisal, E July 1963, 10–16.

Hocken, Peter, 'Edgar Trout' RN 187, Dec. 1991, 23–25.
  'W. B. Grant' RN 188, Jan. 1992, 22.
  'Charles J. Clarke' RN 190, Mar. 1992, 28–9.
  'Harald Bredesen' RN 195, Aug. 1992, 38–40.
  'Cecil Cousen' RN 196, Sept. 1992, 36–7.
  'Eric Houfe's Persistent Quest' RN 203, Apr. 1993, 34–5.
  'The Perceptive Brother Bill' RN 210, Nov. 1993, 27–8.
  'The Charismatic Brother from Devon' RN 213, Feb. 1994, 40–2.
  'Charismatic Rector Fulfilled His Call' RN 214, Mar. 1994, 39–40.
  'The Unquenched Spirit in Molly MacKenzie' RN 218, July 1994, 32–4.
  'The Generous Spirit of Campbell McAlpine' RN 219, Aug. 1994, 34–6.
  'The Prophetic Ministry of Graham Perrins' RN 226, Mar. 1995, 36–8.
  'Donald Gee: Pentecostal Ecumenist?' (contained in bound set of papers
    from EPCRA Conference, Mattersey, July 1995).
Hollenweger, Walter J., 'The House Church Movement in Great Britain' ET
  Nov. 1980, 45–7.
Houfe, Eric A. S. 'An Act of Faith' T Christmastide 1962–1963, 26–27.
  'Victorious Victoria' T Whitsuntide 1965, 18–19.
Houghton, A. T., 'The Best Spiritual Gifts' LF 2 Jan. 1964, 13.
Hughes, Philip E., 'Review of Current Religious Thought' CTO 11 May
  1962, 63.
  'Editorial' C Sept. 1962, 131–5.
Hughes, Selwyn, 'The Spiritual Value of Speaking with other Tongues' RV
  Apr. 1964, 4–5.
Hunt, John, 'Pentecost and the WRU' RT 19 Aug. 1960, 7–8.
Ingram, May T., 'Fire Wind Water' APFRQB 6, Apr. 1961, 8–9.
  'Preparation for Revival' APFRQB 9, Jan. 1962, 4–6.
  'Praying "Until" ' APFRQB 10, Apr. 1962, 4–6.
  'Opposition to Revival' APFRQB 15, Summer 1963, 7–8.
Jones, Bryn, 'Pentecostal Casualties' AVF July–Sept. 1966, 14–16.
Jones, Peter F., 'Cottage near Cuddesdon' CEN 19 Feb. 1965, 6.
Kingston, C. J. E., 'Presidential Diary' EE 21 Nov. 1964, 742.
Kitts, John, 'He Works Through Me' Q July–Sept. 1965, 14–15.
Lamb, The Hon. Roland, 'Thinking Aloud' SR Jan. 1964, 2–7.
Lillie, David G., 'Opening Address' Exmouth, 7–12.
  'The Emergence of the Church in the Service of the Kingdom' Belstone,
    4–13.
  'Opening Address' Mamhead, 5–16.
  'Concerning Spiritual Gifts' Mamhead, 17–22.
  'Panorama' AVF Jan.–Mar. 1965, 6–8.
McAlpine, Campbell, 'Edified and Multiplied' AVF Oct.–Dec. 1964, 13–16.
  'Rise Up and Build' AVF Jan.–Mar. 1965. 9–12.
  'Dig That Well' AVF Apr.–June 1965, 13–16.

'Builders Wanted' AVF Oct.–Dec. 1965, 11–14.

Marsh, Elizabeth P., 'The man who washed his hands in the Thames' RN 7, Feb.–Mar. 1967, 5–6.

Marzetti, Trevor J., 'Headed for the hard road' RN 51, June–July 1974, 12–14.

Massey, R., 'Pentecostal Congregationalism' RT 28 Oct. 1960, 11.

McDougall, Kenneth, 'The Baptism of the Holy Spirit' SR Jan. 1967, 10–14 (also reprinted as 'New World of Reality' RN 9, June–July 1967, 4–8).

Meakin, Rex, 'The Work of the Holy Spirit in a Midland Parish' T Whitsuntide 1965, 22–23.

Munday, Keith W., 'Pentecostal Infiltration' RT 10 Apr. 1964, 34.

North, G. Walter, 'Heaven – Now!' AVF Oct.–Dec. 1962, 9–11.
'The Gifts of the Spirit' AVF Apr.–June 1964, 13–15; AVF July–Sept. 1964, 6–8; AVF Oct.–Dec. 1964, 3–4; AVF Jan.–Mar. 1965, 3–5, 8; AVF Apr.–June 1965, 10–12.
'The Anointing' AVF July–Sept. 1965, 3–5; AVF Oct.–Dec. 1965, 8,10,; AVF Jan.–Mar. 1966, 8–10; AVF Apr.–June 1966, 3–5, 9.

O'Sullivan, Anthony, 'Roger Forster and the Ichthus Christian Fellowship: The Development of a Charismatic Missiology' PN 16/2 (Fall 1994) 247–263.

Palmer, F. Noel, 'Two-Stage Experience?, CEN 17 Jan. 1964, 5.
'The Anointing Spirit' APFRQB 17, Summer 1964, 8,12.

Parsons, Thomas Roy, 'A Personal Letter from One of the New Trustees' LHML 56, Christmas 1967, 2.

Pearson, Trevor, 'More News of Resurgence' Q Apr. 1963, 8–10.

Peppiatt, Martin, 'The Christian's relation to Christ and the Spirit at conversion' RN 4, Aug.–Sept. 1966, 4–6.
'How to live the life that counts' RN 7, Feb.–Mar. 1967, 7–11.

Perrins, Graham, 'The Masterpiece' AVF Jan -Mar. 1966, 12–13, 15.
'David's Tabernacle' AVF Apr.–June 1966, 14–16.
'Joined together' F 10, 12–14.

Petts, David, 'Pentecost in Oxford University' RT 27 May 1960, 12–13.

Potter, O. F., 'Remarkable Outpouring' RT Aug. 25, 1961, 16.

Pusey, Michael, 'A tale of two churches' F 7, 7–8.

Reid, Gavin, 'How did it ever become a best seller?' RN 6, Dec. 1966–Jan. 1967.7–9.

Rhodes, Philip C., 'This New Move' AVF Oct.–Dec. 1957, 3–5.

Richards, Wesley, 'Everything you always wanted to know about Bryn Jones, but were afraid to ask' RS Mar.–Apr. 1989, 28–33.

Robertson, Pat, 'Even the Beatniks Listened' CL Feb. 1966, 14–15.

Saward, Michael, 'The Holy Spirit in the Life of the Church' LF Jan. 16, 1964, 60.

Shaw, R. A., 'Great Things He Hath Done' in *I Received The Holy Spirit*, BPF 10–13.

'From behind the curtain' AVF July–Sept. 1963, 6–7.

Sillitoe, Barry, 'New Power in Africa prison ministry' RN 7, Feb.–Mar. 1967, 22.

Skitch, F. H., 'Pentecost in the Church of England' RT 10 Apr. 10, 6.

Smith, David Rushworth, 'Is Your Miracle Really Necessary?' AVF Jan.–Mar. 1961, 3–4.

'Divine Healing and Evangelical Christians' in *Be Thou Made Whole*, 1st edn., 7–11.

'Divine Healing and the Devil' in *Be Thou Made Whole*, 1st edn., 38–42.

'The Last Outpouring?' LF 14 Feb. 1963, 150.

'Divine Healing – a Work of the Holy Spirit' in *Be Thou Made Whole*, 2nd edn., 34–40.

'Evangelicalism and the Pentecostal' CH 26 May 1967, 11.

'Mid-Week Message: Series on Dynamic Evangelicalism', 1979.

Smith, Douglas, 'The Spirit Level' BW 21 Dec. 1965, 3.

Smith, Kenneth, 'Elim Conference 1963: Report on the Business Sessions' EE 6 July, 1963, 424–7, 429.

Smith, Philip L. C., 'A New Work of the Holy Spirit in a Church of England Parish' RT 25 Oct. 1963, 5–6, (also printed in EC, EE, M, Q, and T; see note 93 to Chapter Ten).

'Glossolalia – a phenomenon rather unusual in contemporary Anglicanism' T Whitsuntide 1964, 30–1.

Stevenson, Herbert F., 'Pentecostalism in Theory and Practice' LF Nov. 4, 1965, 1085, 1094; Nov. 25, 1965, 1175.

'False Fire?' LF 24 Feb. 1966, 172, 184.

'Self-Deceived?' LF 24 Feb. 1966, 184–5.

Stevenson, T. H., 'From My Diary': EE 7 Nov. 1959, 595; EE 23 Jan. 1960, 59; EE 10 Aug. 1963, 503, 508.

'The Work of the Holy Spirit in the Church Today' EE 18 Apr. 1964. 244–5.

Strachan, C. Gordon, 'My Story' PE 1/3, 1964, 11–13.

'The Pentecostalists raise some disturbing questions' LW July 1964, 219 and P 69, Sept.–Nov. 1964, 8.

Stride, Eddy, 'Talking of Tongues' CEN 17 Sept. 1965, 4.

Tattersall, E. W., MR: 'Remarkable Stories of Evangelism and Healing' (11 Apr. 1957 1); 'Question and Answer Evangelism Works Miracles in Plymouth' (18 Apr. 1957, 8); 'Converted Overnight: Plymouth Stories' (25 Apr. 1957, 3); 'Hard Hitting Evangelism Down in Plymouth' (2 May 1957, 7); 'New Life Out of Drunken Bedlam' (9 May 9, 3); 'Success of Plymouth Rescue Work Adds Further Problem' (23 May 1957, 5).

Tee, Alexander, 'Pentecostal Baptisms Everywhere' EE 2 Feb. 1963, 75.

Terhoven, Ken, 'Repercussions of the Matlock Project' LF 26 Sept. 1963, 980, 986

Tomlinson, David, 'The House Church – What's Going On?' RS Nov. – Dec. 1978, 6–9.

Trout, Edgar, 'Revival – Word of Testimony' from papers of the 12th Summer School on the Ministry of Divine Healing of the Presbyterian Church of Wales, 1965, 26–35.

'Gifts of Healings' AVF Jan.–Mar. 1967, 13–16.

Walker, T. W., 'Pentecost – part of normal Christianity' EE 20 June 1964, 387–8.

'Conference Communion' EE 17 June 1964, 411–12.

Wallis, Arthur, 'The Purity of the Church' Exmouth, 24–39.

'The Divine Idea of the Local Church' Belstone, 21–34.

'Revival and the Reformation of the Church' APFRQB 11, July 1962, 2 – 6.

'The Holy Spirit Vitalizing our Witness' Mamhead, 66–82.

'The real and the counterfeit' RN 8, Apr.–May 1967, 6–10.

'Consider Jesus . . . the Apostle' AVF July–Sept. 1965, 10–14.

'The church in the house' RN 52, Aug–Sept. 1974, 14–16.

'Springs of Restoration' RS July–Aug. 1980, 21–24; RS Sept.–Oct. 1980, 6–9.

'Apostles Today? Why Not!' RS Nov.–Dec. 1981, 2–5.

Ward, Ronald A., 'Tongues in Canada' CE 21 Dec. 1962, 5.

Williams, Derek, 'Denominations – the End of the Road?, CR Jan. 1981, 22–6.

Winter, David, 'Speaking with Tongues', LF 28 Mar. 1963, 296.

'Charismata Come to Britain' CL Mar. 1964, 16–17.

Wood, William, 'Order of St. Luke' LHML 7, July 1951, 5.

'Editorial': LHML 17, Christmas 1954, 1–2; LHML 18, Easter 1955, 1; LHML 37, Autumn 1961, 1–2.

'Philadelphia Conference' LHML 23, Christmastide 1956, 5–8.

'About the Mission' LHML 25, Summer, 1957, 2–3.

'The Ecumenical Movement' LHML 29, Christmas 1958, 2.

'Christmas Message' LHML 35, Christmas 1960, 7–8.

'The Spirit Bloweth . . .' LHML 36, Easter 1961, 5–7.

'Gathering Up' LHML 38, Christmas 1961, 16.

'Missioner's Message': LHML 39, Easter 1962, 1; LHML 49, Summer 1965, 1–2; LHML 53, Christmas 1966, 1–2.

'The Leaflets' LHML 43, Summer, 1963, 3.

'Bits of Spiritual Biography' LHML 44, Christmas 1963, 20–1.

'Let's Be Frank' LHML 45, Easter 1964, 1–3.

'Oral Roberts University: First International Seminar' LHML 45, Easter 1964, 15–16.

'Jesus at Work in this Decade' LHML 52, Summer 1966, 7–8.

'Extracts from Monthly Messages, No. 142' LHML 54, Easter 1967, 2.

Wyatt, Stephen E., 'The Blood of Jesus Christ and Healing' in *Be Thou Made*

Whole, 2nd edn., 27–33.
'Divine Healing and the Law of God' in *Be Thou Made Whole*, 2nd edn., 56–62.

Other Articles of Background Relevance

Gunstone, John, 'The Spirit and the Lord's Supper' TR 10, Oct. 1978, 29–32.
'After Seven Score Years and Ten: Celebrating the Oxford Movement' TR 24. July 1983, 18–26.
Hocken, Peter, 'The Charismatic Renewal, the Churches and Unity, OiC 1979, 310–21.
'Jesus Christ and the Gifts of the Spirit' PN 5/1 (1983), 1–16. 'Cecil Polhill: Pentecostal Layman' PN 10/2 (1988) 116–140.
Hollenweger, Walter J., ' "Touching" and "Thinking" the Spirit: Some Aspects of European Charismatics' in *Perspectives on the New Pentecostalism* (ed. Russell P. Spittler), 45–56.
'Charismatic and Pentecostal Movements: A Challenge to the Churches' in *The Holy Spirit* (ed. Dow Kirkpatrick), 209–33.
Martin, Francis, 'Le Baptême dans l'Esprit. Tradition du Nouveau Testament et vie de l'Eglise' NRT Jan.–Feb. 1984, 23–58.
Riss, Richard, 'The Latter Rain Movement of 1948' PN 4/1 (1982), 32–45.

Miscellaneous Items in Periodicals

BT: 'Another vicar resigns over Infant Baptism' (17 Dec. 1964, 2); 'Baptism of the Holy Spirit' (7 Jan. 1965, 1); 'Theological Agreements and Disagreements' (2 Dec. 1965, 3).
BW: 'Peter Parson's Log' (1 Aug. 1963, 9); 'Pentecostal Churches' (30 Apr. 1964, 14); 'Pentecostal Churches' (9 Dec. 1965, 10).
CEN: 'Sound of "tongues" ' (28 Apr. 1961, 10); 'Tongues and Healing' by 'a U.S. correspondent' (4 Aug, 1961, 7); 'Pentecostal trends in England' (8 Sept. 1961, 9); 'Sober Anglicans' (25 Oct. 1963, 8); ' "Baptism of the Holy Spirit" at Beckenham' (15 Nov. 1963, 1); ' "Look to South India" Plea' (10 Jan. 1964, 1); ' "Baptism of the Spirit" should unite, not divide' (10 Jan. 1964, 1); ' "Tongues" Movement Grows' (21 Feb. 1964, 1–2); 'I felt something warm' (15 May 1964, 3); 'Pentecostal Movements by Dr. Coggan' (30 Oct. 1964, 3); ' "Tongues" Vicar Resigns' (11 Dec. 1964, 1); 'Baptism Issue Explodes' (18 Dec. 1964, 1); 'Tongues at Loughborough' (10 Sept. 1965, 1); 'Tongues in Seattle' (5 Nov. 1965, 2); 'Vulgar faith' (3 Dec. 1965, 8).
CH: 'Outpost' (14 June 1963, 11); 'Baptism of the Spirit' (10 Jan. 1964, 1, 12); 'The Spirit in the Church' (31 Jan. 1964, 5); 'Interest in New Pentecostalism' (19 Nov. 1965, 20); 'Big Business in Soho' (26 Nov. 1965, 1, 16);

'Baptist Revival Fellowship: Varied views on the Baptism of the Holy Ghost' (3 Dec. 1965, 3); 'Full Gospel in London' (3 Dec. 1965, 5).

CT: 'Vestments Issue Still Disturbs Evangelicals' (10 Jan. 1964, 1); 'Californian Who Speaks in Tongues' (8 May 1964, 3); 'Indwelling Spirit' (15 May 1964, 10); 'Lee Abbey's Valuable Role Today' (29 Oct. 1965, 17).

EC: 'American Bishop Warns Against "Speaking in Tongues"' (24 May 1963, 12); 'Countryman's Comments' (4 Oct. 1963, 8); 'A New Movement of the Spirit?' (19 June 1964, 5); 'Visitors in Scotland' (7 Aug. 1964, 7).

EE: 'Church Unity' (25 Apr. 1959, 260); 'Episcopalians claim 'Gifts' for today' (15 Apr. 1961, 226); 'Students' Pentecostal Fellowship' (26 Aug. 1961, 539); 'Look at it with Squintus' (3 Feb. 1962, 75); 'A bridge to freedom' (10 Mar. 1962, 146); 'First Annual Student Pentecostal Fellowship Conference' (19 May 1962, 316); 'A Pentecostal invasion' (14 July 1962, 434); 'The spreading flame' (9 Mar. 1963, 146); 'Speaking with tongues' (20 Apr. 1963, 242); 'Passing of a Pope' (29 June 1963, 402); 'The new outpouring of the Spirit' (9 Nov. 1963, 706); 'British Pentecostal Fellowship' (9 May 1964, 293); 'Doctrine and Experience' (16 May 1964, 306).

LC: 'Closely Guarded Secret' (10 July 1960, 5); 'Pentecostal Voices' (17 July 1960, 9).

LHML: 'The Conference Findings' (LHML 35, Christmas 1960, 4–5); 'Healing Advance 1961' (LHML 35, 6; LHML 36, Easter 1961,4); 'The Order of St. Luke' (LHML 36, 13); ' "The Spirit Bade Me Go" ' (LHML 40, Summer 1962, 10–12); 'Agnes Sanford in South London' (LHML 43, Summer 1963, 1); 'Baptism of the Holy Spirit and Healing' (LHML 43, 11); ' "Speaking in Tongues" ' (LHML 44, Christmas 1963, 11); 'Overseas Homes of Prayer and Healing' (LHML 45, Easter 1964. 20); 'Speaking in Tongues' (LHML 45, 26–27); 'Praying in the Spirit' (LHML 46, Summer 1964, 4); 'Extracts from the Constitution of the London Healing Mission' (LHML 50, Christmas 1965, 2).

P: 'The Ever-Widening Pentecostal Revival' (P 56, June–Aug. 1961, 2); 'Pentecostal Ambassador' (P 56, 2); 'In Journeyings Often' (P 61 Sept.–Nov. 1962, 7); 'News of the New Pentecostal Revival' (P 64, June–Aug. 1963, 6, 9).

Q: 'News of Resurgence' (Jan. 1963, 8–12); 'Resurgence News' (Apr. 1963, 4–8); 'More News of the Resurgence Told in Testimonies' (Apr. 1963, 10–12); advertisement for meeting to be addressed by Fr. Francis Maquire (sic) (Apr. 1963, 15); 'Resurgence' (July 1963, 21–24); 'Reports on Swanwick 1963' (Jan. 1964, 5–22).

RN: 'A New Breath of Life' (RN 1, Jan. 1966, 4–10); 'Teaching week-end follows big meetings' (RN 2, Mar.–Apr. 1966, 4–8); 'Fountain Trust January Conference' (RN 2, 9–11); 'Blaze of Glory' (RN15, June–July 1968. 3–4); 'Great Adventure: Leslie Sutton 1894–1968' (RN 15, 23–24);

300 *Streams of Renewal*

'George Ingram: A life lived with God' (RN 24, Dec. 1969–Jan. 1970, 19–20); 'Intercessors Needed' (RN 25, Feb.–Mar. 1970, 18–19); 'Death of Denis Clark' (RN 98, Apr.–May 1982, 11).

RT: 'Campaigns at Congleton Pentecostal Church' (26 Feb. 1960, 15); 'Students' Pentecostal Fellowship' (11 Aug. 1961, 17); 'Colchester Student Crusade' (10 Nov. 1961, 16); 'Student's [sic] Pentecostal Fellowship Meeting' (13 Apr. 1962, 9); 'Revival Blessings at Eastwood, Derbys.' (3 Aug. 1962, 7); 'Report on Yale' (17 May 1963, 16); 'Rector Addresses Convention' (6 Dec. 1963, 14); 'Students' Pentecostal Fellowship Rally' (3 Apr. 1964, 18); 'Great Public Rallies' (12 June 1964, 3–4); 'Spiritual Gifts' (9 Oct. 1964, 2); 'Students' Pentecostal Fellowship London Rally' (18 Dec. 1964, 19); 'Burton Methodists Baptized in Water and the Spirit' (26 Mar. 1965, 18); 'Assemblies of God – Anglican Consultation' (29 Oct. 1965, 20); 'Tongues Speak' (19 Dec. 1965, 2).

RV: 'From the Editor's Desk' RV Nov. 1963, 2; Jan. 1964, 2; Mar. 1964, 2; May 1964, 2; 'Great Blessing Received at the London Deliverance Convention' (RV Mar. 1964, 6); 'On Time' (RV Apr. 1964, 6).

Letters to Periodicals

To CEN: From M. H. Bateman (6 Dec. 1963, 6); George Canty (24 Jan. 1964, 6; 15 May 1964, 6); Geoffrey Carr (18 Dec. 1964, 6); Jennifer Crees (6 Mar. 1964. 6; 18 Dec. 1964, 6); Harry Fisher (6 Dec. 1963. 6); John Gravelle (28 Feb. 1964, 6) Michael Harper (10 Jan. 1964, 6; 22 May 1964, 14); T. L. Livermore (29 Nov. 1963, 6; 3 Jan. 1964, 5); Charles May (22 Nov. 1963, 6; 6 Dec. 1963, 6); John Pearce (18 Dec. 1964. 6); Brian Seaman (27 Dec. 1963, 5); Paul Sharland and others (18 Feb. 1964, 6); Philip Smith (13 Dec. 1963, 18); Gwyneth Vick (3 Jan. 1964, 5).

To CH: From Michael Bennett (11 June 1965, 14; 2 July 1965,4; 23 July 1965, 10); William Boatwright (28 May 1965, 7); F. A. F. Bongers (30 July 1965, 4); James T. Bradley (20 Aug. 1965, 10); Philip G. Chesterman (27 Aug. 1965, 6); David M. Coomes (23 July 1965, 10); R. V. Dinner (20 Aug. 1965, 10); Noel Doubleday (30 July 1965, 4); J. A. Eggo (23 July 1965, 10); S. P. Ferguson (18 June 1965, 7; 9 July 1965, 4; 27 Aug. 1965, 6); W. B. Grant (23 July 1965. 10); Leslie Greening (27 Aug. 1965,6); R. Hubbard (2 July 1965, 4; 13 Aug. 1965, 6); C. Frank Lenton (6 Aug. 1965, 8; 27 Aug. 1965, 6); David Mellar (14 May 1965, 11); G. E. S. Oakley (6 Aug. 1965, 8); Robert A. Penney (3 Dec. 1965, 7); J. Perry (9 July 1965, 4); W. G. Turney (18 June 1965, 7); G. K. D. Vere (2 July 1965, 4); F. D. Walker (18 June 1965, 7); David H. Wallington (30 July 1965, 4).

To CR: From Gordon Strachan (July 1964, 30).

To CT: From Peter Barker (5 June 1964, 12); M. S. P. Boulton (19 Nov. 1965, 12); Michael Harper (26 Nov. 1965, 14); Reginald M. Lester (29 May 1964,

9); Michael Meakin (1 Nov. 1963, 7); Christopher Pilkington (29 May 1964, 9); Alma Trott (22 May 1964, 12).

To EC: From R. Bell (24 Jan. 1964, 9); J. S. Benson (24 July 1964, 10); George Canty (17 Jan. 1964, 10); L. J. England (17 Jan. 1964, 10); W. E. Filmer (6 Dec. 1963, 15); J. Harper (29 Jan. 1965, 9; 5 Mar. 1965, 9); C. J. Holdway (15 Nov. 1963, 9; 20 Dec. 1963, 9); Ena B. Kenadjian (5 Mar. 1965, 9); L. J. Kilbane (1 Nov. 1963, 9); S. E. Lawless (19 Feb. 1965, 9); David Lillie (10 Jan. 1964, 9); J. W. Mears (20 Dec. 1963, 9); Pamela Russell (6 Dec. 1963, 15); Philip Smith (8 Nov 1963, 9); R. H. Tindall Lucas (10 Jan. 1964, 9).

To LF: Eric J. Alexander (7 Oct. 1965, 1000); D. R. Bowman (18 Apr. 1963, 372); Charles F. Brown (18 Apr. 1963, 372, 380); George Canty (16 Jan. 1964, 62, 64; 11 Mar. 1965, 234); Desmond W. Cartwright (4 Mar. 1965, 199); Horace Chappell (4 Apr. 1963, 323, 329); Cecil Cousen (12 May 1958, 402); S. M. Giles (25 Apr. 1963, 402); C. E. Goodman (18 Apr. 1963. 380); I. Grieveson (28 Mar. 1963, 294); Michael Harper (11 Nov. 1965, 1134); Edward A. Hay (11 Nov. 1965, 1133–1134); Roy Hession (11 Apr. 1963, 357–358); Alan C. Hipkiss (4 Apr. 1963, 323); A. T. Houghton (16 Jan. 1964, 64); A. E. Jackson (28 Mar. 1963, 294); H. A. King (21 Mar. 1963, 275, 284); David G. Lillie (18 July 1963, 722, 732; 4 Mar. 1965, 199–200); Ernest Long (25 Apr. 1963, 402); Esther Luscombe (28 Mar. 1963, 294); Donald Macmillan (18 Apr. 1963, 371–372); James B. Pears (4 Apr. 1963, 329); Jon Prentice (25 Apr. 1963, 402); Graham Smith (25 Apr. 1963, 402); R. M. Stephens (11 Apr. 1963, 358); V. F. D. Tarrant (23 Sept. 1965, 930); 'Thunderbolt' (4 Apr. 1963, 323); R. W. F. Wootton (27 Sept 1962, 800); Stephen E. Wyatt (4 Apr. 1963, 329).

To RN: From Kathleen Baker (RN 8, Apr.–May 1967, 13–14); Richard Callender (RN 8, Apr.–May 1967, 12); W. B. Grant (RN 10, Aug.–Sept. 1967, 15); K. Haye (RN 4, Aug.–Sept. 1966, 6); David Lillie (RN 5, Oct.–Nov. 1966, 7–8); Douglas Ross (RN 5, Oct.–Nov. 1966, 9); Hugh Thompson (RN 5, Oct.–Nov. 1966, 7).

To RV: From 'R.D.' (Launceston) (Dec. 1963, 7); 'T.N.' (Farnborough) (Jan. 1964, 6).

To W: From Metcalfe Collier (Dec. 1965, 465); Douglas Duckworth (Nov. 1965, 428); Sunil K. Ghosh (Jan. 1964, 31–2); J. G. Hardwidge (Dec. 1965, 466–467); A. E. Horton (Nov. 1965, 429–430); George A. Hughson (May 1964, 190); D. Minshull (Jan. 1964, 31); Hubert V. G. Morris (Aug. 1965, 309); A. Mulholland (Jan. 1964, 21); P. Parsons (Sept. 1965, 349–350); G. J. Polkinghorne (Dec. 1965, 465); Paul Prosser (Nov. 1963, 432); Alan Reed (Aug. 1965, 309); L. S. Reed (Aug. 1965, 309; Nov. 1965, 428); B. V. Smith (Nov. 1965, 427–8); John Stickland (Dec. 1965, 467); P. Derek Warren (Dec. 1965, 466); Roland J. White (Dec. 1965, 465–466).